FM 3-28

CIVIL SUPPORT OPERATIONS

AUGUST 2010

**HEADQUARTERS
DEPARTMENT OF THE ARMY**

Published by Books Express Publishing
Copyright © Books Express, 2010
ISBN 978-1-907521-63-8
To purchase copies at discounted prices please contact
info@books-express.com

FM 3-28

Field Manual
No. 3-28

Headquarters
Department of the Army
Washington, DC 20 August 2010

Civil Support Operations

Contents

		Page
	PREFACE	v
	INTRODUCTION	vii
Chapter 1	THE DOMESTIC ENVIRONMENT	1-1
	The Army and Civil Support Operations	1-1
	The Constitution of the United States and the Army	1-4
	Army Components and Civil Support Operations	1-5
	Duty Status of Forces Conducting Civil Support Operations	1-7
	Key Aspects of Domestic Operations	1-9
	Primary Civil Support Tasks	1-12
	Fundamentals of Civil Support Operations	1-15
	Training for Civil Support Operations	1-18
Chapter 2	A COMPREHENSIVE APPROACH FOR CIVIL SUPPORT	2-1
	National Policy for Domestic Emergencies	2-1
	Tiered Response from Local through National Level	2-12
	National Guard Civil Support Operations	2-22
	Federal Military Civil Support Operations	2-23
Chapter 3	PROVIDE SUPPORT FOR DOMESTIC DISASTERS	3-1
	The Nature of a Disaster	3-1
	Responsibility for Disaster Response	3-2
	Initial Response from Local and State Authorities	3-4
	National Guard Disaster Response	3-4
	Federal Military Disaster Response	3-9
	Phases of Disaster Response Operations	3-14
	Considerations for Disaster Response Operations	3-16
Chapter 4	PROVIDE SUPPORT FOR DOMESTIC CBRNE INCIDENTS	4-1
	Potential Consequences of Domestic CBRNE Incidents	4-1
	Civilian CBRNE Incident Response	4-7
	National Guard CBRNE Incident Response	4-8
	Federal Military CBRNE Incident Response	4-9

Distribution Restriction: Approved for public release; distribution is unlimited.

	Support for Pandemic Disease Outbreaks	4-13
	Considerations for Domestic CBRNE Incident Response Operations	4-18
Chapter 5	**PROVIDE SUPPORT FOR DOMESTIC CIVILIAN LAW ENFORCEMENT AGENCIES**	**5-1**
	Principal Authorites for Support to Domestic Civilian Law Enforcement Agencies	5-1
	Main Types of Missions for Support to Domestic Civilian Law Enforcement Agencies	5-4
	Protection Against Terrorism	5-8
	Considerations for Support to Domestic Civilian Law Enforcement Agencies	5-9
Chapter 6	**PROVIDE OTHER DESIGNATED SUPPORT**	**6-1**
	Types of Designated Support	6-1
	Requests for Other Designated Support	6-6
Chapter 7	**LEGAL CONSIDERATIONS**	**7-1**
	Powers of a State Governor	7-1
	Authorities for Federal Military Support	7-1
	The Posse Comitatus Act	7-6
	Federal Military Forces and Civil Disturbance	7-7
	Mobilization of the Reserve Component	7-7
	Rules for the Use of Force	7-8
	Intelligence Rules and Restrictions	7-10
	Isolation and Quarantine Authorities	7-14
	Personal Liability	7-15
Chapter 8	**SUSTAINMENT—LOGISTICS AND PERSONNEL SERVICES**	**8-1**
	The Sustainment Warfighting Function	8-1
	Logistics Coordination for Civil Support Operations	8-1
	Logistics Considerations for Civil Support Operations	8-11
	Personnel Services in Civil Support Operations	8-18
Chapter 9	**SUSTAINMENT—HEALTH SERVICE SUPPORT**	**9-1**
	Medical Capabiility Coordination for Civil Support Operations	9-1
	Health Service Support Considerations for Civil Support Operations	9-5
	Medical Logistics for Civil Support Operations	9-9
Appendix A	**PLANNING CHECKLISTS**	**A-1**
Appendix B	**SAFETY**	**B-1**
Appendix C	**NATIONAL GUARD WEAPONS OF MASS DESTRUCTION–CIVIL SUPPORT TEAMS**	**C-1**
Appendix D	**CBRNE ENHANCED RESPONSE FORCE PACKAGE**	**D-1**
Appendix E	**CBRNE CONSEQUENCE MANAGEMENT RESPONSE FORCE**	**E-1**
Appendix F	**AIRSPACE COMMAND AND CONTROL**	**F-1**
Appendix G	**SEARCH AND RESCUE**	**G-1**
Appendix H	**UNMANNED AIRCRAFT SYSTEMS IN CIVIL SUPPORT**	**H-1**
Appendix I	**INCIDENT COMMAND SECTIONS AND SUPPORT FUNCTIONS**	**I-1**
Appendix J	**COMPARISON OF STABILITY AND CIVIL SUPPORT TASKS**	**J-1**

Contents

Appendix K MEDIA CONSIDERATIONS K-1
            GLOSSARY Glossary-1
            REFERENCES References-1
            INDEX Index-1

Figures

Introductory figure—full spectrum operations vii
Figure 1-1. Range of response 1-3
Figure 1-2. Primary civil support tasks with examples 1-13
Figure 2-1. NIMS incident command staff 2-4
Figure 2-2. Example of NIMS command and management structure 2-5
Figure 2-3. Expanded command and coordination under NIMS 2-6
Figure 2-4. An overview of tiered response under the National Response Framework 2-8
Figure 2-5. FEMA regions and headquarters 2-18
Figure 2-6. A joint field office example, with command staff, sections, and branches 2-21
Figure 2-7. An example of National Guard organization within a state 2-23
Figure 2-8. Example of defense coordinating officer and defense coordinating
            element organization 2-25
Figure 2-9. USNORTHCOM and USARNORTH structure 2-27
Figure 2-10. A pre-scripted mission assignment for communications support 2-30
Figure 3-1. Military forces required for a typical incident 3-2
Figure 3-2. Military forces required for a catastrophic incident 3-3
Figure 3-3. State response and National Guard echelons—Illinois example 3-6
Figure 3-4. Relationship of National Guard forces to area commands 3-7
Figure 3-5. The federal request for assistance process 3-11
Figure 3-6. Example of USNORTHCOM structure for DSCA 3-12
Figure 3-7. USNORTHCOM and National Response Framework phases of disaster
            response 3-15
Figure 3-8. Example of parallel command structure 3-19
Figure 3-9. Multistate disaster requiring major commitment of federal military forces 3-20
Figure 4-1. World Health Organization pandemic influenza phases 4-14
Figure 6-1. Geographic area coordination centers for wildland firefighting 6-4
Figure 7-1. An example of a dual-status command 7-5
Figure 7-2. Illustration of the continuum of force 7-8
Figure 7-3. Sample rules for the use of force card carried by National Guard forces 7-10
Figure 8-1. Federal Emergency Management Agency logistics centers 8-3
Figure 8-2. USARNORTH sustainment structure 8-7
Figure 8-3. Illustration of base support installation selection 8-11
Figure 8-5. Example of joint movement center organization 8-18
Figure D-1. Example of CBRNE enhanced response force package organization D-2

Figure D-2. Example of patient flow D-3
Figure E-1. State and federal CBRNE incident response forces E-2
Figure E-2. Organization of the CBRNE consequence management response force E-3
Figure E-3. USNORTHCOM disaster response phases and actions E-5
Figure I-1. Example of a fully manned joint field office I-3
Figure I-2. Example of the operations section of a joint field office I-4
Figure I-3. Example of the planning section of a joint field office I-5
Figure I-4. Example of the logistics section of a joint field office I-6
Figure I-5. Example of the finance and administration section of a joint field office I-7

Tables

Table 1-1. State active duty, Title 32, and Title 10 status summary 1-8
Table 1-2: Key military aspects of domestic operational environments 1-10
Table 2-1. Emergency support function annexes (ESFs) 2-9
Table 2-2. National Planning Scenarios 2-12
Table 4-1. National Planning Scenarios related to CBRNE incidents 4-2
Table 4-2. National Guard CBRNE incident response capabilities 4-9
Table 4-3. Department of Defense CBRNE incident response capabilities 4-12
Table A-1. Initial planning checklist for situational awareness and assessment A-1
Table A-2. Initial planning checklist for a joint task force A-3
Table A-3. Initial planning checklist for Army units A-3
Table A-4. Initial planning checklist for the S-1 .... A-5
Table A-5. Initial planning checklist for the S-2 .... A-6
Table A-6. Initial planning checklist for the S-3 .... A-7
Table A-7. Initial planning checklist for the S-4 .... A-8
Table A-8. Initial planning checklist for the S-6 .... A-9
Table G-1. Disaster response and civil search and rescue comparison chart G-2
Table J-1. Stability and civil support task comparison chart J-1

Preface

PURPOSE

This field manual (FM) provides keystone Army doctrine for civil support operations. It expands on the discussion of civil support operations, the fourth element of full spectrum operations, in FM 3-0. This manual focuses on the planning, preparation, execution, and assessment of civil support operations, which are conducted within the United States and its territories. It discusses the role of Army forces cooperating with and supporting civilian organizations in domestic operational environments, with particular emphasis on how operations conducted by Army forces within the United States differ from full spectrum operations conducted overseas.

All civil support operations buttress the capabilities of civil authorities within the United States. The mechanisms that regulate civil support come from law, policy, regulation, and directive. Civil support operations require Army leaders to understand an environment shaped primarily by federal, state, local, and tribal agencies, and circumscribed by law. Nowhere is this more striking than in the roles of the National Guard. In sharp contrast to stability operations, Army forces may conduct civil support operations with National Guard forces responding under the direction of a governor or alongside active duty forces as part of a coordinated national response. FM 3-28 explains the reasons for the division of forces and provides considerations for the entire Army, including all three components: Regular Army, Army Reserve, and Army National Guard.

The proponent has made every effort to keep Army civil support doctrine consistent with appropriate laws, policies, regulations, and directives of the federal and state governments, the Department of Defense, the Department of the Army, and the National Guard. In any case where Army doctrine differs, the laws, policies, regulations, and directives take precedence.

SCOPE

The manual's primary focus is on the operational Army echelons that conduct civil support operations. These include battalions, brigades, division headquarters, and Army Service component headquarters. However, these echelons require extensive support from the generating force, including Army civilians and contractors, and the FM addresses that support as applicable.

Although two combatant commands, United States Pacific Command and United States Northern Command, conduct civil support operations, this manual uses United States Northern Command terminology and methods throughout. Users located in the United States Pacific Command area of responsibility should refer to theater plans and standing operating procedures for specific civil support procedures in that theater. The fundamentals of civil support operations remain the same, but the unique characteristics of the Pacific region alter some of the details of defense support of civil authorities and National Guard civil support within the United States Pacific Command area of responsibility.

FM 3-28 is organized into nine chapters and eleven supporting appendixes. Chapters 1 and 2 provide an overview of domestic operations and the Army's role in civil support. Chapters 3, 4, 5, and 6 explain the primary civil support tasks—provide support for domestic disasters; provide support for domestic chemical, biological, radiological, nuclear, or high-yield explosives incidents (CBRNE incidents); provide support for domestic civilian law enforcement agencies; and provide other designated support. Chapter 7 provides a legal discussion aimed primarily at unit commanders, providing them with sufficient information to understand what their staff judge advocates should tell them. Chapters 8 and 9 address sustainment (logistics, personnel services, and health service support), but due to the complexity of the subject, logistic and personnel services are in chapter 8, and health service support receives separate discussion in chapter 9.

The appendixes address specific details pertinent to civil support operations—planning, safety, specialized response forces, airspace command and control, search and rescue, unmanned aircraft systems, incident command, media considerations, and Army tactical tasks. Appendixes C, D, and E provide a review of the three Army forces organized specifically for chemical, biological, radiological, nuclear, or high-yield explosives incidents. These three appendixes provide nascent doctrine on these organizations, pending the development of more detailed tactics, techniques, and procedures for each.

Just as civil support and incident management and response continue to evolve within all echelons of government, so too will FM 3-28. The Combined Arms Center plans to replace this edition in 18 months with a multi-Service manual written in conjunction with the Marine Corps. The multi-Service manual will address land force civil support operations. It will capitalize on material not yet available when this edition of FM 3-28 was prepared, such as the *DSCA Tactical Commander's Handbook* (scheduled to be released in late July, 2010), in order to streamline the content.

INSTRUCTIONS ON EFFECTIVE USE OF THIS MANUAL

Readers should review the entire manual. Civil support principles, policies, and terminology—introduced in the first three chapters—are distinct from those used for military operations overseas. All readers should understand chapters 1 through 3 before applying any of the other content.

APPLICABILITY

This publication applies to the Active Army, the Army National Guard (ARNG)/Army National Guard of the United States (ARNGUS), and the United States Army Reserve (USAR) unless otherwise stated. The target audience for this manual is broad. It includes the commanders, leaders, and staff of Army forces involved in civil support operations. It also provides general information to civil authorities at federal, state, local, and tribal levels for use when coordinating with Army forces engaged in civil support operations. This manual is suitable for use by other Services coordinating with Army forces engaged in civil support operations and other organizations (including the Coast Guard) providing support to civilian agencies.

This doctrine does not apply to Army forces engaged in counterterrorism operations, nor does it apply to any state defense force that is not part of the National Guard. It also does not cover operations of the United States Army Corps of Engineers, a direct reporting unit of the Army that provides civil support in accordance with U.S. law and other applicable regulations. Finally, this doctrine does not apply to military activities conducted within a military installation.

ADMINISTRATIVE INFORMATION

Headquarters, U.S. Army Training and Doctrine Command (TRADOC), is the proponent for this publication. The preparing agency is the Combined Arms Doctrine Directorate, U.S. Army Combined Arms Center. Send written comments and recommendations on a DA Form 2028 (Recommended Changes to Publications and Blank Forms) to Commander, U.S. Army Combined Arms Center and Fort Leavenworth, ATTN: ATZL-CD (FM 3-28), 300 McPherson Avenue (Building 463), Fort Leavenworth, KS 66027-2337. The point of contact for FM 3-28 is the Combined Arms Doctrine Directorate at (913) 684-4884; or by e-mail to: leav-cadd-web-cadd@conus.army.mil; or submit an electronic DA Form 2028.

Introduction

Field Manual (FM) 3-0 states that "Army forces combine offensive, defensive, and *stability or civil support* [emphasis added] operations simultaneously as part of an interdependent joint force to seize, retain, and exploit the initiative, accepting prudent risk to create opportunities to achieve decisive results. They employ synchronized action—lethal and nonlethal—proportional to the mission and informed by a thorough understanding of all variables of the operational environment. Mission command that conveys intent and an appreciation of all aspects of the situation guides the adaptive use of Army forces." The introductory figure illustrates how the elements of full spectrum operations can be combined.

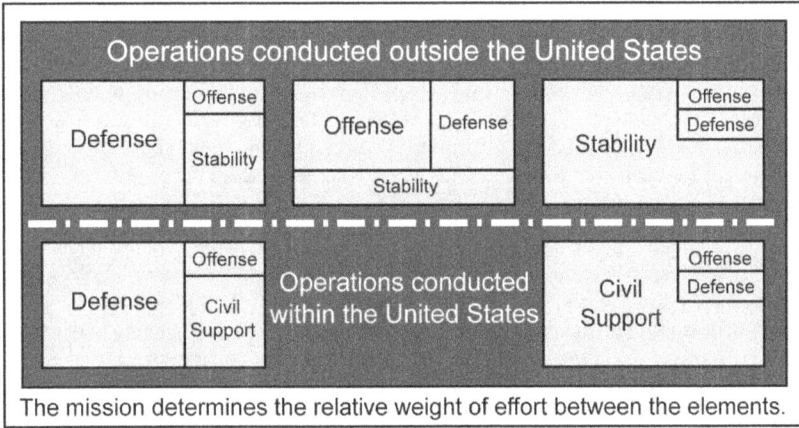

Introductory figure—full spectrum operations

FM 3-28 explains how the Army conducts civil support operations, the fourth element of full spectrum operations. It discusses similarities and differences between civil support operations and the other elements of full spectrum operation. Stability operations and civil support operations are similar in several ways. Both revolve around the civilians on the ground within land areas of operation. Both stability and civil support tasks require Army forces to provide essential services and work with civilian authorities. However, domestic operational environments are quite different in terms of law, military chain of command, use of deadly force, and interagency process.

Protecting the United States from direct attack is the highest priority of the United States Armed Forces. Since the First World War, the Armed Forces have focused primarily on defending the United States by projecting power overseas. According to Section 3062, Title 10, United States Code, the Army ". . . shall be organized, trained, and equipped primarily for prompt and sustained combat incident to operations on land." However, when civil authorities request assistance or if directed by the President, the Armed Forces also have great capability to respond to domestic emergencies and disasters. Department of Defense conducts these operations under civilian control in accordance with the Constitution of the United States. Based on the Constitution, and consistent with America's history, the military does not lead the federal response except by the direction of the President, under conditions of extreme domestic emergency, or threat of war.

Civil support operations encompass support provided by the components of the Army to civil authorities within the United States and its territories. This includes support provided by the Regular Army, Army

Reserve, and National Guard. They conduct civil support operations, either in combination with offensive and defensive operations, or singly, in support of civil authorities.

Substantial portions of the Army's strength reside in the Army National Guard, including 33 of 73 brigade combat teams, and almost half of the Army's multifunctional brigades. The Army National Guard has a dual role for civil support operations. It may serve in a federal capacity, under the command of the President, and integrated with Regular Army units, as part of a federal military joint task force. The Army National Guard also provides the states and territories with the "organized militia" ordained in the sixteenth clause of Section 8, Article I, of the Constitution of the United States. As the direct descendants of the militia formations pre-dating the Revolution, today's National Guard provides each state, territory, and the District of Columbia with military capability to conduct civil support operations when directed by their respective governors, as part of a joint task force–state.

When operating overseas, the distinction between the three components of the Army—Regular, Reserve and National Guard—is irrelevant. All are conducting full spectrum operations under a single joint force commander. When operating overseas, the National Guard is federalized and operates under the same rules, regulations, and guidance as the Regular Army. The majority of Regular and Reserve Soldiers will serve with their National Guard counterparts in this environment and will see them operate under exactly the same rules and conditions as themselves. However, this is not the case when the Regular Army, Army Reserve, and National Guard conduct civil support operations. There are important differences in the rules, regulations, laws, and guidance that guide employment of the components of the Army when operating within the United States, its trusts, and territories. This manual highlights those differences and explains why it is important for each component to understand what these differences are and how they affect the conduct of civil support operations.

For military forces conducting civil support operations, there is a federal response under the control of the President and a state response under the control of a state's governor. Federal military forces operate under the command and control of the President, the Secretary of Defense, and the supported combatant commander. A state's military forces (referred to as state National Guard) operate under the command and control of the governor, exercised through a state joint force headquarters (referred to as a joint force headquarters–state) headed by the adjutant general of that state. While federal and state National Guard forces operate in proximity to one another, they remain under their respective chains of command. Unity of command, as the military defines it, is not applicable between state and federal government agencies in these circumstances. It is also not applicable to the federal military forces and state National Guard, unless the President and the governor formally agree to appoint a dual-status commander. Therefore, achieving unity of effort in civil support operations becomes essential.

Federal military forces normally operate under a joint task force formed by the combatant commander and deployed in support of a federal primary agency. Combatant commanders have authority to alert forces under their command to prepare for civil support, but actual conduct of civil support operations requires authorization from the Secretary of Defense or designated authority. Federal military forces normally augment the federal agencies' ability to assist state and local governments. The response effort typically begins with a declaration of a disaster or emergency by the President, but it may also be initiated by a request for assistance from another federal agency or a state governor. The President may mobilize units of the National Guard for federal service within the United States, but the laws governing the domestic operations of the Regular Army also regulate National Guard Soldiers in federal service.

> **Federal military forces:** Regular Army, Navy, Marine and Air Force personnel and units; mobilized Army, Navy, Air Force and Marine Reserve forces and personnel; and any National Guard forces and personnel mobilized for federal service in accordance with Title 10, United States Code. The President of the United States is their Commander in Chief.
>
> **State National Guard forces:** Air and Army National Guard personnel and units serving under state control, in accordance with Title 32, United States Code. The governor of each respective state has overall command responsibility for the National Guard in that state and is their Commander in Chief. State National Guard forces do not include state defense forces organized outside of the National Guard.

State National Guard forces normally operate as part of a state National Guard joint task force formed from units of the state's Air National Guard and Army National Guard. The governor of each state has overall command and has the authority to alert and deploy their state's National Guard units to support state agencies. The National Guard provides state governors with military capabilities for various emergencies in the states. Because of their proximity, the National Guard is typically the first military force to respond to domestic emergencies. Unless placed in Title 10 status, the National Guard continues to operate under the command of the state governor and state National Guard chain of command. When operating as part of the state National Guard, the National Guard falls under state laws and generally has more flexibility in supporting local authorities.

When federal military forces and state National Guard forces are participating in civil support operations, supported combatant commanders communicate through the National Guard Bureau to the National Guard joint force headquarters–state. The National Guard Bureau serves as the "channel of communications" to the states. If an adjutant general establishes a subordinate task force or joint task force, the supported combatant commander may be given direct liaison authority with the task force or joint task force. In a disaster response situation, the combatant commander may receive permission to coordinate directly with the states or to subordinate commands within the states.

Homeland security and homeland defense are complementary components of the National Security Strategy. *Homeland defense* is the protection of U.S. sovereignty, territory, domestic population, and critical defense infrastructure against external threats and aggression, or other threats as directed by the President (Joint Publication (JP) 3-27). Missions are defined as homeland defense if the nation is under concerted attack from a foreign enemy. Department of Defense leads homeland defense and is supported by the other federal agencies. In turn, Department of Defense supports the Nation's homeland security effort, which is led by the Department of Homeland Security. *Homeland security* is the concerted national effort to prevent terrorist attacks within the United States; reduce America's vulnerability to terrorism, major disasters, and other emergencies; and minimize the damage and recover from attacks, major disasters, and other emergencies that occur (JP 3-28). In both homeland defense and homeland security, the Army conducts civil support operations. The discussion in this field manual emphasizes civil support operations in support of homeland security.

> Note: Coast Guard forces are unique in that they normally operate under Title 14, United States Code, as part of the Department of Homeland Security, but they may come under the operational control of Department of Defense for some missions. In some homeland security missions the Coast Guard may exercise tactical control of federal military forces.

Civil support operations require mastery of a specialized vocabulary derived from national laws and policies. In the interest of clear communication, the Combined Arms Center avoids using shortened forms (acronyms and abbreviations). However, in a few cases the shortened form is easier to say and remember than the full term. In other cases, the shortened form has become commonly used (such as FEMA for Federal Emergency Management Agency), and this manual uses it as such. See the glossary in the back of this manual for a listing of acronyms used.

This page intentionally left blank.

Chapter 1
The Domestic Environment

This chapter provides a broad overview of civil support and how it differs from operations conducted outside the United States. This overview includes definitions of key terms related to civil support operations. This chapter reviews the Army's Constitutional foundation. It also discusses components of the Army and unit status as they relate to civil support operations. The chapter then discusses key aspects of domestic operations. It specifies four primary civil support tasks and identifies five fundamentals that apply to all components of the Army. It concludes with a summary of training requirements.

THE ARMY AND CIVIL SUPPORT OPERATIONS

1-1. Civil support is the fourth element of full spectrum operations. Civil support operations encompass support provided by the components of the Army to civil authorities within the United States and its territories. The range of response includes support provided by the Regular Army, Army Reserve, and National Guard. They may conduct civil support operations either in combination with offensive and defensive operations, as part of homeland defense, or exclusively in support of civil authorities.

1-2. Although not the primary purpose for which the Army is organized, trained, and equipped, civil support operations are a vital aspect of the Army's service to the Nation. The skills that allow Soldiers to accomplish their missions on today's battlefields can support local, state, and federal civil authorities, especially when domestic emergencies overwhelm the ability of government agencies to support fellow Americans. That is not the only thing that the Army can provide. Army equipment developed for combat can assist law enforcement agencies, rescue operations, and a host of other requirements. Army trainers can apply their skills to mentor their civilian counterparts in those things at which the Army excels. The Army has a long history of civil support operations, back to its inception. In any given year, thousands of Soldiers support civilian agencies in missions ranging from disaster response to support for major sporting events.

1-3. Just as commanders need to understand each operational environment in campaigns conducted outside the United States, they need to understand the domestic operational environments in which they conduct full spectrum operations. However, there are important differences about operations conducted in support of civil authorities—principally, the roles of civilian organizations and the relationship of military forces to federal, state, and local agencies. What support Army forces provide (who, when, where, and how) depends on specific circumstances. Soldiers and civilians need to understand the domestic environment so they can employ the Army's capabilities efficiently, effectively, and legally.

DEFENSE SUPPORT OF CIVIL AUTHORITIES DEFINED

1-4. This discussion defines *defense support of civil authorities* and clarifies the usage of the terms *civil support, defense support of civil authorities,* and *National Guard civil support. Civil support* is defined as Department of Defense support to U.S. civil authorities for domestic emergencies, and for designated law enforcement and other activities (Joint Publication (JP) 3-28). *Defense support of civil authorities* (DSCA) is defined as—

> *Support provided by U.S. Federal military forces, National Guard forces performing duty in accordance with Reference (m) [Title 32, United States Code], DOD [Department of Defense] civilians, DOD contract personnel, and DOD component assets, in response to requests for assistance from civil authorities for special events,*

domestic emergencies, designated law enforcement support, and other domestic activities. Support provided by National Guard forces performing duty in accordance with Reference (m) [Title 32, United States Code], is considered DSCA but is conducted as a State-directed action. Also known as civil support.

Department of Defense Directive (DODD) 5111.13

Civil authorities are defined as those elected and appointed officers and employees who constitute the government of the United States, the governments of the 50 states, the District of Columbia, the Commonwealth of Puerto Rico, United States possessions and territories, and political subdivisions thereof (JP 3-28).

1-5. DSCA will replace two older terms. The first term, *military support to civil authorities*, was defined as a mission of civil support consisting of support for natural or manmade disasters, chemical, biological, radiological, nuclear, or high-yield explosive consequence management, and other support as required (DODD 3025.1). In addition, DSCA will replace the term *military assistance to civil authorities*, defined as the broad mission of civil support consisting of the three mission subsets of military support to civil authorities, military support to civilian law enforcement agencies, and military assistance for civil disturbances (DODD 3025.1). The meanings of these terms are included in the definition of DSCA. In general usage, the terms *civil support* and *DSCA* are interchangeable when referring to operations conducted by federal military forces.

NATIONAL GUARD CIVIL SUPPORT DEFINED

1-6. *National Guard civil support* is defined as support provided by the National Guard of the several states while in state active duty status or Title 32 duty status to civil authorities for domestic emergencies, and for designated law enforcement and other activities. This definition is expected to be adopted by National Guard Regulation 500-1.

1-7. The range of response provided by Army forces includes Regular Army, Army Reserve, and state National Guard forces. The term DSCA, however, does not encompass the full range of response. Neither does National Guard civil support encompass the operations of all National Guard forces. Duty status determines whether National Guard forces are conducting National Guard civil support, DSCA, or both. National Guard duty statuses are state active duty, Title 32, or Title 10 (referring to Titles 32 and 10 of the United States Code, or USC). DSCA includes operations of National Guard forces in Title 32 status. DSCA does not include operations of the National Guard in state active duty status. National Guard forces in state active duty status or Title 32 duty status remain under the command of their governor. If National Guard forces become federalized—placed under Title 10—their operations fall under DSCA and not National Guard civil support. In Title 10 status, federalized National Guard forces are under the command of the President. When this manual discusses federal military forces, it refers to all forces in Title 10 status, including federalized National Guard. See paragraphs 1-25 to 1-32 for more information about duty statuses. Figure 1-1, on page 1-3, illustrates the range of response provided by Army forces.

The Domestic Environment

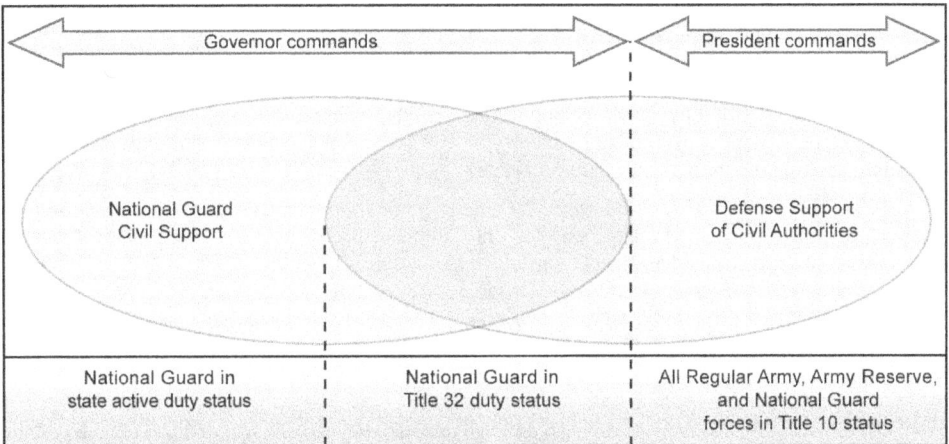

Figure 1-1. Range of response

Note. When a new DODD 3025.1 is approved, the updated definitions of DSCA and National Guard civil support will be incorporated into the joint dictionary. The new DODD 3025.1 will supersede the existing version, and the definitions of military support to civil authorities and military assistance to civil authorities will be eliminated from the joint dictionary. When updated, National Guard Regulation 500-1 will reflect updated definitions of DSCA and National Guard civil support.

1-8. Although the definitions of DSCA and National Guard civil support overlap, the most important distinction—and the one that affects field operations—is the status of the forces providing the support. By law, the National Guard remains under the command of the governor unless federalized, and the all forces in Title 10 status remain under the President's command (under Title 10, USC). The Army supports elected officials with complementary capabilities when and where needed through a unified effort, despite overlapping definitions. DODD 1200.17 states—

> *Homeland Defense and Defense Support to Civil Authorities (DSCA) are total force missions. Unity of effort is maintained consistent with statutory responsibilities in operations involving Federal forces and non-federalized National Guard forces with Federal forces under Federal command and control and non-federalized National Guard forces under State command and control*
>
> DODD 1200.17

1-9. Commanders and key staff need to understand why state National Guard forces and federal military forces operate under different chains of command in civil support. The following sections summarize some of the impacts in terms of—

- The structure of the United States under the Constitution of the United States and its impact on the Army
- The roles of the components of the Army—Regular, Reserve, and National Guard—and their requirements for providing civil support.
- Specific military aspects of civil support operations and how they differ from operations conducted outside the United States.

Chapter 1

THE CONSTITUTION OF THE UNITED STATES AND THE ARMY

1-10. Under the Constitution, the United States is a republic comprising of 50 states, together with various territories and possessions. This system, in which the states share powers with a central national government, is called federalism; it is the basis for division of powers between state and federal government. The Constitution carefully apportions powers within the federal government between the branches of the federal government (executive, legislative, and judicial) and the individual states. Regarding the Armed Forces, the Constitution states—

> *The Congress shall have power . . . To raise and support Armies, . . . To provide and maintain a Navy; To make Rules for the Government and Regulation of the land and naval Forces; To provide for calling forth the Militia to execute the Laws of the Union, suppress Insurrections and repel Invasions; To provide for organizing, arming, and disciplining, the Militia, and for governing such Part of them as may be employed in the Service of the United States, reserving to the States respectively, the Appointment of the Officers, and the Authority of training the Militia according to the discipline prescribed by Congress . . . .*
>
> Article I, Section 8 of the Constitution of the United States
>
> *The President shall be Commander in Chief of the Army and Navy of the United States, and of the Militia of the several States, when called into the actual Service of the United States . . . .*
>
> Article II Section 2 of the Constitution of the United States
>
> *. . . . [The President] shall take Care that the Laws be faithfully executed . . . .*
>
> Article II, Section 3 of the Constitution of the United States

1-11. The framers of the Constitution granted the states authorities concerning the militia, the predecessor of today's National Guard. This requirement is the constitutional basis for the separation of the National Guard from the Regular Army and Air Force. It is the authority that permits the state governors retain command over the National Guard within their respective states. There is not a chain of command in the military sense between the President and the governors. Each has certain powers under the Constitution. The President as head of Executive branch of the federal government and military commander in chief may only exercise the authorities granted by the Constitution and U.S. law. Within their respective states, the governors retain executive authority, including command over their state's National Guard until the President mobilizes it for federal service. The practical impact of this on the Army forces operating domestically is a legal division between the National Guard and federal military forces. This is unique to domestic operational environments, and commanders at all levels need to understand how it affects operations.

1-12. The Constitution also outlines the antipathy of the founding fathers towards the large militaries of the European powers. These men viewed a large standing army answering to the head of state as a continuous threat to civil liberty. Although the founders shared a fear of a large standing army, they also saw the necessity of a national army for the common defense. They balanced this requirement by providing the states with military capabilities. They had ample reasons for this balancing act.

1-13. The Articles of Confederation (1784 to 1787) failed to provide the national government with authority and means to act in the national interest. This led to the Constitutional convention to restructure the Nation's government. The Constitution of the United States (ratified in 1787) included provisions for federal and state forces to enforce the law. It was not long before this was tested. In 1794, the Whiskey Rebellion forced the first President to use armed forces to restore order. President Washington's guidance was that the military was to support local civil authorities, not pre-empt them. President Washington's response established the fundamental precept that the military supports civil authority and remains in law today.

ARMY COMPONENTS AND CIVIL SUPPORT OPERATIONS

1-14. Civil support provided by Regular, Army Reserve, and Army National Guard units varies according to domestic law and Department of Defense (DOD) policies. Each component has different civil support capabilities, requirements, and restrictions. Regular Army forces and Army Reserve units always remain under the command of the President of the United States, exercised through the Secretary of Defense and the various combatant commanders. The National Guard (including the Army National Guard and Air National Guard) are state forces and remain under the command of the governors of their respective states, unless mobilized for federal service under Title 10, USC. This creates a unique environment where Regular Army, mobilized Army Reserve, federalized National Guard, and National Guard forces under state command may conduct civil support operations simultaneously and in proximity while different agencies and under different chains of command. Commanders and civilian agencies need to keep in mind the distinctions between the components of the Army. The following sections highlight the components and their capabilities.

THE REGULAR ARMY

1-15. The Regular Army consists of approximately 550,000 professional Soldiers organized into operational forces intended for deployment and ground combat operations, and the generating force—professional Soldiers supported by civilians that sustain, train, and equip not only the Regular Army, but the other components of the Army as well. The operational forces and the generating force provide DSCA as directed by the Secretary of Defense. The Regular Army provides civilian leaders a menu of capabilities that capitalize on their expeditionary and campaign qualities. The most important of these are size, training and equipment levels, flexibility, and endurance.

1-16. The Regular Army's primary attribute for civil support is this component's ability to generate large forces rapidly and sustain them for long periods in an emergency. The Regular Army can provide large forces in the interim between the time a governor calls out the state's National Guard and the arrival of substantial civilian responders from outside the state (see chapter 3 regarding disaster response operations). When directed and with the support of United States Transportation Command, the Regular Army deploys forces ranging from small detachments to corps-sized formations of 100,000 troops or more, supported by the full resources of DOD. Because they are professionals, Soldiers of the Regular Army spend much more time in training than their reserve counterparts. They are also not under pressure from civilian employers to return to their occupations. In most cases Regular Army units have more modern equipment than the reserve components. All these factors make units of the Regular Army highly adaptive and flexible, mission-focused, and capable of prodigious effort.

1-17. The limitations on domestic employment of Regular forces include proximity, legal, and operational commitments. Regular Army units are concentrated at several large installations spread across the country and may be based far from an incident location. Their ability to respond is less a factor of their readiness than one of intra-theater transportation. While legal considerations affect all Soldiers, there are additional legal limitations on the use of Regular Soldiers, discussed in detail in subsequent chapters. Perhaps the most important limitation on the use of Regular forces is their operational tempo—the rapidity with which Regular Army forces are committed to support ongoing campaigns and other missions outside the United States. The nearest or most suitable Regular Army unit may be committed to operations elsewhere, with some or all of its equipment and personnel in route to another theater.

THE ARMY RESERVE

1-18. The Army Reserve is one of two reserve components of the Army. It consists of approximately 206,000 Soldiers. It includes both units and individuals. Although it does not have any brigade combat teams, it does include supporting units of almost every type. Army Reserve units are located throughout the country.

1-19. The law currently restricts the use of Army Reserve units for civil support missions. In general, Army Reserve units can only conduct civil support operations in two circumstances. First, Army Reserve units may be mobilized by the President in response to a chemical, biological, radiological, nuclear, or high-yield explosives incident. Second, Army Reserve units already on active duty for training may provide immediate response or other civil support when authorized by DOD. However, any time spent on civil support operations is counted against the total training time for that year, and may not exceed the total active duty for training time allotted for that year.

1-20. Individual call-up and augmentation of Regular Army units conducting civil support follows similar rules to those applied in a limited Presidential call-up. Refer to chapter 7 for additional discussion on the restrictions on the use of Army Reserve forces for domestic operations.

THE ARMY NATIONAL GUARD

1-21. The Army National Guard is the other reserve component of the Army. It consists of approximately 360,000 Soldiers. Each state, each territory, and the District of Columbia have National Guard forces, for a total of 54 state and territorial Army National Guard elements. These forces are organized into modular formations identical to those of the Regular Army and Army Reserve. Unlike the Regular Army, however, the Army National Guard has a dual role. As a reserve component of the Army, the President may mobilize the National Guard for federal service. In this capacity, the Army National Guard provides an operational reserve for the Regular Army. This includes eight of the Army's 18 division headquarters, 33 of the Army's 73 brigade combat teams, 47 per cent of the Army's multifunctional support brigades, and 40 per cent of the Army's functional support brigades. Until the President brings any unit of the National Guard into federal service, National Guard forces remain under the command of their respective state or territorial governor. As state forces, the Army National Guard units provide the majority of the Soldiers committed to civil support, and are critical to the state's support of its citizens.

1-22. Army National Guard units have advantages and disadvantages when employed in a civil support role. Their significant advantages are proximity, responsiveness, knowledge of local conditions, tactical flexibility in civil support missions, and closer association with state and local officials. The important disadvantages of National Guard forces are unit distribution between states, limited endurance, and the ability of the states to fund them.

1-23. Because they are state resources, the governor can activate National Guard units based on requirements in that state. During an emergency, Army National Guard units often task-organize with Air National Guard units from that state in state joint task forces. In state service, the National Guard is more flexible in terms of law enforcement and in the range of missions they may be assigned in support of first responders. Quite often, their leaders are personal acquaintances of the other key state officials, which tend to speed communication through state channels.

1-24. Possibly the most important limitation of the Army National Guard is its endurance. Each day the National Guardsman is deployed is a day away from civilian employment. Most employers are generous in allowing time for National Guard call-ups, but deployments for annual training, state civil support missions, and deployment overseas, create serious strains. The endurance of the National Guard is also limited by fiscal considerations. The state has limited funds to pay personnel and operational costs, including health care costs. A third limitation is structural. Although the Army tries to align unit organizations as closely as possible within that state's National Guard, units may still be distributed across more than one state. Thus, the combat organizations with which National Guard units train in annual training may be different than the units that command them in civil support operations.

DUTY STATUS OF FORCES CONDUCTING CIVIL SUPPORT OPERATIONS

1-25. The particular duty status of a unit—the legal standing of the organization—determines its chain of command and in some cases the missions it may undertake within the United States and its territories (the homeland). Depending on their status, units may be described as federal military forces or state National Guard forces. However, the inclusion of National Guard forces within either category varies, as discussed in paragraphs 1-26 to 1-32.

FEDERAL MILITARY FORCES (TITLE 10 STATUS)

1-26. Title 10, USC, governs all federal military forces. For the Army, these forces include the Regular Army, the Army Reserve, and all National Guard units ordered to federal active duty in Title 10 status ("federalized" National Guard). For the other Services, federal military forces include all their components except the Air National Guard unless it mobilizes for federal service. Federal military forces—all forces in Title 10 status, including federalized National Guard—are federal assets under the command of the President. The Posse Comitatus Act restricts federal military forces—all forces in Title 10 status, including federalized National Guard (see chapters 5 and 7 for more information about the Posse Comitatus Act).

1-27. In a large-scale disaster, the President may direct that federal military forces support federal agencies, but these forces will remain under federal, not state command. In most cases, there are separate federal and state chains of command assisting numerous organizations on the ground. Unity of effort across jurisdictions and involving numerous organizations requires significant effort in establishing effective communication.

STATE NATIONAL GUARD FORCES IN STATE ACTIVE DUTY OR TITLE 32 STATUS

1-28. National Guard forces under the control of the governor may be in either a state active duty status or Title 32 status. Although there are legal distinctions between the two statuses, there is no difference in their tactical employment. Therefore, this manual refers to National Guard forces in either status as state National Guard forces. Some states have uniformed forces that are not part of the National Guard and are not considered state National Guard forces. These state defense forces and are discussed in paragraph 1-33.

State Active Duty Status

1-29. When the governor mobilizes the state National Guard, the forces are in state active duty status, under the command and control of the governor. The state government pays the expenses for forces in state active duty status. National Guardsmen on state active duty conduct all missions in accordance with the needs of the state and within the guidelines of state laws and statutes. National Guardsmen on state active duty receive pay from that state and are subject to the state military codes (not the Uniform Code of Military Justice). National Guard forces in state active duty status can perform civil law enforcement missions in accordance with the laws and statutes of their state. Generally, National Guard forces assist with incident management and homeland security operations within the state.

Title 32 Status

1-30. Under certain circumstances, a governor may request that the federal government pay for the costs associated with a state call up of the National Guard for responding to an emergency. When the Secretary of Defense approves, National Guard forces change from state active duty status to Title 32 status. Title 32, USC, is the principal federal statute covering the National Guard. Even though the National Guard forces are on active duty and funded by the federal government, in Title 32 status, National Guardsmen, remain under the command of the governor. Although the distinction between funding lines is important to the respective state and federal treasuries, it has no tactical impact. For Army commanders, the important distinction is that National Guard units in Title 32 status remain under state control and therefore have authority for some missions that Regular Army and Army Reserve units do not. Because forces in Title 32 status remain under the command of the governor, National Guard units may conduct law enforcement missions and are not subject to the restriction of the Posse Comitatus Act.

1-31. The National Guard of one state can assist other states responding to a disaster through formal agreements, such as the Emergency Management Assistance Compact (known as EMAC). Typically, this occurs in state active duty, and may transition to Title 32 status upon approval by the Secretary of Defense. When requested by the supported state's governor and authorized by the supporting state's governor under a separate memorandum of agreement, National Guard elements deploy to the supported state. The supporting National Guard operates under the operational control of the supported state's adjutant general. Typically, deployments under an assistance memorandum are limited to a specific period, such as 30 days. Often, military and civilian officials refer to all National Guard forces as "Title 32 forces," notwithstanding that some of them may be in a state active duty status—without federal funding. Table 1-1 summarizes the types of National Guard duty status.

Table 1-1. State active duty, Title 32, and Title 10 status summary

	State Active Duty	*Title 32*	*Title 10*
Command and control by—	Governor	Governor	President
Where missions are performed:	Within respective state or territory and according to emergency management assistance compact or state-to-state memorandum of agreement	Within respective state or territory and according to emergency management assistance compact or state-to-state memorandum of agreement	Worldwide
Funded by—	State government	Federal government funds, administered by the state	Federal government
Types of missions:	Under state law—missions include riot control, law enforcement, and emergency (incident) response	Missions include service for annual training, drills, disaster and law enforcement missions, and other federal military requirements. Title 32 status for incident response requires a disaster or emergency declaration by the President	Missions include worldwide training and operations, as assigned by joint commander
Discipline:	State military code	State military code	Uniform Code of Military Justice
Conduct law enforcement?	Yes, as authorized by the supported governor	Yes, as authorized by the supported governor	No, strictly limited by the Posse Comitatus Act, standing execute orders, and Department of Defense directives
Pay determined by—	State law	Department of Defense Publication 7000.14-R	Department of Defense Publication 7000.14-R
Travel, lodging, and benefits determined by—	State law	Department of Defense travel regulations (http://www.defensetravel.dod.mil/perdiem/trvlregs.html) and public law	Department of Defense travel regulations (http://www.defensetravel.dod.mil/perdiem/trvlregs.html) and public law

1-32. State and territorial National Guard forces have primary responsibility for providing military support to state and local authorities in emergencies. In most civil support situations, the President will not federalize National Guard forces. National Guard units conduct advance planning with civilian responders Together these organizations—civilian and military—establish coordination plans and procedures based on National policy such as the National Incident Management System, the National Response Framework, and the National Planning Scenarios. Command and control follows the authority under which Service members are ordered to duty: state active duty and state National Guard forces remain under the authority of the respective governor, and federal military forces under federal command and control.

STATE DEFENSE FORCES

1-33. Not all individuals wearing an Army uniform are part of the Army. State defense forces may be present during civil support operations. Twenty-four states have a state defense force of some description, organized under a separate provision of Section 109(c) of Title 32, USC. A state defense force may be a "state organized defense force" or "state guard," or even a named militia unit. However, these forces are not National Guard forces, although they are the responsibility of the adjutant general. They are always under the governor's command. Each state continues to fund its state defense forces regardless of the nature of the disaster response—Title 32 status does not apply. State defense forces may conduct law enforcement missions consistent with states laws and orders by the governor. In some states and territories, the state defense force has law enforcement authority similar to a credentialed law enforcement officer. Many of these units wear standard Army uniforms when in state service. This can lead to confusion, since to civilians they appear to be members of the Armed Forces. The state often employs these elements within their county of residence.

KEY ASPECTS OF DOMESTIC OPERATIONS

1-34. Either a governor or federal civilian agencies may request help from the military when the situation exceeds their capacity to respond. However, DOD support, especially the active components of the military, is only temporary until local, state, and federal authorities resume their normal roles. Commanders keep in mind that federal laws require the supported federal agency (such as the Federal Emergency Management Agency) to reimburse DOD for any support the latter provides. That can be very expensive—Hurricane Katrina expenses that DOD billed to the Federal Emergency Management Agency exceeded five billion dollars.

1-35. Civil support operations are generally not the top priority mission of DOD. War fighting and the homeland defense mission are the top priority, but DOD must be prepared to conduct civil support missions. DOD is not the lead in civil support operations but supports a primary agency. The primary agency establishes priorities and maintains overall direction of the civil support. DOD anticipates requirements from the primary agency, and plans, prepares, and trains for such contingencies. Specific requirements are identified within the Chairman of the Joint Chiefs of Staff standing execute order for DSCA (referred to as the CJCS DSCA EXORD). In any DSCA contingency involving federal military forces, the defense coordinating officer is the Secretary of Defense's primary DOD agent for coordinating support to the federal coordinating officer.

1-36. In civil support operations, there is a federal-government-led response, one or more state-government-led responses, and one or more local-government-led (city, county, tribal) responses. The federal-government-led response is under the command and control of the President, Secretary of Defense and supported combatant commander. The state-government-led response is under the command and control of the governor. The local-government-led response is under the control of the mayor or local official. In civil support operations, all of these levels of responses, local, state, and federal, may be occurring simultaneously. Commanders and staffs need to understand key military aspects of the domestic environment. These aspects are summarized in Table 1-2, pages 1-10 to 1-11.

Table 1-2: Key military aspects of domestic operational environments

Military aspect	Impact on military operations
Army forces conduct civil support operations only in the United States and its possessions and territories. Army forces do not conduct civil support operations overseas.	Civil support operations do not include activities occurring solely within a military installation. Army forces do not conduct stability operations within the United States and its territories. Disaster relief operations overseas in support of a foreign nation are stability operations—foreign humanitarian assistance or foreign consequence management—and Department of State is normally the lead agency.
Department of Defense is not in the lead in civil support operations; Department of Defense supports a primary agency. The state National Guard is not the primary agency for civil support to its respective state. State National Guard forces support state agencies.	Although Soldiers always remain under their military chain of command, a primary civilian agency establishes the priorities. Missions develop in response to civilian requests for assistance.
In civil support operations, numerous relief efforts—local, state, and national—may occur simultaneously. Each has its own chain of command. A city mayor may control a local response. A tribal leader may control a tribal response. A governor may control a state response. The President controls the national response and the federal military response. The Secretary of Defense and supported combatant commander command and control federal military forces.	Military and civilian organizations support a primary agency but in most cases are not directly subordinate to it. Each level of government is sovereign within the limits of the law: a governor is not subordinate to the President, nor is a mayor subordinate to a governor. Two or more distinct military chains of command may operate within the same area. For example, active component and National Guard forces may support and report to different agencies, under different commanders.
Civil support is neither homeland defense nor homeland security. Federal military forces contribute to homeland security by conducting homeland defense and civil support operations. The same is true for state National Guard forces.	Army forces support federal and state homeland security requirements but are not part of Department of Homeland Security or similar state agencies. However, an adjutant general may be *dual-hatted* as a state's director of homeland security or emergency management.
The top priorities of Department of Defense are warfighting and homeland defense, not civil support. Department of Defense must be prepared, however, with trained and ready forces to conduct civil support missions.	Unless the Nation comes under attack by foreign forces, civil support will be the only element of full spectrum operations conducted in the Homeland. Should Army forces be required to conduct homeland defense operations, they may conduct civil support operations simultaneously with offensive and defensive operations.
Department of Defense and state National Guard forces work with the Department of Homeland Security and other agencies to anticipate requirements. This includes planning, preparation, and training for contingencies involving state National Guard and federal military forces.	Planning and preparation for civil support are continuous. They are based on national policy and federal government plans. State National Guard forces prepare to support state, regional, and national contingencies.
In a civil support operation, a defense coordinating officer coordinates with a federal coordinating officer as the Secretary of Defense's primary agent.	Within a joint (interagency) field office, a defense coordinating officer interfaces between the supported federal agencies and supporting federal military forces.
Federal military forces conduct civil support as part of a joint Service and interagency effort, under the command and control of the supported combatant commander.	Army forces—state National Guard forces and federal military forces—cooperate as part of a joint force in support of civil authorities, based on national policy. Military forces coordinate with local, state, and federal civil authorities according to the National Response Framework and the National Incident Management System.
Effective civil support operations depend on coordination with state and federal Interagency partners.	Coordination with civil authorities is critical. The structure of civilian government within the United States makes unity of command during incident response operations impractical, so commanders must do everything in their power to ensure unity of effort.

Table 1-2. Key military aspects of domestic operational environments (continued)

Military aspect	Impact on military operations
Military forces conduct civil support operations under state and federal laws.	Staff judge advocates are critical to mission success. State and federal laws determine how military forces operate within the United States; they limit the tasks military forces may perform. Due to legal requirements, commanders accept a certain amount of inefficiency.
Many tactical civil support tasks are similar to tactical stability tasks, with some important differences.	Although stability and civil support operations share most tactical tasks, the conditions for these tasks are quite different. Therefore, proficiency in stability tasks must be reinforced with specialized training for civil support operations.
Military forces receive reimbursement for the costs of civil support missions only if they maintain a detailed record of operations and associated costs.	In most cases, the law requires civilian agencies to reimburse the military for any operational costs associated with civil support missions. To obtain reimbursement, military forces must account for specific actions and costs in detail and present these figures to the appropriate agency for payment.

DIFFERENCES BETWEEN STABILITY AND CIVIL SUPPORT OPERATIONS

1-37. Civil support operations are conducted only within the United States and U.S. possessions and territories. Civil support is not conducted outside the United States. If DOD conducts disaster relief operations in support of a foreign nation, for example, it is a stability operation and is called foreign humanitarian assistance or foreign consequence management. The Department of State, not DOD, is in the lead for this type of effort.

1-38. Within homeland defense, Army forces combine offensive, defensive, and civil support operations as part of a joint operation to defend the United States from external attack or other threats. Within the framework of homeland security, Army forces, as part of a joint response at the state level, federal level, or both, will normally conduct civil support operations exclusively, often employing capabilities developed for other elements of full spectrum operations as part of civil support.

1-39. Stability operations and civil support have similar tasks. Both revolve around the civilians on the ground within land areas of operation. Both stability and civil support tasks require Army forces to provide essential services and work with civilian authorities. However, domestic operational environments are quite different in terms of law, military chain of command, use of deadly force, and the interagency process.

1-40. When operating overseas, the distinction between the three components of the Army—Regular, Reserve and National Guard—is irrelevant. All are conducting full spectrum operations under a single joint force commander. When operating overseas the National Guard is federalized and operates under the same rules, regulations, and guidance as the Regular Army. The majority of active component Soldiers will have most of their interaction with the National Guard in this environment and will see them operate under exactly the same rules and conditions as themselves. However, this is not the case when the Regular Army, Army Reserve, and National Guard conduct civil support operations. There are important differences in the rules, regulations, laws, and guidance that guide employment of the components of the Army when operating within the United States, its trusts and territories. It is important for to understand what these differences are and how they affect the conduct of civil support operations.

HOMELAND SECURITY AND HOMELAND DEFENSE

1-41. Civil support is not synonymous with homeland security or homeland defense. Civil support contributes to both homeland security and homeland defense. DOD supports homeland security and conducts homeland defense.

1-42. Joint doctrine defines *homeland security* as a concerted national effort to prevent terrorist attacks within the United States; reduce America's vulnerability to terrorism, major disasters, and other emergencies; and minimize the damage and recover from attacks, major disasters, and other emergencies that occur (JP 3-28).

1-43. The Department of Homeland Security describes homeland security as follows:

> *Homeland security is a widely distributed and diverse—but unmistakable—national enterprise. The term "enterprise" refers to the collective efforts and shared responsibilities of Federal, State, local, tribal, territorial, nongovernmental, and private-sector partners—as well as individuals, families, and communities—to maintain critical homeland security capabilities. The use of the term connotes a broad-based community with a common interest in the public safety and well-being of America and American society that is composed of multiple actors and stakeholders whose roles and responsibilities are distributed and shared. As the Commander-in-Chief and the leader of the Executive Branch, the President of the United States is uniquely responsible for the safety, security, and resilience of the Nation. The White House leads overall homeland security policy direction and coordination. Individual federal agencies, in turn, are empowered by law and policy to fulfill various aspects of the homeland security mission. The Secretary of Homeland Security leads the federal agency as defined by statute charged with homeland security: preventing terrorism and managing risks to critical infrastructure; securing and managing the border; enforcing and administering immigration laws; safeguarding and securing cyberspace; and ensuring resilience to disasters. However, as a distributed system, no single entity is responsible for or directly manages all aspects of the enterprise.*
>
> Quadrennial Homeland Security Review Report, February 2010

1-44. Joint doctrine defines *homeland defense* as the protection of United States sovereignty, territory, domestic population, and critical infrastructure against external threats and aggression or other threats as directed by the President (JP 3-27). The operative phrase is "external threats and aggression". Homeland defense begins far from the territory of the United States and depends upon U.S. forces and the assistance of immediate neighbors including Canada and Mexico. DOD takes the lead for homeland defense, and other federal government organizations provide support. For more information concerning homeland defense, refer to JP 3-27.

PRIMARY CIVIL SUPPORT TASKS

1-45. Field Manual (FM) 3-0, 27 February 2008, specifies three primary civil support tasks. FM 3-28 now adds an additional primary civil support task to those specified in FM 3-0, making four primary civil support tasks:

- Provide support for domestic disasters.
- Provide support for domestic chemical, biological, radiological, nuclear, or high-yield explosives incidents.
- Provide support for domestic civilian law enforcement agencies.
- Provide other designated support.

1-46. The expansion to four tasks recognizes the increased emphasis placed on chemical, biological, radiological, nuclear, or high-yield explosives incident response, particularly if terrorist groups employ weapons of mass destruction. Incidents involving chemical, biological, radiological, nuclear, or high-yield explosives threats require specialized capabilities, and the effects of weapons of mass destruction on domestic operational environments may be considerably more complex than other disasters. Similar considerations apply to pandemic response. Figure 1-2 illustrates the four primary civil support tasks with examples of missions for each.

Provide support for domestic disasters
- Response to natural and manmade disasters
- Response to all hazards except CBRNE incidents

Provide support for domestic CBRNE incidents
- Terrorist attacks
- Industrial accidents
- Pandemic influenza
- Human, animal, or crop diseases

Provide support for domestic civilian law enforcement agencies
- Civil disturbances
- Support during disasters
- Equipment and training
- State and federal counterdrug efforts
- Border security

Provide other designated support
- National special security events
- Other special events
- Wildfire response
- Critical infrastructure protection
- Augmentation of federal agencies

CBRNE incident   chemical, biological, radiological, nuclear, or high-yield explosives incident

Figure 1-2. Primary civil support tasks with examples

PROVIDE SUPPORT FOR DOMESTIC DISASTERS

1-47. There are many types of disasters, but they all have one thing in common: people in the disaster area have their lives upended and all too often, lose loved ones. Natural disasters occur throughout the United States and its territories. Some disasters afford some warning beforehand, such as hurricanes, ice storms, or even volcanic eruptions. The Department of Homeland Security, and specifically the Federal Emergency Management Agency, marshals available support in advance of these events and assists local and state officials with evacuation plans and recovery after the disaster. For other disasters, such as an earthquake or a chemical accident, there is usually no warning. Emergency services and law enforcement at every level respond according to prior planning and the availability of resources. Military response occurs at four levels:
- At the direction of the governor for state National Guard forces.
- A declaration by the President requested by the governor of the affected state.
- At the direction of Service Secretaries for capabilities not assigned to the combatant commanders (for example, bases and installations).
- Through immediate response authority.

PROVIDE SUPPORT FOR DOMESTIC CHEMICAL, BIOLOGICAL, RADIOLOGICAL, NUCLEAR, OR HIGH-YIELD EXPLOSIVES INCIDENTS

1-48. Since September 11, 2001, Americans understand the seriousness of an attack on the homeland by terrorists. Congress created the Department of Homeland Security to meet this threat in the wake of the attacks in 2001. The most dangerous threats to the homeland come from terrorist groups armed with weapons of mass destruction. The majority of scenarios discussed in the National Response Framework deal with accidental or deliberate threats posed by chemical, biological, radiological, nuclear, and high-yield explosives. In the aftermath of an attack with a weapon of mass destruction, federal military and state National Guard forces provide specialized capabilities and general-purpose forces in support of civil authorities.

1-49. Not every chemical, biological, radiological, nuclear, or high-yield explosive threat is from terrorists, or even manmade. Pandemic disease outbreaks (known as pandemics) fall under this civil support task. A pandemic is a global disease outbreak. A pandemic occurs when a new disease emerges for which people have little or no immunity and for which there is no vaccine immediately available. The disease spreads easily person-to-person, produces serious illness, and can sweep across the country and around the world in very short time. Pandemic influenza, for example refers to an influenza virus that infects humans across a large area and proves very difficult to contain. The word "pandemic" may confuse people, particularly those who equate it with mass casualties. Actually, the designation of pandemic does not relate to the lethality of the disease, but its spread. Influenza outbreaks are always serious because the virus may mutate into something more lethal as it spreads. Army support to pandemic response is both external and internal. Externally, Army forces respond to lead federal and state agencies request for support in dealing with the disease. Internally, Army installations take all applicable measures to maintain the combat readiness of the force.

1-50. Other outbreaks of infectious disease may prove more serious than a contagious influenza. These include animal diseases such as hoof and mouth disease and crop infestations caused by fungus, bacteria, or viruses. In these incidents, the Army provides support when requested by state or federal agencies, such as the Departments of Agriculture. Although technically not pandemics, these incidents could entail significant support from DOD and the National Guard.

PROVIDE SUPPORT FOR DOMESTIC CIVILIAN LAW ENFORCEMENT AGENCIES

1-51. This task applies to the restricted use of military assets to support civil law enforcement personnel conducting civil law enforcement operations within the United States and its territories. These operations are significantly different from operations outside of the boundaries of the United States. Army forces support civilian law enforcement under U.S. Constitutional and statutory restrictions and corresponding directives and regulations. Army leaders must understand the statutes governing the use of military assets for civil law enforcement. By understanding these statutes, Soldiers can avoid violating laws while achieving desired objectives.

PROVIDE OTHER DESIGNATED SUPPORT

1-52. This task denotes pre-planned, routine, and periodic support not related to a disasters or emergencies. Most often, this is support to major public events, and consists of participatory support, special transportation, and additional security. These events are national special security events such as the Olympics, an Inauguration, or a state funeral. Some missions may involve specific support requested by a federal or state agency to augment their capabilities due to labor shortages or a sudden increase in demands. Such support may extend to augmentation of critical government services by Soldiers, as authorized by the President and directed by the Secretary of Defense. For example, President Reagan replaced striking Air Controllers in the Federal Aviation Administration with like skilled military personnel, until newly hired civilians completed training. Other presidents have used Soldiers to move coal during strikes, or even take over key commercial enterprises when the President believed security considerations justified such radical action.

1-53. One of the missions that either federal military or state National Guard forces receive on a regular basis is firefighting within state and national lands. This is a hybrid mission, sharing aspects of disaster response and planned support to an agency or community. (See chapter 6 for more information about firefighting missions.)

FUNDAMENTALS OF CIVIL SUPPORT OPERATIONS

1-54. A broad set of fundamentals applies to any of the civil support tasks and guides Army leaders at every echelon. While every civil support mission is unique, these fundamentals shape the actions of commanders and leaders in the accomplishment of any civil support mission. Army forces may or may not be among the first organizations to arrive in an incident response operation. However, Army forces should be among the first organizations to complete their tasks, transition responsibilities to civil agencies, and leave. Civil support operations succeed when they create the conditions for civil authorities and nonmilitary groups to carry on the effort without military support. The fundamentals of civil support are—

- The primary purposes of civil support are to save lives, alleviate suffering, and protect property.
- The law defines every aspect of civil support operations—who has jurisdiction, who responds, and the restraints and constraints imposed on Soldiers.
- Civilian officials direct civil support operations. They set the priorities. The Army supports them.
- All costs associated with civil support missions must be documented.
- The military end state is reached when civilian authorities can fulfill their responsibilities without military assistance

THE PRIMARY PURPOSES OF CIVIL SUPPORT ARE TO SAVE LIVES, ALLEVIATE SUFFERING, AND PROTECT PROPERTY

1-55. While there are many potential missions for Soldiers as part of civil support, the overarching purposes of these missions are, in order, to save lives, alleviate suffering, and protect property. Some missions may accomplish these purposes directly. An aircraft crew participating in a search and rescue operation is there to save lives. Regular Army Soldiers fighting fires in a National Forest are guarding public property, as are the National Guard Soldiers patrolling streets in the aftermath of a tornado. Some civil support missions accomplish these purposes indirectly. The Soldiers and civilians assisting with the load-out of medical supplies that are being shipped from an installation to a municipal shelter will not meet the citizens housed there, but their actions help reduce the distress of their fellow citizens. In the absence of orders, or in uncertain and chaotic situations, each Soldier governs their actions based on these three purposes.

THE LAW DEFINES EVERY ASPECT OF CIVIL SUPPORT OPERATIONS—WHO HAS JURISDICTION, WHO RESPONDS, AND THE RESTRAINTS AND CONSTRAINTS IMPOSED ON SOLDIERS

1-56. The law defines almost every aspect of civil support operations. It prohibits many Soldiers from undertaking certain missions, in particular those associated with law enforcement. The law also specifies professional requirements for skills such as medical treatment. Commanders should consult with the staff judge advocate before authorizing Soldiers to execute any task outside of the mission received through the chain of command.

1-57. Domestic operational environments are quite different from other environments outside the United States because of U.S. law. Military forces operating in the domestic environment do not have a status-of-forces agreement as they would when deployed overseas. Disregard of the laws regarding civil support can cause military units to enter a legal minefield that will cripple mission accomplishment. Leaders at every level ensure that their Soldiers comply with applicable U.S. law, even when it hampers rapid accomplishment of the mission. For example, an Army unit storing or transporting ordnance and ammunition may be subject to Environmental Protection Agency restrictions. Unless waived by legal authority, laws restrict Army chaplains from conducting religious services for local citizens.

1-58. Every deploying headquarters requires a staff judge advocate or ready access to a staff judge advocate. Army staff judge advocates know and assess the applicability of federal and state laws when Army forces conduct civil support operations. Commanders concentrate particularly on legal limitations, especially those concerning law enforcement support by Regular Army forces and Army National Guard forces serving in Title 10 status. Unless there is an imminent risk to life or limb, commanders in doubt about the legal consequences of an action ask their higher headquarters for clarification.

1-59. Crises can bring out the best and worst in human nature, including military forces. With this in mind, military units, particularly early responding National Guard units, must be prepared to enforce the laws in environments where civilians' behavior is at its worst. The rules for use of force are restrictive, and leaders review them with their subordinates before every mission. All personnel must understand the standing rules for the use of force and any approved mission-specific rules for the use of force. The rules for the use of force are the equivalent of the rules of engagement, except that they apply in domestic, noncombat situations. The rules of engagement used in combat are permissive; the rules for the use of force are restrictive. Commanders give the same emphasis to rules for the use of force as to rules of engagement in a restrictive environment. Commanders always keep in mind that the first purpose of civil support is to save lives; lethal force is always a measure of last resort. (Chapter 7 discusses legal restrictions on the use of force. See also appendix B of JP 3-28.)

1-60. In civil support, military capability comprises—
- The ability to perform a task effectively and efficiently.
- The ability to perform a task safely.
- The legal authority to perform a task.

1-61. Soldiers are mission-focused and trained to exercise initiative in combat. Even if they lack resources, Soldiers often accomplish missions through non-doctrinal tactics, techniques, and procedures. Soldiers make up for a lack of resources by combining anything at hand with unlimited effort. While effective, it is inefficient. In civil support operations, commanders maintain a balance between the willingness of their subordinates to tackle any mission against the capability to do it.

1-62. Safety and risk management are paramount. Soldiers sometimes attempt to perform tasks without the appropriate training or equipment. In combat, their action may win the engagement. In civil support operations, it could lead to a lawsuit, legal action, an injury, or all three. Therefore, commanders ensure that Soldiers avoid improvising and adhere to all safety procedures. To illustrate, a collapsed building in the aftermath of an earthquake becomes one of the most hazardous places imaginable. If Soldiers attempt an improvised rescue, they may become victims themselves and kill the trapped survivors. Subsequent investigations may assign liability to the commander that proceeded without authority.

CIVILIAN OFFICIALS DIRECT CIVIL SUPPORT OPERATIONS: CIVILIANS SET THE PRIORITIES; THE ARMY SUPPORTS THEM

1-63. In civil support operations, the military works for the civilian agency. The command of military forces remains within military channels, but missions begin as requests for assistance from the supported civilian authorities. One of the biggest mistakes that tactical commanders may make is to assume that they need to take charge upon arrival at the scene of an incident. Military forces operating freely within civilian jurisdictions risk upsetting the balance between civilian authority and the private sector. While a commander may view sidestepping local authority as a faster means of accomplishing the mission, long-term recovery may be negatively affected. Commanders begin by viewing their areas of operations as a mosaic of civil authorities, each with primacy in its jurisdiction. While the mission may constitute a specific military task, commanders realize the end state requires that state, territorial, local, and tribal authorities provide effective support to their citizens, with the assistance of military forces.

1-64. Military forces are not organized or equipped to operate efficiently within the domestic environment, although they may be the most effective means of response early in an emergency. For example, a sapper engineer unit can remove enough debris to clear emergency routes, but a commercial construction company can usually do the job better, faster, and more cheaply when they arrive. In addition, the civilian construction contributes to economic recovery by putting local businesses and people back to work.

1-65. The primary civilian agency establishes the priority of effort in any civil support operation. At the federal level, this is typically the Federal Emergency Management Agency. At the state level, it is the state emergency management agency or equivalent. However, the civilian agencies do not issue orders to military units. Military planners located within a multiagency command structure integrate federal and state National Guard capabilities within priorities established by the primary agency. Typically, this is the defense coordinating officer at the federal joint field office and the state director of military support working with the state emergency manager. These individuals and their staffs ensure that military forces receive the correct priority of effort, and then translate the civilian guidance into mission assignments.

1-66. Army forces, regardless of their duty status, plan to accomplish their tasks and hand over any remaining tasks or duties to appropriate civil organizations as soon as feasible. Army forces complete their missions and redeploy in the least amount of time needed civil authorities to resume providing for citizens and carry on the response without military support. Federal military forces normally complete their tasks before the end state of complete recovery. National Guard forces often experience a double transition. In the first phase, they may take over missions previously assigned to joint federal military forces or National Guard forces sent from other states. In the second phase, they support the transition to a fully civilian-run recovery operation.

1-67. Because the National Guard of each state and territory builds relationships with its civilian counterparts continuously, when National Guard forces arrive to support an incident response they usually integrate with first responders very quickly. Federal forces benefit from the National Guard's contacts to develop amicable and efficient operations with local civil authorities.

ALL COSTS ASSOCIATED WITH CIVIL SUPPORT MISSIONS MUST BE DOCUMENTED

1-68. Another major distinction in domestic operations is the requirement for supported civilian agencies to reimburse DOD for any support provided by joint forces. All civil support provided by DOD is provided on a reimbursable basis unless otherwise directed by the President, or reimbursement is waived by the Secretary of Defense. Cost reimbursement for civil support is usually according to Section 1535 of Title 31, USC, (commonly called the Economy Act), which mandates cost reimbursement by the federal agency requesting support. The Robert T. Stafford Disaster Relief and Emergency Assistance Act (commonly known as the Stafford Act) sets the guidelines for reimbursements to federal agencies and states from federal funds set aside to support missions in response to a Presidential declaration. Federal law also mandates that the States reimburse the Federal Emergency Management Agency for a portion (usually 25 per cent) of any request for assistance that is passed to the federal level. This requires detailed documentation of what civil support state and federal military forces actually provided. Therefore, all military forces engaged in civil support maintain a detailed record of operations, and not just direct expenditures.

1-69. The practical effect on Army commanders is a requirement to document activities in much more detail than they normally would outside the United States. In particular, commanders ensure they document and report all transfers of equipment and supplies (including expendables) to another agency. As a rule, battalion and higher units designate a responsible staff section to document all costs associated with civil support missions and establish procedures for documenting costs within the unit. Subordinate leaders ensure that their subordinates keep logbooks, automated documentation systems, and reports up-to-date. Even in the initial response to a major catastrophe, leaders urge subordinates to record actions taken and resources transferred from their unit to civilians and other military units.

The Military End State Is Reached When Civilian Authorities Can Fulfill Their Responsibilities Without Military Assistance

1-70. The military end state for civil support missions, tactically and operationally, is based on the capabilities of civilian authorities to discharge their responsibilities without military assistance. Measures of effectiveness should be based upon civilian capability to perform a particular task without military assistance. As soon as that threshold is achieved, commanders report it to the supported agency through the military chain of command. This does not imply a complete return to normalcy; it means that civilian resources can continue the mission. For example, an Army unit may be tasked to deliver food and water to a community isolated by a disaster. As soon as the roads reopen, civilian relief organizations move in and begin supplying necessities using contracted vehicles. Although communities are still recovering, civilians can meet their most basic requirements without the military.

TRAINING FOR CIVIL SUPPORT OPERATIONS

1-71. Civil support operations require specialized training for military forces, although many of the tasks implemented at the tactical unit level can be similar to some of the tasks conducted in stability operations. Both focus on the civilians within an area of operations. Mission accomplishment depends on the success of civilian agencies, and not on battlefield victory. Both stability and civil support operations stress the employment of non-destructive means rather than the use of traditional lethal combat power that Soldiers employ during combat operations against enemy forces. However, in other aspects, the two elements of full spectrum operations are different. Operations conducted inside the borders of the United States require Army forces to provide support to civilian agencies through a comprehensive approach laid out in national doctrine and directives. Operations are constrained by different laws to a greater degree than prescribed by the Law of Land Warfare and The Hague and Geneva Conventions. It is accurate to say that both stability operations and civil support operations require similar capabilities—and achieve similar purposes—but Soldiers conduct them under radically different conditions.

Common Tasks by Warfighting Function

1-72. FM 7-15 (*The Army Universal Task List*, known as the AUTL) identifies a comprehensive list of Army tactical tasks (ARTs) and groups them into six warfighting functions. The warfighting functions (ARTs 1 through 6) address movement and maneuver (ART 1), intelligence (ART 2), fires (ART 3), sustainment, (ART 4), command and control (ART 5), and protection (ART 6). Additional larger tasks appear under army tactical task (ART 7), which includes tactical missions, full spectrum operations, and operational themes.

1-73. Appendix J of this manual compares the ARTs for stability and civil support operations. It also highlights tasks unique to stability operations and those that exclusively belong to civil support. Trainers should note that appendix omits the fires warfighting function, which does not contain ARTs directly applicable to stability or civil support operations. Excluding the fires tasks, there is a 78 per cent correlation between stability tasks and civil support tasks. That is, over three-fourths of the tasks units execute in stability operations also occur in civil support operations. The reverse, tasks unique to civil support, is currently very small (only five out of 630). The number of unique tasks will grow as forces cycle through civil support missions and identify additional tasks for the AUTL. For example, civil support operations require the unit to establish unclassified communication bridges between networks with federal, state, and local agencies.

1-74. Although units will perform the same tasks in either stability or civil support, the conditions and standards required for civil support operations will be different. For example, ART 7.3.1, establish civil security, has 19 different measures. Army forces conducting civil support also support civil security, but only in seven measures. The conditions and standards for the task are quite different for security provided in civil support.

TRAINING PRIORITY FOR CIVIL SUPPORT TASKS

1-75. Commanders tasked to prepare for civil support missions assess their unit's proficiency in three warfighting functions; in order of priority, they are command and control, sustainment, and protection. These three take priority because disasters usually occur without warning. The requirement to deploy into a restrictive operational environment, and operate with joint and interagency elements requires a well-drilled command and control system, with flexible Soldiers able to improvise and adapt systems intended for combat into a robust civilian disaster response system based upon National Incident Management System. The majority of missions given to Army forces in a disaster will stress the sustainment warfighting functions. Mission success will hinge upon the units' ability to deliver personnel, medical support, supplies, and equipment, while maintaining their equipment and their Soldiers. This will normally occur in an area devastated by a disaster and lacking potable water, power, and sanitation. This generates the third priority, protection. Even without the threat of attacks by terrorists, a disaster area is a dangerous place. In the event of a chemical, biological, radiological, nuclear, or high-yield explosives incident, it can become a deadly environment for those without proper training and equipment. For those units that have a specific chemical, biological, radiological, nuclear, or high-yield explosives mission, this function becomes their top training priority.

This page intentionally left blank.

Chapter 2
A Comprehensive Approach for Civil Support

This chapter builds on the principles introduced in chapter 1. It describes the national system for integration of all government agencies involved responding to domestic emergencies. It gives an overview of the National Incident Management System and the National Response Framework. After that, it clarifies responsibilities and relationships among civil authorities, Department of Defense, and the Army. In conjunction with defense support of civil authorities, the planning, policies, and procedures established in the national policy documents provide a comprehensive approach to civil support.

NATIONAL POLICY FOR DOMESTIC EMERGENCIES

2-1. The National Incident Management System (NIMS) establishes the national approach for incident management across local, state, and federal levels. (All types of emergencies and disasters generally are known as *incidents*.) In military terms, the NIMS contains the capstone doctrine for coordinated incident management in the United States. The incident management systems described in the NIMS is the foundation for the additional response procedures described in the National Response Framework (NRF). The NIMS and NRF also provide the foundation for National Planning Scenarios, developed for a range of threats from a terrorist nuclear attack to the outbreak of a deadly infectious disease. The Department of Homeland Security (DHS) promulgates and updates the NIMS, NRF, and supporting planning documents. The NIMS and NRF provide policy and guidance for federal agencies, including Department of Defense (DOD). Federal agencies develop supporting plans that implement the requirements established in the NIMS and NRF. Virtually all state, county, and city emergency managers use the NIMS and NRF.

2-2. The NIMS and NRF apply not only across all levels of government, but they also include military forces and nongovernmental organizations. This policy forms a comprehensive approach for responding to domestic emergencies. The NIMS and NRF provide guidance on how to achieve unity of effort across all participating organizations.

2-3. Incident response is a federally planned but bottom-up system, usually progressing from local, to state, to federal level as the magnitude of a particular incident exceeds the resources of the first responders. This is known as a "tiered response." Local first responders take initial action, whether an incident is a routine small-scale emergency or a major disaster requiring further assistance. Initially, local, state, and tribal officers rely on their own law enforcement, firefighting, and other resources, which may include the state's National Guard. Within each state, local chief executive officers (such as mayors, county commissioners, and tribal chief executive officers) assess the situation. If necessary, they request assistance from a neighboring county or municipality. Normally, assistance from neighboring jurisdictions follows established agreements. If an incident overwhelms these capabilities, the local civil authorities request state assistance. If necessary, the governor requests federal support. Federal military installations near the disaster may respond when asked by the local civil authorities (see chapter 3); in such instances, they may be the first Soldiers at the scene of an incident.

2-4. The leaders of tribal nations have the right to request certain federal assistance directly, bypassing the state in which tribal lands are located. In general, tribal nations have authority similar to state authority for incident response operations. However, a request for a Presidential declaration under the Robert T. Stafford Disaster Relief and Emergency Assistance Act (commonly known as the Stafford Act) must go through the governor of the state.

2-5. Even though they support civilian authority, all military forces remain under the operational and administrative control of their respective military chains of command. For the National Guard, this extends upward through the state National Guard command structure to the governor. Regular Army, mobilized Army Reserve, and Marine forces always remain under the command of the President through the Secretary of Defense and through the supported combatant commander or Service secretary. Military units support civilian organizations that follow the national policy in the NIMS and NRF (described in paragraphs 2-6 to 2-37), but Soldiers remain under military command and follow military doctrine, including this manual. Thus, a joint task force providing civil support plans according to the principles and processes described in Joint Publication (JP) 5-0. An Army brigade under operational control of a joint task force follows the Army operations process—plan, prepare, execute, and assess—and uses the military decisionmaking process. Similarly, Army forces exercise command and control through their existing structures; they do not modify their operations center to conform to the NIMS. However, they adapt their procedures and liaison arrangements to interface with their civilian counterparts.

THE NATIONAL INCIDENT MANAGEMENT SYSTEM

2-6. The NIMS has five components: preparedness, communications and information management, resource management, command and management, and ongoing management and maintenance. This discussion highlights the central construct of the NIMS—the command and management component. Individual responders and agencies manage and coordinate their efforts using these flexible elements of the NIMS command and management component:

- The incident command system.
- Multiagency coordination systems.
- Public information.
- NIMS planning process. Broadly similar to the military decision making process, the NIMS planning process guides responders in each tier as they respond to the situation with an incident action plan.

This field manual does not provide an exhaustive discussion of the NIMS. For the complete document, see the Federal Emergency Management Agency (FEMA) Web site at http://www.fema.gov.

Incident Command System

2-7. The NIMS establishes the *incident command system* as the standardized organizational structure for managing all domestic incidents. The incident command system includes common terminology, modular organization, management by objectives, reliance on an incident action plan, manageable span of control, and integrated communications (see the NIMS document online for a thorough discussion). Every incident command organization shares these characteristics, but each incident command structure adapts to the requirements of situation. In the immediate aftermath of any incident, local responders arrive first on the scene. First responders normally include law enforcement, fire, emergency medical services, and hazardous materials teams. At the incident site, local authorities organize the various responders based on the incident command structure.

2-8. Civilian incident management terms such as *single incident command, unified command,* and *area command* (explained further later in this chapter) do not include the idea of giving and receiving military orders. A civilian incident commander directs subordinates within his or her chain of authority. However, for the most part, this civilian commander *manages* other participating organizations and individuals. In this civilian usage of *command*—within a multiagency environment—groups and individuals generally carry out tasks they are willing to perform. Therefore, Army leaders adapt their leadership style not only to cooperate fully with other groups, but also to encourage cooperation among all participating organizations and individuals. Army leaders keep in mind that they serve in a supporting role.

2-9. The incident command system prescribes five major functional areas: command, operations, logistics, planning, and finance. As required, information and intelligence functions are located in the planning section. However, if the situation warrants, the incident command system recommends that the organization break intelligence out as a sixth functional area. The incident command system is flexible to accommodate all circumstances including floods, hazardous material accidents, aircraft crashes, or earthquakes—it is an all-hazards system. It is flexible enough to manage catastrophic incidents involving thousands of response personnel; several levels of command are possible. Options include a single incident command structure, a unified command structure, and an area command.

2-10. A *single incident command* structure refers to situations in which one incident commander has manageable span of control. The single incident commander is normally the senior responder of the local civilian organization with the responsibility for the incident, such as a fire chief or police chief. When there is only one incident commander, he or she establishes an incident command post at a safe distance from but not near the scene of the emergency to direct operations.

2-11. The incident command system provides the flexibility for agencies to coordinate and combine any number of independent efforts in an effective and efficient response. Based on the situation, a *unified command* structure enables agencies with different legal, geographic, and functional responsibilities to plan and coordinate operations. In a unified command structure, the individuals designated by their jurisdictional authorities jointly determine objectives, plans, and priorities and work together to execute them. By working as a team, the unified command overcomes much of the inefficiency and duplication of effort that can occur when agencies from different functional and geographic jurisdictions, or agencies at different levels of government, operate without a common organizational framework.

2-12. The primary difference between the single incident command structure and the unified command structure is that in a single incident command structure, one incident commander is solely responsible for establishing incident management objectives and strategies. Unified command strives for unity of effort as all responding agencies and organizations support the unified command without giving up individual agency authorities, responsibilities, or accountability.

2-13. An incident large enough to require federal military support will usually be multijurisdictional and use a unified command structure. In addition, a very large or complex incident may have separate incident command organizations (any combination of single or unified commands). The primary federal agency may establish an *area command* to coordinate separate incident commands responding to a larger emergency. (State authorities managing a complex, multijurisdictional response without federal assistance may also use an area command.) An area command does not have operational responsibilities—it is a management organization. Its functions include setting priorities, allocating resources according to established priorities, ensuring effective communications, and ensuring that incident management objectives are met and do not conflict with each other or with policy. (An area command becomes a *unified area command* when it is managing more than one multijurisdictional incident. This is different from a *unified command* responding to a single multijurisdictional incident.)

Incident Command Staff

2-14. When an incident requires a team of responders, the incident commander establishes an incident command post as close to the incident as practical. In a small incident command post, the incident command staff typically includes a public information officer, a safety officer, and a liaison officer. Depending on the nature of the incident, the incident commander adds additional staff support as needed. The incident command staff typically consists of operations, planning, logistics, and finance and administration section chiefs. These individuals, along with an incident commander (or unified command) and other qualified emergency management personnel, are known as an *incident management team*. Figure 2-1 illustrates the incident command staff developed by NIMS. (See appendix I for more details about the incident command staff sections.)

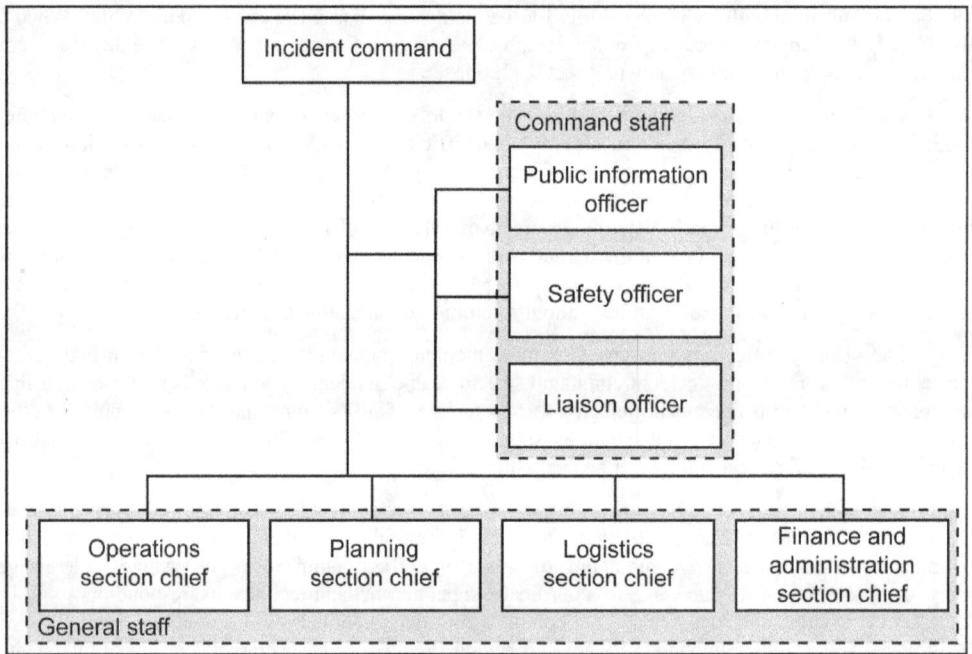

Figure 2-1. NIMS incident command staff

2-15. The incident command staff has three sections identified as command staff. These are the public information officer, the safety officer, and liaison officer. The public information officer is responsible for interfacing with the public, the news media, and other agencies with incident-related information. The public information officer assembles accurate, accessible, and complete information on the incident's cause, size, and current situation, the resources committed, and other matters of general interest for both internal and external audiences. The safety officer monitors incident operations and advises the incident command on all matters relating to operational safety. The safety officer is responsible for developing the incident safety plan. The incident safety plan is a set of systems and procedures for ongoing assessment of hazardous environments, coordination of interagency safety efforts, and implementation of measures to promote incident personnel safety, as well as the general safety of incident operations. The liaison officer is the incident command's point of contact for representatives of governmental organizations, nongovernmental organizations, and private sector organizations. The liaison officer provides information on the incident command's policies, resource availability, and other incident-related matters. In either a single or unified command structure, representatives from cooperating organizations coordinate through the liaison officer.

2-16. An *incident complex* refers to two or more incidents located in the same general area and assigned to a single incident command or a unified command. This management system is used when multiple incidents, such as separate fires burning relatively close together, are more efficiently managed by one incident command system organization.

Multiagency Coordination Systems

2-17. *Multiagency coordination systems* are flexible coordination processes established among related groups of supporting organizations in response to specific incidents. These organizations normally coordinate resources above the field level. The two most common elements of NIMS multiagency coordination systems are multiagency coordination groups and emergency operations centers.

2-18. A *multiagency coordination group* is an ad hoc coordination group usually consisting of administrators, executives, or their representatives. They commit agency resources and funds to support an incident response. Multiagency coordination groups establish coordination procedures (systems) that bridge members' jurisdictional lines and disciplines to support operations on the ground. Multiagency coordination groups communicate and coordinate with the incident command or unified command, usually by placing personnel at or near an emergency operations center (see figure 2-2).

2-19. An *emergency operations center* is a facility where the coordination of information and resources to support on-site incident management activities normally occurs. An emergency operations center may be a relatively small, temporary facility or a permanently established facility. Many cities, most counties, and most states have permanent emergency operations centers. These may be organized by major functional disciplines (such as fire, law enforcement, and medical services), by jurisdiction (such as federal, state, regional, county, city, and tribal), or by some combination (see JP 3-41). Emergency operations centers are called by a variety of different names. An emergency operations center normally includes a full incident command staff performing coordination; communications; resource allocation and tracking; and information collection, analysis, and dissemination. An emergency operations center serves as a central communication point between organizations participating in the incident command system and multiagency coordination groups. In a complex operation, several emergency operations centers may be operating at different jurisdictional levels. An area command may interface between several incident command posts and an emergency operations center. Figure 2-2 illustrates how an emergency operations center coordinates support for an area command. Figure 2-3, on page 2-6, illustrates an expanded response with several operations centers supporting an incident commander.

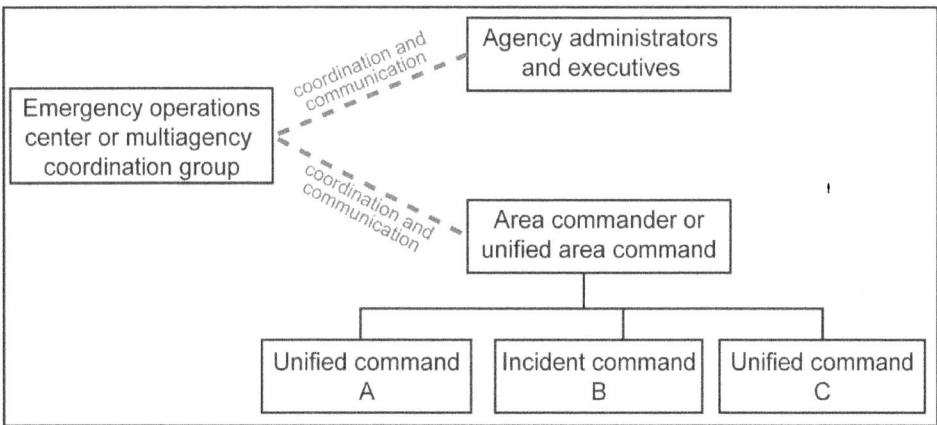

Figure 2-2. Example of NIMS command and management structure

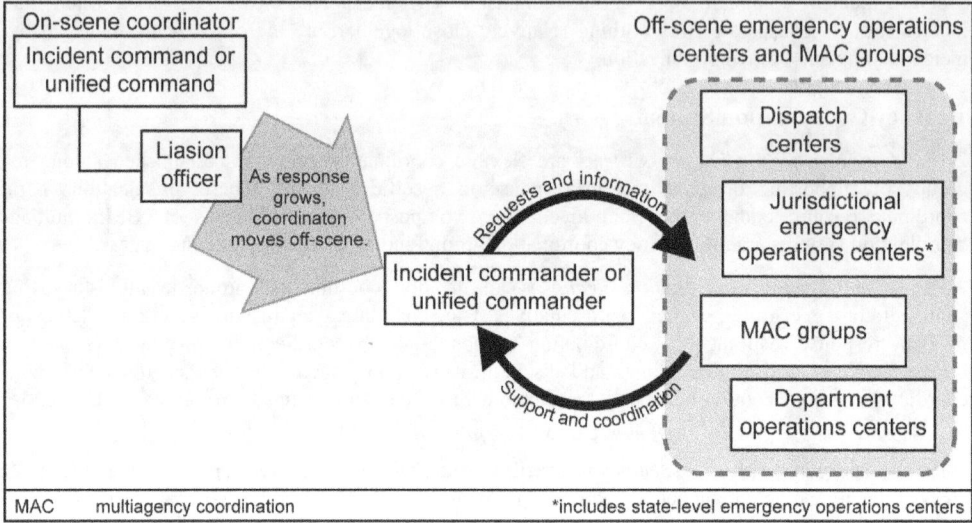

Figure 2-3. Expanded command and coordination under NIMS

Public Information

2-20. In the NIMS, *public information* refers to flexible processes, procedures, and systems used by incident managers to communicate timely, accurate, and accessible information about an incident to the public, responders, and additional stakeholders. In a large, multiagency incident response, the NIMS public information system includes a public information officer, a joint information system, and a joint information center. (The word "joint" means interagency in this context.) A civilian public information officer supports the incident command and management structure as a member of the command staff (refer to figure 2-2).

2-21. A multiagency *joint information center* (a feature of the NIMS communications and information management component) serves as the central location for exchanging public information. A large incident may require more than one joint information center. This component emphasizes the need for a common operating picture (similar to the *common operational picture* in Army doctrine) and interoperability of systems and components. Participating organizations cooperate to establish communications interoperability and standardize their types of communication and their equipment. (See appendix K for more information about media considerations.)

The National Incident Management System Planning Process

2-22. The NIMS describes a planning process for developing an incident action plan. Army officers should be familiar with the NIMS planning process to synchronize planning with civilian counterparts. The NIMS planning process represents a template for planning that includes all steps that an incident commander or unified command and other members of the command and general staffs should take to develop and disseminate an incident action plan. A clear, concise incident action plan template is essential to guide the initial incident management decision process and the continuing collective planning activities of incident management teams.

2-23. The process contains five primary phases that are designed to enable the accomplishment of incident objectives within a specified time. The planning process may begin with the scheduling of a planned event, the identification of a credible threat, or the initial response to an actual or impending incident. The process follows a series of formalized steps for developing a written incident action plan.

2-24. The incident action plan must provide clear strategic direction and include a comprehensive listing of the tactics, resources, reserves, and support required to accomplish each overarching incident objective. The comprehensive incident action plan states the sequence of events for achieving multiple incident objectives in a coordinated way. However, the incident action plan is a living document that is based on the best available information at the time of the planning meeting. Planning meetings should not be delayed in anticipation of future information.

2-25. The primary phases of the planning process are essentially the same for the incident commander who develops the initial plan, for the incident commander and operations section chief revising the initial plan for extended operations, and for the incident management team developing a formal incident action plan. During the initial stages of incident management, planners should develop a simple plan that can be communicated through concise oral briefings. Frequently, this plan must be developed very quickly and with incomplete situation information. As the incident management effort evolves, additional lead time, staff, information systems, and technologies enable more detailed planning and cataloging of events and lessons learned.

2-26. The five primary phases in the planning process are—
- Understand the situation.
- Establish incident objectives and strategy.
- Develop the plan.
- Prepare and disseminate the plan.
- Execute, evaluate, and revise the plan.

Understand the Situation

2-27. The first phase includes gathering, recording, analyzing, and displaying situation, resource, and incident-related information to facilitate increased situational awareness of the magnitude, complexity, and potential impact of the incident. In this phase, the goal is to determine the resources needed to develop and implement an effective incident action plan.

Establish Incident Objectives and Strategy

2-28. The second phase includes formulating and prioritizing measurable incident objectives and identifying an appropriate strategy. The incident objectives and strategy must conform to the legal obligations and management objectives of all affected agencies; they may need to include specific issues relevant to critical infrastructure. Reasonable alternative strategies that will accomplish overall incident objectives are identified, analyzed, and evaluated to determine the most appropriate strategy for the situation at hand. Evaluation criteria include public health and safety factors, estimated costs, and various environmental, legal, and political considerations.

Develop the Plan

2-29. The third phase involves determining the tactical direction and the specific resources, reserves, and support requirements for implementing the selected strategies and tactics for the operational period. Before the formal planning meetings, each member of the command and general staffs is responsible for gathering certain information to support the proposed plan.

Prepare and Disseminate the Plan

2-30. The fourth phase involves preparing the plan in a format that is appropriate for the level of complexity of the incident. For the initial response, the format is a well-prepared outline for an oral briefing. For most incidents that will span several operational periods, the plan will be developed in writing according to incident command system procedures.

Chapter 2

Execute, Evaluate, and Revise the Plan

2-31. The planning process includes the requirement to execute and evaluate planned activities and check the accuracy of information to be used in planning for subsequent operational periods. The general staff should regularly compare planned progress with actual progress. When deviations occur and when new information emerges, it should be included in the first step of the process used for modifying the current plan or developing the plan for the subsequent operational period.

THE NATIONAL RESPONSE FRAMEWORK

2-32. The NRF replaced the earlier National Response Plan in 2004 as the all-hazards doctrine for managing domestic incidents. It elaborates the principles in the NIMS, focusing on prevention, preparedness, response, and recovery. It provides the structure and mechanisms for coordinating federal support to state and local incident managers and for exercising federal authorities and responsibilities based on the NIMS.

2-33. The NRF emphasizes a tiered response structure, with the lowest possible jurisdictional level retaining incident management responsibility. Figure 2-4 illustrates tiered response. Local authorities provide the initial response to every incident, including manmade and natural disasters. When local authorities are overwhelmed, they request assistance from neighboring jurisdictions. When incidents are of such a magnitude that these resources are overwhelmed, local authorities request resources from the state. The state then draws on its own internal emergency response capabilities or requests assistance from neighboring states through mutual-aid agreements. States often deal with large and devastating events this way without any federal assistance. When state resources are overwhelmed, the governor requests federal support. Paragraphs 2-38 to 2-79 discuss tiered response in detail.

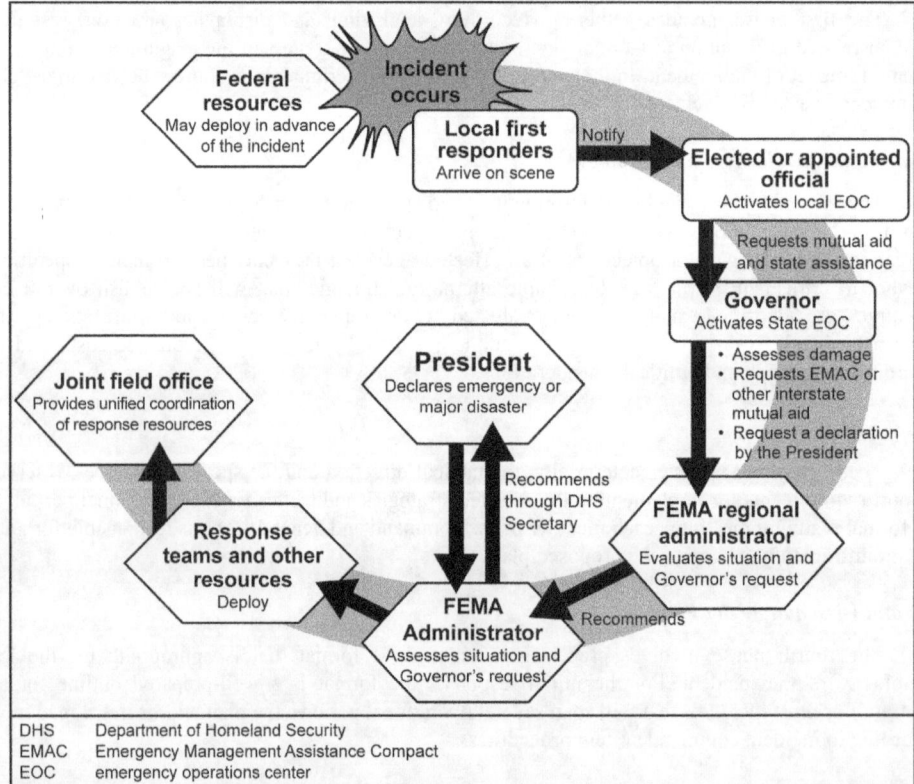

Figure 2-4. An overview of tiered response under the National Response Framework

2-34. The NRF establishes a systematic and coordinated approach to incident response at the field, regional, and federal headquarters levels. It establishes protocols for such activities as reporting incidents, issuing alerts and notification, coordinating response actions, and mobilizing resources. Though the NRF generally seeks to preserve the primary role of state and local bodies as first responders, it recognizes catastrophic events will require a federal government response.

The Five Principles of the National Response Framework

2-35. According to the NRF, the overarching objectives for incident response center on saving lives, reducing suffering, and protecting property and the environment. Five key NRF principles of operations are the basis of the overarching objectives:

- Leaders at all levels communicate and actively support *engaged partnerships* (cooperation) by developing shared goals and aligning capabilities so no one is overwhelmed in times of crisis.
- Incidents are managed at the lowest possible jurisdictional level and supported by additional capabilities when needed, through a *tiered response*.
- As incidents change in size, scope, and complexity, the response is adapted to meet requirements through *scalable, flexible, and adaptable operational capabilities*.
- Organizations participating in a multiagency or multijurisdictional response achieve *unity of effort through unified command*.
- Individuals, households, communities, and governments maintain *readiness to act* balanced with an understanding of risk.

Emergency Support Function Annexes

2-36. A key component of the NRF is the emergency support function annexes (referred to as emergency support functions or ESFs). The ESFs group federal resources and capabilities into fifteen support categories most likely needed for national incident response. ESFs outline responsibilities agreed to by each participating entity. Each ESF designates one entity as the ESF coordinator (sometimes referred to as the lead). Each ESF also has primary and supporting agencies. Table 2-1, pages 2-9 to 2-11, lists the ESFs with the ESF coordinator for each. Below each ESF coordinator are the specific functions organized in that annex. DOD is a supporting agency for 14 of the 15 ESFs, and the ESF coordinator for only one—ESF #3, Public Works and Engineering (United States Army Corps of Engineers). The ESF coordinators work through a regional defense coordinating officer and a federal coordinating officer to obtain federal military support under each ESF.

Table 2-1. Emergency support function annexes (ESFs)

ESF #1: Transportation
ESF #1 Coordinator: Department of Transportation
• Aviation/airspace management and control
• Transportation safety
• Restoration and recovery of transportation infrastructure
• Movement restrictions
• Damage and impact assessment
ESF #2: Communications
ESF #2 Coordinator: Department of Homeland Security (Federal Emergency Management Agency)
• Coordination with telecommunications and information technology industries
• Restoration and repair of telecommunications infrastructure
• Protection, restoration, and sustainment of national cyber and information technology resources
• Oversight of communications

Table 2-1. Emergency support function annexes (ESFs), continued

ESF #3: Public Works and Engineering
ESF #3 Coordinator: Department of Defense (United States Army Corps of Engineers)
• Infrastructure protection and emergency repair • Infrastructure restoration • Engineering services and construction management • Emergency contracting support for life-saving and life-sustaining services
ESF #4: Firefighting
ESF #4 Coordinator: Department of Agriculture (United States Forest Service)
• Coordination of federal firefighting activities • Support to wild land, rural, and urban firefighting operations
ESF #5: Emergency Management
ESF #5 Coordinator: Department of Homeland Security (Federal Emergency Management Agency)
• Coordination of incident management and response efforts • Issuance of mission assignments • Resource and human capital • Incident action planning • Financial management
ESF #6: Mass Care, Emergency Assistance, Housing, and Human Services
ESF #6 Coordinator: Department of Homeland Security (Federal Emergency Management Agency)
• Mass care • Emergency assistance • Disaster housing • Human services
ESF #7: Logistics Management and Resource Support
ESF #7 Coordinator: General Services Administration and Department of Homeland Security (Federal Emergency Management Agency)
• Comprehensive, national incident logistics planning, management, and sustainment capability • Resource support (facility space, office equipment and supplies, contracting services, and others)
ESF #8: Public Health and Medical Services
ESF #8 Coordinator: Department of Health and Human Services
• Public health • Medical • Mental health services • Mass fatality management
ESF #9: Search and Rescue
ESF #9 Coordinator: Department of Homeland Security (Federal Emergency Management Agency)
• Life-saving assistance • Search and rescue operations
ESF #10: Oil and Hazardous Materials Response
ESF #10 Coordinator: Environmental Protection Agency
• Oil and hazardous materials (chemical, biological, radiological, and nuclear) response • Environmental short- and long-term cleanup

Table 2-1. Emergency support function annexes (ESFs), continued

ESF #11: Agriculture and Natural Resources
ESF #11 Coordinator: Department of Agriculture
<ul><li>Nutrition assistance</li><li>Animal and plant disease and pest response</li><li>Food safety and security</li><li>Natural and cultural resources and historic properties protection</li><li>Safety and well-being of household pets</li></ul>
ESF #12: Energy
ESF #12 Coordinator: Department of Energy
<ul><li>Energy infrastructure assessment, repair, and restoration</li><li>Energy industry utilities coordination</li><li>Energy forecast</li></ul>
ESF #13: Public Safety and Security
ESF #13 Coordinator: Department of Justice
<ul><li>Facility and resource security</li><li>Security planning and technical resource assistance</li><li>Public safety and security support</li><li>Support to access, traffic, and crowd control</li></ul>
ESF #14: Long-Term Community Recovery
ESF #14 Coordinator: Department of Homeland Security (Federal Emergency Management Agency)
<ul><li>Social and economic community impact assessment</li><li>Long-term community recovery assistance to states, tribes, local governments, and the private sector</li><li>Analysis and review of mitigation program implementation</li></ul>
ESF #15: External Affairs
ESF #15 Coordinator: Department of Homeland Security
<ul><li>Emergency public information and protective action guidance</li><li>Media and community relations</li><li>Congressional and international affairs</li><li>Tribal and insular affairs</li></ul>

National Planning Scenarios

2-37. The NRF builds preparedness using the National Preparedness Guidelines and the National Infrastructure Protection Plan. (The National Planning Scenarios are part of the National Preparedness Guidelines.) DHS provides these scenarios for use at local, state, and national level to conduct exercises and estimate response capabilities. There are currently fifteen planning scenarios. Each scenario provides the basis for planning and national-level exercises. Table 2-2, page 2-11, lists the scenarios, and illustrates how the scenarios fit into eight categories called key scenario sets. Additional information is available at the FEMA Web site: http://www.fema.gov.

Table 2-2. National Planning Scenarios

Key Scenario Sets	National Planning Scenarios
Set 1: Explosives Attack—Bomb Using Improvised Explosive Device	Scenario 12: Explosives Attack— Bomb Using Improvised Explosive Device
Set 2: Nuclear Attack	Scenario 1: Nuclear Detonation—Improvised Nuclear Device
Set 3: Radiological Attack—Radiological Dispersal Device	Scenario 11: Radiological Attack—Radiological Dispersal Device
Set 4: Biological Attack—with annexes for different pathogens	Scenario 2: Biological Attack—Aerosol Anthrax Scenario 4: Biological Attack—Plague Scenario 13: Biological Attack—Food Contamination Scenario 14: Biological Attack—Foreign Animal Disease
Set 5: Chemical Attack—with annexes for different agents	Scenario 5: Chemical Attack—Blister Agent Scenario 6: Chemical Attack—Toxic Industrial Chemicals Scenario 7: Chemical Attack—Nerve Agent Scenario 8: Chemical Attack—Chlorine Tank Explosion
Set 6: Natural Disaster—with annexes for different disasters	Scenario 9: Natural Disaster—Major Earthquake Scenario 10: Natural Disaster—Major Hurricane
Set 7: Cyber Attack	Scenario 15: Cyber Attack
Set 8: Pandemic Influenza	Scenario 3: Biological Disease Outbreak—Pandemic Influenza

TIERED RESPONSE FROM LOCAL THROUGH NATIONAL LEVEL

2-38. The NRF is based on the capability of civil authorities at each level to respond to extraordinary situations. Each level of government maintains enough capability to carry out its legal responsibilities specified in law. Each has some reserve capability to deal with situations out of the ordinary that occur within its jurisdiction. When a situation exceeds the capacity of that level of government, it calls upon the next higher level of government to provide support. The key players in this tiered response are local government, tribal government, state and territorial government, and the federal government. Acting at all levels, nongovernmental organizations and the private sector work closely with government agencies in response to an incident.

COMPRESSION OF RESPONSE TIMES

2-39. Although tiered response is the guiding principle, actual response can be compressed to such a degree that it begins almost simultaneously at all levels. This is true for the military response to a catastrophic incident, especially if the incident is preceded by a warning period—such as a hurricane. State National Guard forces may receive an alert order through state channels at the same time that federal military forces receive alert and prepare-to-deploy orders through DOD channels. Although the Stafford Act limits the ability of the federal government to provide full assistance until requested by the governor of a state, the President and the Secretaries of Homeland Security and Defense have ample authority to prepare to support even before the formal request from the governor arrives at the President's desk.

FIRST RESPONDERS—LOCAL-TO STATE-LEVEL

2-40. No matter how large an incident becomes, almost every response begins at the local level. First responders normally include police, fire, and emergency medical personnel from the affected community. Homeland Security Presidential Directive–8, National Preparedness, defines *first responder* as—

> . . . those individuals who in the early stages of an incident, are responsible for the protection and preservation of life, property, evidence, and the environment, including emergency response providers as defined in Section 2 of the Homeland Security Act of 2002 (6 U.S.C. 101) [Section 101 of Title 6, United States Code (USC)], as well as

emergency management, public health, clinical care, publics works, and other skilled support personnel (such as equipment operators) that provide immediate support services during prevention, response, and recovery operations.

Homeland Security Presidential Directive–8, paragraph 2.d.

2-41. First responders are trained and certified to perform their specific duties and responsibilities according to the NRF, NIMS, and their state and local laws and emergency operations plan. They participate in numerous types of all-hazard exercises which are appropriate for their locality. They use a NIMS-based incident command system. It is important to keep in mind that a NIMS incident command system is not the same as a military command and control system using echelons such as company, battalion, brigade, or joint task force commanders. (Refer to the NIMS for a thorough discussion of its incident command system.)

2-42. Local first responders, such as police, fire, and emergency management, arrive very quickly and are usually the last to leave an incident site. When a situation requires several departments, such as police, fire, and health services, the primary responding agency designates the (civilian) incident commander. For example, if a large fire causes injuries and disrupts traffic, the fire chief of the responding fire department becomes the incident commander. He or she sets up an incident command post near the scene and assumes control of other assets as they are committed. As other assets arrive, such as fire companies from another city, they report to the incident commander and receive their missions. The incident command post may also receive reinforcements to enable it to increase its span of control and endurance.

2-43. In a major incident, the city or county executive activates an emergency operations center. These centers are usually in or near the city hall, police headquarters, or county administration building. Large municipalities may have a specialized facility. From this location the local government maintains command and control over first responders and coordinates requests for assistance. As the situation develops, the emergency operations center may designate additional incident commanders based on geography and different challenges.

Local Chief Executive Officer—Mayor, Administrator, Manager, or Parish President

2-44. Response to any incident begins at the local level and expands as each jurisdiction becomes overtaxed. This section discusses the basic roles of local, state, and tribal governments involved in incident management. Understanding government structure and responsibilities allows Army forces to better integrate civil support operations. The Homeland Security Act of 2002 defines "local government" as—

. . . a county, municipality, city, town, township, local public authority, school district, special district, intrastate district, council of governments (regardless of whether the council of governments is incorporated as a nonprofit corporation under State Law), regional or interstate government entity, or agency or instrumentality of a local government; an Indian tribe or authorized tribal organization, or in Alaska a Native village or Alaska Regional Native Corporation; and a rural community, unincorporated town or village, or other public entity.

Homeland Security Act of 2002

2-45. Local governments (counties, cities, or towns) respond to emergencies routinely using their own resources. They also rely on mutual aid agreements with neighboring jurisdictions when they need additional resources. A mayor or county manager, as that jurisdiction's chief executive, is responsible for the public safety and welfare of the people of that jurisdiction. This individual may also serve as the principal advisor to the state emergency director or homeland security administrator. The local chief executive officer—

- Is responsible for coordinating local resources to prevent, prepare for, respond to, and recover from disasters.
- Depending on state and local law, may have powers to suspend local laws and ordinances in an emergency. The local chief executive officer may establish a curfew, order evacuations, and, in coordination with the local health authority, order quarantines.

- Provides leadership and plays and a key role in communicating to the public, and in helping people, businesses, and organizations cope with the consequences of any type of disaster.
- Negotiates and enters into mutual aid agreements with other jurisdictions to facilitate resource sharing.
- Requests state assistance through the governor when the situation exceeds the local capability.
- May request emergency assistance to prevent loss of life or property from a nearby military installation.

Tribal Chief Executive Officer

2-46. Tribal governments respond to the same range of emergencies and disasters that other jurisdictions face. They may require assistance from neighboring jurisdictions under mutual aid and assistance agreements and may provide assistance as well. The United States has a trust relationship with Indian tribes and recognizes their right to self-government. As such, tribal governments are responsible for coordinating resources to address actual or potential incidents. When local resources are not adequate, tribal leaders seek assistance from states or the federal government. Tribal governments normally work with the state, but as sovereign entities, they can also elect to deal directly with the federal government for other types of assistance. In order to obtain federal assistance via the Robert T. Stafford Disaster Relief and Emergency Assistance Act (known as the Stafford Act), the state governor must request a Presidential declaration on behalf of a tribe.

2-47. Native American reservations have a special status within incident response operations. They are neither federal property, such as a military base or national park, nor are they part of the state in which they are located. Within the reservation, that particular Indian Nation controls its own affairs. Most tribes have agreements in place with surrounding jurisdictions for emergency assistance such as medical, fire, and hazardous material response. Civil support of tribal authorities, however, remains an extremely sensitive area and occurs only in extraordinary circumstances.

2-48. Both the tribal authorities and the Department of the Interior, specifically the Bureau of Indian Affairs, must approve any military response into a Native American reservation. In a reversal of the normal response sequence, the President could commit federal resources to an emergency on a reservation, while the National Guard of that state remained in a supporting role, outside the reservation. The tribal chief executive officer is responsible for the public safety and welfare of the people of that tribe. The tribal chief executive officer, as authorized by tribal government—

- Coordinates tribal resources to address all actions to prevent, prepare for, respond to, and recover from disasters involving all hazards including terrorism, natural disasters, accidents, and other contingencies.
- May suspend tribal laws and ordinances, and take actions such as establishing a curfew, directing evacuations, and initiating quarantine.
- Provides leadership and plays a key role in communicating to the tribe, and in helping people, businesses, and organizations cope with the consequences of any type of domestic emergency or disaster within the jurisdiction.
- Negotiates and enters into mutual aid agreements with other tribes and jurisdictions to facilitate resource sharing.
- May request assistance directly from the federal government (other than under the Stafford Act), normally through the Bureau of Indian Affairs.
- May request state assistance through the governor of the state.

State or Territorial Governor

2-49. The state helps local governments if they need assistance. States have significant resources of their own, including emergency management and homeland security agencies, state police, health agencies, transportation agencies, incident management teams, specialized teams, and the National Guard. If additional resources are required, the state may request assistance from other States through interstate mutual aid and assistance agreements such as the Emergency Management Assistance Compact (EMAC).

Administered by the National Emergency Management Association, EMAC is a congressionally ratified organization that provides form and structure to the interstate mutual aid and assistance process. If an incident is beyond the local and state capabilities, the governor can seek federal assistance. The state will collaborate with the impacted communities and the federal government to provide the help needed.

2-50. As a state or territories' chief executive, the governor is responsible for the public safety and welfare of the people of that state. The governor—

- Coordinates state resources to address the actions required to prevent, prepare for, respond to, and recover from disasters.
- Under certain emergency conditions, the governor can make, amend, and rescind orders and regulations under certain emergency conditions.
- Provides leadership and plays a key role in communicating to the public and in helping people, businesses, and organizations cope with the consequences of any type of declared emergency within the state.
- Encourages participation in mutual aid from jurisdiction to jurisdiction within the state and enters into mutual aid agreements with other states.
- Encourages tribes and counties to share resources.
- Is the commander-in-chief of state National Guard forces (state National Guard when in state active duty or Title 32 status and the authorized state National Guard forces).
- Requests federal assistance when state capabilities are insufficient or have been exceeded or exhausted.

State-Level Agencies

2-51. Each state has a state emergency director and a state emergency management agency, which is the state's counterpart to FEMA. The actual title and office nomenclature varies by state. This individual serves as the principal advisor to the governor for homeland security and coordinates state level emergency response. He or she receives training on emergency planning and management from the federal government and state experts, and is often an emergency professional. In many states, the adjutant general of the National Guard serves as the chief of staff of the state National Guard, the state director of homeland security, and the state emergency manager. Each state has an emergency operations center, normally manned at minimum levels but rapidly expansible and organized according to NIMS and NRF principles. Some states have mobile command center capabilities, allowing the state emergency operations center to move into a facility nearer the scene of a large emergency, and every state has some sort of mobile forward command post to allow the governor and emergency manager to maintain control. The organization of ESFs within each state varies somewhat, with many states having more than fifteen, and some less.

2-52. Each governor has many capabilities to commit to an incident response. Most states have corresponding agencies to those of the federal government, and these agencies frequently work together. The state agencies have two limitations—fiscal and manpower. Only the federal government has the funds and personnel to respond to a very large emergency, which is why federal laws such as the Stafford Act regulate so much state and federal interaction.

State Coordinating Officer

2-53. A state coordinating officer, appointed by the governor, represents the state government in the unified coordination group (an interagency group of senior leaders within a joint field office—see paragraph 2-79). In addition, a state coordinating officer oversees state-level incident response operations and coordination with local governments, tribal nations, military forces, nongovernmental organizations, and FEMA.

Nongovernmental and Private Sector Organizations

2-54. Within the United States, disaster response brings with it a multitude of organizations and private citizens motivated by a sincere desire to help. Some of these organizations have the charter to do emergency assistance. The American Red Cross, for example, has a charter from Congress to assist in emergencies anywhere in the country. Faith-based organizations often respond to assist with disaster relief. Quite often, ad hoc groups of concerned citizens travel to a disaster and offer their services to relief organizations. Organizations normally link their efforts to government agencies through the local and state emergency operations centers but often simply go to where they perceive a need. Commanders need to coordinate with the leadership of nongovernmental organizations on the ground and establish a collaborative working relationship with them, while emphasizing that requests for assistance need to go through the appropriate coordinating officer. Therefore, part of this relationship will depend on making clear to the nongovernmental organization leadership what Soldiers in the area can and cannot do for them according to laws and policies.

2-55. Nongovernmental and voluntary organizations are essential partners in responding to incidents. To engage these key partners most effectively, local, tribal, state, and federal governments routinely coordinate with voluntary agencies, community and faith-based organizations, and other entities. They develop plans to manage volunteer services and donated goods, establish appropriate roles and responsibilities, train, and conduct exercises before an incident occurs. Working through emergency operations centers and other structures, nongovernmental and voluntary organizations assist local, tribal, state, and federal governments in providing shelter, food, counseling services, and other vital support. Normally, professional American Red Cross personnel operate positions in local and state emergency operations centers. These types of groups often provide specialized services that help individuals with special needs, including those with disabilities.

2-56. Nongovernmental organizations and private sector representatives are good sources of information for military forces. For example, the American Red Cross is an excellent source for incident awareness. American Red Cross professionals and volunteers across the nation possess more response experience than any military organization. They usually arrive early in any disaster. Private sector individuals such as electrical and cable technicians may also have valuable information about the situation. However, Soldiers need to exercise caution when dealing with personally identifiable information on people outside the military—information such as names, addresses, employers, and descriptions. For further information, see chapter 3.

2-57. Forming the foundation for the health of the Nation's economy, the private sector is a key partner in local, tribal, state, and federal response. The private sector is responsible for most of the critical infrastructure and key resources in the Nation and thus may require assistance in the wake of a disaster or emergency. The private sector also provides goods and services critical to the response and recovery process, either on a paid basis or through donations.

2-58. The utility companies throughout the United States have sophisticated emergency response plans and protocols. Their response is multitiered, beginning with the utilities within the state and expanding to a national level effort drawing resources from across the nation. In anticipation of a major incident such as a hurricane, or in response to an unexpected disaster, the utility companies alert and deploy assets to restore essential services. Soldiers will encounter emergency utility teams throughout the affected area. They utility companies coordinate their efforts with the incident commander and local emergency manager as they arrive. In a large disaster, they will provide liaison teams to the state and federal command centers.

FEDERAL GOVERNMENT RESPONSE

2-59. The federal government maintains a wide array of capabilities and resources that can assist state governments in responding to incidents. In addition, federal departments and agencies may also request and receive help from other federal departments and agencies. A general understanding of federal government responsibilities helps National Guard, Regular Army, and Army Reserve commanders integrate civil support with civilian efforts. Any commitment of Army forces, regardless of component, is certain to interact with some part of the federal government. Without the comprehensive approach described in the NIMS and the NRF, Army forces might find themselves bombarded by tasking from every level of government. State National Guard forces receive mission guidance through their state joint force headquarters, which works directly with the state emergency operations center. (In many states, the adjutant general is also the state emergency coordinator.) Based on the NIMS and NRF, a defense coordinating officer serves as the single point of contact for federal military forces supporting civil authorities in any disaster.

Department of Homeland Security

2-60. The Homeland Security Act of 2002 established DHS. The act charges DHS with preventing terrorist attacks within the United States; reducing America's vulnerability to terrorism, major disasters, and other emergencies; and minimizing the damage and recovering from attacks, major disasters, and other emergencies. The agency with which Army forces deal most frequently is FEMA. The Coast Guard is also part of DHS. These two agencies are described in more detail in paragraphs 2-63 to 2-68.

2-61. The Secretary of Homeland Security is responsible for coordinating a federal response in support of other federal, state, local, tribal, or territorial authorities as directed in Homeland Security Presidential Directive (HSPD)-5, *Management of Domestic Incidents*. In this role, the Secretary will coordinate federal resources used in response to a pandemic influenza outbreak when any one of the following four conditions applies:

- A federal department or agency acting under its own authority has requested DHS assistance.
- The resources of state and local authorities are overwhelmed and federal assistance has been requested.
- More than one federal department or agency has become substantially involved in responding to the incident.
- The President directs the Secretary to assume incident management responsibilities.

2-62. DHS comprises several agencies with law enforcement responsibilities. These include Customs and Border Protection, Immigration and Customs Enforcement, Transportation Security Administration, and the United States Secret Service. Any of these agencies may request military support. All of them provide support under the NRF for a variety of scenarios. Additional information is available through DHS web site at http://www.dhs.gov/index.shtm. Under the Department of Justice, the Bureau of Alcohol, Tobacco, Firearms, and Explosives also may seek military support related to civilian law enforcement activities.

Federal Emergency Management Agency

2-63. FEMA is part of DHS. Its missions are planning for disaster response and coordinating disaster responses. For incident response, the Nation is divided into ten FEMA regions as shown in Figure 2-5, page 2-18. Alaska falls within Region X, Hawaii and the Pacific territories within Region IX, and Puerto Rico and the Atlantic possessions within Region II. The alignment of the islands in Pacific and Atlantic Oceans minimizes the likelihood of a disaster in that region affecting the continental and island areas simultaneously.

2-64. Each FEMA region has a regional coordination center located within its offices. This center activates during any significant and stays manned until response operations conclude and recovery operations pass to the control of an on-site recovery center. FEMA coordinates with organizations across each region for preparation and incident response. The agency oversees NIMS, the NRF, disaster response training, and national planning and preparation for all hazard emergencies. DOD works directly with FEMA in each region to plan responses to disasters and terrorist attacks. Defense coordinating officers are permanently co-located with each FEMA regional office. For a full listing of their responsibilities, go to http://www.fema.gov.

Chapter 2

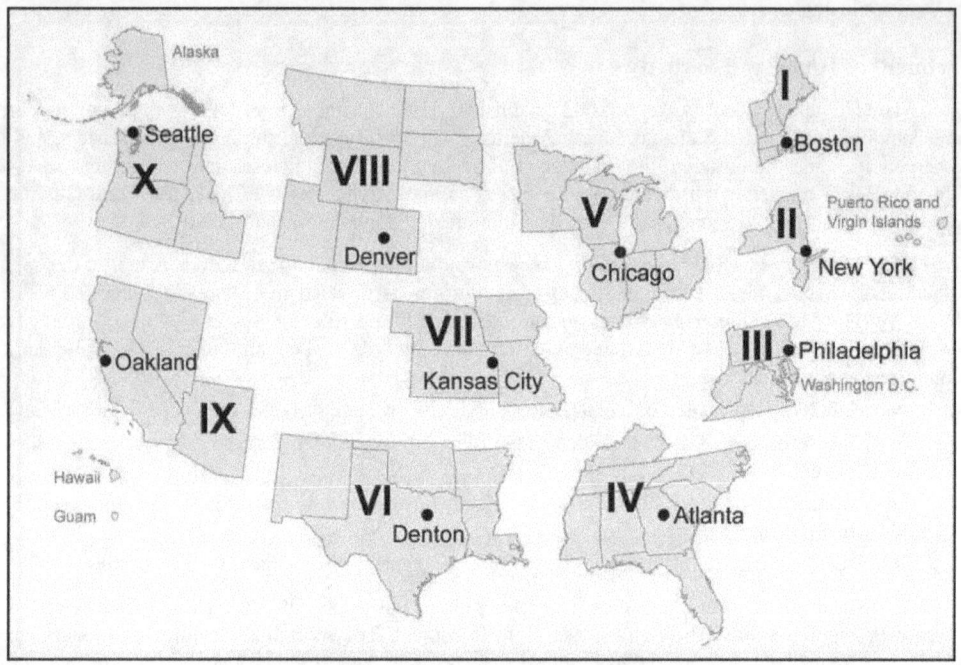

Figure 2-5. FEMA regions and headquarters

The Coast Guard

2-65. The Coast Guard is the fifth Armed Service, but it falls under Title 14, USC, not Title 10 or Title 32. It is a law enforcement agency as well as a military Service, and it has offices and units across the country. The Coast Guard has a unique position among the Armed Services. Because of its unique status, the Coast Guard supports and is supported by the other Armed Services. In homeland defense, for example, units of the coast guard may be under Navy control. In homeland security, Navy warships and aircraft may provide support to a Coast Guard operation. Because of its Title 14 responsibilities and as part of DHS, the Coast Guard frequently supports civil authorities, and vice versa. Army units conducting civil support operations may support or receive support from Coast Guard elements. In a large incident, the senior Coast Guard officer in charge could exercise tactical control over some or all responding federal military forces.

2-66. In the reorganization of the federal government after 9/11, the Coast Guard moved from Department of Transportation to DHS. The Coast Guard's homeland security missions include port, waterway, and coastal security; drug interdiction; control of illegal immigration; and other law enforcement. Non-homeland security missions include marine safety, search and rescue, aids to navigation, living marine resource protection (fisheries enforcement), marine environmental response, and icebreaking. This array of missions endows the Coast Guard with many civil support capabilities.

2-67. The Coast Guard Deployable Operations Group provides organized, equipped, and trained deployable, specialized forces to the Coast Guard, DHS and civilian incident commanders. These forces deploy in support of national requirements as tailored, integrated force packages, across the United States and other high interest areas. The Deployable Operations Group has approximately 3,000 Coast Guard personnel from twelve Maritime Safety and Security Teams, the Maritime Security Response Team, two Tactical Law Enforcement Teams, eight Port Security Units, the National Strike Force Coordination Center, and three National Strike Teams.

2-68. The Coast Guard has some of the best-trained and equipped personnel for hazardous material incidents in the Nation. Although most Coast Guard capabilities and personnel are stationed in the coastal cities, they can deploy highly trained teams anywhere in the country using Coast Guard, commercial, and DOD transport. Once they arrive, Coast Guard forces can support Title 10 and state National Guard forces interchangeably.

Department of Justice

2-69. The Attorney General of the United States has lead responsibility for criminal investigations of terrorist acts or terrorist threats by individuals or groups inside the United States. The Attorney General acts through the Federal Bureau of Investigation and cooperates with other federal departments and agencies engaged in activities to protect national security. The Attorney General and these departments and agencies coordinate the activities of other members of the law enforcement community to detect, prevent, preempt, and disrupt terrorist attacks against the United States.

Department of State

2-70. The Department of State has international coordination responsibilities for domestic disaster assistance to the United States. The Secretary of State also is responsible for coordinating international prevention, preparedness, response, and recovery activities relating to emergencies or disasters. When the United States suffers a disaster, other nations may offer material, financial or military assistance. The Department of State coordinates the receipt of foreign assistance. When the assistance includes foreign military forces, Department of State officials coordinate between the foreign government, DOD, and gaining combatant commanders prior to their employment.

Other Federal Departments

2-71. During an incident, other federal agencies may play primary, coordinating, or supporting roles, or any combination, based on authorities, resources, and the nature of the incident roles and responsibilities outlined in the ESFs. Although DOD usually supports DHS, any agency may request federal military support if its own resources are overtaxed. Several federal agencies have responsibility to declare disasters or emergencies, and DOD may support these agencies in their response. Some examples include—

- Department of Agriculture.
- Department of Commerce.
- Department of Health and Human Services.
- Department of the Interior.
- Department of Energy.

2-72. The Secretary of Agriculture may declare a disaster in certain situations when a county sustained production loss of 30 percent or greater in a single major enterprise, authorizing emergency loans for physical damages and crop loss. The Forest Service (a part of the Department of Agriculture) provides wildland fire fighting teams and incident command system teams suitable for supporting emergency response.

2-73. The Secretary of Commerce may make a declaration of a commercial fisheries failure or fishery resources disaster. The National Oceanic and Atmospheric Administration Commissioned Corps operates ships, aircraft, and diving teams suitable for supporting emergency response.

2-74. The Secretary of Health and Human Services may declare a public health emergency. The Secretary of Health and Human Services directs the national response to communicable diseases such as pandemic influenza (see chapter 4). The United States Public Health Service Commissioned Corps provides teams of health professionals prepared to support emergency response.

2-75. The Department of the Interior includes the Bureau of Indian Affairs, Bureau of Land Management, and the National Park Service. They provide wild land fire fighting teams and incident command system teams suitable for managing emergency response.

2-76. Department of Energy is involved with incidents involving nuclear facilities security and incidents and is the emergency coordinator for ESF #12. In the event of an accident involving an American nuclear weapon, Department of Energy works directly with DOD according to carefully developed plans and procedures.

The Federal Coordinating Officer and the Joint Field Office

2-77. In most cases, the federal government assists an incident response operation following a Presidential disaster or emergency declaration and a request by a governor. The NRF describes the coordination structures for federal departments and agencies in its third chapter and in the ESFs. These structures are in addition to the systems described in the NIMS.

2-78. When the federal government joins a disaster response operation, the Administrator of FEMA and the Secretary of Homeland Security recommend a *federal coordinating officer* for that operation, and the President makes the appointment. The federal coordinating officer represents FEMA in the unified coordination group and ensures integration of federal activities. Normally, the federal coordinating officer selected for a specific operation is a full-time, permanent federal coordinating officer from within the FEMA region affected by the incident. In some cases, a federal coordinating officer from another FEMA region becomes the federal coordinating officer for the operation because of availability. Initially, FEMA may deploy specialized teams to support state and local jurisdictions. These teams can deploy on short notice, before a joint field office can be established.

2-79. When required, FEMA establishes a joint field office ("joint" in this context means interagency) to coordinate the national-level response. A joint field office is a temporary federal facility for coordination and liaison across agencies and jurisdictions. FEMA organizes every joint field office according to the NIMS and adapts its makeup to meet the requirements of the situation. Therefore, every joint field office has a similar broad division of major responsibilities but is staffed differently. It has, for instance, an operations section, a planning section, a logistics section, and a finance and administration section, directed by a *unified coordination group*. The unified coordination group includes key state and federal officials involved in managing the response. A joint field office may be geographically grouped or functionally grouped, with air operations or evacuation functions included. The NRF specifies that DOD may support every ESF, based on the situation. Figure 2-6 illustrates a notional fully staffed joint field office with all ESFs activated. See Appendix I for a more detailed view of the various incident command system staff sections.

A Comprehensive Approach for Civil Support

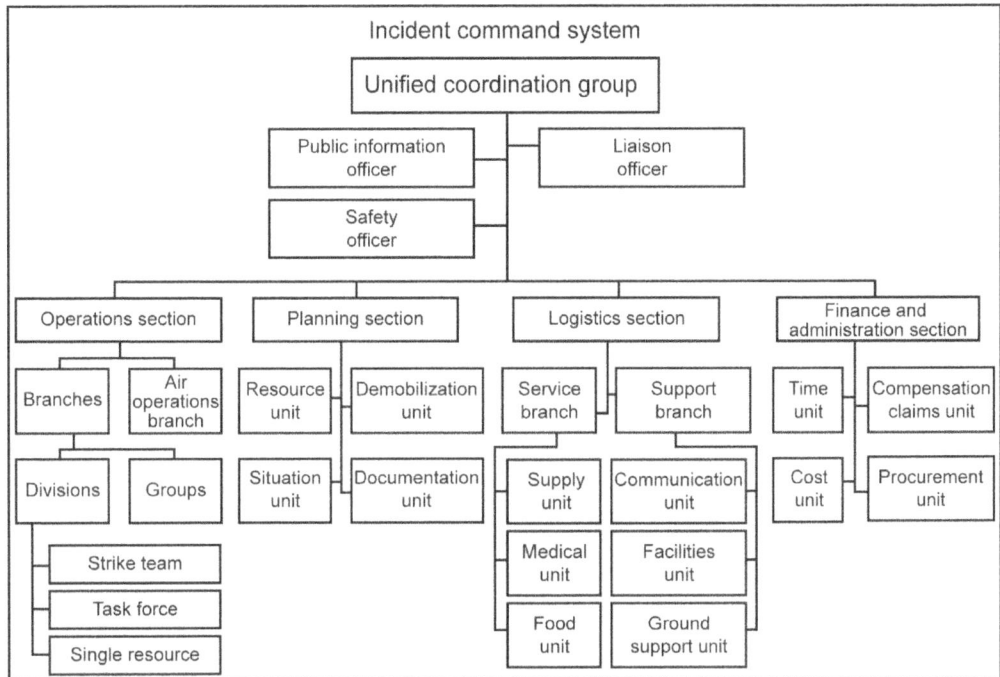

Figure 2-6. A joint field office example, with command staff, sections, and branches

2-80. The Secretary of Homeland Security or the President may designate a regional team leader to ensure effective management of federal support for a catastrophic or unusually complex incident involving several states, and hence, several joint field offices. A regional team leader, when designated, represents DHS in the unified coordination group. However, for most incidents requiring a federal response, the federal coordinating officer is the senior federal official.

> Note: Under older nomenclature the regional team leader was called a *principal federal official*. Some responders still refer to this individual as the principal federal official.

2-81. A regional team leader is distinct from a federal coordinating officer. He or she does not have directive authority over a federal coordinating officer or other members of the unified coordination group. The regional team leader promotes multiagency collaboration, resolves interagency conflict, and presents policy issues to the Secretary of Homeland Security. A regional team leader, when designated, interfaces with federal, state, tribal, and local jurisdictional officials regarding the overall federal incident management strategy and acts as the primary federal spokesperson for coordinated media and public communications.

NATIONAL GUARD CIVIL SUPPORT OPERATIONS

2-82. The National Guard is a crucial capability available to state governors in any emergency. State National Guard forces have equipment and expertise in communications, logistics, search and rescue, law enforcement, and decontamination.

THE ADJUTANT GENERAL

2-83. A state's adjutant general is an Air Force or Army general officer who serves as the commander of the state's National Guard and is the joint forces commander for all military forces under the governor's command and control. National Guard Regulation 500-1 establishes the adjutant general as a joint position, with authority over subordinate Air and Army National Guard forces of that state or territory. The adjutant general recommends National Guard response options to the governor and designates the National Guard commander for any National Guard response. The adjutant general has a joint staff that includes full-time National Guard officers and state civilian employees. During any incident, the adjutant general coordinates with adjutant generals from other states and with the National Guard Bureau for emergency assistance. In states with constituted militia units, the adjutant general serves as an intermediary with state National Guard forces.

2-84. In many states, the National Guard adjutant general is the governor's homeland security advisor as well as commander of the state's military forces. For example, in the state of Washington, the state's homeland security apparatus is embedded in the [state of] Washington Military Department. The adjutant general is therefore responsible for military operations, emergency management, emergency telecommunications, and policy-related interaction with executive and legislative branches of local, state, and federal governments.

ORGANIZATION OF NATIONAL GUARD FORCES

2-85. National Guard forces are permanently organized under a joint force headquarters–state (JFHQ–state). The JFHQ–state oversees the administrative requirements for the Guard units and coordinates with the National Guard Bureau in Washington, D.C.

2-86. Each state's National Guard varies in composition and size; there is no standard response organization for all 54 Guard entities. In most incidents, the adjutant general establishes a headquarters known as a joint task force–state (JTF–state). The JTF–state (designated in contingency plans) has operational control of all Air and Army National Guard forces from all participating states. These partnerships have already been established and reinforced through joint and multiagency exercises. The JTF–state commander task-organizes units into task forces for particular missions. Within an operational area, these state task forces work alongside federal task forces. Figure 2-7, page 2-22, shows an example of a National Guard response organization with a state.

A Comprehensive Approach for Civil Support

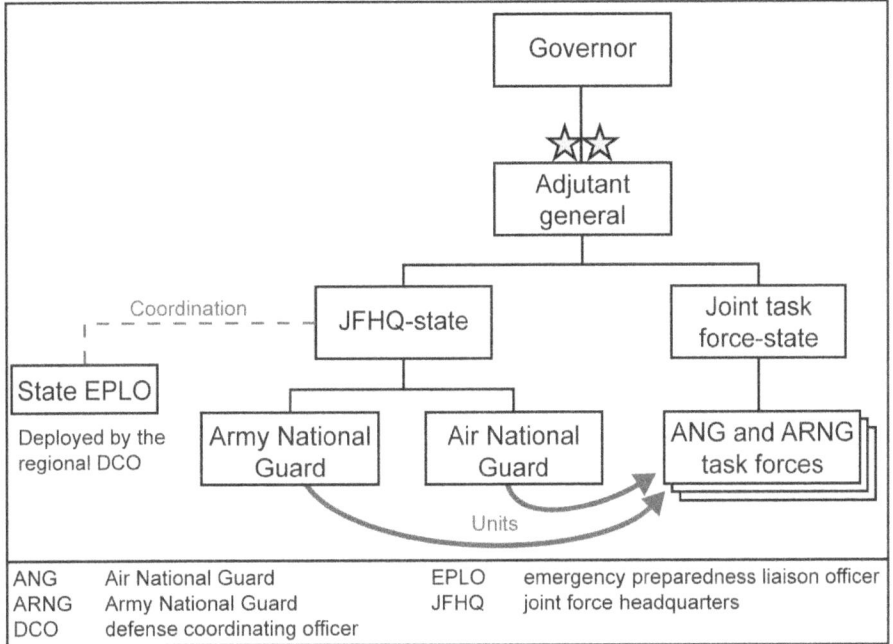

Figure 2-7. An example of National Guard organization within a state

Note: The reader should avoid confusing the joint force headquarters–state (JFHQ–state) with combatant commander's standing joint task force headquarters (SJFHQ).

2-87. Each state has existing contingency plans for different incidents and updates these plans to adjust for Guard units serving in Title 10 status. These task forces employ Air Guard and Army Guard personnel completely integrated at the small-unit level. This is routine in most National Guard response forces.

CHIEF OF THE NATIONAL GUARD BUREAU

2-88. The Chief of the National Guard Bureau is the liaison between the state and territorial National Guards and the federal military components. The Chief of the National Guard Bureau coordinates National Guard support between the states. The Chief of the National Guard Bureau communicates, collaborates, and coordinates with combatant commands. This coordination facilitates continuity and integration with state, territorial, and federal military capabilities. The Chief of the National Guard Bureau also coordinates closely with federal civil authorities and adjutants general of the states.

2-89. The Army National Guard Office in Washington D.C. maintains a continuously manned National Guard operations center that keeps the Chief of the National Guard Bureau informed about National Guard forces committed to civil support operations and to operations overseas. Although the Army National Guard office does not control any of the 54 National Guard elements, it provides critical coordination between the various National Guards before and during any emergency. The Army National Guard office can identify units, personnel, or equipment available for loan between state forces in an emergency.

FEDERAL MILITARY CIVIL SUPPORT OPERATIONS

2-90. The primary mission of DOD and its components is national defense. As directed by the President or the Secretary of Defense, DOD provides support to a primary federal agency as part of a coordinated federal response to any incident that exceeds local and state capabilities, following a request for assistance from civil authorities. However, DOD resources are not typically required to mitigate domestic incidents. For example, in 2005, the President declared 65 major disasters or emergencies. Federal military forces responded to only three.

2-91. The Services can provide many types of federal military support under various authorities. When deciding to commit DOD resources, military readiness, cost, lethality, risk, appropriateness, and whether the response is in accordance with applicable laws and regulations all factor into the decision.

2-92. The Secretary of Defense orders the use of federal military forces for domestic incidents as directed by the President. The decision to employ regular military forces requires assessment of the impact on combat readiness, or when operations and appropriate under the circumstances and the law. The Secretary based the decision primarily on combat readiness. The Secretary of Defense or the Assistant Secretary of Defense for Homeland Defense and America's Security Affairs is the approval authority for any requests from lead federal agencies for any actions that might require lethal force by federal military forces. This includes the authorization for any Soldier in Title 10 status to carry weapons during a defense support of civil authorities (DSCA) mission.

2-93. The joint director of military support, located in the Pentagon, is the DOD action agent for federal civil support. The joint director of military support interfaces with FEMA and the regional defense coordinating officers when civil authorities request federal military support for incident response. The joint director of military support works with the Joint Chiefs of Staff and Service Secretaries to analyze the request and develop a recommendation. Once analyzed, the request goes to the Secretary of Defense for approval, who then passes that decision to the Joint Chiefs of Staff for sourcing from the appropriate combatant commander.

DEFENSE COORDINATING OFFICER

2-94. DOD appoints twelve full-time defense coordinating officers—one in each of the ten FEMA regions and two in the outlying territories. Each defense coordinating officer works closely with federal and state emergency agencies in each FEMA region and develops personal ties with the key representatives. Although the defense coordinating officer is not an ESF manager, each defense coordinating officer has a permanent work space inside FEMA's regional coordination center, next to the ESF desks. A defense coordinating officer is serves as the single point of contact for DOD at a joint field office. These officers are selected carefully and retained in their assignment for long periods. Defense coordinating officers serve as the vital link between the state emergency operations center, state National Guard joint headquarters, federal agencies, and federal military forces.

2-95. Generally, requests for DSCA originating at a joint field office are initially coordinated with and processed through the defense coordinating officer. The defense coordinating officer has a defense coordinating element consisting of a staff and military liaison officers who facilitate federal military support to activated ESFs. Specific responsibilities of the defense coordinating officer usually include coordinating requests for military support (see figure 3-5, page 3-11), forwarding mission assignments to the appropriate military organizations through DOD channels, and assigning military liaisons, as appropriate, to activated ESFs. A defense coordinating officer does not process requests for assistance from United States Special Operations Command, United States Army Corps of Engineers, or National Guard forces operating under state active duty or Title 32 status (not in federal service). In some circumstances, a defense coordinating officer does not process requests for federal military forces in support of the Federal Bureau of Investigation.

2-96. At the start of any incident, or when warning precedes an incident, the defense coordinating officer establishes a watch office (manned by the defense coordinating element) within the FEMA regional coordination center. For most incidents, FEMA does not require federal military support, and the defense coordinating officer remains at the regional coordination center to monitor the situation. If and when the FEMA region establishes a joint field office, and there is a likelihood of federal military forces deploying, DOD activates the regional defense coordinating officer and defense coordinating element. Activation means DOD designates the defense coordinating officer as the single point of contact between the primary agency and DOD.

2-97. In some situations, DOD may commit small military detachments when the states require specialized federal military support. When directed by United States Northern Command (USNORTHCOM), a defense coordinating officer exercises tactical control over these forces and coordinates with USNORTHCOM and local officials for their sustainment. Figure 2-8 illustrates an example of the organization of a defense coordinating officer and defense coordinating element.

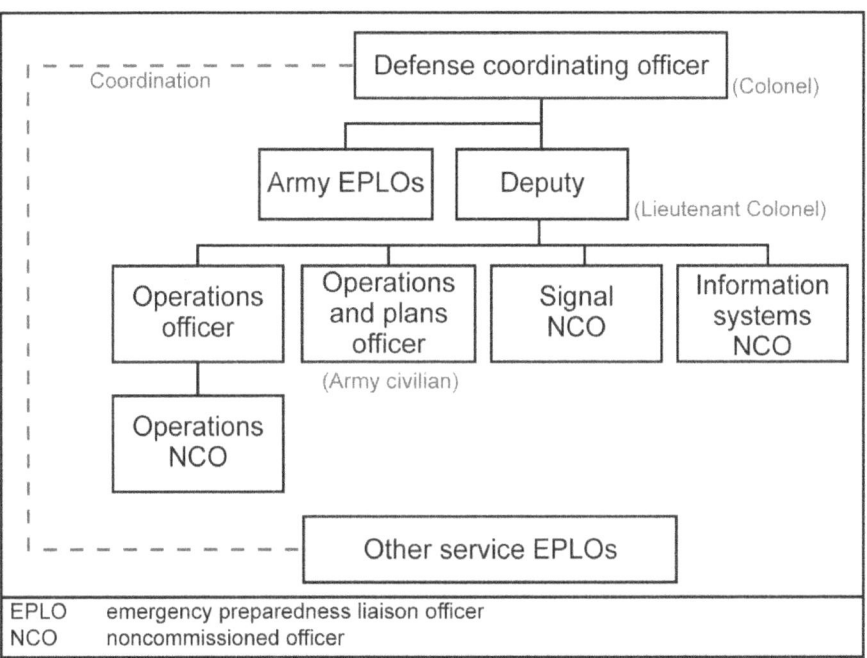

Figure 2-8. Example of defense coordinating officer and defense coordinating element organization

2-98. An *emergency preparedness liaison officer* is a senior reserve officer or noncommissioned officer who, when activated, assists the defense coordinating officer and serves as the subject matter expert for their Service. An emergency preparedness liaison officer can assist ESF planners conduct planning and coordination involving military forces. Emergency preparedness liaison officers are directed by the defense coordinating officer and work in close coordination with the defense coordinating element. An emergency preparedness liaison officer may serve as a liaison to the JFHQ–state or at a DOD installation when tasked by the defense coordinating officer. An emergency preparedness liaison officer identifies potential federal military support requirements for incidents.

2-99. Each state emergency preparedness liaison officer is a member of the Armed Forces Reserve Title 10 Reserve. When mobilized, they are under the control of the defense coordinating officer. When directed by the defense coordinating officer, they facilitate planning, coordination, and training for civil support operations. They serve as Service component liaisons to the adjutants general of the states, the joint force headquarters–state, and the state emergency management agencies. They develop a habitual relationship with respective state and National Guard officials through training and real-world incident management.

2-100. Regional emergency preparedness liaison officers are also Title 10 reserve officers. Unlike the state emergency preparedness liaison officer, they are not aligned to a particular state. They provide the defense coordinating officer with a team of senior professionals available to act as liaison officers at regional military bases, and to augment the state emergency preparedness liaison officer and defense coordinating element. The emergency preparedness liaison officer and regional emergency preparedness liaison officer may be from any of the Armed Services, and officers from Services other than the Army may be referred to by their Service. There are typically between ten and twenty regional emergency preparedness liaison officers within each FEMA region.

COMBATANT COMMANDS

2-101. The President and Secretary of Defense command federal military forces through the combatant commands. There are two geographic combatant commands with primary DSCA responsibilities: USNORTHCOM and United States Pacific Command (USPACOM). The other combatant commands provide capabilities to USNORTHCOM and USPACOM for DSCA as directed by the Secretary of Defense. USNORTHCOM and USPACOM control five standing joint tasks forces that have primary missions associated with DSCA.

United States Northern Command

2-102. USNORTHCOM anticipates and conducts homeland defense and civil support operations involving federal military forces within its area of responsibility to defend, protect, and secure the United States and its interests. The USNORTHCOM area of responsibility includes air, land, and sea approaches and encompasses the continental United States, Alaska, Puerto Rico, the Bahamas, Turks and Caicos Islands, and the U.S. Virgin Islands. It also includes the Gulf of Mexico, the Straits of Florida, and the water surrounding the continental United States out to approximately 500 nautical miles. Additionally, the USNORTHCOM area of responsibility includes Canada and Mexico. As directed by the President or Secretary of Defense, USNORTHCOM conducts operations through assigned Service components, designated functional commands, and subordinate standing joint task forces.

2-103. In accordance with the Chairman of the Joint Chiefs of Staff standing execute order for DSCA (referred to as the CJCS DSCA EXORD) the USNORTHCOM Commander has the authority to alert and prepare to deploy assigned and allocated forces in support of a primary agency such as FEMA. The Combatant Commander may request, deploy, and employ selected forces upon notification from the Chairman of the Joint Chiefs of Staff and the Secretary of Defense, in support of a validated request for assistance from a primary agency. The intent of the order is to provide the combatant commander the maximum latitude to posture federal military forces to respond immediately to an incident.

2-104. If required, USNORTHCOM may deploy its standing joint force headquarters, a joint command and control element organized within USNORTHCOM headquarters. This command and control element rapidly deploys to enable the stand-up of a joint task force headquarters or to augment existing joint task forces. In addition, USNORTHCOM may deploy a situation awareness team as an advance joint liaison element.

United States Army North

2-105. United States Army North (USARNORTH) is the Army component command assigned to USNORTHCOM. USARNORTH is the joint forces land component command within USNORTHCOM. As the joint forces land component command, USARNORTH commands and controls federal land forces conducting DSCA. USARNORTH has a main command post, based at Fort Sam Houston, and two contingency command posts, each capable of operating as a joint task force with augmentation. The contingency command posts organize for rapid land and air deployment anywhere within the USNORTHCOM area of responsibility. Both command posts have joint and interagency compatible communications systems, with satellite links.

2-106. USNORTHCOM has standing joint task forces (see paragraphs 2-107 to 2-108) subordinated to USARNORTH. The defense coordinating officers and defense coordinating elements for all ten FEMA regions also belong to USARNORTH. In response to any incident requiring large numbers of federal troops, USARNORTH initially deploys a contingency command post near the joint field office. Figure 2-9 shows USNORTHCOM and USARNORTH command and control.

A Comprehensive Approach for Civil Support

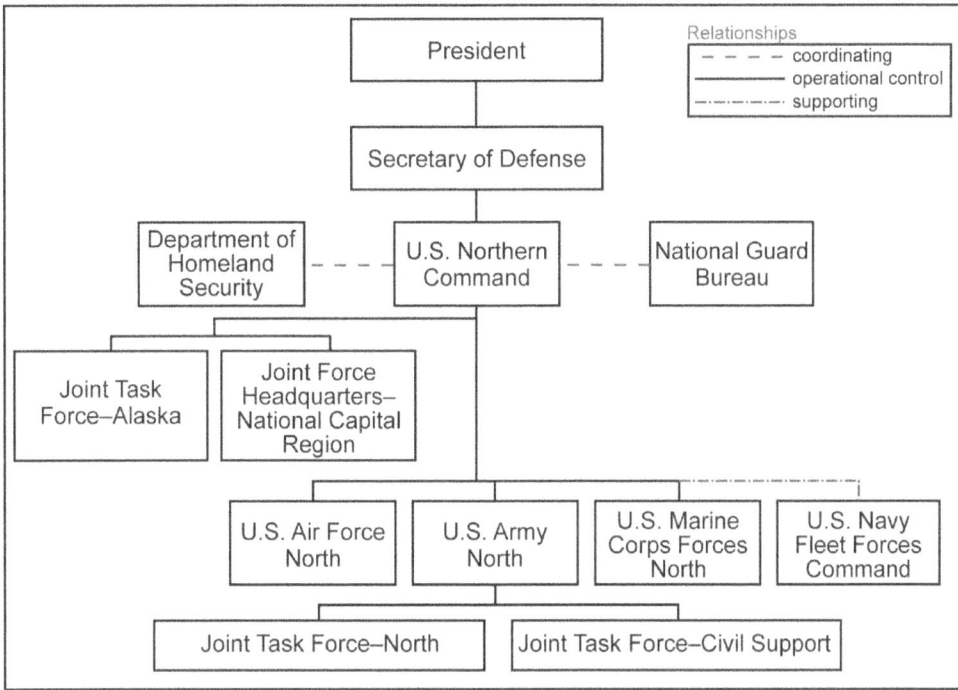

Figure 2-9. USNORTHCOM and USARNORTH structure

Joint Task Force-Civil Support

2-107. Joint Task Force–Civil Support is a standing joint task force headquarters assigned to USNORTHCOM and under the operational control of USARNORTH. It plans and integrates federal military support for chemical, biological, radiological, nuclear, or high-yield explosives incidents (referred to as CBRNE incidents). During support for CBRNE incidents (this *support* is also called CBRNE consequence management) Joint Task Force–Civil Support forces consist mainly of CBRNE consequence management response force units as provided to USNORTHCOM in an annually updated execute order for CBRNE incident response operations. When directed by the Secretary of Defense, the commander of USNORTHCOM deploys Joint Task Force–Civil Support to establish command and control of federal military forces at a CBRNE incident site. The CBRNE consequence management response force provides capabilities such as casualty decontamination, security, medical triage and treatment, aviation, logistics, and transportation. USNORTHCOM may deploy Joint Task Force–Civil Support to the USPACOM area of responsibility to provide CBRNE incident support within U.S. territory. (See chapter 4 and appendix E of this manual, and also Field Manual (FM) 3-11, for more information.)

Joint Task Force-North

2-108. Joint Task Force-North is under the operational control of USARNORTH. It employs military capabilities in support of federal civilian law enforcement agencies for threats to the homeland. Chapter 5 discusses support to domestic civilian law enforcement agencies in detail.

Joint Force Headquarters-National Capital Region

2-109. The Joint Force Headquarters-National Capital Region plans, coordinates, and maintains situational awareness in the National Capital Region to safeguard the Nation's capital. As directed, this headquarters employs forces for civil support.

Joint Task Force–Alaska

2-110. Joint Task Force–Alaska, headquartered at Elmendorf Air Force Base, is a subordinate command of USNORTHCOM. It is comprised of Soldiers, Sailors, Airmen, and DOD civilian specialists. Joint Task Force–Alaska's mission is to deter, detect, prevent and defeat threats within the Alaska joint operations area to protect U.S. territory, citizens, and interests, and as directed, conduct civil support. Within its joint operations area, Joint Task Force–Alaska plans and integrates DOD homeland defense efforts and provides DSCA to civilian agencies such as FEMA.

Other Units

2-111. Other allocated or theater committed military assets for homeland defense and DSCA include a theater sustainment command, an air and missile defense command, a contracting brigade, and a human resources command.

United States Pacific Command

2-112. USPACOM conducts civil support in Hawaii, Guam, and American Samoa, and the U.S. territories within its area of responsibility. Due to the large distances within the USPACOM area of responsibility and the distribution of U.S. forces in the region, USPACOM maintains flexible command and control arrangements for civil support. USPACOM conducts civil support operations through assigned Service components and designated functional components. It has one standing joint task force, Joint Interagency Task Force–West, which supports civilian law enforcement agencies in USPACOM's area of responsibility. It can also activate Joint Task Force–Homeland Defense to perform DSCA and homeland defense missions.

2-113. In accordance with the CJCS DSCA EXORD, the USPACOM Commander has the authority to alert and prepare to deploy assigned and allocated forces in support of a primary federal agency. The combatant commander may request, deploy, and employ forces upon notification from the Chairman of the Joint Chiefs of Staff and Secretary of Defense, in support of a validated request for assistance from a primary agency. The intent of the order is to provide the combatant commander with the maximum latitude to posture federal military forces to respond immediately to an incident.

Joint Interagency Task Force–West

2-114. Joint Interagency Task Force–West is the USPACOM executive agent for federal military support to law enforcement for counterdrug and drug-related activities. The mission of Joint Interagency Task Force–West (formerly Joint Task Force–5) is to detect, disrupt, and dismantle drug-related transnational threats in Asia and the Pacific. Joint Interagency Task Force–West does this by providing interagency law enforcement intelligence, supporting U.S. law enforcement, and developing partner nation capacity to protect U.S. security interests at home and abroad. Joint Interagency Task Force–West provides U.S. and foreign law enforcement agencies with interagency information and analysis, counterdrug training, and infrastructure development support.

Joint Task Force–Homeland Defense

2-115. USPACOM forms Joint Task Force–Homeland Defense by combining a Service headquarters (such as an Army Division), a joint signal element, personnel from a joint manning document, and DHS liaison. The primary mission of Joint Task Force–Homeland Defense is DSCA within the USPACOM area of responsibility, excluding Alaska. Current plans focus on developing the Task Force–Homeland Defense into a standing joint task force that represents all five armed Services and various government agencies.

UNITED STATES ARMY CORPS OF ENGINEERS

2-116. The United States Army Corps of Engineers (USACE) manages components of the nation's public works infrastructure. This includes maintenance and management of the national waterways, environmental remediation and recovery operations, real estate, disaster recovery operations, and general project management functions. The Corps of Engineers is responsible for infrastructure protection and emergency repair to support states in reconnaissance and emergency clearance of debris from damaged areas.

2-117. USACE coordinates ESF #3, *Public Works and Engineering*. It provides technical assistance, engineering, and construction management resources and support during response activities. This includes preparedness, response, and recovery actions. It also extends to construction management, contracting and real estate services, providing emergency repair of damaged public infrastructure and critical facilities, and support to the FEMA Public Assistance Program and other recovery programs. The Public Assistance Program provides supplemental federal disaster grant assistance for debris removal and disposal; emergency protective measures; and the repair, replacement, or restoration of disaster-damaged public facilities and the facilities of certain qualified private nonprofit organizations. See also the USACE Web site at www.usace.army.mil.

JOINT TASK FORCE

2-118. The combatant commander normally establishes a joint task force to command federal military forces (excluding USACE resources). The joint task force normally exercises operational control over all federal military forces and installations within its assigned joint operational area. When the joint task force is established, consistent with operational requirements, its command and control element will co-locate with the joint field office to ensure coordination and unity of effort. If that is not operationally feasible, the joint task force commander places a liaison officer with the defense coordinating officer at the joint field office.

2-119. The defense coordinating officer and joint task force commander have distinct roles and responsibilities. The defense coordinating officer serves as DOD's single point of contact at the joint field office for requesting assistance from DOD. With few exceptions, requests for federal military support originating at the joint field office are coordinated with and processed through the defense coordinating officer.

2-120. Based on the complexity and type of incident, and the anticipated level of federal military resources needed, DOD may also elect to designate a joint task force commander to command federal (Title 10) military activities in support of the incident objectives. If a joint task force is established, consistent with operational requirements, its command and control element will be co-located with the senior on-scene leadership at the joint field office to ensure coordination and unity of effort. The co-location of the joint task force command and control element does not replace the requirement for a defense coordinating officer and defense coordinating element as part of the joint field office unified coordination staff. The defense coordinating officer remains the DOD single point of contact in the joint field office for requesting assistance from DOD.

PRE-SCRIPTED MISSION ASSIGNMENTS

2-121. Part of the CJCS DSCA EXORD addresses pre-scripted mission assignments. Based on careful analysis of previous DSCA missions and DOD capabilities, the Joint Staff develops a menu of capabilities and identifies each as a force package. The CJCS DSCA EXORD does not specify types of military units; rather, it identifies force packages with specific capabilities that a supported agency (such as FEMA) likely will require from DOD. The joint director of military support provides the CJCS DSCA EXORD to FEMA and other agencies. This provides FEMA a menu of military capabilities from which it can select. The supported agency selects the DOD capability, and the request for assistance flows very rapidly up to the Pentagon and back to the requesting agency. Simultaneously, the Joint Staff (normally the joint director of military support) sources the request to a supporting combatant command or Service. The alert and deployment orders follow rapidly. The use of a pre-scripted mission assignment expedites much of the coordination between the civilian agency and DOD for determining what the civilian agency needs and the approximate cost of providing it. As an example, a pre-scripted mission assignment for communications support is shown in figure 2-10. Note that cost figures are included in a pre-scripted mission assignment.

UNCLASSIFIED

DEPARTMENT OF DEFENSE

Title: DoD ESF #2, 25-User Communications Package (Fixed Site Teams) (FOS/DFA)

Block II – Assistance Requested:
Provide 25-User Communications Package (fixed site teams) in support of disaster operations in response to [*incident*] in the State of [*State*]. All local, State, and non-DoD national assets are exhausted or do not have the capacity to meet this requirement.

Block IV – Statement of Work:
As requested by and in coordination with FEMA and (*list ESF lead agency being supported*), the DoD will provide voice, data, and video communications solutions (24-hour operations) at a fixed location for a staff of up to 25 personnel who provide coordination of initial assessment teams and other first responders. Provide Internet reachback (UNCLASSIFIED).

Specific capabilities required include:
- Satellite phone such as Iridium or Globalstar
- UHF TACSAT, VHF, and UHF Line-of-Sight (LOS) radios
- Non-secure voice/telephone
- Non-secure data (Internet) connectivity
- Non-secure facsimile/printer/scanner
- Non-secure radio
- Non-secure VTC

NOTE: Systems operate with commercial power, rechargeable batteries, vehicle batteries, solar panels, and/or portable generators.

POC for positioning teams is _____ (name) at _____ (contact information)

24-hour support required? Y / N   Estimated period of support _____ days.

All equipment and supply purchases must be coordinated with FEMA. Prior FEMA approval is necessary to ensure reimbursement.

FEMA logistical support required:
- Safe, secure, and environmentally protected work space
- Parking facilities
- Access to power source
- Messing facilities/MREs
- List of approved lodging
- Access to fuel for generators and rental vehicle

Total Cost Estimate: ~ $91,250
Includes 15 military personnel TDY for a 10-day period

Current cost information and other relevant data should be used to complete this document when it is prepared for submission to the Department of Defense.

FINAL FEMA PSMAs for DOD 9.9.09.doc   Page 11 of 31

UNCLASSIFIED

Figure 2-10. A pre-scripted mission assignment for communications support

Chapter 3
Provide Support for Domestic Disasters

This chapter discusses the first primary civil support task—provide support for domestic disasters. The doctrine in this chapter builds on chapters 1 and 2. The discussion begins by explaining the general nature of a disaster. It then explains how civil authorities fulfill their responsibilities for responding, starting from the lowest level of government and eventually incorporating support from military forces. It discusses National Guard support for disaster response operations, followed by federal military support for disaster response operations. It briefly explains military and civilian operational phases. It concludes with an extended discussion of doctrinal considerations specific to disaster response.

THE NATURE OF A DISASTER

3-1. There is an adage among emergency responders that "every disaster has a zip code." This is a reminder that any disaster is both a personal and a community experience for the victims. After a disaster, the affected communities often experience a collective shock that inhibits the local response, compounded by the destruction. Until Soldiers have been part of a disaster response effort, the misery and loss experienced by the victims—and the degree of disruption that inhibits even the most basic services—lie beyond their experience. Only combat operations create similar effects within civilian communities, and even then the destruction may not equal the aftermath of a tornado or hurricane. The compensating factor for Soldiers is that no operational experience is likely to produce the same sense of satisfaction as assisting their fellow citizens' recovery, even though the mission is exhausting and often frustrating.

3-2. A disaster can strike anytime, anywhere. It can take many forms—a hurricane, an earthquake, a tornado, a flood, a fire or a hazardous spill, an act of nature, or an act of terrorism. It may build over days or weeks, or it may hit suddenly and with no warning. Every year, millions of Americans face a disaster and its terrifying consequences. A disaster can quickly produce an overwhelming demand for resources and reduce the ability of local, state, and tribal governments to respond effectively. A disaster can result in many deaths and injuries or cause extensive damage to critical infrastructure. Besides hurricanes, earthquakes, and floods, potentially devastating events include large, powerful winter storms, regional droughts, and contagious disease outbreaks. Naturally occurring plant and animal disease strains reaching epidemic infection levels could have a devastating effect on the nation's food supply and the economy. The destruction of or inability to access communications systems, transportation, and shelter may further complicate governments' ability to assist the victims.

3-3. Natural or manmade disasters may start a chain of subsequent disasters such as chemical spills, biological hazards, and potentially explosive material. Each subsequent disaster creates a cascading chain of harmful effects. For example, a chemical spill caused by a tanker truck accident on a bridge over a flooded major river causes numerous complications. The chemical enters the potable water system and compounds the effects of the flooding on waterborne shipping traffic. The food supply is contaminated as the chemical is deposited on flooded cropland. Lack of sanitation after flooding can cause serious diseases to appear.

3-4. Military support in response to a disaster varies from loaning equipment to local authorities to committing major units of the National Guard and regular and reserve military components. At the peak of the response to Hurricane Katrina, over 75,000 military personnel from the regular and reserve components supported civil authorities at the local, state, and national level.

RESPONSIBILITY FOR DISASTER RESPONSE

3-5. The primary responsibility for responding to domestic disasters and emergencies (also called incidents) rests with the lowest level of government able to manage the response. As discussed in chapter 2, if a situation exceeds local capability, local authorities first seek assistance from neighboring jurisdictions, usually under a mutual aid agreement. Requests work their way up from the lowest level to the highest level, as each lower level's resources become insufficient. If the capabilities of neighboring jurisdictions are overtaxed, or responders anticipate additional requirements, they go to the state for assistance. If state capabilities prove insufficient, state authorities then ask for assistance from other states under existing agreements and compacts (including requests for support from nonfederalized National Guard units). In a smaller incident, state authorities normally exhaust state resources, including support from states within their region, before requesting federal assistance.

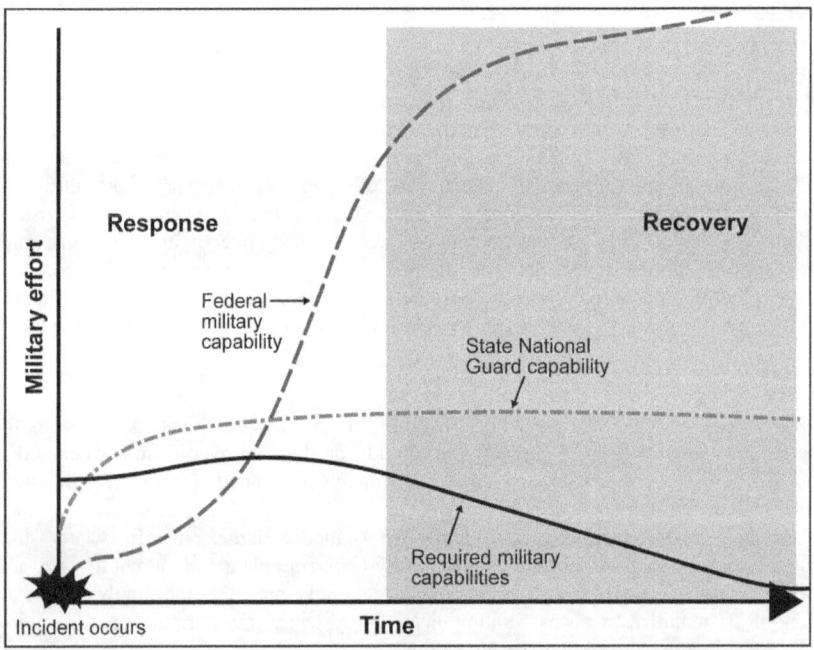

Figure 3-1. Military forces required for a typical incident

3-6. For most incidents, a state's National Guard capabilities are sufficient; no additional military support is needed. Studies show that more than 90 per cent of declared emergencies require no federal military forces, even in incidents requiring significant support from the Federal Emergency Management Agency (FEMA). Figure 3-1 illustrates this using a solid line for the total military effort needed, and dotted lines representing the military capability that state National Guard and federal military forces can generate. Given advance warning, the capability gap can be reduced. It may also be reduced through immediate response authority (see figure 3-2, page 3-3) of federal military forces from nearby installations.

Provide Support for Domestic Disasters

3-7. A catastrophic incident always exceeds the immediate capability of responders at every level. The effect of the disaster on local responders—disaster victims themselves—compounds the requirements. Although a formal request under Robert T. Stafford Disaster Relief and Emergency Assistance Act (commonly known as the Stafford Act) for federal assistance follows the process illustrated in chapter 2, in practice, the President commits federal aid simultaneously with the governor's commitment of state resources. Based on initial assessments from the Department of Homeland Security and supported combatant commander, the Secretary of Defense authorizes support from federal military forces. Even before the formal authorization, the combatant commander places available forces on alert. After the state's civilian and National Guard responders arrive, federal military forces fill the capability gap until national resources can meet requirements. Figure 3-2 illustrates the requirements in a major catastrophe as a solid line and the relative capabilities of the National Guard and federal military forces as dotted lines.

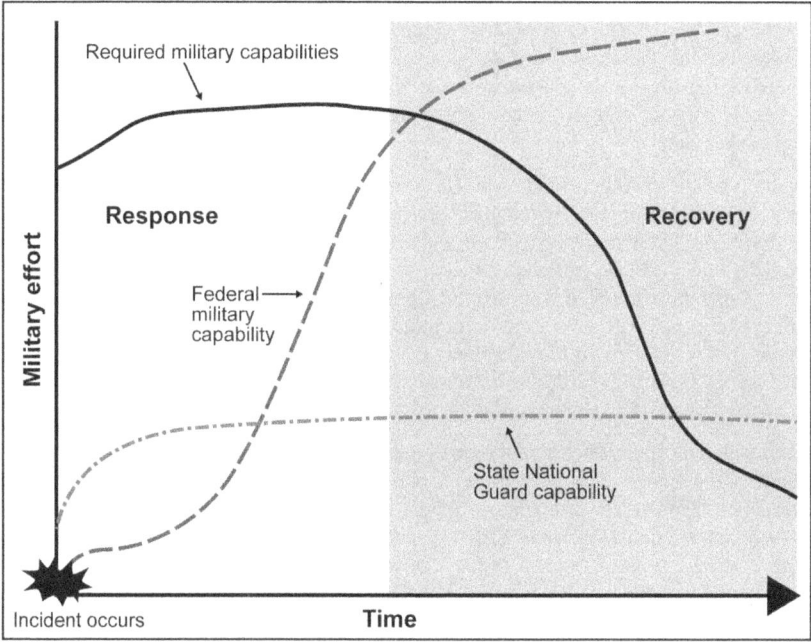

Figure 3-2. Military forces required for a catastrophic incident

3-8. To close the initial capability gap, federal military forces support response and recovery efforts (usually led by FEMA) as fast as they can deploy. The capability gap, though it will decline quickly, may remain until the bulk of federal military forces arrive. Deploying and receiving large forces in disaster areas takes time; initial response will always lag requirements. Means of deployment must be re-tasked from other commitments. (Even in a major catastrophe, however, the federal military support available will rapidly exceed the need.) During the initial deployment period, commanders should expect criticism from media representatives who demand to know why more is not being done. Despite this, commanders do everything within their scope of authority to ensure that unity of effort is achieved.

3-9. Civilian agencies will eventually reach their full capacity, recovery will begin, and military forces will no longer be needed. Transition for military forces usually follows the reverse order of alert and deployment. Federal military forces redeploy to their home stations first. Any of their remaining missions pass to federal agencies (usually executed by civilian contract), National Guard units, and state agencies. However, should conditions deteriorate, the President can increase federal military support at any time. As state and local agencies recover, National Guard units begin to redeploy, with priority normally given to National Guard units assisting from other states under mutual aid agreements. Until the governor is satisfied that citizens' needs can be met by civilian means alone, that state's National Guard forces continue to support local authorities in a reduced, "steady state" posture by rotating units and personnel.

INITIAL RESPONSE FROM LOCAL AND STATE AUTHORITIES

3-10. Before and during an incident, city, county, and tribal emergency managers assess their jurisdictions' ability to respond. They consider the incident commanders' assessments, experience with similar incidents, training based on the National Incident Management System (NIMS) and the National Response Framework (NRF), estimates developed from the National Planning Scenarios, and advance coordination with their counterparts in adjacent states or territories. They determine if they will need support from outside their jurisdictions.

3-11. In some types of disasters, such as hurricanes, there is a warning period—sometimes up to a week. This allows planners to initiate evacuations, pre-position supplies, and mobilize additional responders. Unfortunately, many disasters occur with no warning. Local emergency manager request assistance from adjacent jurisdictions and state officials as soon as possible when a disaster strikes unexpectedly. Prior planning and preparation, coupled with support from outside the disaster area, mitigates the effects of the incident somewhat. Local officials from adjoining communities normally have agreements in place that authorize their first responders to provide emergency assistance when requested. Similar agreements allow commercial services, such as utilities, to assist their counterparts across an entire region. However, adjacent communities may be unable to provide assistance if the incident also affects them.

3-12. When local authorities determine they will not be able to manage the response through support from their neighbors, they request assistance from the state. The state activates its emergency operations center, and representatives from state emergency support functions (see chapter 2 for more information about emergency support functions, known as ESFs) report to it. The state emergency operations center normally initiates operations from its permanent offices. However, the governor or state emergency manager may displace it if the permanent location is affected by the disaster and would degrade the response, or if the governor needs to be closer to the disaster area. The latter is particularly true in the larger states, when movement by air may require refueling stops.

NATIONAL GUARD DISASTER RESPONSE

3-13. When any municipality or county activates an emergency operations center, it notifies the state emergency manager. The state emergency manager then passes a situation report to the joint force headquarters–state and then to the National Guard watch desk. The adjutant general or a designated representative may deploy a liaison team from the joint force headquarters–state to assess and monitor the situation. A National Guard liaison team is likely to deploy if the situation is unclear and has the potential to require additional resources. If the adjutant general anticipates local authorities needing additional assistance, the joint force deploys additional teams.

3-14. National Guard commanders may provide immediate response to a local community, but under state laws. The local emergency managers may have contingency agreements in place with local armories and nearby National Guard training installations. Alert for the National Guard begins with the activation of the alert roster—usually initiated by full time Guard personnel. This alerting message is the notification the Guard members receive to report to their home station. The National Guard local commander is not a permanent full time member and is alerted by his or her alert roster. The supporting commander assesses the situation within the larger context of the likely state response. Soldiers committed locally in an immediate response may be needed for a larger call-up of National Guard forces by the governor. The local commander may limit the immediate assistance in order to support higher priority missions. Frequently, National Guardsmen muster at their units even before an official alert order; their experience enables them to anticipate quite accurately when they will be needed. The Tennessee National Guard's response to damaging tornadoes in 2008 provides an example of a state response.

> **Tennessee National Guard Responds to Tornadoes**
>
> Strong tornados struck Arkansas, Tennessee, Kentucky, Mississippi and Alabama in February, 2008. Two thirds of Tennessee suffered damaging storms. Tornadoes killed 32 people, injured 149, and destroyed over 750 homes, making it the worst storm to hit the state in 75 years. Many of the counties hit by the storm were overwhelmed with storm debris and lacked the means to clear roads and initiate response and recovery operations. Macon, Sumner, and Trousdale counties reported a swath of destruction over a mile wide. The storm nearly destroyed some communities. The Tennessee Governor called out the National Guard to help in the recovery efforts.
>
> The 230th Engineer Battalion, Tennessee National Guard, received the alert to deploy within 48 hours. Their mission was to support the Tennessee Department of Transportation. The Tennessee National Guard deployed 27 large dump trucks, eight large bucket loaders, troops with chain saws, and a logistics support package. Over a two-week period, the unit collected, hauled, and dumped over 9,000 cubic yards of debris.

The Joint Force Headquarters–State

3-15. Under National Guard Regulation 500-1, each state maintains a joint force headquarters–state (JFHQ–state) to unify command of its Air and Army National Guard forces. The JFHQ–state functions as the joint staff for the adjutant general, who directs the state National Guard's operations. The JFHQ–state co-locates with the state's emergency operations center and allocates resources to National Guard forces. One of the most important functions of the JFHQ–state is coordinating requests for assistance by state National Guard forces. Simultaneously, the JFHQ–state provides situation reports to the National Guard Bureau joint operations command center in Washington D.C. During a disaster response, however, most states exercise operational control of their deployed forces through a joint task force headquarters in the operational area.

3-16. The adjutant general alerts state National Guard forces through emergency communications networks that tie together subordinate National Guard armories, installations, and commanders. Based on standing contingency plans, the adjutant general organizes one or more joint task forces formed around one of the state's battalions or larger sized units. This may be a brigade headquarters with Air National Guard personnel and state civilians. Although other states have different arrangements, the support follows similar patterns. The adjutant general supports the governor, and the JFHQ–state supports the state emergency operations center. The joint task force exercises operational control of committed forces and works with the civilian incident command organization (see chapter 2) on-scene. Figure 3-3 illustrates the relationships between civilian command organizations and National Guard echelons during a large, state-level multijurisdictional disaster response, as used in Illinois. This example shows a joint task force. In some states, the military response may include only Army National Guard, and the force headquarters may be a task force. A civilian *area command* may not be needed, depending on the extent of the disaster (refer to chapter 2).

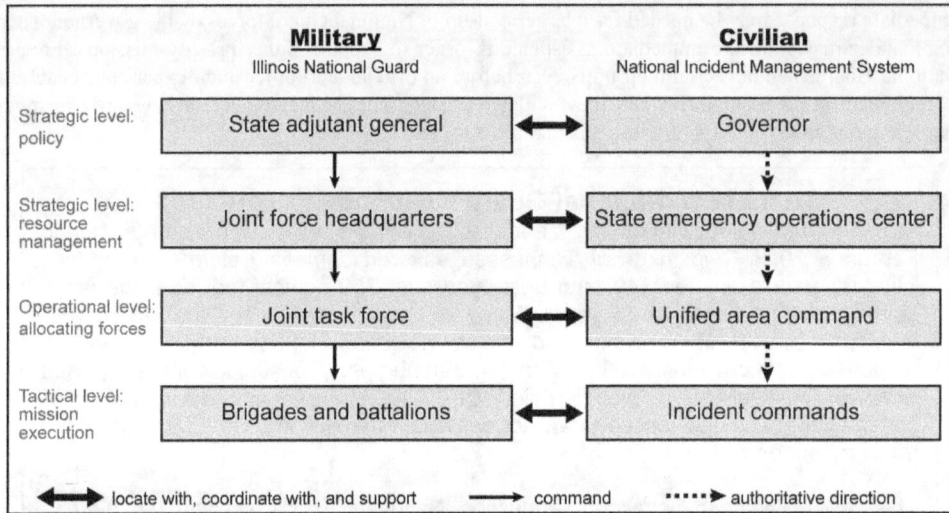

Figure 3-3. State response and National Guard echelons—Illinois example

3-17. Even in states where the adjutant general is also the state emergency coordinator, National Guard forces remain in support of civil authority. State constitutions echo the principles in the Constitution of the United States and respect the authorities of elected and appointed officials within their jurisdictions. The relationship between National Guard leaders and their civilian counterparts may intertwine considerably. This occurs for practical reasons and also because National Guard and state officials work closely together for years and often form teams to respond to incidents.

3-18. When a disaster involves many counties, such as in a hurricane or major winter storm, the affected state may employ several area commands and incident commands. The adjutant general organizes joint or single Service task forces and places them in direct support of the area commands. This streamlines the command and control process by allowing the civilian incident commanders to pass requests for assistance directly to supporting task force commanders, who then issue fragmentary orders to the appropriate units. Task force commanders inform the JFHQ–state of their status and pass on requests for reinforcements or additional equipment and sustainment. This arrangement capitalizes on mission command and individual initiative. Figure 3-4, page 3-7, illustrates the relationships of National Guard task forces to incident commands.

Provide Support for Domestic Disasters

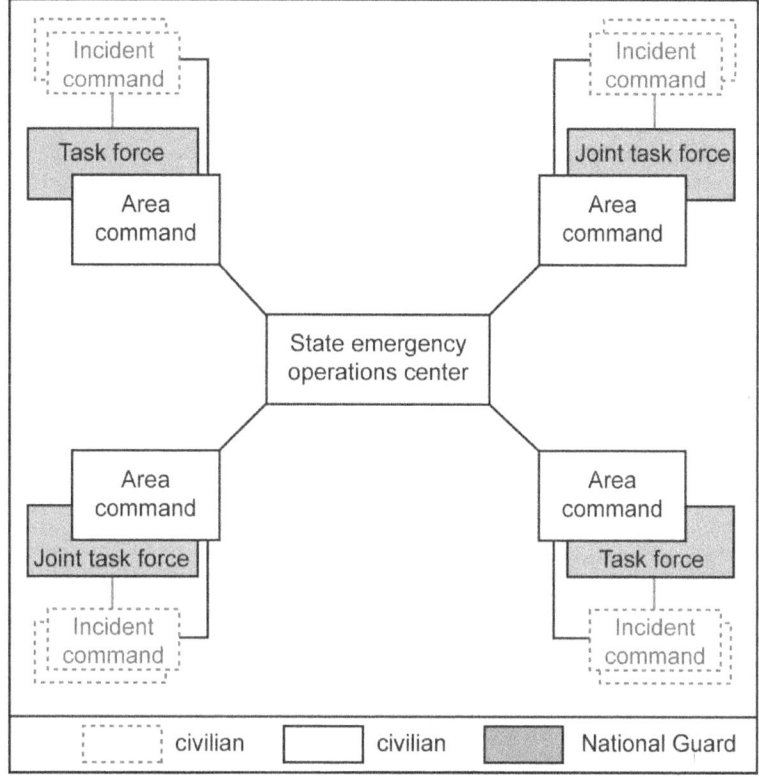

Figure 3-4. Relationship of National Guard forces to area commands

Planning Considerations for State National Guard Units

3-19. State National Guard contingency planners consider several factors when preparing for potential disasters. Some factors are common to Army unit planning, but several are unique to the National Guard. These include—
- Proximity of the unit to the disaster.
- Deployed personnel and equipment.
- Distribution of tactical units.

Proximity Of The Unit To The Disaster

3-20. The closer the unit's armory is to the disaster, the more rapidly it can respond, and the more familiar key leaders will be with the area and local civilians. However, the unit is also more likely to suffer in the disaster, with some or all of its capability severely degraded.

Deployed Personnel And Equipment

3-21. National Guard units deploy overseas more frequently today than at any time during the Cold War. The adjutant general continually updates plans based upon the availability of forces within the state. By coordinating with adjacent states and the National Guard Bureau for support under assistance agreements (see paragraphs 3-24 to 3-29), the adjutant general manages the state's disaster response capabilities. If a disaster strikes and one of the state's units is preparing for deployment but not yet federalized, the governor may commit the unit to the disaster, under state control. The adjutant general works through the National Guard Bureau to coordinate adjustments to deployment and training schedules.

Distribution of Tactical Units

3-22. Unlike the Regular Army, the various tactical units that make up the brigades and divisions of the National Guard are widely distributed. Units are not necessarily co-located with their heavy equipment. For example, a National Guard brigade combat team may have its battalions distributed across armories throughout the state. In some cases, one of the battalions may belong to another state's National Guard. Disaster response plans within each state adjust task-organizations based on availability of forces, proximity of units to one another, and unit equipment. Early in the response, a task force may consist of small units from many units, and larger forces gradually assemble their table of organization and equipment configuration.

3-23. National Guard planners also assess requirements against capabilities they will provide during civil support operations. These include security; chemical, biological, radiological, nuclear, and high-yield explosives consequence management; communications; logistics; engineer support; medical support; transportation; aviation; and maintenance. Refer to National Guard Regulation 500-1 for additional discussion.

Emergency Management Assistance Compact

3-24. The Emergency Management Assistance Compact (EMAC) grew out of several states helping each other after Hurricane Andrew in 1992. The EMAC is a comprehensive agreement similar to a treaty between nations. It establishes a legal framework for interstate mutual aid. The National Emergency Management Association administers the EMAC. All states, the District of Columbia, Puerto Rico, and the Virgin Islands are members of EMAC. For more information, see Web site http://www.emacweb.org/.

3-25. When incidents occur, governors enter into contractual agreements between their states based on prior EMAC arrangements. States request assistance on an EMAC request form (known as a REQ-A). On the form, requesting states provide details about support sought from neighboring states, including costs for reimbursement. Requesting states prepare a separate request to each neighboring state from whom they seek support. Support under EMAC requires an emergency declaration from the requesting state's governor but not from the President of the United States.

3-26. If National Guard forces support another state based on an EMAC agreement, they normally serve in a state active duty status. National Guard forces do not serve in Title 32 status unless approved by the Secretary of Defense. The EMAC does not pertain to federalized National Guard forces, in Title 10 status.

3-27. Article XIII of the EMAC prohibits EMAC agreements for using National Guard forces from one state for civil disturbance or law enforcement operations in another state. This type of support requires a separate memorandum of understanding. The Gulf States have executed memoranda with each other for civil disturbance and law enforcement support. The terms of their agreements cover the use of armed National Guardsmen from another state, including command relationships, immunity, carrying and loading of weapons authority, law enforcement authority, and training on state rules on the use of force requirements.

3-28. State National Guard forces provide their interstate support agreements to the National Guard Bureau. Because the Bureau monitors the status of the total National Guard force, it can identify resources to match requirements and assist with the details. In an emergency, the National Guard Bureau in Washington, DC, assists with additional agreements between states, but the respective governors must execute their memorandum of understanding concerning the use of out-of-state forces.

3-29. Whenever state National Guard forces respond in support of another state, each state's joint force headquarters ensures the following coordination requirements are met:

- The memorandum of understanding specifies the duration of the commitment with the supported state. (Most National Guard commitments are for 30 days.) The agreement normally specifies the "time on station" and excludes mobilization, movement, and demobilization time. The supported adjutant general specifies the command relationship between the gaining unit and the supporting unit. The preferred relationship is operational control, with specific coordinating instructions concerning logistics and health service support.
- The supporting state retains administrative control throughout the deployment.
- The supporting unit deploys with a minimum of 72 hours of sustainment.
- The agreement must clearly specify the authorities for law enforcement duties granted by the supported governor and approved by the supporting governor.
- The gaining state designates and operates the reception, staging, onward movement, and integration facility and procedures for all incoming units and personnel from supporting states.
- The supporting unit commander provides the gaining unit commander with a complete unit status report when the unit arrives, and updates it according to the gaining unit's standing operating procedure. Forces avoid needless operational and administrative difficulties by ensuring accurate status reporting.
- The supporting unit brings or maintains access to any professional licenses necessary (such as medical or veterinary licenses) for personnel provided under a mutual aid agreement that are not validated under EMAC. The supported state must specify which licensing requirements are waived or restricted.
- Both states agree to the documentation needed for reimbursable expenses and procedures not covered in National Guard regulations.
- The gaining and supporting unit commanders coordinate actions related to disciplinary matters. Unless modified by the respective governors, Soldiers remain subject to their state's military codes.

FEDERAL MILITARY DISASTER RESPONSE

3-30. Federal military forces provide support during emergencies and incidents in two general categories. The first is immediate response authority, under which an installation commander may assist a local community in an emergency. This support is limited in time and scope. The second category is in response to a Presidential declaration of emergency or disaster. In the latter case, federal military support may range from installation support up to commitment of major portions of the Regular Army.

IMMEDIATE RESPONSE AUTHORITY

3-31. Although federal military forces are seldom first responders, they can support local authorities in an emergency, under immediate response authority. In the absence of a federally declared disaster, installation commanders and responsible officials from Department of Defense (DOD) may provide support to save lives, prevent human suffering, and mitigate great property damage. This includes mutual aid for fire protection and immediate response as directed by the Secretary of Defense. This response must be consistent with the Posse Comitatus Act. (See chapters 5 and 7 for more about the Posse Comitatus Act.) The Chairman of the Joint Chiefs of Staff standing execute order for DSCA (referred to as the CJCS DSCA EXORD) dated 14 August 2009 states—

> *When time does not permit prior approval from higher headquarters, local military commanders, or responsible officials of other DOD components, may in imminently serious conditions, upon request from local authorities, provide support to save lives, prevent human suffering, or mitigate great property damage. Such immediate response should be provided to civil agencies on a cost-reimbursable basis, but requests for immediate response should not be delayed or denied because of the inability or unwillingness of the requester to make a commitment to reimburse the Department of*

> *Defense [DOD]. Commanders, or responsible DOD, officials will report all actions and support provided through the appropriate chain of command to the National Military Command Center (NMCC), . . . and provide a copy to the Geographic CCDR [combatant commander]. After 72 hours of employment, respective military departments will coordinate continued operations with the Geographic CCDR.*
>
> CJCS DSCA EXORD, 14 August 2009

3-32. According to Section 1856a of Title 42, United States Code (USC), each agency charged with providing fire protection for any property of the United States may enter into agreements with local fire-fighting organizations (including nearby military installations) to provide assistance in fighting fires. This includes personal services and equipment required for fire prevention, the protection of life and property from fire, fire fighting, and emergency services. Emergency services include basic medical support, basic and advanced life support, hazardous material containment and confinement, special rescue events involving vehicular and water mishaps, and extractions from trenches, buildings, or confined spaces.

3-33. Requests for assistance under immediate response authority usually go directly from local civilian authorities to local military commanders. Requests may also go to DOD officials. The installation commander may provide all assets with the exception of those that have a potential for lethality. The Secretary of Defense must approve deployment of weapons and munitions, including bayonets. Deployed forces remain under military command and function in direct support of the requesting local authority. Typical missions include—

- Search and rescue.
- Evacuation, decontamination, fire-fighting, medical treatment, restoration of medical capabilities and public services.
- Removal of debris, rubble, or hazards to permit rescue or movement.
- Recovery, identification, and registration, and disposal of the dead of deceased persons.
- Detecting, assessing, and containing a chemical, biological, radiological, nuclear, or high-yield explosives incident.
- Collecting, safeguarding, and distributing essential food items and supplies.
- Damage assessment.
- Communications.
- Explosive ordnance disposal.

Note: The installation senior commander will not approve any civilian jurisdiction request for law enforcement support outside the installation, including interdicting vehicles, conducting searches and seizures, making arrests or apprehensions, surveillance, investigation, or undercover work.

FEDERAL MILITARY FORCES DISASTER RESPONSE—PRESIDENTIAL DECLARATION

3-34. Usually, the commitment of federal military forces for civil support operations follows a presidential disaster declaration under the Stafford Act. After the disaster declaration, a primary federal agency (usually FEMA) coordinates with the defense coordinating officer (DCO) to prepare a request for DSCA and submit it to the DOD executive secretary. (See paragraphs 2-94 to 2-100 for details about the DCO.) However, a federal coordinating officer may initiate the request, or another federal agency could request federal military support. In addition, the President may bypass the usual request process and order the military to provide support. Figure 3-5, page 3-11, illustrates the usual process that leads to committing federal military forces. Paragraphs 3-45 to 3-48 provide more information about how requests for assistance develop into mission assignments.

3-35. Concurrently with the DSCA request to joint director of military support, the appropriate combatant commander, either United States Northern Command (USNORTHCOM) or United States Pacific Command (USPACOM) develops the concept of operations and support and submits a request for forces to

Provide Support for Domestic Disasters

the Joint Staff. The Secretary of Defense designates the supported combatant commander and any supporting combatant commands. When validated, the request for forces becomes an order to the supporting combatant commanders to provide the forces. In support of this process, the Army Service component commander coordinates with Department of the Army and United States Army Forces Command (for most Army units) concerning required capabilities.

3-36. Based on the Army force generation process, the United States Army Forces Commander and Department of the Army identify the required forces to the supporting combatant commander (normally United States Joint Forces Command). The Secretary of Defense specifies the command relationship of forces to the gaining combatant command, either operational control or attached. The Secretary of the Army may direct modifications to administrative control; if not, administrative control remains with the providing Army headquarters.

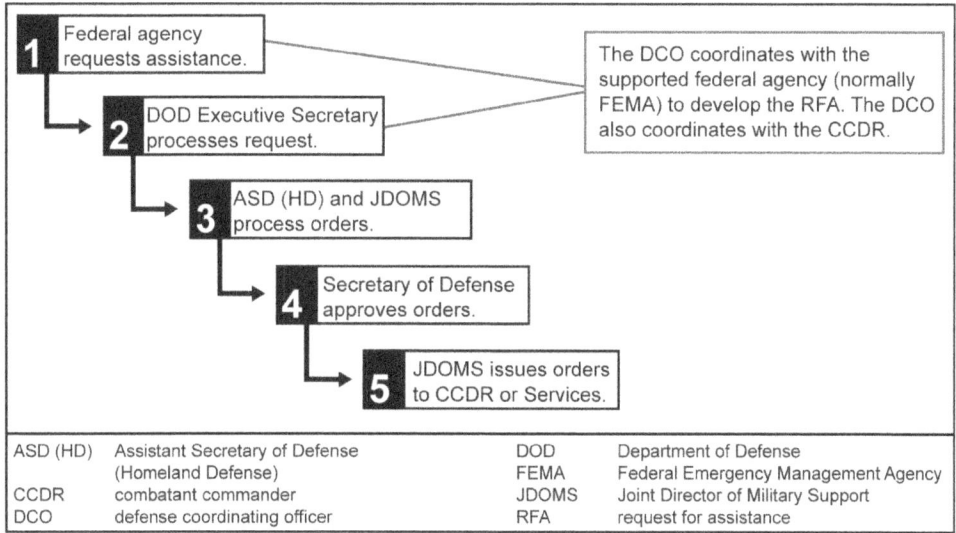

Figure 3-5. The federal request for assistance process

3-37. If approved by the President, the Secretary of Defense may mobilize National Guard forces for federal service. These forces pass to the operational control of the gaining combatant commander. National Guard units conducting DSCA in federal military (Title 10) status change their administrative control to the gaining Army Service component command—usually United States Army North (USARNORTH). However, the Army Service component commander coordinates with the providing adjutant general to continue as much of the administrative control support as feasible through the respective states. The Secretary of Defense may also direct the Service secretaries to place selected installations in a support relationship to the supported combatant command.

3-38. For any federal military force operating in the USNORTHCOM area of responsibility, the joint force land component commander determines the required capabilities and the appropriate command relationships, depending on the situation. The determination of command and control arrangements is one of the most important joint force land component command decisions. Figure 3-6 illustrates an example of USNORTHCOM structure for DSCA.

3-39. If the requirement for federal military support only consists of a small number of troops, the joint force land component commander may place the detachment under operational control of the DCO, rather than a joint task force. The joint force land component commander provides the DCO with any additional assets to support the detachment. The DCO coordinates missions with the federal coordinating officer and issues orders to the detachment commander. The DCO and staff—the defense coordinating element—coordinate for support through the joint force land component command and other federal agencies.

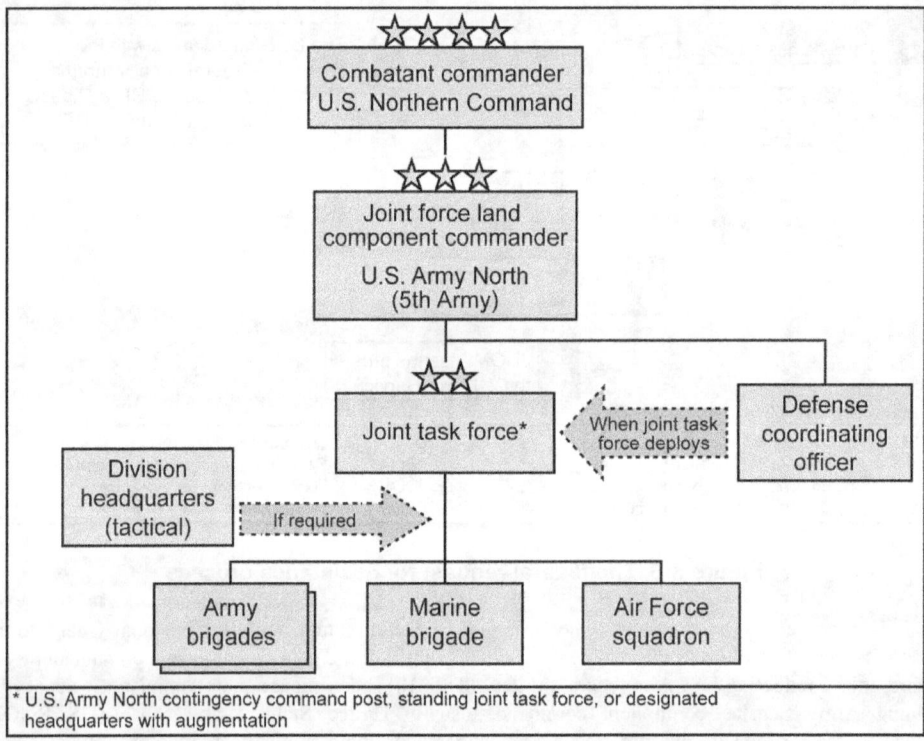

Figure 3-6. Example of USNORTHCOM structure for DSCA

3-40. Anything larger than a small element necessitates more extensive command and control than the joint force land component command and defense coordinating element can provide. Within the USNORTHCOM area of responsibility, the combatant commander and USARNORTH assesses the command and control requirements needed to control federal Army and other federal military land forces. The USNORTHCOM commander decides whether to commit Joint Task Force–Civil Support. USARNORTH may employ either of its two contingency command posts as a joint task force or land component command; conversely, it may designate an incoming headquarters as the joint task force or land component.

3-41. The USNORTHCOM commander identifies the base support installation. The base support installation is normally a DOD installation with an airfield and suitable support facilities. The base support installation is the domestic equivalent to a theater base in other areas of responsibility. The base support installation becomes the aerial port of delivery and joint reception, staging, onward movement, and

Provide Support for Domestic Disasters

integration facility for the Army forces. USARNORTH establishes and controls the joint reception, staging, onward movement, and integration facility, usually at the base support installation or very near it. In addition to joint reception, staging, onward movement, and integration, the base support installation may become a training facility and principal supporting base for the federal relief efforts. If a suitable DOD installation is not nearby, USNORTHCOM may request permission to use a National Guard base. However, National Guard bases usually support no more than one or two battalions at a time and may require extensive additional military and contract support. (See chapters 8 and 9 for more information about sustainment.)

3-42. Both USNORTHCOM and USARNORTH routinely deploy situational assessment teams to disaster areas in advance of a decision to commit federal military forces. These teams deploy to the incident area and come under the operational control of the DCO. The DCO facilitates coordination and information sharing between the assessment teams and the various emergency support functions. If required, the DCO can coordinate for information sharing between the assessment team, the state emergency operations center, and the JFHQ–state. Because DCOs work full-time in their FEMA regions, each DCO is usually well-acquainted with state emergency managers, state coordinating officers, and state emergency preparedness liaison officers. Once the assessment team provides its findings to its parent headquarters, it becomes part of the defense coordinating element. As part of the defense coordinating element, the assessment teams continue to provide situation updates to their former headquarters through the DCO's situation report.

3-43. USNORTHCOM or USARNORTH also sends liaison teams to DOD installations nearby to assess the potential basing requirements. If deployment of federal military forces is likely, USARNORTH deploys a contingency command post to the vicinity of the joint (interagency) field office. From there, the command post coordinates requirements between the DCO and USARNORTH, assists the defense coordinating element, and begins the process of tying in military command and control with the joint field office.

3-44. The liaison team members achieve efficiency by combining interpersonal skill with professional competence. If the situation is severe enough to require federal military forces, civilians at the joint field office and a state emergency operations center will be under great stress. Bringing newly arrived federal military personnel up to speed may seem like an additional burden in a chaotic situation. Before deployment, the liaison teams and the contingency command post coordinate through the DCO with senior federal and state officials. They obtain as much information as possible. Upon arrival, the liaison team leaders further coordinate through the defense coordinating element in order to support civilian incident commanders and deployed National Guard forces.

3-45. In situations other than a disaster, a federal agency or state government may request DOD assistance. The request follows the same general process as an emergency under the Stafford Act. However, requests for assistance in circumstances other than a declared emergency or disaster come under the Economy Act. This law prohibits the use of DOD capabilities in lieu of similar capabilities within the requesting agency or state. The law also requires the supported agency to reimburse DOD for all operating expenses. Tactically, the Stafford and Economy Act have no significant effect on operations.

MISSION ASSIGNMENTS

3-46. Federal military forces receive their missions when they arrive in the disaster area. Within the (civilian) joint field office, ESF coordinators analyze the requirements and capabilities in coordination with the federal coordinating officer and DCO. Together, they identify potential requests for assistance from federal military forces. The DCO determines if the requests are feasible. The DCO also assesses whether the requests are appropriate—evaluating resources and legal issues. If the requests meet the criteria (listed in paragraph 3-46), the DCO submits the requests according to the process illustrated in figure 3-5.

3-47. Beginning with the DCO and continuing through the chain of command, each request for DOD assistance receives an evaluation based on six factors (sometimes referred to by the acronym CARRLL):

- **Cost.** Who will pay or reimburse DOD for the assistance rendered?

- **Appropriateness.** Who normally provides and is best suited to satisfy the request for assistance? Is it in DOD's interest to provide the assistance? Have other options been considered to meet the request? Is DOD the best provider of the requested assistance under the circumstances?
- **Readiness.** Does the assistance have an adverse impact on the responding unit's ability to perform its primary readiness, training, deployment missions?
- **Risk.** What is the potential health or safety hazards to federal military forces and their equipment, vehicles, or aircraft? Can these risks be mitigated?
- **Legality.** What is the legal authority that permits or prohibits the requested assistance?
- **Lethality.** Is there any potential for lethal force to be used by or against Federal military? If yes, has the Secretary of Defense authorized the carrying of weapons?

3-48. The defense coordinating element performs a critical function by performing a modified mission analysis on each request for assistance. First, they determine if the request for assistance expresses the right mission. Often this means translating civilian terms into military terms. Second, they translate the approved mission assignment into a mission tasking order, suitable for the joint task force to analyze and execute. Ideally, the federal coordinating officer and DCO determine what capabilities are required, not how to do the mission, allowing mission command. The joint task force commander translates the mission tasking order into an operations order that allows the joint task force maximum flexibility. For example, rather than asking the joint task force for "one UH-60 helicopter to fly the federal coordinating officer and FEMA Director at a specific date and time and location", the DCO may revise it into a mission tasking order, to "provide command and control aviation support to the federal coordinating officer."

3-49. Broader issues of support may require discussion among the members of the unified coordination group (see paragraph 2-79) and military commanders. When required, the federal military joint task force commander and the state joint task force commander participate in the discussions with their respective DCO or state coordinating officer, but their inclusion is not required.

PHASES OF DISASTER RESPONSE OPERATIONS

3-50. The NRF divides disaster response into three broad phases: prepare, respond, and recover. USNORTHCOM plans for DSCA use six phases: shape, anticipate, respond, operate, stabilize, and transition. (Army doctrine does not specify operational phases. See Field Manual (FM) 3-0, chapter 6.) Figure 3-7 illustrates the relationship between the NRF phases and the USNORTHCOM phases. Commanders conducting civil support operations should be familiar with these phases and understand their relationships. USARNORTH applies the USNORTHCOM phases for sustainment planning (see chapter 8).

Provide Support for Domestic Disasters

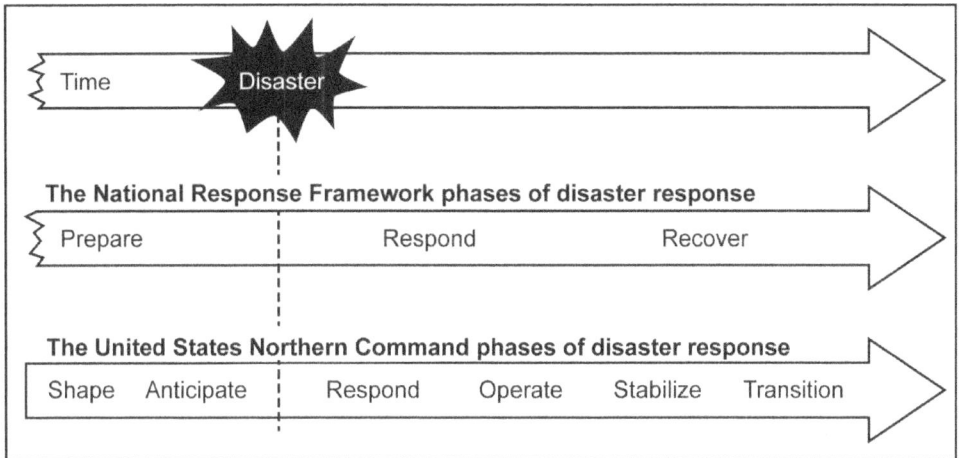

Figure 3-7. USNORTHCOM and National Response Framework phases of disaster response

3-51. Phase 0 (zero), shape, refers to continuous situational awareness and preparedness. Actions in this phase include interagency coordination, planning, identifying capability gaps, conducting exercises, and public affairs activities. USNORTHCOM plans synchronize Phase 0 activities, which are ongoing.

3-52. Phase I, anticipate, begins with the identification of a potential DSCA mission, a no-notice incident, or when directed by the President or Secretary of Defense. This phase ends when federal military forces deploy or when the determination is made that federal military forces are not needed. Phase I is completed with deployment of the DCO, the defense coordinating element, emergency preparedness liaison officers, and other required personnel.

3-53. Phase II, respond, begins with the deployment of initial federal military response capabilities. This phase ends when federal military forces are ready to conduct operations in the joint operations area. This phase is completed when sufficient forces are deployed to accomplish the mission.

3-54. Phase III, operate, begins when federal military forces commence operations. Phase III ends when federal military forces are close to completing their missions and no further requests for assistance are anticipated.

3-55. Phase IV, stabilize, begins when military and civil authorities decide that federal military support will scale down. Military and civil authorities establish criteria for transition to civilian management of the response without federal military support. Phase IV is successful when all operational aspects of mission assignments are complete and federal military support is no longer needed.

3-56. Phase V, transition, begins with the redeployment of remaining federal military forces. This phase ends when federal military forces have redeployed and operational control is returned to their parent commands. Phase V is complete when federal military forces have transitioned all operations back to state National Guard forces or civil authorities.

PLANNING SUPPORT FOR CIVILIAN EMERGENCY MANAGERS

3-57. Early in an operation, a catastrophic disaster may overburden the civilians managing the response. Urgent requirements force emergency managers to concentrate all their efforts on the next 24 or 48 hours. Longer planning horizons may become a low priority. Army planners can support civil authorities by offering to develop long-term plans. Before offering to support long-term planning, the senior commander must earn the trust and confidence of civilian leaders. Army commanders always keep in mind that they serve in a supporting role. Once accepted, Army planners help the civilian staff develop a phased plan (keeping in mind NRF phases) with an achievable end state. Similar assistance, offered where needed in

Chapter 3

the joint field office or within other parts the incident command system (such as incident command posts and emergency operations centers), contributes to effective unified action.

TRANSITION FROM MILITARY TO CIVILIAN SUPPORT

3-58. The Army's role in disaster response ends as soon as practical. The ultimate task of federal and state disaster response efforts is to assist the local community in returning to self-sufficiency. When directed by the federal coordinating officer or state coordinating officer, Army forces complete their mission assignments and turn over responsibility for further efforts to civilian agencies and commercial enterprise. Commanders coordinate with appropriate interagency and military groups (including joint field offices, emergency operations centers, incident commands, and defense coordinating elements) to avoid gaps in necessary support. The goal of the recovery effort is to allow state authorities to control as much of the long-term recovery as feasible and return federal forces to their parent installations.

3-59. In addition, commanders at every level keep in mind the human aspects of the transition to civilian organizations and account for it in their assessments. In a disaster, Soldiers form friendships and professional relationships with civic and group leaders with whom they work. Communities form a relationship with the Soldiers they see every day. When military units are near the end of a mission, they need to coordinate the transition with their civilian counterparts. Each situation is different, but commanders make sure they plan for the human aspects of transition as well as the details of transferring missions.

3-60. National Guard forces may supplant federal military forces as communities begin to recover. This is likely in incidents involving immediate response authority. Federal military forces that arrive immediately at an incident site may be relieved by National Guard forces as the latter reach the scene. In other cases, federal military forces may receive a mission assignment to replace National Guard units so that state National Guard forces can enforce public order, while federal troops take over humanitarian efforts. The transition between federal military forces and state National Guard forces is planned and coordinated through the joint field office between the federal coordinating officer, DCO and state coordinating officer. In addition to specific coordination requirements specified in fragmentary orders, the outgoing and incoming commander exchange information on the situation and environment.

CONSIDERATIONS FOR DISASTER RESPONSE OPERATIONS

3-61. In this section and in succeeding chapters, FM 3-28 discusses operational and tactical considerations for civil support operations. This discussion includes selected considerations organized by the Army doctrinal concepts of battle command and the elements of combat power. The emphasis is on tactical considerations that require additional planning and on measures that complement civil support operations or distinguish them from stability operations.

3-62. FM 3-28.1 discusses many other tactical considerations. Commanders and staff can also find related information in Center for Army Lessons Learned, National Guard Lessons Learned, and Joint Lessons Learned publications. The USNORTHCOM Web site, http://www.northcom.mil/, also provides a portal for extensive reference material.

BATTLE COMMAND

3-63. Battle command drives the operations process in civil support just as battle command drives it in full spectrum operations overseas. Commanders understand, visualize, describe, and direct while assessing and leading. However, certain aspects of civil support require a different command perspective than combat situations. The most obvious is the lack of a thinking, adaptive enemy. Although Soldiers may encounter some criminal behavior by civilians during civil support operations, from the Soldier's perspective the civilians are citizens and not enemy combatants. Commanders also adjust the way they understand, assess, and lead, adapting the particulars of battle command to domestic operational environments.

Understand

3-64. Command in civil support begins with understanding the operational environment. Understanding the physical environment, particularly in the aftermath of a disaster or terrorist attack, requires first-hand knowledge. To achieve this, commanders travel to their subordinate's location to get their subordinate's assessment of the situation and measure that against personal observation, just as they would in combat. Reports and statistics may be useful summaries of activity but cannot convey the actual impact of the incident on the community. Commanders speak with citizens throughout the area and ascertain for themselves the situation in the community. They make sure their subordinates do the same. There is no substitute for face-to-face discussions to build understanding of the situation at a human, neighborhood level and then assemble that level of understanding into an appreciation of the larger situation.

3-65. To understand the environment, commanders need to know their role and that of their units within the environment. Commanders begin with their own chain of command. In many operations, the task organization combines units and headquarters that have not worked together previously. For many of the Regular Army units, this may be their first deployment in a domestic emergency. The command arrangements for civil support will differ from those used in combat operations. Commanders at each level meet with their seniors and subordinates early and often. As soon as they understand their military organization and commanders' intent, they do the same with leaders of other military forces and the civilian agencies. This parallels how commanders develop understanding in stability operations—the role of that unit within the larger context. Military forces are there to support citizens, working in conjunction with local, state and federal authorities.

Assess

3-66. Commanders stress assessment of the situation to their staffs and subordinates. They build situational awareness through coordination with supported and supporting agencies, other military forces, volunteer organizations, and contacts with the media. On the ground, leaders are certain to encounter misinformation and rumors, particularly in the early stages of response. Inoperable and incompatible communications, overloaded incident command centers, distraught citizens, and exaggerated or inaccurate news media coverage contribute to confusion. Although it may not be battle command as FM 3-0 defines it, the chaos surrounding a disaster poses challenges found in combat situations. Commanders keep in mind that the effectiveness of civil support depends not on the success of military missions, but on the effectiveness of the civilian agencies in meeting the citizens' needs.

3-67. Initial assessment is vital. The initial assessment provides the responding commander with information and recommendations to make timely decisions for the response. Initial assessment identifies specific needs on the ground and actual coordination requirements, including but not limited to items covered in local, state, and federal disaster plans. Prior planning and exercises are invaluable, but disasters never occur exactly as anticipated. The initial assessment provides information to help verify on–the-ground conditions. This information helps the commander make required decisions in order to provide the most effective military support for civil disaster response. During the initial assessment, the commander may determine that an existing plan fits a very different incident and can rapidly orient the unit on measures developed in response to that scenario, adapted for the situation.

> **Earthquake Plans Adapted to an Ice Storm**
>
> In February of 2009, a severe ice storm paralyzed western Kentucky. The storm left more than 100,000 citizens, many in rural areas, in dire circumstances. They had no electric power, no way to call for help and all the roads were blocked by broken trees. The Adjutant General of Kentucky, who was also the state's emergency manager, did not have a specific plan for a winter storm of this severity. However, he did have plans for dealing with an earthquake. He quickly realized that the effects of the ice storm were similar to those predicted for the earthquake. He ordered civilian responders and National Guard emergency forces to adapt the plan they had rehearsed in March of 2008 as part of an emergency response simulation. Subordinates took the initiative and executed ice storm relief effort based upon plans for a major earthquake. BG Heltzel, adjutant general of Kentucky, attributed the success of the relief effort to prior planning, even if it was for a very different emergency than actually occurred.

Lead

3-68. In civil support operations, commanders focus not only on their subordinates, but on their civilian counterparts. They work to develop trust and confidence between military and civilian personnel. This is an art, and it depends on human qualities. There is no checklist for how to do this, but it is essential for commanders to promote unified effort. Military commanders begin by demonstrating their willingness to support and not take charge of the various field offices. Close cooperation and honesty break down friction. Army leaders look for interagency shortfalls in personnel, communication, and situational awareness, and offer assistance if available. They stress that their Soldiers and personnel are there to help and to learn, and they demonstrate it by personal example.

COMMAND AND CONTROL OF MILITARY FORCES DURING DISASTER RESPONSE OPERATIONS

3-69. Probably the most challenging aspect of civil support is the command and control adjustments required to adapt Army forces to their supporting role within a multiagency environment. Specific areas that require attention include command and support relationships, command post operations, and communications, liaison, and control measures.

Parallel Command

3-70. In many large-scale civil support operations, state National Guard and federal military forces operate in overlapping areas but under separate chains of command. The parallel command structure is one of the means to enhance unity of effort, but its success depends on continuous coordination between all of its components. Within a parallel command structure, there is no single force commander and therefore no unity of command in the military sense. Both the federal and state militaries retain control of their respective forces. Decisions regarding the operation require the collective effort of all participating leaders: state and federal governmental leaders, and state and federal senior military leaders. These leaders collaborate within the NRF to develop common goals, unify their efforts, and accomplish the mission. Figure 3-8 shows an example of a parallel command structure.

Provide Support for Domestic Disasters

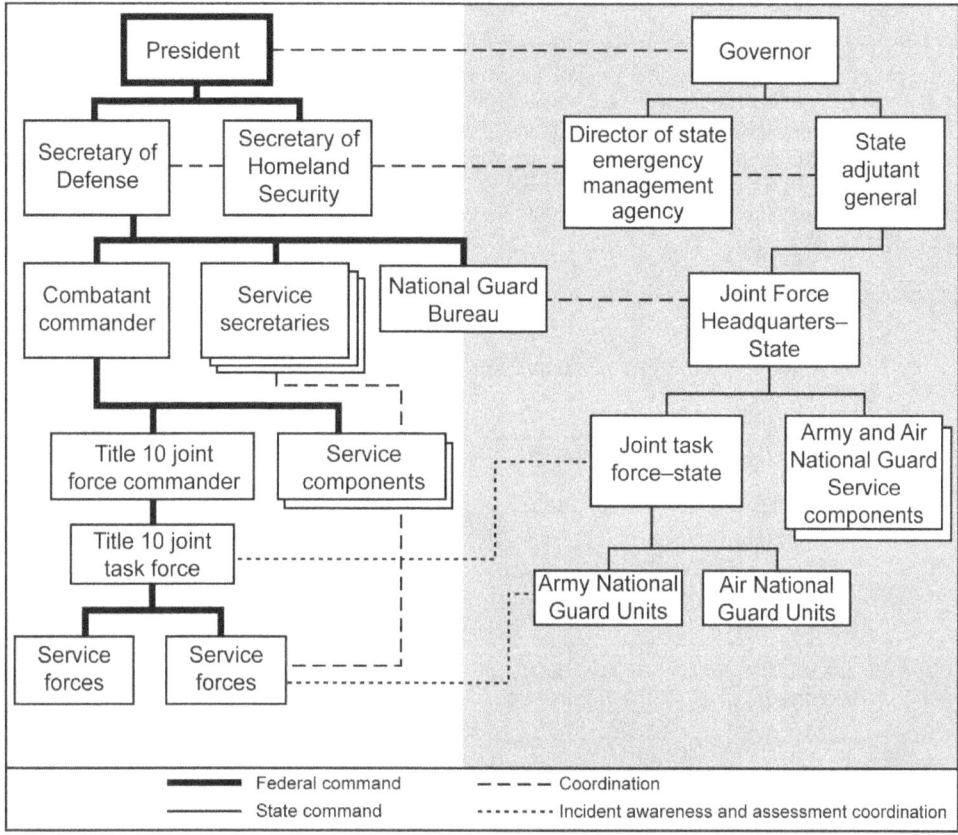

Figure 3-8. Example of parallel command structure

3-71. The challenge in using a parallel command structure for DSCA is its dependence on the efficient and effective use of available forces by the state and federal military chains of command. Therefore, its effectiveness depends on a close working relationship between commanders. Physically co-locating command posts or exchanging high-quality liaison officers at the command posts facilitates this coordination.

Comand in Multistate Disasters

3-72. A major catastrophe such as a major earthquake may affect several states simultaneously. This makes a coordinated national response imperative. The military commitment could involve thousands of Soldiers from every component. Within the affected states, all National Guard forces will support their respective state's first responders. However, in a multistate disaster, existing agreements for support from adjacent states may be overridden by the extent of the catastrophe. The National Guard Bureau will work with all unaffected states to coordinate for additional National Guard forces to deploy and reinforce the state National Guard forces within the affected states.

3-73. A multistate disaster will require FEMA to activate at least one joint field office per state. In those states where federal military forces join the response effort, a DCO will operate within each joint field office. In order to oversee the multiple responses FEMA may expand the regional coordination center within the disaster area (if still operational) to direct the regional response efforts. Note that DCOs from other FEMA regions would have to deploy to joint field offices established in each state since the regional DCO remains with the regional coordination center and principal federal official. The Department of

Homeland Security and FEMA would coordinate the National response efforts from the National Operations Center in Washington, DC.

3-74. Figure 3-9 illustrates command and control for a very large federal military forces response to a major catastrophe in the continental United States. In this hypothetical response, an earthquake on the scale of the 1811 New Madrid Quake (see vignette on page 3-20) strikes a region of the United States, devastating a three state region (states A, B, and C). State B suffers the greatest damage, including severe damage and large loss of life within a major metropolitan area. Other states beyond state A, B, and C are affected, but their state National Guard forces can meet military requirements. Supporting combatant commands, principally United States Joint Forces Command, provide federal military forces to USNORTHCOM.

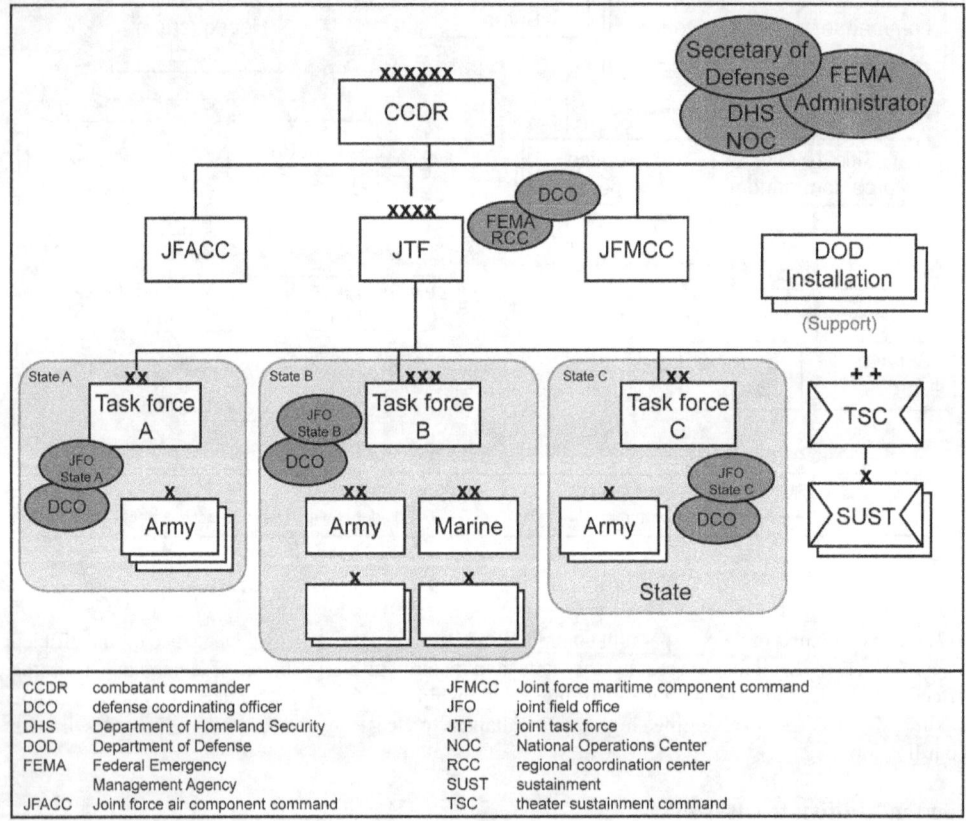

Figure 3-9. Multistate disaster requiring major commitment of federal military forces

> **The New Madrid Earthquake**
>
> In 1811 a massive earthquake devastated the Mississippi Valley region near modern Carbondale, Illinois. The quake was so violent that the Mississippi River reversed its course for a period and sections of the surrounding valley "liquefied" from the shaking. The quake was powerful enough to ring church bells on the East Coast of the United States. Other severe earthquakes followed in succeeding months. If the New Madrid Quake were to occur today, it could devastate several states along with major cities such as St. Louis and Memphis and shatter transportation and energy infrastructure crossing the Mississippi River. Today the New Madrid Earthquake scenario features prominently in FEMA and state planning for catastrophic disasters.

Command and Support Relationships

3-75. Command and support relationships require careful attention. Military forces remain under military chain of command, but state National Guard and federal military forces have different chains of command. Unless directed by the President as specified in law, the chains of command remain separate. Although the chains of command remain separate, the forces are often intermixed geographically.

> Note: The U.S. Army Corps of Engineers operates separately from both state National Guard forces and federal military forces. The United States Army Corps of Engineers is the ESF coordinator for ESF #3 and receives priorities from the joint field office directly. Federal military forces may also receive mission assignments under ESF #3, but they remain under the joint task force's command.

3-76. National Guard commanders may enhance unity of effort through judicious use of support relationships, which differ from command relationships under Army doctrine (see FM 3-0, appendix B). For example, the joint task force-state may place a National Guard company in direct support of a local incident commander. The National Guard commander receives his priorities directly from the incident commander, but retains operational control over all Guardsmen in the company.

3-77. Federal military forces are attached or under operational or tactical control to the federal military joint task force. The joint task force commander further task-organizes subordinate units based on mission assignments, normally specifying operational control by the gaining headquarters. Administrative control remains with the original providing component headquarters, subject to modification by the Secretary of the Army.

3-78. Support relationships can facilitate unified action when federal military and state National Guard forces operate in the same area, subject to mission assignments. Following requests from FEMA or the state, a federal military installation or unit may support a National Guard force, particularly in cases where the federal installation is supporting FEMA efforts. However, because the command lines remain separate, any supporting relationship requires approval by both DOD and the affected state's adjutant general, in coordination with their respective federal and state coordinating officers.

Command Post Operations

3-79. Command post operations pose different challenges from those encountered in a stability operation. Whenever possible, the joint task force headquarters should co-locate with their supported civilian coordinating officer. The state joint task force positions itself within or near the state emergency operations center, and the federal military joint task force co-locates with the joint field office. This eases communications challenges between the joint task force and the DCO. In practice, the joint field office positions itself near the incident area (50 to 100 miles away). If locating the joint field office near the state emergency operations center does not degrade support to the incident area, the federal coordinating officer will do so.

3-80. In some instances, it is not feasible to locate the federal military joint task force command post near the joint field office. The most practical solution is for the joint task force headquarters to remain at the base support installation (see chapter 8). The commander employs a small, mobile command post as a tactical command post to allow face-to-face contact with subordinate commanders while maintaining situational awareness between the DCO and joint task force main command post.

3-81. Similar considerations apply for subordinate units. Units position their command post close to their civilian counterpart's field facilities. If the civilian agencies have multiple facilities from which they are coordinating their response, the tactical unit selects a command post that provides rapid access to civilian locations by foot or vehicle. Units select command post facilities in coordination with their higher headquarters that—

- Allow communication with the higher and subordinate commanders. Disruption of civilian communications and the limitations of tactical radios become the primary considerations.
- Allow rapid road movement between higher and subordinate command posts
- Comply with requirements of state and local officials. Normally, the controlling joint task force headquarters negotiates contracts with local agencies for facilities, whether an existing structure or field location. Unit commanders may recommend a suitable facility based on advance party reconnaissance, but the approval remains with civilian authorities.

3-82. Access to the military command post should be as unrestricted as possible, consistent with force protection posture. Civilian officials and news media require frequent access. If space permits, the staff should designate an area where visitors can observe the command post, coordinate with various staff officers, and obtain reports. If the unit requires a work area for classified information (this seldom occurs), physically separate it from the rest of the tactical operations center and restrict access. Keep in mind that the local, state, and federal agencies all operate on unclassified networks; therefore, reports sent to any civilian agencies must be unclassified.

3-83. In the initial stages of operations, units deploy and operate their command posts in accordance with their standing operating procedures. As soon as practical, the commander should adjust the staff functions to align with the incident command system. This realignment will assist other agencies that coordinate with the unit and save time when processing requests and information. Initially, this can be as simple as placing the appropriate sections together and hanging an incident command system functional designation from the ceiling. Commanders should give careful consideration to their intelligence staff section. One option is to consolidate the S-2 and S-3 functions under the S-3 as the operations section. This can assist the commander in complying with the restrictions on intelligence in domestic environments. (See the discussion of intelligence in paragraphs 3-115 to 3-121, and in paragraphs 7-40–7-52.)

Communications

3-84. Based on studies conducted by the National Communication System and real world incidents (such as 9/11 and Hurricane Katrina), there is a high probability that commercial wired and wireless communication infrastructure will be highly saturated for an indeterminate period. This is due to several factors such as a higher than normal percentage of usage due to first responders, personnel staying home from work or school and personnel attempting to locate information on their loved ones potentially involved in the incident. Depending on the incident, there could also be a large percentage of the commercial communication system degraded or destroyed (electromagnetic pulse and cell towers being destroyed, for example). Power to cell phone towers remains problematic for an extended period due to back up batteries and generators shutting down communication nodes. Units cannot assume that wired (landline phones etc) or wireless communications will be functional during an incident and must plan for alternate forms of both communication and power without relying on the commercial communications system. Units should consider bringing additional iridium telephones (including dialing instructions, directory, battery charger, and case) to support civilian partner communications needs. Providing satellite telephones (with training) to key civilian leaders can greatly enhance communications and coordination.

3-85. Other communications equipment may be incompatible among various organizations. USARNORTH deployable headquarters have communications systems that are compatible with civilian and military communications systems, as do many National Guard forces. Regular Army and Army reserve forces may have a range of communications capabilities, including legacy systems such as mobile subscriber equipment, newly fielded tactical command and control systems such as command post of the future, and developmental systems. Initially, federal military units may need to provide communications equipment and network access to civilian responders until the civilian communications grid is restored.

3-86. Upon alert, communications officers verify the communications systems required. They obtain frequency lists approved by FEMA and the Federal Communications Commission through their controlling joint task force headquarters. If a unit system is incompatible with local emergency systems, and gaining headquarters, the unit should coordinate with the gaining combatant command and DCO for additional capability for its liaison teams. Units plan for expedient communications that include—

- Liaison teams with unit-compatible communications deployed to the gaining headquarters and supported incident commander or civilian incident command post.
- Satellite telephones. Satellite telephones such as iridium can provide voice communications regardless of the state of the local cellular telephone network or power grid.
- Couriers. A Soldier with a high mobility vehicle can drive to a command post and deliver messages and orders. If roads are passable, a rental or General Services Administration vehicle is more efficient. A very expensive alternative is a helicopter.
- Additional signal units and capabilities. Communications officers should identify ground radio relay as well as single channel satellite communications requirements to ensure they are included in the force package.
- Use of the internet. Most communications will travel via commercial telephone networks or the internet. Signal planning must include the ability to access commercial internet, commercial telephone, and video teleconference (VTC) networks. With internet access (wireless or landline), virtual private network (VPN) software, and Army Knowledge Online (AKO) addresses, units can create a command and control network able to handle almost all of their requirements.

3-87. Federal military units should be prepared to integrate communication systems with civilian agencies. Commanders should not assume that military tactical radio equipment would be able to communicate with civilian equipment, due to equipment differences, spectrum requirements, and the geography at the incident. Interoperability should include radio bridging devices that can connect varied devices such as tactical radios to cell phones, and sharing data through a common information management plan. Army forces that support civilian responders in the field (such as medical, logistics, and aviation) must be able to communicate with civilian responders in order to receive instructions and coordinate. When assisting civilian first responders, federal military units will not only be responsible for communicating with other military units, but also with supported civilian responders. Available technology will assist in bridging these capability gaps. For example, radio bridging equipment allows military tactical equipment to communicate with common civilian radio equipment.

Liaison Officers

3-88. Deployed units supporting the disaster need many liaison officers. Commanders plan for additional liaison teams as part of the force package. During relief efforts in Hurricane Katrina, for example, the U.S. Army Corps of Engineers and other engineer units requested and obtained officers from United States Army Training and Doctrine Command and United States Army Forces Command to increase their liaison capability. Depending on connectivity, these officers can be very effective when equipped with a laptop, cell phone, and rental car. However, they will require satellite-based communications to coordinate in incident areas where the cellular communications are not working.

3-89. In addition to unit requirements, the DCO is inside the joint field office with a defense coordinating element to provide technical expertise and coordination. When required, the DCO requests augmentation for the defense coordinating element from the supported combatant commander. The DCO deploys emergency preparedness liaison officers to National Guard headquarters and military installations to serve as liaison between state National Guard and federal military forces and installations.

3-90. Differences in equipment, capabilities, doctrine, rules for the use of force, and law are some of the interoperability challenges that mandate close cooperation by supporting forces. State National Guard and federal joint task force headquarters should exchange qualified liaison officers at the earliest opportunity. The primary function of the liaison officer is coordination to increase situational understanding. Commanders ensure liaison officers or teams deploy with sufficient communications equipment to permit real-time communication between their respective commanders. Commanders ensure liaison officers are operationally proficient, innovative, tenacious, diplomatic, and have the authority to speak for their parent commander.

Areas of Operations

3-91. National Guard commanders normally use *areas of operations* (see Joint Publication (JP) 3-0) as a primary control measure in disaster response. Before assigning an area of operations, commanders consider the factors described in paragraphs 3-92 to 3-95.

3-92. Unlike combat operations, assignment of an area of operations does not determine the supported commander. It only delineates the area in which a military unit concentrates its support to civil authorities. Legal responsibilities remain with the established jurisdictions unless modified by the governor or the President.

3-93. Commanders should designate areas of operation based upon civilian administrative boundaries such as precincts, municipal boundaries, and county lines whenever possible. Within those boundaries, deployed units should support civil authorities as specified in their mission assignments. Wherever possible, commanders align a specific unit within a civilian jurisdiction. For example, a National Guard rifle company may support a police precinct. Its area of operations would be the precinct boundaries.

3-94. The area of operations for a joint task force–state should coincide with the declared disaster area. The governor normally requests disaster declarations based on county jurisdictions. National-level support, directed by FEMA, will encompass the same area.

3-95. The federal joint task force commander may establish a *joint operations area* (see JP 3-0) to aid in control of federal military forces. Federal military forces do not normally receive an area of operations. They operate in general support of the federal civilian agencies across the disaster area, providing functional support such as distribution of supplies, support to hospitals and shelters, and movement of personnel. An exception may involve an incident occurring on federal lands, when Army units have responsibility for support within a defined area such as a canyon or lake. Another exception involves incorporation of supporting installations within the joint operations area. The joint force commander may extend the joint operations area to include supporting military installations.

PROTECTION DURING DISASTER RESPONSE OPERATIONS

3-96. There are many important considerations related to protection. Safety is just as important in civil support as in other elements of full spectrum operations. Composite risk management is one of the processes commanders use to integrate these and other protection considerations. Appendix B provides a more detailed discussion of safety. Other important considerations include rules for the use of force, restrictions on weapons, and force health protection.

3-97. Rules for the use of force prescribe graduated levels of force used against citizens in a domestic environment, based on the citizen's behavior and threat posture. They share with the more commonly known rules of engagement one fundamental—Soldiers may use lethal force if they are in imminent risk of death or major injury. Beyond that, they differ. Rules of engagement are permissive and intended to allow commanders to fight enemy combatants and avoid inflicting unnecessary losses on noncombatants. Rules for the use of force are restrictive and intended to restrict lethal and nonlethal force according to the risk. A classified Chairman of the Joint Chiefs of Staff instruction (CJCSI) establishes policies and procedures for *standing rules for the use of force* (SRUF) for all federal military forces conducting civil support and certain other missions. (See appendix B of JP 3-28 for a discussion of these policies and procedures as they relate to civil support. See also the current CJCS DSCA EXORD.) The joint task force commander may modify the SRUF only by making them more restrictive. See chapter 7 for more information about rules for the use of force.

3-98. Each state has rules for the use of force and National Guard commanders ensure that all Guardsmen train on them. The rules for the use of force vary widely from state to state. While there are many similarities between the joint SRUF and state rules for the use of force, there may be key differences between the two. Commanders should always consult their servicing judge advocate to determine the current rules for the use of force and the potential effect that the current rules for the use of force may have on operations. Each National Guardsmen carries a rules-for-the-use-of-force instruction card and small unit leaders review the rules before each mission.

3-99. The decision to deploy National Guard troops with weapons in state active duty or Title 32 status remains with the governor. His or her decision will depend upon requirements for law enforcement, and protect critical infrastructure. Arming posture or arming order conventions may vary from state to state and should be communicated to any National Guard forces deploying from other states.

3-100. The Secretary of Defense alone makes the decision to 1) deploy federal military forces with weapons, and 2) to direct federal military forces to carry weapons and ammunition. Should the situation require arming of federal military forces, the joint task force commander will submit a request to arm them through the chain of command to the Secretary of Defense. If approved by the Secretary of Defense, the joint task force commander issues necessary orders to subordinate units that require weapons to accomplish their mission. Soldiers authorized to carry weapons also carry ammunition; Soldiers should not carry weapons to create an appearance of capability that they do not actually possess. In general, the decision to arm some or all federal troops is based upon the threat posed to Soldiers performing disaster response or securing critical infrastructure by criminal elements. When authorized to deploy with weapons, unit commanders establish field arms rooms as prescribed by regulation.

3-101. All Army forces involved in disaster response should monitor the exposure of their Soldiers to environmental contaminants. In a disaster, safety and health hazards are everywhere. Toxic chemicals contaminate structures, water, and soil. Floods often contain enough bacteria from decomposing debris and sewage to infect anyone working near it. Rabies and insect borne diseases become a serious threat. Commanders stress safety and force health protection to their subordinates and demand field discipline from their Soldiers. Leaders and medical personnel continuously check personnel for hot or cold weather injuries, minor trauma, infections, and stress. The supply system needs to push items such as insect repellant, mosquito netting, work gloves, disposable overalls, surgical masks and latex gloves, commercial breathing equipment and filters, and a host of other items. Personal hygiene is as important in civil support as it is in combat. In a flood response, for example, units should have a system to launder every Soldier's uniform and equipment daily, and provide replacement clothing frequently. However, commanders should ensure that they comply with environmental regulations before authorizing field expedient measures for laundry, garbage and waste disposal. Contracted support for portable latrines, laundry facilities, and mess halls become priority issues for commanders. Finally, the chain of command needs to be alert for the effects of fatigue, particularly when Soldiers are operating equipment. The decision to operate around the clock on recovery tasks requires establishment of policy for work and rest. All leaders continuously assess the capability of Soldiers to operate safely during around the clock operations.

MOVEMENT AND MANEUVER DURING DISASTER RESPONSE OPERATIONS

3-102. The purpose of maneuver in disaster response is two-fold: restore mobility and concentrate supporting assets at the point of greatest need. Army forces have several capabilities to make them valuable in disaster response. Most tactical vehicles are able to operate in rougher terrain than commercial vehicles. In the aftermath of a disaster, the ability to provide relief to the victims and often depends on the ability of vehicles to move across debris and flooded areas. Army vehicles do both. However, many of the newer wheeled vehicles such as mine-resistant trucks, have heavy armor, and require experienced drivers in order to operate them on and off road, particularly around obstacles. Using high mobility vehicles, Soldiers can deliver supplies, assist in evacuating stranded citizens, and move Soldiers into the area to remove obstacles and assist first responders. Tactical radio communications, mobility, command and control assets designed for austere environments, and a mission focus make Army units an excellent complement to first responders.

SUSTAINMENT FOR MILITARY FORCES DURING DISASTER RESPONSE OPERATIONS

3-103. Disaster response operations depend upon flexible and effective sustainment. Within the United States, sustainment operations benefit from a huge and diversified economic base centered on commercial activity and utilizing unmatched transportation capabilities. This allows for a greatly reduced logistics footprint. However, it also means that logisticians have a completely different set of challenges when sustaining the force. Success depends upon unity of effort with federal, state, and commercial partners; continuous coordination is critical. Disaster response stresses the logistical system, which needs to respond very rapidly and often in an austere local environment. Sustainment will often require resources from outside the disaster area, since local supply and transportation within the joint operations area may be dysfunctional. See chapters 8 and 9 for more detail on sustainment.

Deployment of Military Forces

3-104. Deployment of military forces to the disaster area requires flexible planning and effective RSOI. In response to disaster, responding forces deploy using multiple deployment means.

3-105. National Guard forces from within that state normally self deploy using organic transportation, chartered commercial busses, and rental vehicles. Advance parties and liaison teams typically self-deploy from their armories using personal, state-owned, and rental vehicles. In the immediate reaction phase, the armory dispatches military vehicles using individual dispatch procedures if convoy clearance is not required. Larger groups of forces deploy in convoy from their armory or training center, using movement credits coordinated through the state emergency operations center. National Guard aircraft follow pre-coordinated procedures with the Federal Aviation Administration to deploy to the incident site. Reception, staging, onward movement, and integration occur at the armory or state mobilization center.

3-106. Out of state National Guard units committed under the EMAC and appropriate memorandums of agreement normally move by military and commercial vehicle. If air movement is required, the National Guard Bureau coordinates with the supported state, supporting state Air National Guard wings, and United States Transportation Command (USTRANSCOM), to initiate airlift using National Guard resources. If supporting forces deploy by air, the supported adjutant general coordinates for reception, staging, onward movement, and integration at the aerial port of debarkation.

3-107. Federal military forces also move by a combination of surface, sea, and air movement. USNORTHCOM planners coordinate with USTRANSCOM for air and surface movement to a base support installation. This is normally the nearest Active component military installation capable of receiving airlift and of supporting joint reception, staging, onward movement, and integration. Within USTRANSCOM, The Military Surface Deployment and Distribution Command coordinates movement by vehicle or rail with the deploying and receiving installations, as well as federal and state authorities for movement control. Intratheater (C-130) aircraft will provide most airlift; other personnel and some equipment may move using commercial aircraft. Oversized systems will await strategic airlift or move by ground transportation. The deploying installation transportation office uses the same procedures required in intercontinental movement, although more equipment may move by convoy. (See chapter 8 for more information about deployment.)

Provide Support for Domestic Disasters

Sustainment for State National Guard Forces

3-108. Once deployed, National Guard unit commanders should coordinate with government agencies and nongovernmental organizations in the area and determine how the state joint task force will assist with relief operations. They pass this information back through the joint task force-state to improve situational awareness across the state. Soldiers may provide immediate assistance with unloading relief items or helping to recover a stuck vehicle. However, National Guard leaders need to politely refuse direct requests for labor and assistance and direct the civilian organization to the appropriate ESF for programmed assistance. In addition, National Guard forces—

- Use an advance party to coordinate with the gaining headquarters (normally the joint task force-state) for a suitable area to establish a support base. Prior to arrival of sustainment forces, they establish the layout in that area.
- Coordinate through higher headquarters to the joint task force-state for resupply operations.
- Identify civil authorities needing assistance or coordinating relief efforts, and notify higher headquarters if there appears to be a need for assistance. Assist the civilians with planning if they want the assistance.
- Coordinate with supporting military units and civilian organizations to pre-position supplies and construction material at or near the point of planned use or at a designated location. This reduces reaction time and ensures timely support during the initial phases of an operation.
- Comply with military and civilian regulations for the movement of hazardous cargo. Always ask for assistance from military and civilian authorities if leaders are unsure what safeguards need to be enforced.
- Maintain an accurate personnel status, and establish centralized procedures for movement of personnel to and from their home stations.
- National Guard forces may coordinate with DOD for use of federal military installations for bed-down of forces and other support.

Sustainment for Federal Military Forces

3-109. The gaining command transmits sustainment instructions to the federal military forces alerted for DSCA in an operation order or fragmentary order. In general, sustainment for federal military forces is coordinated through the theater sustainment command, which provides the principal sustainment. Federal military commanders account for the considerations discussed in paragraphs 3-108 to 3-112.

3-110. Units should arrive in the joint operations area with 72 hours of consumables (principally water and food). The guiding principle is not to add to the sustainment burden on an already overtaxed area.

3-111. One of the most important issues will be capability and requirements for the home installation support to the deployed force, particularly in the initial stages of response. Although USARNORTH will support joint reception, staging, onward movement, and integration and bulk resupply, in the short-term, immediate requests for additional equipment and specialized maintenance may go back to the parent headquarters. Planners determine the transition criteria for support requirements from the home installation to the base support installation.

3-112. Military forces comply with military and civilian regulations for the movement of hazardous cargo. Leaders will verify and adhere to all local safeguards that need to be enforced. If the parent installation requires additional information, the gaining combatant command will assist.

3-113. Military forces maintain an accurate personnel status. They establish centralized procedures for movement of personnel to and from their home stations.

3-114. The deployed joint task force commander coordinates through the joint force land component command or the DCO for any additional support.

Intelligence During Disaster Response and Other Civil Support Tasks

3-115. Questions on the use of DOD intelligence capabilities during civil support operations are complex and subject to different interpretations. USPACOM and USNORTHCOM planning documents and operating procedures provide specific guidance on intelligence activities. Intelligence officers should analyze each fragmentary order carefully for intelligence-related support and identify potential restrictions. If necessary, they consult with the command judge advocate and higher headquarters, particularly regarding the functions of the S-2 and G-2 staff. Related issues may involve the use of tactical intelligence units such as a battlefield surveillance brigade. The command judge advocate provides the commander and intelligence officer legal advice regarding intelligence directives and regulations, restrictions concerning information on persons and organizations not affiliated with DOD, and legally acceptable courses of action. See paragraphs 7-40 to 7-52 for more information.

Incident Awareness and Assessment

3-116. Army forces involved in civil support conduct "incident awareness and assessment," which is a distilled version of intelligence, surveillance, and reconnaissance operations used by forces in combat. Incident awareness and assessment is based on the same concepts as intelligence, surveillance, and reconnaissance operations. However, incident awareness and assessment addresses only those information requirements permitted by law within a domestic environment. Due to policy issues and a history of intelligence abuses in the 1960s and 1970s, domestic intelligence, surveillance, and reconnaissance activities do not occur without express permission of the Secretary of Defense. Further, any use of intelligence capabilities for purposes other than traditional use—support of combat operations—must be expressly approved by the Secretary of Defense.

> Note: The only exceptions to the use of intelligence capabilities are those detailed in the CJCS DSCA EXORD, in paragraph 4.D.7, in support of incident awareness and assessment through the use of Secretary of Defense pre-approved packages (per the 14 August 2009 CJCS DSCA EXORD). The only collection of information concerning U.S. persons, permissible under the 14 August 2009 CJCS DSCA EXORD, is detailed in paragraph 9.L.2.

3-117. The key to incident awareness and assessment is an informed intelligence professional. If alerted to prepare for a DSCA mission, unit staffs should obtain the governing operation plan and standing operating procedures from their gaining combatant command joint task force. Before units begin deployment, G-2s and S-2s should clarify all contentious intelligence areas with their higher headquarters. Intelligence personnel must become familiar with the DOD directives (DODDs) and their specific Service regulations concerning all aspects of domestic incident operations.

3-118. Commanders and staffs modify priority information requirements during civil support operations. When units are conducting civil support operations priority information requirements consists of essential environmental information requirements, and friendly force information requirements. Essential environmental information requirements include information about the physical environment, environmental hazards, and infrastructure. Friendly force information requirements include information about the status of agencies, units, and installations conducting civil support under direction of state and federal coordinating officers.

3-119. Instead of conducting intelligence preparation of the battlefield, the staff conducts a modified process called situation assessment. Situation assessment requires the entire staff to continuously analyze the mission variables (METT-TC) as they relate to that civil support mission.

Limits on the Handling of Sensitive Information

3-120. Information on individuals and specific organizations outside DOD (such as a corporation or faith-based organization) falls within the broad classification of sensitive information. Sensitive information is any personal information about any individual not affiliated with DOD that is collected, stored, or disseminated during DSCA operations. This includes criminal intelligence on individuals obtained from civilian law enforcement agencies. Sensitive information also includes specific information about any the organization and activities of any U.S. organization (private and public sector) outside DOD that is collected, stored, or disseminated during DSCA operations.

3-121. The production, analysis, storage, and distribution of sensitive information require special attention from commanders and intelligence officers at every level. DOD components may collect information concerning the activities of persons and organizations not affiliated with the DOD only as authorized by DODD 5200.27. This directive summarizes public law and Presidential Directives. It carefully limits the types of information that intelligence organizations may collect, process, store, and disseminate about the activities of persons and organizations not affiliated with DOD. It also delineates certain exceptions to the general prohibitions including the acquisition of information essential to protection of DOD functions and property, personnel security, and operations related to civil disturbances. The directive is explicit and commanders and intelligence personnel should refer to it when determining how to handle any information concerning civilians and civilian organizations. Army Regulation 381-10 provides additional instructions and guidance for all Army intelligence organizations.

This page intentionally left blank.

Chapter 4
Provide Support for Domestic CBRNE Incidents

This chapter discusses the second primary civil support task—provide support for chemical, biological, radiological, nuclear, or high-yield explosives incidents. The chapter discusses potential consequences of these types of incidents, National Guard and federal military (Department of Defense) response capabilities, and related considerations for incident response. Because of certain shared characteristics among chemical, biological, radiological, nuclear, or high-yield explosives incidents and pandemic disease outbreaks, pandemic disease outbreaks (including agricultural disease) are included in this civil support task. This chapter builds on doctrine discussed in chapters 1, 2, and 3.

POTENTIAL CONSEQUENCES OF DOMESTIC CBRNE INCIDENTS

4-1. A *chemical, biological, radiological, nuclear, or high-yield explosives incident* is defined as an emergency resulting from the deliberate or unintentional release of nuclear, biological, radiological, or toxic or poisonous chemical materials, or the detonation of a high-yield explosive (Joint Publication (JP) 3-28). It is also known as a CBRNE incident. The Nation's strategic and conventional deterrent may not dissuade terrorists from using chemical, biological, radiological, nuclear, or high-yield explosives, and conventional forces have limitations when supporting CBRNE incidents. The potential consequences are enormous. Public fear, the need to decontaminate infrastructure, and economic losses can protract the effects of CBRNE incidents for months and even years. Although an affected area may become safe to reoccupy, individuals, businesses, and local agencies might relocate, close, or postpone returning to the area. Threats include "dirty bombs," nuclear weapons, biological agents, toxins, refined battlefield chemical agents, or the "weapons of convenience" found in many modern industrial materials. Examples of sophisticated or improvised delivery methods may include insect sprayers, envelopes, backpacks, vehicles, and missiles. In addition, international conflicts, technological advances, information sharing, and commercial spin-offs in the fields of biology, chemistry, and nuclear sciences increase the risk.

4-2. CBRNE incidents can cause massive numbers of casualties without warning. In addition to actual casualties, CBRNE incidents lead to large numbers of patients known as "worried well." This refers to people who *believe* they have been exposed to hazardous materials. Medical practitioners sometimes use the non-pejorative term "low risk patients" to acknowledges that these individuals may have been exposed and may require some type of medical care (to include psychological) but do not need immediate treatment. Medical practitioners expect worried well to outnumber actual casualties by a factor of ten. Actual casualties and the worried well who self-present at hospitals can overwhelm facilities and potentially spread contamination. Lacking recognizable injuries, victims suffering from blast-induced internal injuries or contamination further complicate response efforts.

4-3. The Nation's capability for CBRNE incident response (sometimes referred to as CBRNE consequence management) continues to evolve. The Defense against Weapons of Mass Destruction Act of 1996 directed the Secretary of Defense to enhance the federal government's capability to prevent and respond to terrorist attacks involving weapons of mass destruction. These initiatives led to the establishment of the National Guard's weapons of mass destruction–civil support teams (known as WMD–CSTs) and various Department of Defense (DOD) units. Following the terrorist attacks of 2001, several Homeland Security Presidential Directives (HSPDs) were issued to further improve the Nation's preparedness for terrorist attacks. A classified directive issued in 2006 provides broad guidance for responding to CBRNE incidents. The *Quadrennial Defense Review Report* of 2010 initiated additional changes in the federal and state National Guard forces identified for CBRNE incident response missions. These steps complement the National Incident Management System (NIMS) and the National Response Framework (NRF) to improve the Nation's all-hazards response capability (see chapters 1, 2, and 3). The NRF and the NIMS documents are available at http://www.fema.gov.

NATIONAL PLANNING SCENARIOS

4-4. The federal interagency Scenario Working Group developed scenarios to implement HSPD–8, *National Preparedness*, in setting priorities for national planning. The fifteen National Planning Scenarios depict a credible range of terrorist attacks and disasters. The scenarios are organized into eight key scenario sets. Eleven of the National Planning Scenarios refer to CBRNE incidents. Two of several *incident annexes* in the NRF (not to be confused with *emergency support function annexes*) discuss CBRNE incidents (the *Biological Incident*, and the *Nuclear/Radiological Incident* annexes). The NRF"s incident annexes support the key scenario sets (see chapter 2 for more information, or visit http://www.fema.gov). Emergency support function annex (ESF) #10, *Oil and Hazardous Materials Response*, covers response to a chemical incident caused by accidents or attacks involving dangerous chemicals. Table 4-1 lists National Planning Scenarios related to CBRNE incidents. This is not a complete list of national planning scenarios.

Table 4-1. National Planning Scenarios related to CBRNE incidents

Scenario #	Type of incident
1	Nuclear Detonation – Improvised Nuclear Device
2	Biological Attack – Aerosol Anthrax
3	Biological Disease Outbreak – Pandemic Influenza
4	Biological Attack – Plague
5	Chemical Attack – Blister Agent
6	Chemical Attack – Toxic Industrial Chemicals
7	Chemical Attack – Nerve Agent
8	Chemical Attack – Chlorine Tank Explosion
11	Radiological Dispersal Device
13	Biological Attack – Food Contamination
14	Biological Attack – Foreign Animal Disease

4-5. Military forces conduct CBRNE incident preparedness and response operations under appropriate laws, regulations, and policies. These include the hazardous waste operations and emergency response standard (Title 29, Code of Federal Regulations, Part 1910, Occupational Safety and Health Standard Number 1910.120) and the Comprehensive Environmental Response, Compensation, and Liability Act (Sections 9601 to 9675 of Title 42, USC). Responders at every level plan and operate in accordance with these laws. These and other laws define—

- Response authorities for public and private agencies.
- Hazardous substances, emergency planning, and "community right to know."
- Clean-up requirements.
- Required protective measures and training for responders within the United States.

The federal government provides a billion-dollar fund for public and private agencies to respond to and recover from incidents involving hazardous materials. The NRF integrates governmental jurisdictions, incident management and emergency response disciplines, nongovernmental organizations, and the private sector into a coordinated CBRNE incident response. The Department of Homeland Security uses the National Fire Protection Association Standard 472, "Standard for Competence of Responders to Hazardous Materials/Weapons of Mass Destruction Incidents," to establish the qualifications for personnel conducting domestic CBRNE incident response. During domestic CBRNE incident response operations, national laws subordinate military doctrine and military authority outside of DOD installations while defining command structures within the NRF and the NIMS. They also require that when requested, DOD supports civil authorities. DOD is not the lead unless an incident occurs on a DOD installation.

CHEMICAL THREATS

4-6. Military doctrine classifies chemical weapons by their effects—persistent, nonpersistent, blister, choking, and blood agents. Nonpersistent agents include G-series nerve agents, often referred to by their military designations, "sarin" and "soman." These agents typically volatilize rapidly, immediately affect people, and dissipate quickly. Persistent agents produce casualties through liquid contact and inhalation and remain potent for many hours. The nerve agent O-Ethyl S-Diisopropylaminomethyl Methylphosphonothiolate, known as VX, is the best-known persistent nerve agent. Because persistent agents dissipate slowly they can shut down entire facilities until they are thoroughly decontaminated. Mustard or H-series chemicals are also persistent agents and create severe skin blistering and lung injuries. Hydrogen cyanide, cyanogen chloride, and carbon monoxide are blood agents. Choking agents include phosgene and chlorine. Nerve and blister agents are weapons, while cyanides, chlorine, and phosgene are common chemicals. A nonpersistent chemical weapon using sarin or chlorine or a toxic industrial chemical such as ammonia can continue producing death and injuries for hours if released indoors or in a densely populated area (see vignette about the Graniteville derailment). A persistent hazard such as VX or a carcinogenic toxic industrial chemical such as benzene cause lethal or adverse health effects for days or weeks. Highly persistent chemical weapons such as mustard gas are stable and can produce casualties for decades.

> **The Graniteville Derailment**
> On 6 January 2005, near Graniteville, South Carolina, a train moving chlorine gas derailed and killed 8 people, injured dozens, and sickened hundreds. Over 5000 people evacuated from their homes for nearly two weeks. The accident released approximately 90 tons of chlorine, a deadly chemical. Chlorine attacks the soft tissues of the lungs, leading to death from a form of drowning. Chlorine is also corrosive—exposed metals, cell phones, computers, machinery and other equipment in the area were damaged or destroyed. Corrosion also damaged metal roofs, nails, and other materials around the crash site. The wreck suspended business and affected traffic and civilian life throughout the area for weeks. In addition to lost lives, the derailment resulted in significant litigation and long-term economic losses.

4-7. Chemical warfare agents require specialized production, handling, and storage. Some agents are unstable and break down if improperly stored. In addition, sophisticated chemical weapons such as thickened nerve agent require "precursor" compounds that law enforcement and intelligence agencies may be able detect. In contrast, potentially deadly toxic industrial chemicals are commonly found in large quantities. Some industrial hazards exceed the lethality and toxicity of World War I chemical weapons. In Iraq, insurgents have used chlorine and other toxic industrial chemicals as terror weapons. Using commercial activities as a screen, terrorists might use a toxic industrial chemical as a weapon in the United States.

4-8. Most Army units are not equipped to detect or protect against toxic industrial chemicals although they may have protective capabilities that exceed those of some local police and civilian organizations. Most chemical hazards degrade in hours or days, and first responders hasten the process by a variety of decontaminants. However, working around lethal chemicals requires training and protective equipment, including decontamination capabilities.

4-9. Two events illustrate the panic, loss of lives, economic disruption, and political impact of chemical incidents. In India in 1985, an American subsidiary plant belonging to Union Carbide inadvertently released methyl isocyanate, a heavy gas. Design failures and negligent operation created a catastrophe. More than 10,000 people in the Bhopal region died, and thousands more were injured. In 1995, the Aum Shin Riko cult placed small sarin containers in several Tokyo subway trains. This terrorist attack killed twelve people and injured thousands. Had the cult employed weapons-grade sarin, the loss of life would have been much greater. Both incidents resulted in hundreds of millions of dollars spent in response, litigation, economic loss, and legislation, in addition to having large international impacts. Panic in both incidents overwhelmed facilities and contributed to even greater loss of life.

4-10. Local, state, and federal responders, with National Guard augmentation as required, manage most domestic chemical incidents. These organizations organize, train, and equip to respond to CBRNE incidents and mitigate the consequences. Identification of the hazard, isolation of the affected area (including evacuation), and rapid decontamination of victims and responders are essential to the initial response. First responders and hospital personnel handle the majority of these situations. A larger incident requires additional resources. The Environmental Protection Agency and Coast Guard provide command and control and significant capabilities in accordance with ESF #10. For incidents beyond minor industrial accidents, the state emergency manager and state director of military support may commit a National Guard civil support team. A persistent hazard requires repeated decontamination of personnel and equipment for an indefinite period of time. A responding civil authority may request and receive additional National Guard capabilities, such as a CBRNE enhanced response force package. A catastrophic incident may lead to requests for federal military support such as the CBRNE consequence management response force to transport, secure, sustain, and decontaminate for a protracted period of time. DOD has contingency plans to manage any accident involving stored chemical weapons or incidents at chemical weapons disposal sites.

BIOLOGICAL THREATS

4-11. Of all the potential CBRNE incidents, biological weapons pose the greatest threat to United States. Current threat estimates focus on biological attacks because of the potential for terrorists to produce biological weapons in secrecy and with limited resources. Hostile regimes could develop or refine biological agents with the potential to disrupt the economy and cause mass casualties. Biological agents are lethal in tiny quantities and have a small manufacturing footprint compared to other CBRNE agents. The delivery of a biological agent often leaves no trail. An attacker may spread biological agents by mail (see vignette about an anthrax attack), insects, a pathogen-soaked cloth, or food. Feedlots, food stockpiles, and individuals are targets for biological terrorism. Biological hazards can disrupt a population for weeks. Distinguishing between a manmade or natural biological incident may be difficult or impossible.

> **Anthrax Attack**
>
> Anthrax is a deadly and hardy pathogen, ideally suited for a biological weapon. In September 2001, an individual mailed a small amount of anthrax to media and government targets. The disease killed five people and infected dozens. The anthrax spores spread throughout buildings and mail handling systems, contaminating other mail. The attack closed government buildings, shut down mail distribution, and resulted in thousands of false and malicious white powder incidents. Thousands of congressional staffers, media personnel, responders, and postal workers received antibiotics as a precaution. Thousands of "worried well" demanded antibiotics, while thousands more purchased protective masks. Efforts in New York, Connecticut, the District of Columbia, and Florida reflect the strength of cooperation among private organizations; local, state, and federal governments; and state and federal military forces working under the incident command system. The 44th Civil Support Team in Florida worked with the Environmental Protection Agency, Coast Guard, contractors, and local government to respond to anthrax in a contaminated building in Boca Raton, Florida. In the District of Columbia, the Marine chemical–biological incident response force, Environmental Protection Agency, and Coast Guard worked to identify anthrax in the Hart Senate Building.

Biological weapons come in two types: pathogens and toxins. Pathogens are alive; they reproduce and spread to other organisms. Tularemia, anthrax, and smallpox are pathogens that can be used in biological weapons. Toxins are complex poisons produced by an animal, plant, or microbe. They may be incredibly toxic but do not reproduce. Ricin and botulinum toxin are examples of biological toxins. Though deadly, biological weapons are not perfect. The risk to the individuals creating the weapon, laboratory requirements, and natural degradation of the agent(s) are just a few limitations.

NUCLEAR AND RADIOLOGICAL THREATS

4-12. Nuclear weapons are more destructive than any other type. If a nuclear device were to explode in an urban area, casualties could exceed 100,000, with massive destruction and widespread contamination. Fortunately, nuclear threats are not likely to materialize for several reasons. They require extensive resources to develop and safeguard, so terrorists are unlikely to build their own. However, they could acquire a nuclear weapon from a rogue entity. This is not very likely since nations that have begun nuclear programs have had difficulty producing nuclear weapons, especially weapons that are easily transportable. Finally, the use or threat of use of nuclear weapons risks massive U.S. retaliation against both the perpetrators and their partners.

4-13. A radiological dispersal device threat is very similar to that of a chemical weapon, but the threat is from radiation. Often called "dirty bombs," radiological dispersal devices require less technology than nuclear weapons but are also far less destructive. Instead of a nuclear explosion, a radiological dispersal device uses conventional explosives to spread a radiological contaminant such as cesium. While less lethal, even a low-grade radiological dispersal device presents the ability to terrorize a population, requires significant clean-up, and denies use of an area for a prolonged period.

4-14. The probability of accidents involving radioactive materials is lower than other threats. U.S. authorities plan for accidents involving nuclear reactors. The most publicized incident in the United States occurred in Pennsylvania at the Three Mile Island reactor. Operator mistakes turned a small problem into a near disaster. Fortunately, the containment system worked and only small amounts of radiation leaked. Lessons learned from the incident have helped to improve response and coordination at every level. The Nuclear Regulatory Commission oversees the operation of all civilian reactors. DOD, Department of Energy, and Environmental Protection Agency also have contingency plans to manage any accident involving an American nuclear weapon or nuclear propulsion plants. Like other CBRNE incidents, the threat of contamination can create panic far beyond the actual affected area. (The vignette on page 4-6 briefly describes the 1986 Chernobyl disaster.)

4-15. The Post-Katrina Emergency Management Reform Act of 2006 and the NRF designate Department of Homeland Security, through the Federal Emergency Management Agency (FEMA), as the coordinator for the national response to a nuclear or radiological incident. See chapter 2 for more information about interagency incident response operations.

4-16. Department of Energy provides vital support to the response. Department of Energy capabilities include response teams, radiological isotope identification, response assets deployed across eight Department of Energy regions, and watch centers staffed with subject matter experts. In accordance with the NRF, the Interagency Modeling and Atmospheric Advisory Center provides the single federal hazard prediction model for domestic nuclear incidents. Based on computer-generated models, planners can determine staging areas, evaluate lines of communications, and predict the spread of contamination. Other supporting civilian agencies and DOD capabilities provide downwind contamination monitoring, decontamination support, transportation, water purification, security around impacted areas, and support to the ESFs.

> **Chernobyl**
>
> The April 1986 Chernobyl disaster remains the worst nuclear accident in history. A reactor explosion and fire spewed radioactive fallout across the Soviet Union, Western Europe, and parts of North America. It contaminated huge areas of Russia, Belarus, and Ukraine. The International Atomic Energy Agency estimates that 56 people died, and hundreds of thousands suffered exposure to high doses of radioactivity. The area around Chernobyl remains uninhabitable. The response, ongoing medical care, and environmental monitoring costs have totaled billions of dollars. Foreign criticism and a clumsy Soviet cover-up undermined internal support for the communist regime. Russian military and civilian responders prevented an even greater catastrophe through their unparalleled courage; many knowingly sacrificed their lives to save others and contain the radioactivity.

HIGH-YIELD EXPLOSIVES THREATS

4-17. Explosives remain a prevalent killer, nationally and internationally. Terrorists have employed them against individuals, businesses, and government offices within the United States for decades. The deaths, injuries, long-term health effects, and economic effects of terrorist explosive scar the collective memory of Americans. Although increased restrictions on CBRNE hazards and precursors are in place, information regarding explosives is easily accessible. Soldiers and civilian response agencies may face fertilizer bombs and other homemade explosives, along with improvised explosive devices. The first blast is not the only casualty producer. Collapsed structures near the target area also create challenges for responders.

4-18. Both the Oklahoma City and World Trade Center attacks destroyed large buildings. Managing a collapsed structure such as those requires trained search and rescue teams. A catastrophic collapse may create additional hazards such as asbestos exposure, which can cause long-term health problems and endless litigation. Collapsed structures may require decontamination. FEMA search and rescue teams, augmented as required by trained military search and extraction teams, are essential to collapsed structure rescue operations. The governor and President may commit specialized military units from the Reserve and Active components to augment civilian resources. National Guard CBRNE enhanced response force packages and chemical-biological incident response forces can operate in a contaminated environment.

4-19. Police bomb squads typically respond with fire and emergency medical service to bomb threats and incidents. Military explosive ordnance disposal units have long provided civil support to incidents such as the Oklahoma City bombing, the World Trade Center attack, and other explosives incidents, and often work with the Federal Bureau of Investigation's explosives unit. In situations involving both explosives and chemical hazards, the National Guard provides civil support teams as directed to complement the capabilities of first responders. The vignette on page 4-7 briefly describes the largest industrial explosion in U.S. history.

> **Deadly Industrial Accident**
>
> On 16 April 1947, the SS Grandcamp, a cargo ship carrying 2,300 tons of ammonium nitrate fertilizer, exploded at the Texas City port. The subsequent fire led to the detonation of the cargo, creating a 15-foot tidal wave and sending debris for miles. Secondary fires destroyed tons of crude oil and spread to a nearby ship, the High Flyer. It also exploded with 961 additional tons of ammonium nitrate. Five hundred and eighty-one persons died in the explosions, and thousands more were injured. Over 600 vehicles, tons of crude oil, a chemical factory, and over 500 homes were destroyed by blasts that shattered windows 40 miles away. The Texas City disaster remains America's largest industrial accident.

CIVILIAN CBRNE INCIDENT RESPONSE

4-20. Any CBRNE incident requires numerous specialized assets and equipment. Much of the nation's capacity for responding to these events resides with the Department of Energy, Environmental Protection Agency, Coast Guard, private industry, and local hazardous materials teams. First responders, together with state and federal agencies, augmented as required by military capabilities, manage incidents involving hazardous materials. As described in chapter 2, the response begins when local responders such as the fire department move to the incident site and establish an incident command. If the incident requires more resources, nearby cities, state, and private resources begin to assist (when requested). When local, tribal, and state authorities request federal assistance for a CBRNE incident, the NRF identifies primary federal agencies that take the lead in coordinating the federal response. Concurrent to a CBRNE incident, the Department of Justice conducts investigations with the Federal Bureau of Investigation's hazardous materials response unit or explosives units.

4-21. One of the most difficult and potentially dangerous challenges facing immediate responders is that of determining the nature of the hazard they face. They are familiar with accidents and hazardous spills. Most, however, have never experienced a CBRNE incident. Initial reports are often late or wrong as agencies try to gain situational awareness. In the immediate aftermath of an incident, responders may rush to rescue victims and unwittingly spread contamination beyond the incident site. Obtaining an accurate assessment of requirements is compounded by the suddenness of a CBRNE incident. Like the Texas City incident or Oklahoma City bombing, the emergency occurs without warning or even rational explanation. In the immediate aftermath, victims, witnesses, and relatives deluge emergency responders with reports and requests for help. Faced with the threat of secondary devices and rapidly changing situations, first responders might not have the time or ability to assess a developing CBRNE incident. Defining external resource requirements and enacting mutual aid agreements with adjacent cities during a CBRNE incident becomes challenging.

NATIONAL GUARD CBRNE INCIDENT RESPONSE

4-22. The National Guard CBRNE incident response capabilities consist of a WMD–CST, CBRNE enhanced response force package, National Guard response force, joint force headquarters–state (JFHQ–state), National Guard joint task force, and National Guard joint enabling team. These forces may work together, support other agencies, or remain separated across a large area. Geography, type of hazards, number of response agencies, and size of the incident determine the employment of these forces. The weapons of mass destruction–civil support teams were created specifically for domestic CBRNE incident response operations by congressional law and a presidential decision directive. A National Guard response force is a rapid-response general-purpose force available to each state. Although not a specialized CBRNE element, it can provide incident site security. A National Guard response force can deploy independently or as a headquarters that can assume control of weapons of mass destruction–civil support team and CBRNE enhanced response force package elements deployed to the incident.

JOINT FORCE HEADQUARTERS–STATE

4-23. The JFHQ–state provides consequence management command and control for Army and Air National Guard forces within a state. The JFHQ–state can serve as a command and control element for single or multiple weapons of mass destruction–civil support teams, CBRNE enhanced response force packages, National Guard response forces, and other intra- or interstate National Guard forces during an incident. For additional communications, the JFHQ–state employs the Joint Incident Site Communications Capability secure communications system to augment or replace civilian communications. Based on forces available and geography, states often employ a subordinate joint task force–state for CBRNE consequence management command and control. Most states either have a prearranged joint task force or a designated unit headquarters identified for immediate activation to provide additional command and control of CBRNE enhanced response force packages, weapons of mass destruction–civil support teams, and explosive ordnance disposal, medical, communications, or other units during a CBRNE incident.

4-24. Joint enabling teams alert and deploy when directed by the National Guard Bureau, based upon the Bureau's assessment. Joint enabling teams have internal communications, provide situational awareness to the National Guard Bureau staff, provide subject matter expertise, and facilitate requests for assistance through the Emergency Management Assistance Compact. Table 4-2, page 4-9, summarizes National Guard capabilities.

Provide Support for Domestic CBRNE Incidents

Table 4-2. National Guard CBRNE incident response capabilities

Unit[1]	Size	Capabilities	Availability	Limitations
Weapons of Mass Destruction–Civil Support Team	22 full-time National Guard personnel. 57 teams, one in every state (California, New York and Florida have 2 teams) and territory (District of Columbia, Guam, Puerto Rico, and the Virgin Islands).	Rapid identification of CBRNE agents. Assessment of current and projected consequences. Advice on response measures. Assistance with requests for additional support. Analytical Laboratory System Unified Command Suite—incident communications systems.	Able to deploy to a WMD, HAZMAT, or natural disaster incident within 90 minutes of notification. Able to deploy across state boundaries based on a verbal agreement between affected governors. Civil support teams routinely respond together to support large incidents. Up to 22 teams have been deployed in support of a response.	Cannot be deployed outside the United States or its territories while in Title 32 status.
CBRNE Enhanced Response Force Package	200 personnel.	Casualty search and rescue. Decontamination. Emergency medical care.	Within 6–48 hours. 17 CBRNE enhanced response force packages. At least one CBRNE enhanced response force package in each FEMA region.	8–12 hour sustained capability in contaminated environment.
National Guard Joint Task Force[2]	12,500–25,000 personnel.	Force protection. Aviation support. Mass decontamination. Communication. Medical support. Engineer support. General purpose tasks.	First elements within 24–72 hours.	Larger elements require significant transportation assets.
CBRN chemical, biological, radiological, and nuclear CBRNE chemical, biological, radiological, nuclear, and high-yield explosives			FEMA Federal Emergency Management Agency HAZMAT hazardous materials WMD weapons of mass destruction	
Note[1]: See paragraph 4-26 for a discussion of homeland response force; this is a future capability. Note[2]: There are 2 National Guard joint task forces available—Division East and Division West. Each National Guard joint task force has a division headquarters plus task-organized brigades and battalions with attached CBRN units.				

PLANNED NATIONAL GUARD CBRNE FORCES

4-25. During the 2010 Quadrennial Defense Review, DOD and the National Guard Bureau conducted a comprehensive review of military management capabilities and identified gaps at the regional and national levels. The homeland response force is a new force design. When fully staffed and designated, each FEMA region will have one homeland response force that can deploy by road to a CBRNE incident within 24 hours. A homeland response force will be a CBRNE incident force organized from existing CBRNE enhanced response force packages and weapons of mass destruction–civil support teams and reinforced by various National Guard CBRNE incident response forces located within each FEMA region.

FEDERAL MILITARY CBRNE INCIDENT RESPONSE

4-26. A CBRNE incident may overwhelm a single state's consequence management capabilities, and immediate help under the Emergency Management Assistance Compact (EMAC) may not be immediately accessible. When requested, federal military forces will respond, which may include federalized National Guard forces. Federal military support may range from small, highly qualified teams, through correspondingly large forces, each capable of responding to a larger incident. These elements might work directly for a defense coordinating officer during a smaller incident or under United States Army North (USARNORTH) or United States Northern Command (USNORTHCOM) element during a larger response.

4-27. DOD supports civil authorities during a CBRNE incident with a full range of capabilities. Several organizations have the training and equipment for this mission. National Guard teams routinely practice their roles in consequence management in conjunction with USNORTHCOM. Federal military forces and state National Guard forces also work very closely during national special security events such as the Olympics or national political conventions.

4-28. For any serious incidents, DOD may commit Joint Task Force–Civil Support, a specialized standing joint task force assigned to USNORTHCOM and the CBRNE consequence management response force. Highly trained and specialized CBRNE units such as technical escort units and Defense Threat Reduction Agency teams may augment the DOD response. In large CBRNE incidents, DOD installations serve as staging areas for resources and agencies. Federal military forces also play a key supporting role. During anthrax responses in 2001 and 2002 for example, DOD laboratories, resources, and personnel played critical response roles to mitigate incident effects and costs to the public. As in other disasters, a large CBRNE incident will require military forces to provide security and essential services. Food distribution points as well as the National Pharmaceutical Stockpile or inoculation sites will require security measures during a pandemic influenza or following a CBRNE incident. Water supply, trash collection, medical screening, and augmentation of local government might be required support missions during an incident recovery. All are possible requests for DOD assistance.

4-29. As the joint forces land component command, USARNORTH may deploy one or both contingency command posts configured as a joint task force. USNORTHCOM has deployable headquarters capable of commanding large contingents of federal military. Based upon the initial situation reports from the defense coordinating officer, the USNORTHCOM commander alerts USARNORTH of a potential CBRNE incident response requirement. Joint assessment and liaison teams from USNORTHCOM, USARNORTH, and Joint Task Force–Civil Support deploy as directed to the affected state emergency operations center and regional defense coordinating officer. These teams augment the defense coordinating element and assist the emergency preparedness liaison officers, allowing those elements to focus on supporting their state and federal agencies while the USNORTHCOM liaison elements determine potential employment options of federal military forces. Based on the situation, the defense coordinating officer recommends that the USNORTHCOM Commander alert and deploy some or all of the CBRNE consequence management response forces. The Secretary of Defense approves the USNORTHCOM commander's request for CBRNE consequence management response force capabilities. USARNORTH normally deploys Joint Task Force–Civil Support to provide command and control of CBRNE incident response units under its operational control. In the case of an immediate Presidential decision, the Secretary of Defense directs deployment of USNORTHCOM to deploy and employ a CBRNE consequence management response force.

4-30. Joint Task Force–Civil Support is a standing joint task force staffed and equipped for joint CBRNE consequence management command and control. It exercises operational control of CBRNE consequence management response force units and other forces during a catastrophic domestic CBRNE incident. When deployed, Joint Task Force–Civil Support deploys to the supported joint field office and coordinates federal military support response efforts with the incident command staff and National Guard forces. Joint Task Force–Civil Support trains for and specializes in CBRNE consequence management, but is prepared to respond to all hazards. Joint Task Force 51 and Joint Task Force 52, (USARNORTH contingency command posts) train specifically for all hazards and typically receive augmentation during an incident. In the event of a catastrophic incident, one of the USARNORTH deployable command posts may become the land component joint force land component commander's forward command post, and assume operational control of Joint Task Force–Civil Support and other federal military forces.

4-31. Currently, a CBRNE consequence management response force is a multibrigade force of Army, Marine, and Air Force units that provides federal military assistance to a primary agency in a domestic CBRNE incident. The CBRNE consequence management response force normally deploys with its units task-organized into three subordinate commands: task force–operations, task force–medical, and task force–aviation. These forces bring security, mortuary affairs, transport, medical treatment, logistics and many other resources to an incident site. The Marine Corps chemical–biological incident response force (sometimes known as CBIRF) is the largest CBRNE element within the CBRNE consequence management response force. Additional Army CBRNE units provide decontamination, detection, and reconnaissance capabilities. Army units provide most of the logistical and aviation support. The Air Force provides specialized engineering capability and medical treatment facilities. Refer to appendix E for details on the CBRNE consequence management response force.

4-32. The composition of the CBRNE consequence management response force varies according to the Army force generation cycle. DOD identifies units for the CBRNE consequence management response force through United States Joint Forces Command and the National Guard Bureau, based on requirements and force readiness. The force consists of a mix of active, reserve, and National Guard Forces. National Guard forces committed to the CBRNE consequence management response force remain under state control until USNORTHCOM requires the CBRNE consequence management response force, at which time the President mobilizes and federalizes them. Each CBRNE consequence management response force task force is subject to a CBRNE incident response posture level with "prepare to deploy" time lines determined by the Commander of USNORTHCOM, and the Secretary of Defense.

4-33. Within United States Pacific Command (USPACOM), the Joint Task Force–Homeland Defense has a domestic CBRNE consequence management mission. Although it may require augmentation from a joint manning document, many of its capabilities, subject matter experts, and resources are already within U.S. Army Pacific (USARPAC). Joint Task Force–Homeland Defense works with state, territorial, and military organizations to ensure response across a large area of responsibility. Because of the vast geographical distances within the Pacific, each territory and base has plans to respond to a variety of threats, with forces in place, since any external forces will have to come by air or sealift. The USPACOM consequence management plan includes flexible task-organizations from Services, components, and capabilities that include weapons of mass destruction–civil support teams, CBRNE enhanced response force packages, federal fire departments, Army explosive ordnance disposal teams, Navy explosive ordnance disposal teams, and active component chemical companies.

ADDITIONAL DEPARTMENT OF DEFENSE CBRNE INCIDENT RESPONSE ASSETS

4-34. Explosive ordnance disposal teams and technical escort teams from the 20th Support Command (CBRNE), respond to CBRNE incidents in support of a combatant commander. If requested, they respond to USNORTHCOM and USPACOM for specialized domestic CBRNE incident support. Typical requests include responding to unknown explosive hazards, support to federal installations, movement of munitions, and disposal of unusual unexploded ordnance. The 20th Support Command has CBRNE incident response reams that provide CBRNE incident response capability if requested. These units frequently deploy for national special security events. The CBRNE incident response teams deploy with mission-specific sustainment capabilities, but life-support assistance comes from the supported combatant commander.

4-35. The Marine Corps maintains specialized units for dealing with biological threats and chemical weapons. The Marine chemical–biological incident response force includes decontamination, medical evacuation and treatment, and field detection capability for many hazards. All personnel in the basic package have approved hazardous materials protective equipment. The chemical–biological incident response force may deploy as reinforcement to either federal or state National Guard CBRNE incident response forces.

4-36. The Defense Threat Reduction Agency specializes in analysis of weapons of mass destruction and disposal of weapons of mass destruction. This agency has a variety of specialized capabilities which deploy as teams to deal with chemical, biological, radiological, and nuclear weapons. During a CBRNE incident these teams may support to both federal and state National Guard forces. Table 4-3, page 4-12 summarizes DOD CBRNE response capabilities.

Table 4-3. Department of Defense CBRNE incident response capabilities

Unit[1]	Size	Capabilities	Availability	Limitations
CBRNE Consequence Management Response Force[2]	5000 personnel (composition varies depending on ARFORGEN alignment).	CBRNE assessment, MEDEVAC, and medical treatment. Some rescue support. Incident support. All terrain mobility. Rotary-wing air support. Infrastructure protection. Advanced C2. Flexible task organizations.	Contingency force on order of Secretary of Defense. Requires air and ground movement. Deployment begins within hours.	Deployment times vary with proximity and available lift. Subject to higher priority missions (Federal military elements).
Chemical-Biological Incident Response Force (USMC)	500 Marines.	CBRNE casualty assessment, MEDEVAC and medical treatment. Area decontamination. Limited search and rescue. Incident support. All terrain mobility. Infrastructure protection. Rotary-wing aviation. Flexible task organizations can expand into a large task force.	24 hours, depending on tactical airlift.	72 hours sustainment. May not be available if committed to a CBRNE consequence management response force.
US Army Medical Research Institute of Infectious Diseases	Variable.	Lab analysis and determination of infectious diseases.	24 hours, depending deployment means.	May require sustainment and security.
US Northern Command Joint Task Forces	Various command posts each with 150–250 personnel.	Rapid deploying C2 with military and civilian communications. C2 of task force through division-sized forces. May become a joint task force with augmentation. May function as the JFLCC forward CP controlling other federal military forces.	First elements of the CP within 4 hours. Contingency CP within 12 to 24 hours. Main CP allows reachback anywhere within DOD.	Contingency CPs may require unit liaison teams to augment tactical communications die to wartime C2 systems within subordinate units.
Regular Army Divisions	Typically two or more brigade combat teams with various modular support brigades. 10,000–25,000 personnel.	Intratheater deployment using air, rail, and vehicular movement. Advanced C2 capabilities, trained commanders and staffs, and robust sustainment. Flexible tactical employment. Units with CBRNE defensive equipment and life support.	Alert and prepared for initial deployment within 18–24 hours. Unlimited endurance.	CBRN training and equipment designed for combat. Training focused on combat operations; knowledge of DSCA may be limited. Availability may be limited.

ARFORGEN	Army force generation		DSCA	defense support of civil authorities
C2	command and control		FEMA	Federal Emergency Management Agency
CBRN	chemical, biological, radiological, and nuclear		JFLCC	joint force land component commander
CBRNE	chemical, biological, radiological, nuclear, and high-yield explosives		MEDEVAC	hazardous materials
			USMC	United States Marine Corps
CP	command post		WMD	weapons of mass destruction
DOD	Department of Defense			

Note[1]: See paragraph 4-38 for a discussion of the defense CBRNE response force; this is a future capability.
Note[2]: The CBRNE consequence management response force includes the Joint Task Force–Civil Support plus Regular Army, Air Force, and Marine units and mobilized National Guard.

PLANNED DEPARTMENT OF DEFENSE CBRNE INCIDENT RESPONSE CAPABILITIES

4-37. Following the 2010 Quadrennial Defense Review, DOD and USNORTHCOM initiated development of the defense CBRNE response force, which will replace the CBRNE consequence management response force in fiscal year 2011. This concept builds on experience gained from the CBRNE consequence management response force, while complementing the homeland response forces under development by the National Guard. When fielded, the defense CBRNE response force will be a joint federal military force that can be tailored and deployed rapidly to any CBRNE incident site. Compared with the existing CBRNE consequence management response force, the defense CBRNE response force will deploy more quickly (primarily by strategic airlift) and bring federal military capabilities urgently required for the initial response. Follow-on forces will be task-organized for extended response and transition to recovery. The new force will have more helicopters, emergency medical capability, chemical, biological, radiological, and nuclear reconnaissance and decontamination, and search and rescue. Follow-on force packages will add capabilities needed to complete the initial response and transition to recovery operations. As required, the defense CBRNE response force can be reinforced to more than divisional size (20,000 Soldiers, Marines, and Airmen) with general purpose forces and scalable command and control. Concurrently with the defense CBRNE response force evolution, DOD, National Guard Bureau, and other agencies will develop a "chemical, biological, radiological, and nuclear enterprise" to integrate capabilities from every level into a unified consequence management effort.

SUPPORT FOR PANDEMIC DISEASE OUTBREAKS

4-38. A pandemic disease outbreak, often referred to as a pandemic, is a global disease epidemic. A flu pandemic occurs when a new influenza virus emerges for which people have little or no immunity and for which there is no vaccine. The disease spreads easily person-to-person, produces serious illness, and can sweep across the country and around the world in very short time. The "black death", for example, depopulated large parts of Europe in the 14th century. The great influenza epidemic of 1918–1919 killed 43,000 American Soldiers and millions of civilians in the United States and abroad. Even today, urgent research continues into its origins because a recurrence could have similar or greater effects.

4-39. The designation of pandemic does not relate to the lethality of the disease, but its spread. The World Health Organization categorizes disease outbreaks according to six phases or contagion, followed by three levels of declining threat. Phases 1, 2, and 3 correlate with preparedness, including capacity development and response planning activities, while Phases 4–6 clearly signal the need for response and mitigation efforts. Periods after the first pandemic wave (through phase 6) are elaborated to facilitate post-pandemic recovery activities. The World Health Organization pandemic phases are—

- Phases 1 through 3: predominantly animal infections but few human infections.
- Phase 4: sustained human-to-human transmission.
- Phases 5 to 6: widespread human infection.
- Post peak period: possibility of recurrent events.
- Post pandemic period: disease activity at seasonal levels.

Figure 4-1, page 4-12, illustrates the World Health Organization's pandemic phases.

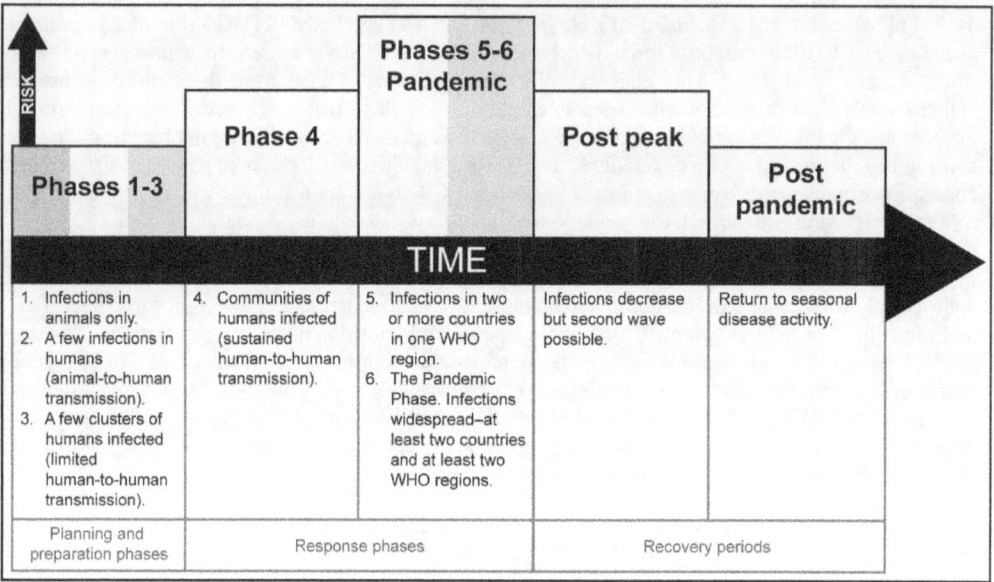

Figure 4-1. World Health Organization pandemic influenza phases

4-40. Although biological weapons are a significant threat to homeland security, naturally occurring diseases continue to pose a greater threat. For example, ricin and anthrax attacks have killed relatively small numbers; West Nile Virus and influenza can kill tens of thousands. Pandemics have occurred intermittently over centuries. The last three pandemics produced millions of fatalities. Animals are the most likely reservoir for emerging viruses; avian viruses played a role in the last three influenza pandemics. The 2009 pandemic influenza may have originated with domestic pigs, quite possibly in North America. Although the timing is unpredictable, history and science suggest that the United States will face additional pandemics in this century. In a world of rapid movement of people and animals across intercontinental distances, the outbreak of flu as serious as the outbreak of 1918 could produce far more fatalities. Viruses remain difficult to combat. Vaccines for a new type of flu may take years to develop and produce, and their effectiveness may vary widely, particularly as the virus continues to evolve rapidly. Generally, flu vaccines improve resistance and may help reduce the severity of the infection, but the more novel the virus, the less effective the vaccine.

4-41. A flu pandemic may cause political, social, economic instability while affecting military readiness. While the flu will infect adversarial forces, it may not degrade their readiness and operational capability in the same manner or at the same time as U.S. and allied forces. The degree to which countries can mitigate morbidity and mortality during the pandemic influenza and reintegrate recovering individuals into society will have considerable impact on military force capabilities. Countries with more advanced and robust health care systems will be better able to mitigate many of the pandemic influenza effects.

SECURITY CONCERNS DURING A PANDEMIC

4-42. Key security concerns could arise during a period of turmoil caused by a pandemic. These include opportunistic aggression, opportunities for violent extremists to acquire weapons of mass destruction, reduced partner capacity during and after pandemic influenza, instability resulting from humanitarian disaster, and decreased production and distribution of essential commodities. The prevalence of pandemic influenza coupled with political, social and economic instability may result in reduced security capabilities, providing an opportunity for military aggression and economic collapse, humanitarian crises, and dramatic social change. The potential for pandemic influenza to reduce the number of mission-capable forces can place DOD mission accomplishment at risk. Therefore, DOD's objective is to prevent and reduce transmission and illness within federal military installations so operational capabilities are preserved. DOD's ability to prevent or reduce transmission or illness and to regenerate, recruit, and sustain the force will become critical. Efforts must include timely force health protection measures, requirements identification and prioritization, proactive procurement, responsive and tailored logistic support, and continuity of essential services.

DEPARTMENT OF DEFENSE READINESS FOR PANDEMICS

4-43. DOD policy and directives stress the importance of state-level planning and preparation before an outbreak requires military resources. The priority of effort goes to installation readiness and force health protection measures. The installation commander plays a pivotal role by coordinating installation response planning and preparation. The flu will not distinguish between Regular military, National Guard and Reserve Component forces, and DOD civilians. Most estimates predict that between 30 per cent and 40 per cent of Soldiers or civilians would not report for duty (either because they are sick, or family members are ill). A pandemic could degrade readiness so that units could not carry out their missions. This could occur due to lack of a pandemic influenza vaccine, lack of antiviral drugs, lack of personal protective equipment, and the lack of education on hygiene and social distancing. Therefore, the installation commander ensures that the civilian workforce remains prepared for a possible influenza outbreak. Commanders ensure their Soldiers receive flu vaccinations regularly. Post agencies develop plans to operate at reduced manning levels by prioritizing missions and ensuring that critical positions have cross-trained replacements. Military forces stress inoculation of personnel and develop plans to augment essential services. They also work with the installation to ensure that families are prepared for an outbreak.

4-44. Training emphasizes casualty manning requirements for combat; commanders may need to implement their casualty response plans before deployment. Commanders emphasize to junior leaders the importance of having someone ready to step up to replace other members of the team when they are unavailable. If deployment is imminent, commanders coordinate with higher headquarters for individual movement of recovered Soldiers. Most important, commanders hold every leader responsible for basic preventative measures shown to be highly effective at containing influenza:

- Sanitation, particularly constant hand washing.
- Rest and proper diet.
- Isolation of infected Soldiers.

Commanders should coordinate with their supporting installation medical activity for guidance about antiviral drugs and other treatment for deploying Soldiers.

COORDINATED NATIONAL RESPONSE TO PANDEMIC DISEASE OUTBREAKS

4-45. The NRF provides the overall architecture for pandemic influenza response, but there are marked differences to federal response for other incidents. The Department of Health and Human Services is the supported agency for pandemic influenza response. USARNORTH works closely with Department of Health and Human Services and FEMA to plan for defense support of civil authorities (DSCA) in a pandemic.

4-46. The scope and pace of an influenza pandemic may defy accurate prediction. The disease may appear in many different parts of the Nation almost simultaneously. It may occur in only one or a few communities, and if not contained there, proceed to affect other communities. In either case, the Secretary of Health and Human Services may have reason to exercise his or her authority under the Public Health Service Act to declare a public health emergency before or coincident with activation of the NRF.

Chapter 4

4-47. The mission of DOD in a pandemic is to preserve the U.S. combat capabilities and readiness and to support U.S. government efforts to save lives, reduce human suffering and slow the spread of infection. Military actions before and during a major influenza outbreak focus on three areas:
- Planning and preparation for a possible outbreak.
- Maintaining combat readiness.
- Support to state and federal agencies.

In any major outbreak of disease, public health workers and medical supplies will require security.

4-48. USNORTHCOM and USPACOM commanders will control federal military support to federal authorities within their respective areas of responsibility.

> Note: Federal military commanders should coordinate carefully with their chain of command to clarify information handling requirements for personal identifying information concerning citizens outside DOD assisted by the military.

Possible missions include military support to—
- Deploy non-countermeasure components of international stockpile and diagnostic reagents to support outbreak investigation, as well as technical and medical assistance.
- Rapidly assess conditions and likelihood of international containment or slowing of pandemic spread.
- Support international deployment of countermeasures to affected regions.
- Work with other countries to implement host country pre-departure screening and initiate U.S. en route and arrival screening at U.S. ports of entry.
- Consider travel or routing restrictions from the affected area and for countries that do not have adequate pre-departure screening.
- Implement protocols for cargo handling that allow trade to continue, when possible.
- Implement protocols to manage or divert inbound international flights with suspected cases of pandemic influenza and prepare to limit domestic ports of entry to manage increased demand for screening, as needed.
- Activate domestic quarantine stations and ensure coordination at state, local, and tribal level, especially with health care resources.
- Prepare to provide military bases and installation support to federal, state, local, and tribal agencies.
- Review domestic pandemic plans and prepare for response, placing critical staff on recall and pre-deploying assets where appropriate.
- Prepare to implement surge plans at federal medical facilities.
- Activate domestic emergency medical personnel plans.
- Deploy pre-pandemic vaccine to state and tribal entities and to federal agencies, and initiate vaccination.
- Limit non-essential passenger travel in affected areas and institute protective measures and social distancing, and support continued delivery of essential goods and services.
- Maintain continuous situational awareness of community needs, triage, and direct federal support of health and medical systems, infrastructure, and maintenance of civil order as feasible.

4-49. National Guard forces will support their state emergency managers in a similar fashion, with one important addition. National Guard commanders may provide Soldiers and Airmen to reinforce police departments unable to provide full law enforcement support to their communities due to absences from illness.

4-50. Public communication during a pandemic is the responsibility of federal and state health officials through their joint information centers. As part of their daily preparation for the mission, Soldiers should receive a situation briefing stressing the facts, and including key information that they can pass on to citizens asking for help.

ENFORCEMENT OF ISOLATION AND QUARANTINE

4-51. A public health emergency may require isolation and quarantine measures to protect the public by preventing exposure to infected or potentially infected individuals. Isolation refers to the separation and the restriction of movement of people who have a specific infectious illness from healthy people to stop the spread of any communicable illness. In most cases, quarantine refers to the separation and restriction of movement of people exposed to an infectious disease. They may not be ill, but they may pose a risk of spreading the disease inadvertently before they manifest clear symptoms. Isolation and quarantine of civilians are normally voluntary but in extreme cases may be compulsory.

4-52. Because compulsory isolation or quarantine is a law enforcement function, Soldiers support law enforcement officials only when authorized by the supported civilian agency through the mission assignment process. Although Hollywood movies depict Regular Army troops enforcing quarantine, this would not be the case in an actual health emergency. Federal military forces do not enforce quarantine. National Guard Soldiers provide the majority of the military support required by their state's officials, and support compulsory measures only as authorized by their governor. See paragraphs 7-53 to 7-58 for more information about legal considerations related to isolation and quarantine.

State Authority for Isolation and Quarantine

4-53. A state's public health authority to enact statutes and issue regulations to compel isolation and quarantine within its borders (intra-state) is derived from the 10th Amendment to the Constitution of the United States and its inherent "police power." As a result of these authorities, states have primary responsibility to enact laws and regulations to promote health, safety, and welfare of its citizens. Consistent with this authority, states may provide for isolation and quarantine restrictions within their borders and conduct these activities in accordance with their respective statutes and regulations.

4-54. The governor of a state may impose isolation and quarantine restrictions in accordance with their respective statutes and regulations. There is variation among states regarding the issue of compelled isolation and quarantine. In general, a governor can declare a public health emergency to initiate isolation or quarantine restrictions. Upon discovery of the need for quarantine or isolation by first responders, the request is forwarded through the appropriate state agency to the governor for approval. The governor assesses the requirements against the resources, and decides whether additional support must be provided by the National Guard. If required such support is provided in state active duty status, unless the President approves a request for support

Federal Government Authority for Isolation and Quarantine

4-55. The federal government has authority under the Commerce Clause of the Constitution to prevent the spread of disease into the United States (foreign) or from one state to another (interstate). The Department of Health and Human Services is the lead federal agency for isolation and quarantines. The Director of the Center for Disease Control and Prevention has been delegated the authority from the Secretary of Health and Human Services to determine whether measures taken by health authorities of any state are insufficient to prevent the spread of any communicable diseases from such state to another state, and to take such measures to prevent the spread of the disease as he deems reasonably necessary.

4-56. The President may authorize federal civilian authorities to detain, examine, and isolate individuals that may have dangerous infectious diseases. This includes cholera, diphtheria, infectious tuberculosis, influenza caused by novel or re-emergent influenza viruses, plague, severe acute respiratory syndrome (known as SARS), smallpox, yellow fever, and viral hemorrhagic fevers that require isolation and quarantine. The Secretary of Health and Human Services coordinates support from state and local authorities for the enforcement of federal quarantine regulations. Such assistance may include National

Guard forces, but the decision to employ National Guard Soldiers belongs to the governor, not the President or the Secretary of Defense. The Secretary of Health and Human Services cooperates with states in the enforcement of their quarantine. At the request of state authorities, Secretary of Health and Human Services may extend temporary assistance to a state in meeting health emergencies. Such assistance may include support provided by federal military forces as authorized by the Secretary of Defense.

4-57. Upon approval by the Secretary of Defense, federal military may be used to support a state quarantine or isolation only by providing logistical, medical, transportation, communications, and other appropriate disaster assistance support as requested by a primary federal agency under the Robert T. Stafford Disaster Relief and Emergency Assistance Act (commonly known as the Stafford Act). This assistance follows the mission assignment process. Unless the President specifically authorizes an exception, federal military cannot be used to enforce a quarantine or isolation (see paragraphs 7-53 to 7-58).

4-58. Because enforcing an isolation or quarantine is a "police power" function, public health officials at the federal, state, and local level may seek the assistance of their respective law enforcement community. At the federal level, this would be primarily the Department of Justice, Federal Bureau of Investigation, United States Marshals Service, Drug Enforcement Administration, and Coast Guard.

Agricultural Diseases

4-59. Pandemic disease threats exist to plants and animals. An outbreak of hoof-and-mouth disease could cost the livestock industry and the U.S. economy billions of dollars. The loss of a crop due to disease or blight also creates economic impacts and could result in food shortages. For example, the potato famine in Ireland forced millions to emigrate or starve in the 19th century. The outbreak was caused by a fungus. Crops, feedlots, and food transportation networks are all at risk for contamination. Operating in support of civil authorities, federal military could play a key role in a response to a biological hazard in the agriculture industry.

4-60. In the case of agriculture, quarantine is often mandatory. Unfortunately, this often requires the destruction of entire herds of livestock. The scale of the infection can rapidly overwhelm county and state officials, and the governor may call up National Guard units to assist with disposal of euthanized animals. Although this has not happened recently in the United States, European military forces assisted officials following large-scale outbreaks of "mad cow" and hoof-and-mouth infections. The Secretary of Agriculture is authorized to cooperate with foreign countries, states, and other jurisdictions, to prevent, regulate, and eliminate burdens on interstate commerce and foreign commerce. The Secretary of Agriculture may request assistance from DOD in order to protect the agriculture, environment, economy, and health and welfare of the population by preventing, detecting, controlling, and eradicating diseases and pests of animals. When federal military support is requested, it will be provided under the Economy Act. Federal military forces providing assistance will receive specific constraints and restraints on their activities through the mission assignment process.

CONSIDERATIONS FOR DOMESTIC CBRNE INCIDENT RESPONSE OPERATIONS

4-61. Actual and suspected CBRNE incidents have triggered response to a single incident site such as the attack on the Pentagon in 2001 or to multiple sites in different states in response to the anthrax attacks of 2001. Responding military forces included both National Guard and Regular military units. For any large incidents, DOD may commit some or all of Joint Task Force–Civil Support, the CBRNE consequence management response force and other specialized CBRNE units such as technical support forces, and various Defense Threat Reduction Agency teams. In large disasters or CBRNE incidents, DOD installations serve as staging areas for resources and agencies. During anthrax responses in 2001 and 2002 for example, DOD laboratories, resources, and personnel played critical response roles that helped mitigate incident impacts and costs to the public. As in other disasters, a large CBRNE incident will require military forces to augment security and essential services.

COMMAND AND CONTROL FOR DOMESTIC CBRNE INCIDENT RESPONSE

4-62. In accordance with the NRF and NIMS, federal military will support a civilian incident command structure with many agencies during civil support operations (see chapter 2). The incident command team is responsible for managing the response. The incident command staff develops an incident action plan, a type of operations order that assigns work tasks. The incident command staff determines safety measures, technical reference, reach-back, personnel protective equipment, logistics, and other requirements. The incident command staff, together with law enforcement, public health, Environmental Protection Agency, Department of Energy and other agencies develops specific mission requirements such as obtaining samples, setting decontamination standards, monitoring exposure levels The most difficult command and control challenge during a CBRNE incident response is maintaining situational awareness at all levels and across all agencies involved. Commanders plan for this by deploying liaison personnel who help the commander to maintain constant communication with both military and civil authorities

4-63. Commanders must integrate composite risk management and operational risk management in their planning to mitigate and manage hazards and ensure force protection when working with civilian agencies. Tailored situational awareness teams perform the following tasks during CBRNE incidents:
- Attend daily incident command planning meetings to anticipate mission requirements.
- Describe to the incident command staff DOD capabilities and limitations.
- Describe to the incident commander legal limitations for federal military and state National Guard forces.
- Provide liaison between other federal military and state National Guard forces in the area.
- Secure resources not provided by DOD.
- Clarify or translate civilian work requirements into tasks related to DOD.
- Establish communications links.
- Augment the incident command staff with CBRNE specialists.

4-64. Most command and control systems developed for combat are incompatible with civilian systems unless the military provides specialized connections. Developing situational awareness and building a common operational picture is critical to effective response. Many state and local emergency operations centers use commercial communications software. State agencies, the National Guard Bureau, and USNORTHCOM continually improve tools that facilitate information sharing at CBRNE and other incident sites.

PUBLIC AFFAIRS AND DOMESTIC CBRNE INCIDENT RESPONSE

4-65. CBRNE incident response activities are likely to be highly publicized and can place great pressure on leaders. The public information and education efforts are essential to easing fear and protecting the public during CBRNE incidents. Accurate information regarding the incident and efforts to protect the public should be disseminated to all subordinates as soon as the incident command staff makes it available. To ensure a unified message, public affairs information is coordinated through the incident command staff during civil support operations. Military public affairs personnel work directly with incident command's joint information center to synchronize efforts.

4-66. Commanders, leaders, and Soldiers play a key role in information. The actions of Soldiers on the ground communicate far more powerfully than other media. Those actions must be in accordance with the command's public affairs guidance. Civilians may assume that uniformed personnel know more about the situation than others do. Rumors will be rampant during the initial response. Disruption to civilian broadcasts may limit routine sources of information. Therefore, federal military may be able to provide updated, factual information to the local populace. Commanders must brief their personnel daily on the public affairs guidance. See appendix K for more information about public affairs.

Protection During Domestic CBRNE Incident Response

4-67. Conventional battlefield protective and detection systems cannot meet all battlefield and homeland security CBRNE requirements. Commanders must understand the limitations of their equipment and personnel. During a CBRNE incident, the incident command staff determines the level of protective garment required based on the hazard.

Chemical Protection

4-68. Conventional forces are not equipped to detect or protect against toxic industrial chemicals and materials. Joint Service Lightweight Integrated Suit Technology (JSLIST) and protective masks do not meet civilian chemical protection standards or protect against most toxic industrial materials. Battlefield chemical detection systems detect specific battlefield threats. Presently weapons of mass destruction–civil support teams, CBRNE consequence management response force units, and attached chemical, biological, radiological, and nuclear defense units along with elements of the 20th Support Command have enhanced CBRNE and industrial chemical protection and detection capabilities. These capabilities are being issued to conventional chemical units in the modular brigades.

Biological Protection

4-69. Battlefield protective equipment will protect Soldiers against biological hazards. Most biological detection systems screen for battlefield biological hazards. Current biological detection and analytical equipment require extensive training and laboratory support for confirmative results. Weapons of mass destruction–civil support teams possess mobile analytical laboratory systems and train to meet standards required by civilian agencies and laboratory networks. In civil support operations, public health departments and other agencies handle the majority of biological sampling and identification.

Nuclear Protection

4-70. U.S. military forces are equipped to deal with the domestic consequences of a nuclear or radiological incident. Battlefield radiological detection equipment and protective gear are suited for civil support operations. Post-blast nuclear and radiological devices present standard exposure levels and decay rates. Conventional radiological detection systems can detect and monitor radioactive materials. However, these systems require training to use properly.

Decontamination

4-71. Battlefield decontamination equipment and measures work well against CBRNE hazards. Sunlight, household disinfectants, and inclement weather also break down some chemical and biological contaminants. Equipped with commercial equipment, the CBRNE enhanced response force package, chemical-biological incident response force, and CBRNE consequence management response force units can support the decontamination of mass casualties or responders during large incidents. Commanders and leaders of CBRNE decontamination units coordinate with their headquarters concerning the location and procedures for operating the station. If available, team leaders should consult with civilian experts from Defense Threat Reduction Agency, Environmental Protection Agency, and other organizations. In particular, senior commanders need to confirm the proposed location and protection measures at the decontamination site with the unified coordination group to ensure hazardous substances are controlled and eliminated safely.

Hazard Prediction Models

4-72. Hazard prediction modeling programs graphically depict the impacts of CBRNE hazards for commanders and incident commanders. Under the NRF, the Interagency Modeling and Atmospheric Advisory Center employs the National Atmospheric Release Advisory Center, which is the single hazardous airborne and dispersion prediction model used during a federal response. In a CBRNE incident, models can provide information on casualty estimates, contaminated areas, road block locations, local hospitals, airfields and hazards concentrations. This information helps the incident command staff and supporting agencies organize staging areas, define work zones, conduct downwind monitoring, and determine evacuation measures. Units operating near a CBRNE incident site should obtain prediction models through the incident command for situational awareness and force protection. The Defense Threat Reduction Agency, weapons of mass destruction–civil support teams, and fire departments employ hazard prediction models.

Protective Equipment

4-73. Battlefield protective equipment and civilian personal protective equipment terminologies and employment are different. Required protective equipment levels vary throughout a response based on the nature of the hazard, distance from a hazard, weather conditions and work being completed. Flexibility in employing personal protective equipment or military protective gear and Soldier safety are priorities. Some CBRNE responses might require light gloves and eyewear rather than a full protective overgarment. Civilian personal protective equipment is categorized by levels A, B, C, and D. Level A is a fully encapsulated vapor protective suit with a self-contained breathing apparatus (SCBA). Level B is a hooded protective suit and SCBA. Level C is a hooded protective suit with a filtered air purifying respirator. Level A, B, and C suits use many types of flexible flash and or chemical protective materials from laminated fabrics and plastics. Level D is a response duty uniform that might include earplugs, gloves, protective footgear and eyewear. Battlefield protective levels do not match civilian personal protective equipment levels. Based on the CBRNE hazards, military protective equipment may not be appropriate. The use of level A, B, C, and D personal protective equipment requires special training and certification.

4-74. Special attention must be given to heat injury prevention to personnel using personal protective equipment. The civilian incident commander will normally determine the level of personal protective equipment based on the hazard. In a large federal response, Environmental Protection Agency, Centers for Disease Control, Department of Energy, response organizations, and the safety officer might contribute to personal protective equipment decisions. When the hazard is unknown, Level A personal protective equipment is chosen.

MOVEMENT AND MANEUVER DURING DOMESTIC CBRNE INCIDENT RESPONSE OPERATIONS

4-75. The incident staging area is the equivalent of an intermediate staging base. Units move to an incident staging area determined by an incident command staff prior to moving into a CBRNE incident site. The staging area personnel receive the unit's personnel and equipment accountability information and provide details regarding the incident. Before leaving the staging area, a unit receives it mission, safety briefings, and updated information regarding the incident. Debris, contaminated areas, other responding agencies, and terrain might delay movement.

4-76. Contaminated areas present a serious hazard to movement near any CBRNE incident. One of the key tasks that Army forces may anticipate is establishing and maintaining security around a contaminated area, sometimes known as a "hot zone." In an urban area this task can be manpower intensive. It requires close coordination with the incident command and unified area command to ensure its proper placement, security, and maintenance. Commanders keep in mind that the contaminated area may shift suddenly due to weather or other factors. Army forces directed to move into a contaminated area plan and rehearse prior to executing the mission. Ideally, the unit is equipped for CBRNE incidents. Otherwise, if a unit is responding to an emergency, Soldiers should follow the unit standing operating procedure for movement techniques in a contaminated environment. Some combat systems provide much better protection than other vehicles, particularly against radiation and chemical threats. Stryker nuclear, biological, and chemical reconnaissance vehicles have overpressure and detection systems and their armor reduces radiation exposure. The M-88 Hercules also has heavy steel armor, and can maneuver in radioactive areas. The armor on these vehicles can attenuate the effects of gamma radiation, and extend the time that rescue or recovery personnel can spend in the hot zone.

4-77. Movement in or near a contaminated area requires decontamination support. Unless decontamination support is available, commanders should not send Soldiers into or near a contaminated area. Commanders must coordinate with the supporting decontamination element to ensure that they can conduct the necessary detection and decontamination before committing Soldiers.

4-78. Aviation unit commanders must review current instructions for operating in or near a contaminated area. A helicopter is almost impossible to decontaminate completely once exposed to hazardous agents or radiation. Aircraft generally should avoid flying near contaminated areas, if possible. If the mission requires exposing the aircraft and crew to hazardous materials, the aviation unit must establish protective procedures for immediate decontamination, and train the air crew in protective measures.

4-79. Engineering support to a CBRNE incident response is extensive and supports all of the other functions. The key capabilities the engineers provide include—
- Force bed down and marshalling support.
- Emergency route opening (use of any available means to enable ground emergency movement into and out of the affected area).
- Engineer site assessment.
- Infrastructure repair.
- Geospatial information support. (Paragraphs 8-81–8-82 discuss geospatial support. Chapter 7 discusses legal considerations related to information.)

SUSTAINMENT FOR DOMESTIC CBRNE INCIDENT RESPONSE OPERATIONS

4-80. A large scale CBRNE incident can quickly exhaust the capabilities of local, state, and federal emergency responders. CBRNE emergency responders develop sustainment plans that include the coordination for and establishment of logistics systems to ensure continuous replenishment of consumables, personnel, spare parts, and maintenance. DOD installations should plan for sustainment of its CBRNE emergency responder preparedness programs as well as establish contact with the appropriate state and federal emergency response officials within the installations respective FEMA region.

CBRNE Incident Response Equipment

4-81. Equipment requirements vary depending upon the nature of the CBRNE incident. Equipment could be provided by FEMA, USARNORTH, Joint Task Force–Civil Support, fire departments, state agencies, military stocks or local purchase. CBRNE response units should deploy to an incident site with the ability to sustain themselves for two to three days and then submit resupply requirements through their chains of command.

National Guard Consequence Management Support Center

4-82. The National Guard's weapons of mass destruction–civil support teams and CBRNE enhanced response force package forces receive support from the consequence management support center. The consequence management support center provides weapons of mass destruction–civil support teams and CBRNE enhanced response force packages full replacement of shelters, light sets, air compressors, CBRNE detection, decontamination, batteries, calibration gases, masks, protective garments, self-contained breathing apparatus and analytical equipment required to sustain an extended CBRNE incident response mission. The consequence management support center rapidly deploys equipment stocks to an incident site. In extended response, the consequence management support center forward deploys personnel and equipment to directly support the CBRNE enhanced response force packages and weapons of mass destruction–civil support teams.

Federal Emergency Management Agency Sustainment

4-83. FEMA supplies pre-positioned equipment to replenish and reconstitute state, local, and tribal responders incident site. This equipment includes protective equipment, detection instruments, medical supplies, decontamination equipment, and logistics.

Sustainment from Military Installations During CBRNE Incident Response

4-84. Some military installations have equipment for responding to CBRNE incidents. They may have a fire department with appropriate assets. During an emergency, installations might provide protective equipment, air compressors, fire trucks, decontamination systems, power generation, detection equipment and other resources. Installations also serve as staging areas providing food, shelter, fuel, headquarters facilities, and vehicles to responding units.

4-85. Mortuary affairs personnel may support CBRNE incidents. Team leaders should verify procedures for handling remains through higher headquarters and through the defense coordinating officer to the primary agency responsible for the appropriate emergency support function (normally ESF #8). Specific procedures on identifying and handling contaminated remains are according to the existing civilian plans and JP 4-06 to the controlling National Guard and federal military joint task force.

INTELLIGENCE CAPABILITIES DURING DOMESTIC CBRNE INCIDENT RESPONSE OPERATIONS

4-86. Domestic intelligence remains a sensitive area in civil support, and incident awareness and assessment during CBRNE incidents may be subject to additional regulatory requirements. See chapter 7 for more information about legal considerations. Commanders should carefully review instructions concerning intelligence capabilities in their specific execution orders. The majority of military intelligence support pertains to ongoing terrorist activities and CBRNE incident investigation. The Department of Justice, Department of Homeland Security, Central Intelligence Agency, and other law enforcement agencies provide domestic intelligence to military commanders daily. Intelligence on domestic terrorists and criminals will come through secure law enforcement channels. The need for intelligence in CBRNE incidents drives the requirement for secure communication between all participating agencies and the military. Military communication systems will tie in with the civilian Joint Incident Site Communications Capability secure communications system. FEMA and other agencies provide this capability to share classified or sensitive information.

4-87. Environmental and safety information receives the widest possible dissemination. The incident command operations staff provides all unclassified information and analysis on the hazardous area to ensure the safety of responders, hospitals, and others impacted by the incident. Intelligence staff members can provide mapping, situational awareness, liaison support, and weather support during a CBRNE incident response.

4-88. The incident command operations and planning sections manage CBRNE incident information. A hazardous materials working group under the operations staff might form in order to coordinate incident information and direct operations. The incident command operations staff receives CBRNE and other hazardous materials survey reports from fire fighters, Department of Energy, DOD, Environmental Protection Agency, and other agencies responding and monitoring an incident site. This information refines hazard prediction models to develop a common operational picture of the hazardous locations. The Interagency Model and Atmospheric Advisory Center provide the contamination prediction model for all federal responses. Field measurement and reporting confirms or alternatively, modifies the predictive models.

This page intentionally left blank.

Chapter 5

Provide Support for Domestic Civilian Law Enforcement Agencies

This chapter covers general concepts for military support to civilian law enforcement agencies. It summarizes the important laws and policy that govern support. It discusses the types of law enforcement missions that commanders could receive, and provides considerations for the employment of forces, particularly in civil disturbance scenarios.

PRINCIPAL AUTHORITES FOR SUPPORT TO DOMESTIC CIVILIAN LAW ENFORCEMENT AGENCIES

5-1. State and federal law carefully limits the support that Army forces may provide to civilian law enforcement agencies. Federal laws, Presidential directives, and Department of Defense (DOD) policy constrain the use of federal military forces from enforcing laws and providing security except on military installations. When authorized by the Secretary of Defense, federal military forces may provide support to law enforcement agencies, but that support is limited to logistical, transportation, and training assistance except in life-threatening emergencies. The governors of the 54 states and territories can use National Guard forces under state command for civilian law enforcement; however, use of state National Guard forces for support to law enforcement is a temporary expedient. Governors have some flexibility in employing state National Guard forces for law enforcement. Chapter 7 provides additional information on the legal considerations for law enforcement support. Department of Defense Directive (DODD) 3025.12 summarizes the responsibilities of civil authorities for law enforcement:

> *The primary responsibility for protecting life and property and maintaining law and order in the civilian community is vested in the State and local governments. Supplementary responsibility is vested by statute in specific Agencies of the Federal Government other than the Department of Defense. The President has additional powers and responsibilities under the Constitution of the United States to ensure that law and order are maintained.*
>
> DODD 3025.12

5-2. Domestic law enforcement missions differ substantially from similar stability tasks associated with civil security and civil control. Except in extreme emergencies, during domestic law enforcement operations the rights of the citizens take precedence. Military forces supporting law enforcement typically have less authority to enforce the law than when conducting stability operations. When circumstances dictate, the governor of a state may call up National Guard forces to assist local and state law officers. The National Guard's authority derives from the governor's responsibility to enforce the laws of that state. Even with that authority, the governor carefully regulates the amount and nature of the support. The governor may employ the state National Guard for law enforcement duties and support in state active duty status or in Title 32 status. Federal laws (principally the Posse Comitatus Act) restrict the role of any National Guard forces in Title 10 status for law enforcement support (see chapter 7) unless a specific exemption is applicable.

5-3. Military support to civilian law enforcement agencies occurs in two general circumstances: in response to an emergency or in response to a request for support from a law enforcement agency. The more difficult case occurs as part of an emergency. Federal Army forces may provide indirect support to federal, state, and local law enforcement organizations reacting to civil disturbances, conducting border security and counterdrug missions, preparing for antiterrorism operations, and providing other related support to law enforcement, but such support requires the approval of the Secretary of Defense. Before approval, the DOD legal staff normally conducts a comprehensive legal review of the request and advises the Secretary of Defense on their conclusion.

5-4. Upon approval of the governor, state National Guard forces may support state law enforcement agencies within their respective states and within the limits prescribed by state law. State National Guard forces in either Title 32 status or state active duty status from another state operating under the Emergency Management Assistance Compact (EMAC) or a memorandum of agreement between the states may only support civilian law enforcement as specified in a memorandum approved by both governors.

LAW ENFORCEMENT SUPPORT UNDER THE POSSE COMITATUS ACT

5-5. The Posse Comitatus Act restricts the use of the federal military forces for direct support to civilian law enforcement. Except as expressly authorized by the Constitution of the United States or by another act of Congress, the Posse Comitatus Act and DOD directives prohibit the use of the Army, Air Force, and—through DOD policy—the Navy and Marine Corps as enforcement officials to execute state or federal law and perform direct law enforcement functions. The Navy and Marine Corps are included in this prohibition as a result of DOD policy articulated in DODD 5525.5. However, the Posse Comitatus Act does not apply to state National Guard forces operating in state active duty status or in Title 32 status. Due to the state National Guard's statutory law enforcement functions, the Posse Comitatus Act does not apply. Nor does the Posse Comitatus Act restrict the Coast Guard, even when it falls under the operational control of the Navy due to the fact that the Coast Guard has inherent law enforcement powers under Title 14, United States Code (USC). Commanders should understand that the Posse Comitatus Act specifies severe criminal penalties if violated. Chapter 7 provides additional detail on the Posse Comitatus Act.

5-6. A catastrophic disaster may overwhelm local law enforcement, particularly when they are responding with a disrupted command and control system. National Guard forces support law enforcement when the governor authorizes that state's military command to assume designated law enforcement duties. The specific legal authority for National Guard members to conduct law enforcement functions are derived from state law and vary from state to state. Federal military forces require special authorization, from the Secretary of Defense, to support civilian law enforcement officials outside of federal military installations. In extreme cases, the state attorney general, in coordination with the Secretary of Defense, may recommend that the President invoke the Insurrection Act (see chapter 7). The restrictions on federalized military forces are derived from Posse Comitatus Act case law and are summarized in the Chairman of the Joint Chiefs of Staff standing execute order for DSCA order (referred to as the CJCS DSCA EXORD) dated 14 August 2009:

> *Unless specifically authorized by law, no DOD personnel in a Title 10, United States Code (USC), status (Federal military forces) will become involved in direct civilian law enforcement activities, including, but not limited to, search, seizure, arrest, apprehension, stop and frisk, surveillance, pursuit, interrogation, investigation, evidence collection, security functions, traffic or crowd control, or similar activities, except in cases and under circumstances expressly authorized by the President, Constitution, or Act of Congress.*
>
> CJCS DSCA EXORD, 14 August 2009

5-7. DODD 5525.5 provides guidance on the type of assistance DOD can provide to local authorities when it is primarily for a military purpose and does not violate the Posse Comitatus Act. This guidance is known as the "Military Purpose Doctrine." Such support cannot degrade combat readiness or the capacity of DOD to fulfill its primary mission. In general, the less directly related the situation is to civilian law enforcement and the more it supports a military purpose, the less applicable is the Posse Comitatus Act. "Military Purpose" actions include:

- Investigations and other actions related to the enforcement to the Uniform Code of Military Justice.
- Investigations and other actions related to the commander's inherent authority to maintain law and order on a military installation or facility.
- Protection of classified military information or equipment.
- Protection of DOD personnel, DOD equipment, and official guests of the DOD.
- Other actions that are undertaken primarily for a military or foreign affairs purpose.

LAW ENFORCEMENT SUPPORT UNDER EMERGENCY AUTHORITY

5-8. In an extreme situation, federal military commanders may commit their forces to uphold the law and protect federal property. Only two circumstances for emergency authority are allowed by DODD 5525.5.

5-9. The first circumstance is when a situation demands immediate federal action, including use of military forces, to prevent loss of life or wanton destruction of property and to restore governmental functioning and public order. The need for federal military forces might arise because of sudden and unexpected civil disturbances, disasters, or calamities. Incidents such as these may seriously endanger life and property and disrupt normal governmental functions to such an extent that duly constituted local authorities are unable to control the situation. The Posse Comitatus Act's restrictions on direct participation in law enforcement still apply in this situation unless another exemption exists.

5-10. The second circumstance is when a situation requires federal military forces to protect federal property and federal government functions. The need might arise when there was an immediate and discernable threat, and duly constituted local authorities were unable or declined to provide adequate protection.

5-11. In either of these situations, federal military commanders responsible for authorizing action under emergency authority must determine that obtaining prior approval from the President through the chain of command is not feasible. Commanders will continue to use all available means to seek specific authorization from the President through their chain of command while operating under their emergency authority.

MARTIAL LAW

5-12. Martial law involves use of the military to exercise police powers; restore and maintain order; ensure essential mechanics of distribution, transportation and communication; and conduct necessary relief measures. In such cases, the ordinary law, as administered by the ordinary courts, is superseded for the time being by the order of a military commander. See page 5-4 for a summary of the historical use of martial law in the United States.

> **Historical Use of Martial Law**
>
> Martial law was first used in the United States by General Andrew Jackson in 1814, during the War of 1812. Later, during the Civil War, Confederate territory taken by Union forces was governed under martial law. Additionally, the Secretary of War issued an order under President Lincoln's authority suspending the writ of habeas corpus. In other words, individuals were arrested and detained indefinitely by a military commander without trial. After the Civil War, the Supreme Court in the seminal case of Ex Parte Milligan reviewed and declared this martial law invalid. It said when it is extremely necessary to furnish a substitute for civilian government and the only authority left is the military, then martial law exercised by the military was permissible and could be implemented. However, where the civilian courts were open and capable of exercising their law enforcement jurisdiction and trying individuals who violated civil laws, as they were in this case, then martial law could never properly exist. "Public necessity" creates martial law, justifies it, and limits its duration. Other instances of martial law occurred during World War II, when Hawaii's governor placed the territory under martial law from December 1941 to October 1944, and in 1954 when Alabama's governor declared martial law in Phenix City, enforced by the Alabama National Guard.

5-13. Only the President may order federal military forces to impose martial law. DODD 3025.12 states that federal military commanders shall not take charge of any function of civil government unless absolutely necessary under conditions of extreme emergency. Any commander who is directed, or undertakes, to control such functions shall strictly limit military actions to the emergency needs, and shall facilitate the reestablishment of civil responsibility at the earliest time possible.

5-14. Other officials may be authorized to impose martial law within a particular state under that state's law, but the restraints are similar to the federal level. The state and federal supreme courts may review any imposition of martial law for legality.

MAIN TYPES OF MISSIONS FOR SUPPORT TO DOMESTIC CIVILIAN LAW ENFORCEMENT AGENCIES

5-15. Support to civil law enforcement agencies usually falls under four general mission areas. Military forces may provide indirect support for counterdrug activities, border security and protection from terrorism. Military forces may provide direct and indirect support during civil disturbance operations. Another category is critical infrastructure protection and is addressed in chapter 6. The military force with primary responsibility for direct law enforcement support (for example, involving face-to-face contact with offenders) is the National Guard, under state command and control.

5-16. Although federal military forces have limitations on direct enforcement of the law, DOD provides indirect support to civilian law enforcement regularly. Indirect assistance facilitates the supported civilian agency's ability to enforce the laws, while maintaining separation between the Soldier and the civilian offenders. DOD policy provides federal military commanders with guidance on indirect federal military support to civilian law enforcement agencies. DOD policy allows indirect federal military support to civilian law enforcement based on the following criteria:

- Assistance is limited to situations when the use of persons not affiliated with DOD would be unfeasible or impractical from a cost or time perspective and would not otherwise compromise national security or military preparedness concerns.
- Assistance may not involve DOD personnel in a direct role in law enforcement operation, except as otherwise authorized by law.

Provide Support for Domestic Civilian Law Enforcement Agencies

- Except as otherwise authorized by law, assistance by DOD personnel will occur at a location where there is not a reasonable likelihood of a law enforcement confrontation.
- Military departments and defense agencies may provide expert advice to federal, state, or local law enforcement officials in accordance with Title 10, USC. This does not permit regular or direct involvement of military personnel in activities that are fundamentally civilian law enforcement operations, except as otherwise authorized.
- Use of DOD personnel to operate or maintain or to assist in operating or maintaining equipment is limited to situations when the training of persons not affiliated with DOD would be unfeasible or impractical from a cost or time perspective and would not otherwise compromise national security or military preparedness concerns.

COUNTERDRUG SUPPORT

5-17. DOD supports federal, state, and local law enforcement agencies in their effort to disrupt the transport or transfer of illegal drugs into the United States. Illicit drug trafficking, smuggling of every sort, and the regional and global movement of terrorists are closely linked by financial, political, and operational ties.

5-18. Countering illegal drugs is a high priority mission. DOD functions and responsibilities related to counterdrug support are based on statutory authority. DOD supports counterdrug operations to enhance national security and international cooperation. The Armed Forces of the United States also assist partner nations in their counterdrug efforts.

5-19. The strategic goals of the National Drug Control Strategy are preventing drug use before it starts, intervening and healing those who already use drugs, and disrupting the market for illicit substances. In support of this strategy, Army forces assist law enforcement officials indirectly through loan of equipment (without operators), use of facilities (such as buildings, training areas, or ranges), transfer of excess equipment, and training conducted in military schools.

5-20. Indirect support by federal military forces to counterdrug agencies requires approval by the Secretary of Defense or a designated representative. Three standing joint task force headquarters provide indirect support to domestic civilian law enforcement agencies. Joint Task Force–North supports counterdrug efforts within the United States Northern Command (USNORTHCOM) area of responsibility. Joint Task Force–West does the same in the United States Pacific Command (USPACOM) area of responsibility. The Joint Interagency Task Force operates in the United States Southern Command area of responsibility. The missions vary widely and may include ground reconnaissance; detection and monitoring; communications support; aerial reconnaissance; marijuana eradication; linguist support; air and ground transportation; intelligence analysis; tunnel detection; engineering support; and maintenance support.

Note: Military forces are prohibited from using herbicides.

5-21. There are 54 state and territory National Guard counterdrug support programs, governed by National Guard regulations. Additionally, there are four regional National Guard counterdrug schools. The Secretary of Defense, in accordance with Section 112 of Title 32, USC, may provide resources though the Chief, National Guard Bureau, to states with approved National Guard counterdrug support plans. In addition to requiring approval by the Secretary of Defense, the state National Guard counterdrug support plan requires approval from the state's attorney general and adjutant general. The Secretary of Defense, (under Section 1004, National Defense Authorization Act for Fiscal Year 1991, as amended) may provide funding through the Chief of the National Guard Bureau to a state receiving Secretary of Defense approval of a counterdrug school execution plan for National Guard Training Support. The National Guard Bureau funds a full-time Title 32 Active Guard and Reserve counterdrug coordinator position in each state for administration and management of the state counter drug program. The counterdrug coordinator serves as the focal point for all counter drug mission validations, approval authority, and the prioritization for counterdrug mission tasking under appropriate policies, instructions, and directives. National Guard support can include linguist support (translators), investigative case and analyst support, operational or investigative case support, engineer support, subsurface diver support, domestic cannabis suppression support, transportation support, maintenance or logistical support, cargo or mail inspection, counterdrug-related training, training law enforcement agency or military personnel, ground reconnaissance, aerial reconnaissance, and demand reduction support.

BORDER SECURITY

5-22. The Department of Homeland Security may request support from federal military forces. Requests for assistance go from Department of Homeland Security to the Secretary of Defense or the Assistant Secretary of Defense (Homeland Defense and America's Security Affairs). If approved by the Secretary of Defense, federal military forces provide indirect support to border security and law enforcement personnel, as well as immigration and naturalization officers. Joint Task Force–North exercises tactical control over federal military assets within the USNORTHCOM area of responsibility.

5-23. State National Guard forces also provide support to Department of Homeland Security border security programs. Under Section 112 of Title 32, USC, National Guard Soldiers assist in border security by operating surveillance systems, analyzing intelligence, installing fences and vehicle barriers, building roads, and providing training. Although state National Guard units could participate in direct law enforcement activities related to border security, under DOD policy they normally provide indirect support, under the control of their governor.

5-24. DOD may indirectly support border security efforts under legislation contained in Title 10, USC, Sections 371 through 374. This is provided through Joint Task Force–North. Joint Task Force–North does not directly enforce the laws pertaining to homeland security. Its mission is to improve the capabilities of Department of Homeland Security agencies to carry out their law enforcement missions.

HOMELAND DEFENSE ACTIVITIES

5-25. Under Sections 901 to 908, Title 32, USC, the Secretary of Defense may provide DOD funding for National Guard Soldiers in a Title 32 status to conduct homeland defense activities within their state. The National Guard Soldiers performing this type of homeland defense duty remain under the command and control of the governor. The duration of this duty is limited to 180 days, but the governor may extend the tour by 90 days with the concurrence of the Secretary of Defense.

CIVIL DISTURBANCE

5-26. When large numbers of people disregard the law—through mob behavior and rioting, for example—local and state police may become unable to protect lives and property, particularly if the mob is armed. Large civil disturbances have occurred throughout U.S. history and frequently have turned deadly. The most recent instance of both federal forces and state National Guard forces controlling a large civil disturbance occurred during the Los Angeles riots in 1992. National Guard forces under state control are responsible for direct support to law enforcement in civil disturbance operations.

5-27. United States Army North (USARNORTH) categorizes civil disturbances according to three general scenarios:
- Violent–destructive–nonconfrontational.
- Violent–destructive–confrontational.
- Nonviolent–nondestructive–confrontational.

Using these scenarios helps commanders determine mission requirements. In all types of scenarios, planners maintain situational awareness and assessment so supporting forces can anticipate requirements and prepare for contingencies. They coordinate with civilian law enforcement agencies as needed.

5-28. The first scenario—violent–destructive–nonconfrontational—is the most likely to require federal intervention. One example is the Los Angeles riots of 1992. This scenario is considered nonconfrontational because the violence is not targeted at authorities. Mobs behave violently toward other civilians and destroy property. The civil disorder is dispersed and intermittent. A variety of causes may lead to this type of situation, including hurricanes that destroy infrastructure. In this scenario, violence can quickly overwhelm state capabilities. Popular discontent can cause violence to spread to several localities. This type of scenario may be the costliest in terms of property damage. It typically requires the quickest response and is the most dangerous to supporting forces.

5-29. The second scenario—violent–destructive–confrontational—refers to concentrated demonstrations of limited duration and focused at points with psychological significance. Antagonism is directed at authorities. Examples are the 1967 march on the Pentagon and the 1973 Wounded Knee standoff. These incidents may start as a planned, lawful protest or special event. If violence erupts, however, it happens suddenly.

5-30. The third scenario—nonviolent–nondestructive–confrontational—refers to peaceful demonstrations against civil or military authorities. This is the least likely to require federal forces. For example, peaceful protesters might block the entrance to a public building or trespass on a military installation.

State National Guard Forces

5-31. The governor may call out the National Guard to quell any civil disturbance when it threatens lives or property. National Guard forces disperse unlawful assemblies and patrol areas to prevent unlawful acts. They assist in the distribution of essential goods and the maintenance of essential services. Military forces also establish traffic control points, cordon off areas, release smoke and obscurants, and serve as security or quick-reaction forces. The National Guard joint task force commander provides liaison teams to each affected law enforcement agency and normally positions the joint task force headquarters near the police headquarters. In addition to support for law enforcement agencies, National Guard forces provide security for emergency responders, particularly fire fighters. After review by the state attorney general, the governor approves the rules for the use of force.

Note: There is no standard military nomenclature for *rules for the use of force* between the 54 states and territories.

Federal Military Forces

5-32. Federal military forces may reinforce law enforcement agencies responding to civil disturbances. Federal military support for civil disturbances does not, technically, fall under support to civilian law enforcement agencies when the Insurrection Act or other exemptions to the Posse Comitatus Act are used. The primary reference for civil disturbance is DODD 3025.12. The President may employ the Armed Forces of the United States, including the National Guard, within the United States to restore order or enforce federal law when requested by the state legislature, or when not in session, by the governor, and when the authorities of the state are incapable of maintaining public order. The President normally initiates action by ordering the dispersal of those obstructing the enforcement of the laws. The President may also act unilaterally to suppress an insurrection or domestic violation without the request or authority of the governor in order to protect the federal government, enforce federal law, or protect the constitutional rights of citizens.

5-33. Responsibility for coordinating the federal response for civil disturbances rests with the Attorney General of the United States. The Attorney General appoints a senior civilian representative as his or her action agent. Any federal military employed in civil disturbance operations remain under military command at all times. Forces deployed to assist federal and local authorities in a civil disturbance adhere to the rules for the use of force approved by the combatant commander.

5-34. USNORTHCOM develops and maintains plans for civil disturbance operations. These plans provide the foundation for civil disturbance support and standardize most military activities and command relationships. Tasks performed by military forces may include joint patrolling with law enforcement officers; securing key buildings, memorials, intersections and bridges; and acting as a quick reaction force.

Training for Civil Disturbance Operations

5-35. Civil disturbance missions require unit training prior to employing crowd control tactics. This normally requires a mobile training team from the military police or trained law enforcement personnel. Note that effective employment of shields and batons requires frequent drilling, and small-unit leaders should put their subordinates through these drills during any available time between commitments. Even in an urgent situation, commanders need to drill their forces repeatedly until small unit leaders can execute maneuvers under extreme stress. Training should be all-arms, emphasizing treatment and evacuation procedures, detention and movement of citizens, and use of authorized nonlethal systems.

PROTECTION AGAINST TERRORISM

5-36. Protecting against terrorism in the United States is a civilian law enforcement responsibility. The Department of Justice—specifically, the Federal Bureau of Investigation (FBI)—has primary federal responsibility for combating terrorism. Responsibilities include measures to anticipate, prevent, and resolve a threat or act of terrorism. The FBI works closely with local, state, and federal agencies to detect and preempt terrorist activity.

5-37. The FBI continually assesses intelligence and reports of terrorist activity. When there is a credible threat, the FBI is responsible to disrupt it and prevent an attack. Should there be an incident, the FBI neutralizes any on-scene threat and conducts the criminal investigation. The FBI special agent in charge supervises the law enforcement activities at the incident scene. To do this, the FBI establishes a *joint operations center* (an ad hoc federal government law enforcement organization for coordinating an interagency response). Based on the National Response Framework's *Terrorism Incident Law Enforcement and Investigation* incident annex, the joint operations center is co-located with the joint field office (see chapter 2). Other FBI actions can include deploying a domestic emergency support team—a rapidly deployable special interagency team that provides advice to the FBI on-scene coordinator. The special agent in charge may also request the FBI hostage rescue team.

5-38. In response to a terrorist incident, several federal law enforcement agencies will deploy assets to the scene. Depending on the seriousness of the incident, the Attorney General of the United States designates the ranking FBI agent as the senior federal law enforcement official to coordinate the activities of not only the FBI, but also all other federal law enforcement agencies. The senior federal law enforcement official works within the joint field office.

5-39. The principal Army contributions to this effort are antiterrorism and force protection. State and federal military forces take effective antiterrorism and force protection measures to prevent attacks and, by complicating the terrorists' activities, increase the likelihood of their detection and apprehension.

ANTITERRORISM SUPPORT AND FORCE PROTECTION

5-40. Antiterrorism efforts within the United States require force protection and indirect support to civilian law enforcement agencies for training and material assistance. Antiterrorism and force protection programs are interrelated; commanders must ensure their application and integration in all civil support operations. Force protection is an overarching mission that ties together all mission assurance functions. Force protection activities include actions taken to prevent or mitigate hostile actions against personnel (including family members), resources, facilities, and critical information. Activities contributing to the force protection mission include antiterrorism, critical infrastructure protection, continuity of operations, logistics, medical activities, legal activities, and safety.

5-41. Antiterrorism involves defensive measures used to reduce the vulnerability of individuals and property to terrorist acts, to include limited response and containment by local military forces and civilians. Antiterrorism programs form the foundation for effectively combating terrorism. The basics of such programs include training and defensive measures that strike a balance between the level of protection, the mission, individual freedoms, and resource availability.

COUNTERTERRORISM SUPPORT

5-42. In very limited circumstances, federal military forces may support domestic counterterrorism operations. The FBI may request specialized federal military counterterrorism support. The FBI on-scene coordinator notifies the FBI Director and the Attorney General of the United States of any request for DOD assistance. The FBI also informs the Assistant Secretary of Defense (Special Operations and Low-Intensity Conflict) of the pending request and provides details of the incident. The Assistant Secretary of Defense (Special Operations and Low-Intensity Conflict) advises the Secretary of Defense, and the Attorney General confers with the Secretary of Defense on the deployment request. They, in turn, confer with the President. The President or Secretary of Defense must approve all federal military support to counterterrorism within the United States.

CONSIDERATIONS FOR SUPPORT TO DOMESTIC CIVILIAN LAW ENFORCEMENT AGENCIES

5-43. State National Guard forces frequently support civilian law enforcement during disaster response. Missions include conducting joint patrols with law enforcement officers, securing evacuated neighborhoods, and providing surveillance support. The disruption and confusion associated with a disaster typically cause numerous problems with these missions. Commanders should evaluate the potential for law enforcement mission as part of their unit's initial reconnaissance and provide their assessment to their state joint task force headquarters. Simultaneously, they impress upon their subordinates that they must refrain from law enforcement activities except as authorized.

5-44. Federal military forces, when authorized, may support law enforcement activities in a major disaster or a serious CBRNE incident. Their mission assignments could include providing technical assistance, logistical support, and communications assistance. Indirectly, they support law enforcement by relieving National Guard Soldiers of non-law-enforcement missions, allowing that state's forces to assist with direct law enforcement support. This complementary employment of federal military and state National Guard forces maximizes the effectiveness of military support to law enforcement agencies.

COMMAND AND CONTROL FOR DOMESTIC LAW ENFORCEMENT SUPPORT OPERATIONS

5-45. Domestic law enforcement support requires expert legal advice to leaders at every level. The command staff judge advocate should review plans and orders carefully, even if this delays their release. Plans and orders should identify measures that require legal consultation, command approval, or both. Supporting commanders should plan for additional liaison personnel and communications to the supported law enforcement agency. Commanders ensure their Soldiers know their chain of command and which law enforcement agency they are supporting. Federal military forces and state National Guard forces may operate in proximity although they remain under separate chains of command. On the ground, however, commanders from both forces co-locate so they can coordinate all operations very closely.

INFORMATION AND INTELLIGENCE FOR DOMESTIC LAW ENFORCEMENT SUPPORT OPERATIONS

5-46. When Army units support civilian law enforcement, they must be very careful about the types of units providing assistance, the nature of the assistance, and the capabilities involved. This is particularly important regarding information about civilians. Just as in the military, civilian law enforcement operations rely on information to ensure success of the mission. Civilian law enforcement agencies comply with strict legal limits on information: who provides it, what is collected, how it is collected, and how it can be used. Military forces supporting civilian law enforcement agencies are even more limited. Commanders must ensure laws, military regulatory authorities, and DOD policies are not violated.

5-47. Many intelligence, surveillance, and reconnaissance capabilities can support law enforcement officials during a disaster or CBRNE incident if their use is approved by the Secretary of Defense. For example, robotic systems used to detect explosives in combat operations can serve similar purposes in the aftermath of a domestic incident to assist in search and rescue operations. Few if any civil law enforcement agencies have this sophisticated equipment or the personnel to operate it. Similarly, two of the most important capabilities employed by Soldiers are night vision systems and integrated suites of surveillance systems. Both capabilities become vital in the aftermath of a major disaster, when power grids are damaged. Use of sophisticated night vision capabilities such as forward looking infrared requires approval of the Secretary of Defense. Army aviation, equipped with surveillance systems and flown by night-qualified aviators increases the nighttime capabilities of law enforcement officials significantly. Although remotely piloted aircraft have similar surveillance capabilities, airspace control procedures may limit or prohibit their use (see appendix H). Military forces using intelligence capabilities to support civil law enforcement agencies are subject to different restrictions than for intelligence activities related to combat.

5-48. Employment of intelligence systems domestically remains a sensitive legal area, particularly when used in support of law enforcement agencies. Commanders must understand the differences between *information* and *intelligence* activities. Any nontraditional use of intelligence, surveillance, and reconnaissance capabilities in support of law enforcement requires approval by the Secretary of Defense. Refer to chapter 7 for a more extensive discussion of legal restrictions on military intelligence.

MOVEMENT AND MANEUVER FOR DOMESTIC LAW ENFORCEMENT SUPPORT OPERATIONS

5-49. In any mission that has the potential for lethal force, such as a civil disturbance, commanders should designate a reserve whenever possible. The reserve may be small, even two or three Soldiers, but even a small reserve can become a critical asset when a situation deteriorates. In planning for the reserve, the commander should—

- Provide the reserve with sufficient mobility to move to any area of the operational area quickly. In a civil disturbance environment, the reserve should have wheeled armored vehicles.
- Ensure the reserve has tactical communications and monitors the command network. Position the reserve near the command post, where the reserve leader can monitor the common operational picture.
- Task-organize the reserve to enable it to use lethal force according to the rules for the use of force (refer to chapter 7; see also appendix B of Joint Publication (JP) 3-28).
- Retain the decision to commit the reserve personally.

5-50. Joint patrols involving state National Guard and local law enforcement officers have proven to be a highly effective and efficient use of Soldiers in the aftermath of disasters and disturbances. The typical joint patrol combines a section of three or four Soldiers, a high-mobility multipurpose wheeled vehicle with tactical radios, night vision equipment, and one police officer familiar with the area. The patrol combines mounted and dismounted security activity with presence. The inclusion of the police officer allows for rapid administration of law enforcement and facilitates arrest and detention. It also solves many perplexing intelligence issues. The police normally carry nonlethal weapons, allowing for discriminate application of force. The presence of the Soldiers provides command and control even when emergency traffic overwhelms police communications. The military vehicle provides increased mobility, and the night vision equipment provides the patrol with tactical advantages over looters. As with any law enforcement support, the controlling joint task force coordinates within its higher chain of command for the authority to commit Soldiers to law enforcement support of any type. Small unit commanders should always confirm rules for the use of force through their headquarters before combining Soldiers with police officers. When employing joint patrols, the commander coordinates carefully with the supervising police chief to plan the patrols and ensures that the military patrol leader conducts necessary preparation and coordination with the supported police department before each patrol.

5-51. Generally, only National Guard members are authorized to conduct point patrols in state active duty or Title 32 status. Title 10 members may conduct joint patrols if the Insurrection Act has been implemented or under other exceptions to the Posse Comitatus Act.

PROTECTION FOR DOMESTIC LAW ENFORCEMENT SUPPORT OPERATIONS

5-52. Soldiers assigned to protect critical facilities such as a public utility, transportation nodes, or similar critical infrastructure vital to public health and safety, must understand how to apply the standing rules for the use of force, especially the use of deadly force, to protect that particular facility.

Protective Equipment

5-53. A wide variety of specialized protective equipment enables Soldiers to conduct civil disturbance operations. Personnel protectors provide the individual Soldier with added protection to the sensitive and vital areas of his body. They provide excellent protection for the individual Soldier from trauma often inflicted by thrown objects such as rocks, bricks, sticks, and bottles. Some examples include nonballistic face shields and body shields. Additional protective equipment includes ballistic full-body shields and face shields, leg protectors, and other equipment to protect individuals from small arms fire. Soldiers may carry these items of equipment in lieu of or in combination with the individual ballistic armor based on the situation.

The Use of Force

5-54. Federal military forces supporting law enforcement often have severe restrictions on the use of force. Soldiers in Title 10 status may only use deadly force when all lesser means have failed or cannot reasonably be employed and it is reasonably necessary—

- To protect federal military when the commander reasonably believes a person poses an imminent threat of death or serious bodily harm.
- To protect yourself and other federal military from imminent threat of death or serious bodily harm.
- To protect persons not affiliated with DOD in the vicinity from the imminent threat of death or serious bodily harm, if directly related to the assigned mission.
- To prevent the actual theft or sabotage of assets vital national security or inherently dangerous property.
- To prevent the sabotage of a national critical infrastructure.
- To prevent a serious offense that involves imminent death or serious bodily harm against any person, if directly related to the assigned mission.

5-55. In civil disturbance and other tense situations, commanders take extra precautions concerning the employment of weapons. The preferred means is for company commanders to maintain designated marksmen under their personal control. The marksmen should be trained marksmen armed with precision systems. The marksmen may occupy over-watch positions or remain in reserve at the commander's location. Their orders to engage come from the commander personally; at all other times they observe but do not engage. All other subordinate leaders control their Soldiers and stress that they only employ their weapons in self-defense, to save the life of an innocent citizen, or to protect designated critical infrastructure.

5-56. Commanders should plan for the use of exclusion warnings and barriers around any protected facility. In sharp contrast to combat situations, these markings and barriers should be highly visible and as easily understandable as possible. Units should set up warning signs, entry control points, and crowd control measures intended to prevent any accidental confrontation with security forces. Barrier material, particularly concertina, should be clearly marked and visible at all times. If possible, Soldiers should establish an outer barrier of traffic pylons, police tape, or wooden rails to keep citizens from accidentally injuring themselves on barbed wire. Often a well-informed Soldier posted at a likely primary contact point provides the best means of public control.

Nonlethal Weapons

5-57. Nonlethal weapons provide an effective alternative means of employing force to reduce the probability of death or serious injury to noncombatants and the individual Soldier while still mitigating the threat. Commanders should evaluate the use of nonlethal weapons in domestic operations plans and rules for the use of force. Additionally, commanders should plan for and conduct rehearsals of rules for the use of force to prepare their personnel for operations that may employ nonlethal weapons.

5-58. Nonlethal capability sets provide commanders with flexible options to accomplish mission objectives relating to homeland security and homeland defense. Primarily used by the National Guard reaction forces, the National Guard Bureau nonlethal capability sets include personal protective gear (face shields, body shields, and shin guards), counter personnel equipment (restraints, electronic stun devices, and chemical spray) and training devices like strike pads and simulation cartridges. With 240 total sets distributed to all states and territories, 36 additional sets available from a central source, plus over 380 instructors, the National Guard can provide indirect and direct support to law enforcement agencies across the United States.

5-59. The primary doctrine for Soldiers on the employment of nonlethal weapons tactics during civil disturbance operations is in Field Manual (FM) 3-19.15 and TC 3-19.5. Additional information may be found in FM 3-22.40.

5-60. Commanders must ensure that they and their subordinates understand when and how to employ nonlethal weapons. Nonlethal weapons continue to evolve, and Soldiers must be trained to use them properly. Before employing any new nonlethal weapon, the command staff judge advocate should review all pertinent orders and instructions for its use. Use of nonlethal weapons, like the use of all weapons, will require approval from higher headquarters. Use of riot control agents by Soldiers requires additional authorization from appropriate authorities (state or federal). Soldiers need to understand that all nonlethal weapons are not equal; different classes of weapons require different rules for the use of force. Most nonlethal weapons require approval from higher headquarters, and use of riot control agent by Soldiers must be specifically authorized by the joint task force (state or federal). Soldiers should never use a nonlethal weapon that is still in development.

SUSTAINMENT FOR DOMESTIC LAW ENFORCEMENT SUPPORT OPERATIONS

5-61. Civil disturbance operations may require specialized equipment and munitions, as well as barrier material. The G-4 or S-4 should review the required equipment list and coordinate with the controlling joint task force concerning equipment and ammunition on hand. Additional items may include riot batons, concertina wire and pickets, flexible cuffs, face and body shields, protective mask filters, additional stretchers, portable firefighting equipment, and assorted batteries. Critical infrastructure security missions may require additional supplies, such as marking tape, to delineate the secure area.

5-62. Military departments and defense agencies may make equipment, base facilities, or research facilities available to federal, state, or local civilian law enforcement officials for law enforcement purposes, according to DOD directives. Additionally, DOD personnel can operate, maintain, or assist in operating or maintaining DOD equipment, when the training of persons not affiliated with DOD would be unfeasible or impractical from a cost or time perspective and would not otherwise compromise national security or military preparedness concerns. This must be approved by the Secretary of Defense or a designated representative. (See DODD 5525.5.)

Chapter 6
Provide Other Designated Support

This chapter discusses the fourth primary civil support task—provide other designated support. It describes five types of support that Army forces provide under this task. It provides basic information about how civilian organizations request these types of support.

TYPES OF DESIGNATED SUPPORT

6-1. The Army conducts a range of civil support missions not directly related to disasters; chemical, biological, radiological, nuclear, or high-yield explosives incidents; and civilian law enforcement. In fact, they are hybrid missions, combining aspects of incident response, law enforcement, and public relations, to accomplish different ends. Missions that fall under this task include support for special events, direct support to federal agencies, protection of critical infrastructure, wildland firefighting support, and community support activities.

SUPPORT FOR SPECIAL EVENTS

6-2. Department of Defense (DOD) provides other support as directed for a variety of special events. Events typically requiring federal military support include large recreational or sporting events such the World's Fair, the Super Bowl, the Olympics, or the World Series. Events requiring federal military support also include important political events such as a Presidential inauguration, joint sessions of Congress, or meetings involving world leaders. Certain events receive special status not only because of large crowds, but also because of security requirements for the participants and the threat of civil disturbance. Events such as these are known as "national special security events." National special security events are characterized by political, economic, social, or religious significance that may cause them to become the target of terrorism or other criminal activity. The Department of Homeland Security designates national special security events. The Secretary of Homeland Security establishes a special working group for each event. The working group normally includes representatives from DOD and the National Guard Bureau. The United States Secret Service, as part of Department of Homeland Security, is the primary agency for coordinating support to national special security events. The Secret Service designs and implements the operational security plan. Events in this category normally allow sufficient time for planning. Numerous federal and state agencies may cooperate. Planning for possible transition to disaster support is inherent in these operations. The United States Northern Command (USNORTHCOM) and United States Pacific Command (USPACOM) commanders monitor national special security events in their respective areas of responsibility. If an incident occurs at a national special security event, the Federal Bureau of Investigation leads the law enforcement and criminal investigation efforts, and Federal Emergency Management Agency (FEMA) coordinates incident management.

6-3. State National Guard forces provide other support as directed for civilian law enforcement agencies, national special security events, protecting critical infrastructure, and other activities. The general focus of state National Guard missions is usually on supporting security. Normally, some level of threat or hostility is anticipated. Some general, ongoing planning and preparation may be possible for these types of missions. Normally, mission-specific planning and training will be required once National Guard support has been requested and approved. The supporting state National Guard forces are typically force packages task-organized, trained, and equipped for the mission. The duration of these National Guard missions is typically weeks to months.

6-4. National special security events may combine National Guard, Regular Army, and Army Reserve forces. During the Presidential inauguration of 2009, National Guard, Regular Army, and Army Reserve forces provided both ceremonial and security support. More than 10,000 National Guard troops from numerous states assembled under the command of the District of Columbia adjutant general. All the Regular Army and Army Reserve forces fell under the control of the Joint Task Force–National Capitol Region. The federal military and state National Guard commanders coordinated closely throughout operations. This event is an excellent model of effective parallel command structure for federal military and state National Guard forces working together. Based on this model, Army officers tasked with similar responsibilities should—

- Integrate plans between federal military forces and state National Guard forces as early as possible.
- Establish joint and interagency planning protocols and provide liaison officers to key command centers.
- Establish a mobile reserve large enough to handle contingencies. Position the reserve closely enough that it can respond quickly, yet far enough away that it is not visible to the crowds, or impeded by them.
- Maintain operational security.

6-5. Because a national special security event entails detailed planning, preparation, and execution, there is time to appoint a dual-status commander for the event. In most cases, this will be a senior National Guard officer from the state hosting the event. See chapter 7 for a discussion of dual-status command.

6-6. For other special events, the joint director of military support plans, coordinates, and monitors federal military support according to priorities assigned by the Department of Homeland Security special events working group. DOD focuses on support related to public safety and security, including, but not limited to, physical security, aviation, logistics, communications, joint operations and command centers, and explosive ordnance disposal. Federal military support for special events may be reimbursable or nonreimbursable depending on the type of support provided and the nature of the event.

DIRECT SUPPORT TO FEDERAL AGENCIES

6-7. Certain domestic situations may require contingency military support outside the National Incident Management System framework. In such cases, DOD provides support in response to a request from a federal government agency or at the direction of the President. These incidents fall into three general categories.

6-8. In the first case, the President may direct the Secretary of Defense to augment the federal civilian work force of an agency experiencing labor problems. For example, in 1982, the President used military personnel to replace the striking air traffic controllers. Earlier Presidents used the Army to deliver the mail during postal strikes. This may occur based upon a request from the supported agency, or may be based upon a Presidential decision.

6-9. In the second case, the President may authorize military support to a federal government agency that suddenly expands its responsibilities due to an incident. Examples include support for animal or plant disease eradication, oil and hazardous substance spills, and wildfires. DOD supports the Department of Agriculture for emergencies requiring the containment and eradication of plant or animal diseases. The Environmental Protection Agency and Department of Homeland Security (Coast Guard) have responsibilities related to the National Oil and Hazardous Substances Pollution Contingency Plan (known as the National Contingency Plan and found in Title 40, Part 300, Code of Federal Regulations). DOD contributes support either under the Robert T. Stafford Disaster Relief and Emergency Assistance Act (commonly known as the Stafford Act), or the Economy Act. The response to the oil drilling accident in the Gulf of Mexico in 2010 illustrates such support. In this instance, reimbursement costs were assumed by the owning corporation, while DOD assets supported the clean up. The National Interagency Fire Center, a joint Department of Agriculture and Department of Interior organization, coordinates the federal response to wildfires. DOD provides resources for the containment, control, and extinguishing of wildfires on lands owned by the federal government. (See paragraphs 6-15 to 6-19.)

6-10. The third case involves a sudden mass immigration to the United States. This could result in DOD providing support, when directed, to other federal agencies support such as housing, security, and logistics while the federal government resolves the administrative requirements for migrants to enter the United States. For example, Regular Army and Army Reserve forces provided extensive support to federal authorities during the Mariel Boatlift in 1980. Thousands of Cubans took advantage of Castro's relaxation of his immigration policy to come to the United States. Local authorities were overwhelmed, and the Army provided extensive support to temporarily house, secure, and move the immigrants.

PROTECTION OF CRITICAL INFRASTRUCTURE

6-11. Law enforcement support and protection of critical infrastructure share certain similarities. Both missions require Soldiers to be prepared to use force to protect individuals and facilities. Both require close cooperation with civilian security elements. These missions differ in other respects. Federal military units may be tasked to protect nonmilitary critical infrastructure by the President, and critical military infrastructure by the President or Secretary of Defense. Within the specific limits of their infrastructure protection mission, federal military forces may remove, detain, and use force against individuals that pose a threat to designated facilities without violating the Posse Comitatus act. Any use of force must remain within the rules for the use of force specified for that mission (see chapter 7). National Guard forces under state command may receive a specific protection mission by their governor or may deploy to protect certain facilities in accordance with pre-existing contingency plans when ordered. Certain USNORTHCOM and USPACOM plans require National Guard forces under federal command (Title 10 status) to alert and deploy security elements for either homeland defense or homeland security missions.

6-12. The President has authority to order federal military forces to protect critical infrastructure. This authority is derived from the President's position as the Commander in Chief of the Armed Forces of the United States, under Article II of the Constitution of the United States. The President may direct federal military to protect critical infrastructure in either a homeland security or a homeland defense role. The distinction between these roles is critical for two reasons. First, DOD is the lead federal agency for a homeland defense operation, but not for a homeland security operation. Second, with the exception of defense critical infrastructure protection (functions normally a part of DOD's core mission), DOD participates in homeland security missions only if approved by the Secretary of Defense, consistent with existing legal constraints, and only if they do not negatively affect DOD's primary warfighting missions.

6-13. Normally, the President will provide justification prior to exercising authority under Article II, either by issuing either a national emergency declaration or through executive order. This declaration or order would also trigger the authority the Secretary of Defense, combatant commanders, and on-scene commanders to exercise their authority to protect defense critical infrastructures, assets, and property. Before any federal military forces can use deadly force to protect any infrastructure or asset, the President must designate it as either a "national critical infrastructure" or "asset vital to national security," or an on-scene commander must have designated the property as "inherently dangerous property."

Chapter 6

6-14. Critical infrastructure protection requires careful planning and effective small-unit leadership. The primary consideration is the application of the rules for the use of force. Soldiers with the mission to protect designated public utilities, transportation nodes, or similar critical infrastructure vital to the public health and safety must understand how to apply the rules for the use of force to protect that particular facility. The unit leader should coordinate in detail with the manager of the facility and any security personnel employed at the facility.

WILDLAND FIREFIGHTING SUPPORT

6-15. The federal government manages vast areas of land within the United States. Some of this land is provided for national parks; some is owned and managed by the United States government for wildlife habitat and natural resources. Each state also has an array of parks and resource preserves. Wildfires occur on these lands every year, and federal and state forestry services maintain robust firefighting capabilities to combat them. However, when wildfires exceed civilian firefighting capabilities, the primary agency requests assistance from federal military forces, the National Guard, or both. The types of support vary, but they range from surveillance to air movement of personnel and equipment and may include augmenting firefighting personnel with military units. Military forces support wildland firefighting under the Economy Act.

6-16. The National Interagency Fire Center is located in Boise Idaho. It coordinates the mobilization of national resources for wildland fire and other fire incidents throughout the United States. The National Interagency Fire Center operates and maintains the National Incident Coordination Center. The National Incident Coordination Center dispatches heavy air tankers, lead planes, smokejumpers, hotshot crews, incident management teams, area command teams, medium and heavy helicopters, infrared-equipped aircraft, military resources, telecommunications equipment, remote automated weather stations, and large transport aircraft. Geographic area control centers control manage wildland firefighting within their regions. Figure 6-1 illustrates the geographic area coordination centers with their respective regions.

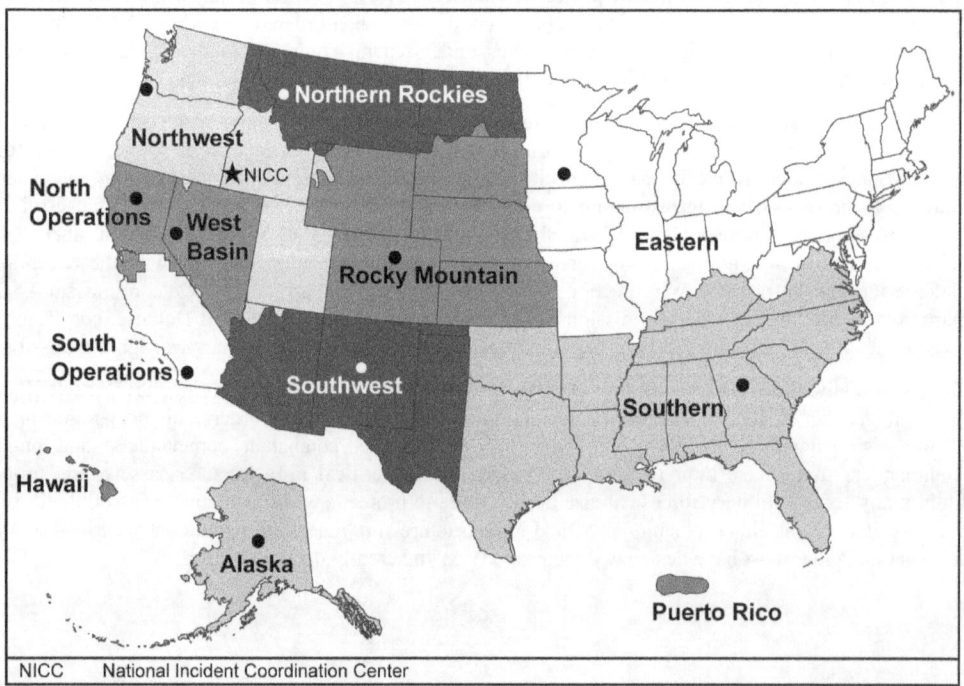

Figure 6-1. Geographic area coordination centers for wildland firefighting

6-17. Wildfire firefighting is a hybrid mission that combines aspects of disaster response with other types of support. It involves response to an incident but also entails specialized planning, training, and command and control. Although military forces remain under the command of their military leadership, civilian professionals direct the tactical employment of supporting military forces. First responders need disciplined manpower they can rapidly convert into large numbers of personnel along the fire line. They also need reserves to fill gaps created when civilian firefighters reach exhaustion.

6-18. Any large wildfire creates a very dangerous environment for neighboring residents and first responders alike. Fighting fires can be lethal, and Soldiers supporting firefighting agencies must receive special training and equipment. The National Interagency Fire Center has developed an intensive training program that prepares Soldiers and leaders for service on the fire lines. The National Interagency Fire Center conducts training in conjunction with joint reception, staging, onward movement, and integration of supporting military units. Commanders need to understand the U.S. Forest Service reorganizes its small units into firefighting teams and places them under the tactical control of an experienced firefighter. The Forest Service also provides equipment, protective garments, and communications as part of the training. It provides communications and life support to all personnel not directly involved in firefighting, such as truck drivers and administrative personnel.

6-19. Force health protection becomes a primary concern of commanders in any wildfire support mission. While the Forest Service can train personnel, it cannot condition them or enforce field discipline. Commanders must stress the role of the small-unit leader in caring for subordinates. Medical personnel need to conduct frequent checks on the health of Soldiers and be prepared to treat heat injuries, burns, and trauma.

COMMUNITY SUPPORT ACTIVITIES

6-20. Commanders take an active interest in their relationships with civilian officials by supporting appropriate community events. They initiate and support activities of common interest and benefit. They establish productive relationships with national, state, and community officials that benefit the Army and civilian communities. Army installation commanders often appoint a community relations committee to review community assistance requests. Such civil support falls outside the definition of DSCA.

6-21. There are limitations on the use of Army forces for community support. Army forces do not compete with resources and services commercially available in the community. Commanders may not authorize military support when local businesses can provide the same or similar support. Army participation in community assistance is never provided for profit. Leaders ensure that no unit realizes a monetary profit, a gratuity, or remuneration in any form unless provided for by public law or regulation.

6-22. Periodic planned community assistance activities can be national missions that focus on developing public support for the Army. They also can be civilian organization or local community missions focused on improving the community, its infrastructure, and quality of life. However, certain programs do not fit neatly into one category or the other. Programs established by DOD or Department of the Army require execution at the installation level. Many require the energy and initiative of the commander to foster successful partnerships to form new partnerships.

6-23. Army aviation units may fly emergency medical evacuation missions to transport civilians to community hospitals. This is similar to immediate response authority, but there are administrative differences. The civilian agency is not required to reimburse DOD. Army aircraft must perform the mission from their home airfield and return upon completion. In other words, the aircrew cannot relocate to another state to support emergency services away from their home base.

REQUESTS FOR OTHER DESIGNATED SUPPORT

6-24. Paragraphs 6-25 to 6-27 discuss how civilian organizations normally request other designated support. Requests may be addressed to National Guard forces of a particular state, to DOD, or to specific installation commanders.

REQUESTS TO THE STATE NATIONAL GUARD

6-25. The requesting civilian organization may contact a state's National Guard directly. All state National Guard headquarters have established processes for community support requests, generally through their public affairs offices. Civilian organizations may search for specific contact information online by entering the name of the state and the words "National Guard" into a search engine.

REQUESTS TO DEPARTMENT OF DEFENSE

6-26. Civilian organizations may submit requests for federal military support, through public affairs channels, to the Office of the Assistant Secretary of Defense for Public Affairs, Attn: Directorate for Community Relations and Public Liaison as Community Relations/Public Affairs Support. Organizations use DD Form 2535 (Request for Military Aerial Support) or DD Form 2536 (Request for Armed Forces Participation in Public Events (Non-Aviation)). Either form can be submitted through Army, Navy, Marine, or Air Force public affairs officers for processing. (See http://www.defense.gov/faq/comment.html for more information.)

REQUESTS TO INSTALLATION COMMANDERS

6-27. Installation commanders may provide support when it meets the requirements of innovative readiness training (under Section 2012, Title 10, United States Code). Innovative readiness also refers to support to a civilian organization that provides training to the military unit involved. Applications are available at http://irt.defense.gov/index.html.

Chapter 7
Legal Considerations

This chapter identifies the primary mission authorities for military forces participating in civil support, with an emphasis on authorities affecting federal military forces. It summarizes the authorities of state governors, the President, the Secretary of Defense, and military commanders to respond to requests for assistance from civil authorities. This chapter also discusses the most common legal issues commanders face when conducting civil support operations—particularly those issues related to rules for the use of force, information and intelligence, isolation and quarantine, and liability.

POWERS OF A STATE GOVERNOR

7-1. Governors serve as commanders in chief of their state National Guard forces and may assume special powers upon the declaration of a disaster, emergency, enemy attack, or riot. The authority of the governor is circumscribed or limited by United States Code (USC) and each state's law and statutes. Although the governors' powers vary from state to state, emergency powers in all states generally include authorities to—

- Suspend statutory and regulatory provisions that otherwise might hinder response to a disaster.
- Require hospitalization for those injured during a disaster.
- Control ingress and egress into the emergency area to direct the evacuation of residents and prescribe transportation routes.
- Provide temporary shelter.
- Commandeer property (with compensation).
- Control or suspend utility services.
- Limit or suspend the sale and possession of alcohol and explosives following a disaster or emergency.

7-2. Governors also issue executive orders declaring "states of emergency" and ensure that state agencies plan for actions in the event of a disaster. Once a disaster occurs, the governor determines how to respond to a local government's request for assistance. If appropriate, the governor declares a state of emergency, activates the state response plan, and may call up the National Guard (under state orders). The governor gives the National Guard its mission(s) and determines when to withdraw National Guard forces. The governor informs the Federal Emergency Management Agency (FEMA) regional director of his or her actions.

AUTHORITIES FOR FEDERAL MILITARY SUPPORT

7-3. The U.S. military has provided support to civil authorities in response to civil emergencies and natural disasters throughout its history. The terminology applied to this function has varied over the years: military assistance or military support to civil authorities, military support of civil defense, and employment of military resources in natural disaster emergencies within the United States. The change in terminology reflects the evolving changes in authorities granted to Department of Defense (DOD) by the President and the Congress.

Chapter 7

AUTHORITIES OF THE PRESIDENT

7-4. Although Article II of the Constitution of the United States and laws passed by Congress provide the primary basis for the present-day authorities of the President, the scope of Presidential authority is much broader. The President possesses inherent authority derived not from specific constitutional provisions or statutes, but from the aggregate of presidential responsibilities as the Nation's Chief Executive, Commander in Chief of the Armed Forces, and the highest law enforcement authority. Supreme Court decisions have held that the President has the inherent authority to preserve order and ensure public health and safety during a national crisis or an emergency, according to the necessities of the situation. This inherent authority empowers the President to act in response to an incident.

7-5. When confronted with a national crisis or emergency where there is no expressed Constitutional or statutory authority, the President can either present the matter to the Congress and wait for legislation that will authorize him or her to act, or take immediate action on the basis of the President's inherent authority when no one other than the President is capable of doing so.

The Robert T. Stafford Disaster Relief and Emergency Assistance Act

7-6. The Robert T. Stafford Disaster Relief and Emergency Assistance Act (known as the Stafford Act) is the primary federal statute giving the President the authority to direct federal agencies to provide assistance to state and local authorities during an incident. The purpose of this assistance is to save lives, alleviate human suffering, protect public health and safety, and lessen or avert the threat of a catastrophe. The Stafford Act allows four ways for the President to provide federal—including military—support to civil authorities. Within these four categories, military support may include aviation, communications, engineering, logistical, medical, public affairs, and other capabilities.

Major Disaster Declaration

7-7. The President may declare a major disaster when an incident is severe enough to necessitate federal assistance to save lives, protect and preserve property, and provide for the public health and safety. The declaration follows a request from the governor of the affected state. The President acts through FEMA to authorize any appropriate federal agency to support state and local authorities.

Emergency Declaration

7-8. In cases where the President does not declare a major disaster, he or she may declare an emergency. This declaration is either before (in anticipation of) or following an incident necessitating federal assistance to save lives, protect property, provide for the public health and safety, and lessen or avert the threat of a catastrophe. The amount of damage either anticipated or actual is less severe than for a major disaster. Again, a request from the governor of the affected state is required. The President, through FEMA, may authorize any federal agency to use personnel, equipment, facilities, and technical and advisory services to support state and local authorities.

The National Emergencies Act

7-9. The National Emergencies Act of 1976 (Sections 1601-1651, Title 50, USC) gives the President broad authorities to respond to emergencies, subject to Congressional regulation of these emergency powers. Under the powers delegated by this statute, the President may seize property, organize and control the means of production, seize commodities, assign military forces aboard, institute martial law, seize and control all transportation and communication, regulate the operation of private enterprise, restrict travel, and, in a variety of ways, control the lives of United States citizens. Moreover, Congress may modify, rescind, or render dormant such delegated emergency authority.

Department of Defense Ten-Day Emergency Work Authority

7-10. The President may direct the Secretary of Defense to send federal military forces on an emergency basis to preserve life and property for a period not to exceed ten days. This DOD ten-day emergency work authority includes removal of debris and wreckage and temporary restoration of essential public facilities and services. It follows a request from a governor for assistance. A Presidential major disaster or emergency declaration is not required. However, the President may issue a declaration following the ten-day period, if additional federal assistance is requested and necessary.

Federal Primary Responsibility Authority

7-11. The President may, without a request for assistance from a governor, unilaterally issue an emergency declaration and send federal assets, including federal military forces, to an area or facility over which the federal government exercises exclusive or primary responsibility by virtue of the Constitution or a federal statute. This may include federal missions, personnel, equipment, and property.

Reimbursement Under The Economy Act And Stafford Act

7-12. Once approved by the Secretary of Defense, federal military forces may perform civil support on a reimbursable basis. The Economy Act of 1932 (Section 1525, Title 31, USC) is the fiscal authority for a federal agency to reimburse DOD for goods and services that agency ordered and DOD rendered (when a more specific statutory authority does not exist). Under the Economy Act, reimbursement may be provided for DOD's total costs.

7-13. If the President issues a major disaster or emergency declaration under the Stafford Act, then the requesting federal agency reimburses DOD for the incremental costs of support provided. Reimbursement policies and procedures differ depending on the authority under which services are performed. Commanders must work closely with their supporting financial management offices to ensure costs are captured and reported appropriately.

AUTHORITY OF THE SECRETARY OF DEFENSE

7-14. The Secretary of Defense, subject to the direction of the President, has the statutory authority to direct and control DOD. The Secretary of Defense also has the statutory authority to issue regulations to manage federal military personnel, property, and facilities. This includes the authority to delegate to subordinate officials the authority vested in the Secretary of Defense. Under these authorities, the Secretary of Defense has issued several DOD directives pertaining to civil support, such as Department of Defense Directives (DODDs) 3025.15 and 3025.1. The Secretary of Defense designated the Assistant Secretary of Defense for Homeland Defense and America's Security Affairs (ASD(HD&ASA)) as the DOD domestic crisis manager, in DODD 5111.13. The ASD(HD&ASA) has policy, planning, advice, and approval authority for civil support operations, except for civil disturbance and chemical, biological, radiological, nuclear, and high-yield explosives incidents, direct support to civilian law enforcement agencies, and the use or potential use of lethal force by federal military forces—which the Secretary of Defense retains.

7-15. The joint director of military support is the action agent for the ASD(HD&ASA) for civil support. Once DOD receives a request for assistance, the joint director of military support evaluates and processes it for the ASD(HD&ASA) and issues an execute order approved by the Secretary of Defense. The joint director of military support also recommends to the Secretary of Defense designation of United States Northern Command (USNORTHCOM) or United States Pacific Command (USPACOM) as the supported commander, depending on the geographic location of the incident.

AUTHORITY OF THE COMBATANT COMMANDER

7-16. The Secretary of Defense has authorized the commanders of USNORTHCOM and USPACOM to provide limited civil support on their own within their respective areas of operation. Specifically, they are authorized to perform the following actions with their assigned and allocated forces and certain aviation, communication, transportation, and medical units:

- Place them on a 24-hour prepare-to-deploy alert for up to seven days.
- Deploy them for up to 60 days, first notifying to the Secretary of Defense and the Chairman of the Joint Chiefs of Staff.
- Employ forces in an emergency after personally approving a request for immediate assistance from a primary federal agency such as FEMA, first notifying the Secretary of Defense and the Chairman of the Joint Chiefs of Staff.

AUTHORITY OF A DUAL-STATUS COMMANDER

7-17. Federal law permits the use of a dual-status military commander to integrate federal and state National Guard forces, reduce duplication of effort, and ensure unity of effort during a national-level (interagency) incident or national special security event. In practice, the authority is used only in pre-planned special events. In most emergencies and disasters, the federal military and state National Guard chains of command remain separate, the former supporting the joint (interagency) field office and the latter the state emergency management authority. In a large, protracted response, particularly one limited in geographic scope to a single state, the President and governor may agree to appoint a dual-status commander. Note that in any extreme emergency, and particularly in case of an external attack on the United States, the President may consolidate all military forces under DOD by federalizing the National Guard and exercising command through USNORTHCOM or USPACOM. This is not dual-status command.

7-18. Under Section 325 of Title 32, USC, a National Guard officer may serve on active duty in a federal status (under Title 10) while retaining his or her National Guard status, if the President authorizes service in both duty statuses, and if the governor of the affected state consents. Under Section 315 of Title 32, USC, the President may approve a Title 10 active duty officer who is detailed to duty with the state National Guard by a Service Secretary to accept a commission from a governor into the state National Guard and serve concurrently in both a federal and nonfederal status. Only the commander is in a dual status; subordinate forces are not.

Note: The dual-status commander may elect to combine or keep separate sections of the staff.

7-19. Four documents are necessary to implement this arrangement:
- Presidential authorization.
- Governor's consent.
- Order by the appropriate Service Secretary bringing the designated dual-status commander onto active duty.
- A memorandum of agreement between the two chains of command.

7-20. A memorandum of agreement must be signed by the governor and the President or their respective designees before a dual-status commander can be established. The purpose of the memorandum of agreement is to avoid future complicating liability determinations and confusion over the application of the Posse Comitatus Act. This memorandum of agreement between the two chains of command should define, at a minimum—

- An agreement that each chain of command will not attempt to issue orders to the dual-status commander that concern forces or missions assigned to the other chain of command.
- Delineation of missions to be performed by forces in each chain of command and that the federal missions will not involve law enforcement duties.

- The military justice authority that can be exercised by the dual-status commander in each of his or her statuses.
- The successor of command authority for each chain of command.
- Rules for the use of force for both chains of command.
- Procedures to resolve any conflicts that may arise.

7-21. A dual-status commander may receive orders from both the federal and state chains of command. However, both chains recognize and respect that the dual-status commander cannot exercise dual authority simultaneously on behalf of two mutually exclusive sovereign governments. Instead, a dual-status commander exercises authority in a completely mutually exclusive manner, (either in a federal or nonfederal status), but never in both statuses at the same time. In other words, a dual-status commander holds a federal hat in one hand and a nonfederal hat in the other hand but can wear only one hat at a time. Figure 7-1 shows an example of a dual-status command structure.

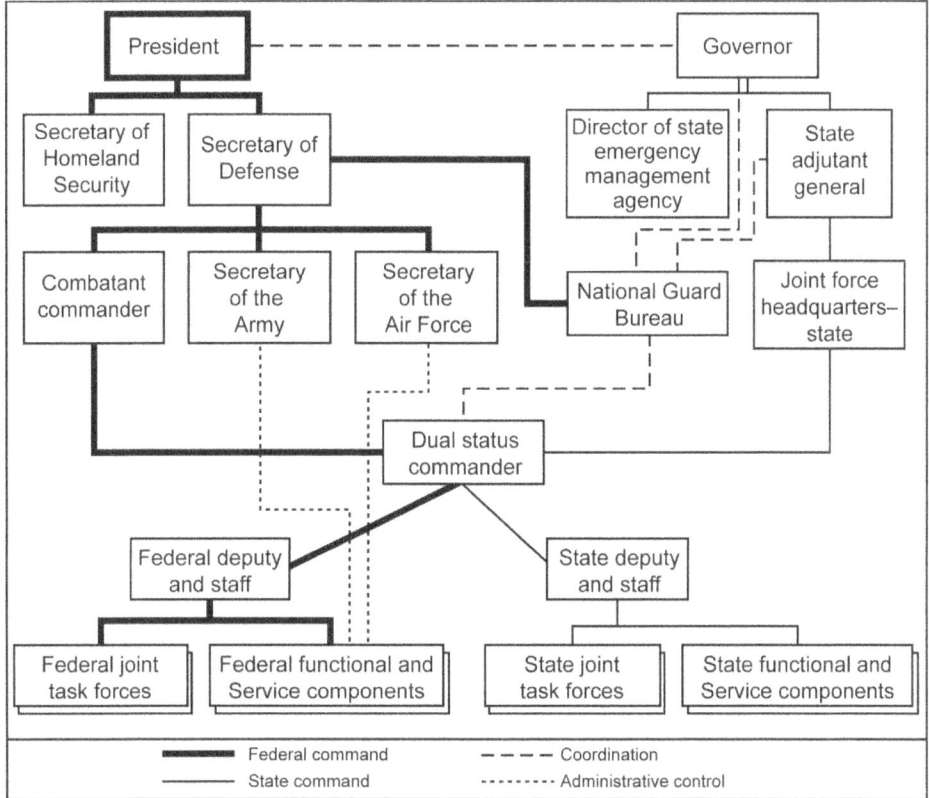

Figure 7-1. An example of a dual-status command

7-22. When in a federal status, the dual-status commander takes orders from the President or those officers the President and the Secretary of Defense have ordered to act on their behalf, and may issue orders to federal forces under his or her command. When in a nonfederal status, the dual-status commander takes orders from the governor through the adjutant general of the state and may issue orders only to National Guard Soldiers serving in a nonfederal (Title 32 or state active duty) status under his or her command.

THE POSSE COMITATUS ACT

7-23. The Constitution does not explicitly bar the use of military forces in civilian situations or in matters of law enforcement, but the United States has traditionally refrained from employing troops to enforce the law except in cases of necessity. The Posse Comitatus Act (Section 1385, Title 18, USC) punishes those who, "except in cases and under circumstances expressly authorized by the Constitution or Act of Congress, willfully use any part of the Army or the Air Force as a *posse comitatus* or otherwise to execute the laws...." Questions arise most often in the context of assistance to civilian law enforcement agencies. In this context, courts have held that, absent a recognized exception, the Posse Comitatus Act is violated (1) when civilian law enforcement officials make "direct active use" of military investigators, (2) when the military "pervades the activities" of civilian officials, or (3) when the military is used so as to subject citizens to the exercise of military power that is "regulatory, prescriptive, or compulsory in nature." The Act applies by regulation to the Navy and Marines. It does not prohibit activities conducted for a military purpose (base security or enforcement of military discipline) that incidentally benefit civilian law enforcement bodies. The Act does not apply to the state forces, but state law may impose similar restrictions.

7-24. Congress has provided for a number of statutory exceptions to the Posse Comitatus Act by explicitly vesting law enforcement authority either directly in a military branch (the Coast Guard) or indirectly by authorizing the President or another government agency to call for assistance in enforcing certain laws. There are several exceptions to the Posse Comitatus Act, including those under—
- The Prohibited Transaction Involving Nuclear Materials statute.
- The Insurrection Act.
- The Emergency Situations Involving Chemical or Biological Weapons of Mass Destruction statute.

7-25. Under the Prohibited Transaction Involving Nuclear Materials statute (Section 831, Title 18, USC), if the Attorney General and the Secretary of Defense jointly determine that the Nation faces an emergency, the Secretary of Defense may authorize federal military forces to provide direct support to civilian authorities to protect nuclear materials.

7-26. Section 333 of Title 10, USC (found in chapter 15, *Insurrection*), referred to the Insurrection Act, governs the President's ability to deploy federal military forces and federalized National Guard forces within the United States to put down lawlessness, insurrection, and rebellion with or without the consent of the governor depending on the situation. The Insurrection Act is discussed further in paragraphs 7-28 to 7-29.

7-27. Under the Emergency Situations Involving Chemical or Biological Weapons of Mass Destruction statute, (Section 382, Title 10, USC) if the Attorney General and the Secretary of Defense jointly determine that the Nation faces an emergency involving an attack using chemical, biological, radiological, or high-yield explosives, the Secretary of Defense may provide resources and personnel to assist civil authorities regarding the enforcement of this statute.

7-28. Although not an exception to the prohibition against direct engagement in the execution of the law, federal military forces may assist state and local civilian law enforcement agencies within limits. Federal law allows federal military forces to provide "indirect" support to federal, state, and local civilian law enforcement agencies. This includes passing information relevant to a violation of federal or state laws; providing equipment, supplies, spare parts, and facilities; supplying sensors, protective clothing, antidotes, or other supplies appropriate for use in responding to a chemical or biological incident; training in the operation and maintenance of equipment; giving expert advice; and allowing personnel to maintain and operate certain detection and communications equipment. The Secretary of Defense or a designee exercises approval authority for this level of support.

FEDERAL MILITARY FORCES AND CIVIL DISTURBANCE

7-29. Congress has delegated authority to the President to call up federal military forces during an insurrection or civil disturbance. The Insurrection Act authorizes the President to use federal military forces within the United States to restore order or enforce federal law after a major public emergency when requested by the state governor or when the President determines that the authorities of the state are incapable of maintaining public order. The President normally executes this authority by first issuing a proclamation ordering the dispersal of those obstructing the enforcement of the laws. The President may act unilaterally to suppress an insurrection or domestic violation against the authority of the United States without the request or authority of the state governor.

7-30. The Insurrection Act has been used to send the Armed Forces to quell civil disturbances a number of times during U.S. history, most recently during the 1992 Los Angeles riots and during Hurricane Hugo in 1989, during which widespread looting was in reported in Saint Croix, Virgin Islands. During the civil rights movement, a few governors of southern states attempted to defy federal law and court orders, necessitating action by the President under the Insurrection Act. In 1957, President Eisenhower federalized the Arkansas National Guard at Central High School in Little Rock. In 1962, President Kennedy invoked the Act when rioting broke out at the University of Mississippi in Oxford upon the admission of a black student. It was again invoked by President Kennedy on June 11, 1963, and September 10, 1963, to enforce court decrees opening public schools to blacks in the state of Alabama. The statue was also invoked by President Lyndon Johnson as a preemptive measure in 1965 to federalize National Guardsmen and deploy federal military forces when state officials in Alabama refused to protect participants during a civil rights march.

MOBILIZATION OF THE RESERVE COMPONENT

7-31. When the President declares a major disaster or emergency under the Stafford Act, the Reserve Component may support the relief effort. Under Section 12304 of Title 10, USC, the President has the authority to involuntarily call-up no more than 200,000 members of the Selected Reserve. There are specific limitations on mobilization of Army Reserve Units and National Guard for civil support. This authority cannot be used for any civil disturbance or a domestic incident, except to respond to an emergency involving a weapon of mass destruction, a terrorist attack, or a threatened terrorist attack in the United States that results or could result in significant loss of life or property. Thus, the President may use this statutory authority to federalize and deploy the National Guard civil support teams of several states in the event of a chemical, biological, radiological, nuclear, or high-yield explosives incident in another state.

> Note: Section 12304(c) of Title 10, USC restricts the involuntary call up of Reserve Components. They may not be used under this authority for disaster response or to repress rebellions. The latter situation requires Insurrection Act authority.

7-32. Soldiers on inactive duty for training (battle assembly) or annual training may be available to perform a civil support mission and may support relief operations during these training periods, subject to the approval of the Secretary of Defense or under immediate response authority. Under Section 10147(a)(2) of Title 10, USC, an Army Reserve unit's annual training may be extended, upon the approval of United States Army Reserve Command, to continue to perform civil support operations for up to 29 days (including travel time).

RULES FOR THE USE OF FORCE

7-33. Soldiers deployed to a combat zone overseas follow rules of engagement established by the Secretary of Defense and adjusted for theater conditions by the joint force commander. Within the United States and its territories, Soldiers adhere to rules for the use of force. There are many similarities between them, for example in the inherent right of self-defense, but they differ in intent. Rules of engagement are by nature permissive measures intended to allow the maximum use of destructive combat power appropriate for the mission. Rules for the use of force are restrictive measures intended to allow only the minimum force necessary to accomplish the mission. The underlying principle is a "continuum of force," a carefully graduated level of response determined by civilians' behavior. The application of rules for the use of force also differs somewhat between National Guard forces and federal military forces. Figure 7-2, page 7-8, illustrates the continuum of force and the graduated response required of Soldiers. Civilian behavior, on the left, rises from cooperative (behaves as ordered by the Soldier) to potentially lethal. The corresponding military response is on the right.

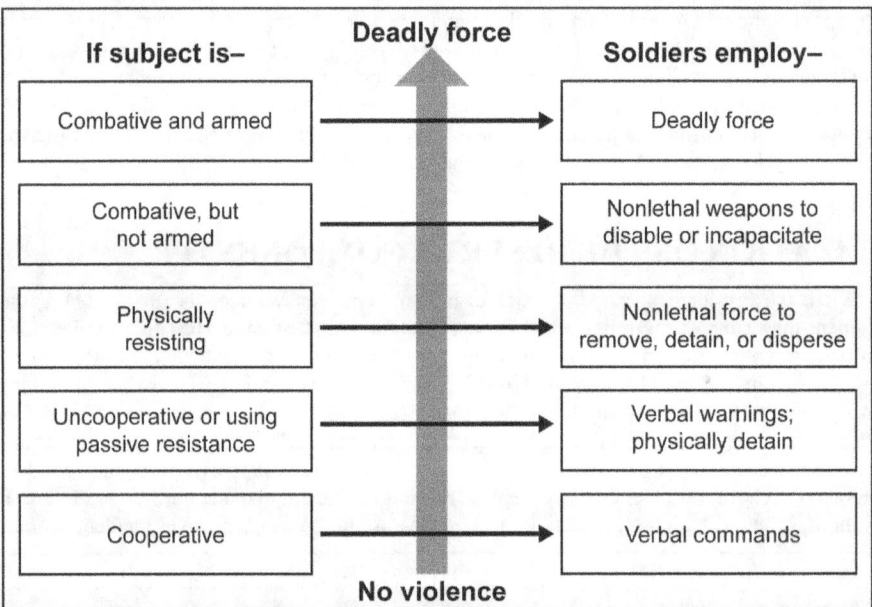

Figure 7-2. Illustration of the continuum of force

7-34. When deployed, both National Guard and Regular Army forces will encounter situations where Soldiers and small-unit leaders will have to know and adhere to the rules for the use of force. Therefore, leaders at every level review the rules for the use of force with their subordinates as part of their pre-mission inspections and confirm that the Soldiers know the rules. Commanders should obtain and issue a rules-for-the-use-of-force summary card to each Soldier before deploying from home station, and the small unit leaders should inspect to ensure that the Soldiers have it. The potentially confusing situations associated with infrastructure and property protection require particular attention from commanders. The Soldiers securing a facility or area must understand the rules for the use of force as they apply to that specific location. Above all, the unit leader must understand if, when, and how he or she may use lethal force to protect the facility.

FEDERAL MILITARY FORCES AND STANDING RULES FOR THE USE OF FORCE

7-35. All federal military forces involved in civil support must follow the *standing rules for the use of force* (SRUF) specified in a classified Chairman of the Joint Chiefs of Staff Instruction (CJCSI). Appendix B of Joint Publication (JP) 3-28 provides more information. See also the current Chairman of the Joint Chiefs of Staff standing execute order for DSCA, referred to as the CJCS DSCA EXORD. The Secretary of Defense approves SRUF, and the supported combatant commander incorporates them into plans and orders for various civil support missions. The SRUF also apply to federal military forces performing a homeland defense mission on land within U.S. territory. They apply to federal forces, civilians, and contractors performing law enforcement and security duties at all federal military installations (and off-installation, while conducting official DOD security functions), unless otherwise modified by the Secretary of Defense. This includes protection of critical U.S. infrastructure both on and off federal military installations, federal military support during a civil disturbance, and federal military cooperation with federal, state, and local civilian law enforcement agencies.

7-36. Before employment in civil support, all Soldiers require training on the appropriate rules for the use of force. Training focuses upon the particular rules for the use of force in the operation plan issued by the gaining joint force commander, but in the absence of the plan commanders should train according to the SRUF. Commanders should include a staff judge advocate to assist with leader training. SRUF cards should be issued to each person during training and personnel should not deploy until they are trained in SRUF. Supported combatant commanders submit a request for mission-specific rules for the use of force to the Chairman of the Joint Chiefs of Staff, for approval by the Secretary of Defense. Unit commanders may further restrict mission-specific rules for the use of force approved by the Secretary of Defense, but may not make them more permissive. Unit commanders notify their chain of command up through the Secretary of Defense of any additional restrictions (at all levels) they place on approved rules for the use of force. In time-critical situations, notification to the Secretary of Defense occurs concurrently with notification to the Chairman of the Joint Chiefs of Staff.

NATIONAL GUARD FORCES AND STATE RULES FOR THE USE OF FORCE

7-37. State law governs rules for the use of force for National Guard forces in a state active duty status. As such, each state must take into account its own specific criminal laws when drafting rules for the use of force. As an example, in the case of the airport security mission conducted by the National Guard following the September 11, 2001 terrorist attacks, there were over 50 different rules for the use of force used by the various states and territories conducting the mission. Although virtually identical, all of these rules for the use of force addressed similar subjects, the specific implementation of these subject areas varied from state to state because of their differing state and territory legal foundations.

7-38. Note that states that provide National Guard forces in state active duty or Title 32 duty status to another state normally will adopt the rules for the use of force of the supported state for those forces while they deployed. The states involved will normally specify in their memorandum of agreement on the rules for the use of force the forces will follow before deployment. As an example, states worked through this process with Louisiana, Texas, and Mississippi following Hurricanes Katrina and Rita.

7-39. Note also that there is no single term used to describe state rules for the use of force. Each state uses a different term. States may refer to them as rules of engagement, rules for the use of force, rules on the use of force, and rules of interaction. "State rules for the use of force," as used in this field manual, is a generic term intended to refer to rules of the fifty-four National Guards based on the criminal laws of the individual states or territories. Each state prepares and issues a reference card for its rules for the use of force. Figure 7-3, page 7-10, illustrates the type of card that a Guardsman might carry.

Chapter 7

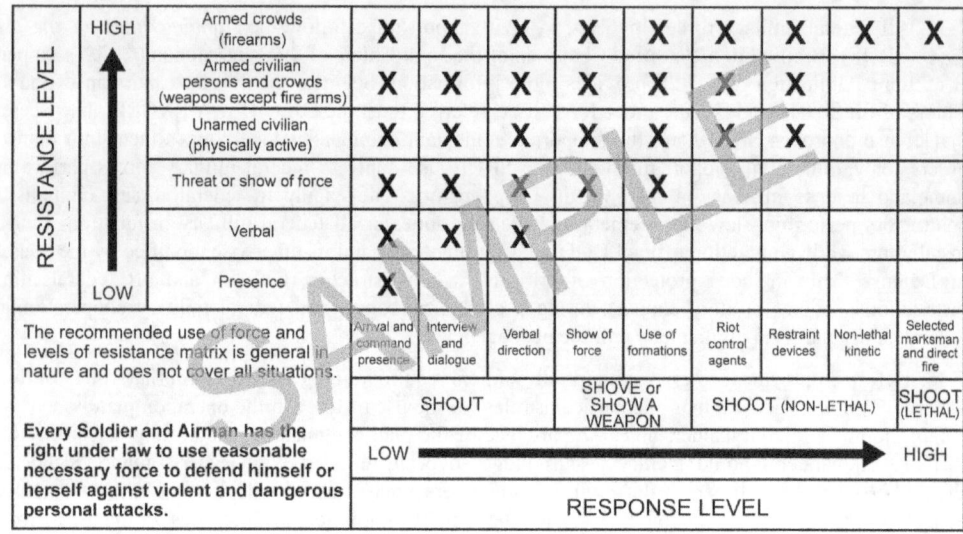

Figure 7-3. Sample rules for the use of force card carried by National Guard forces

INTELLIGENCE RULES AND RESTRICTIONS

7-40. Intelligence oversight refers to the law and regulations that balance the Constitutional right of individuals to privacy with the need for the federal government to collect intelligence for national security purposes. Commanders need to understand that DOD directives and Service regulations restrict the military from collecting or possessing information on U.S. citizens, whether individuals and groups. Because of the difficulty of determining an individual's legal status, DOD imposes restrictions on collection and storage of any civilian personal indentifying information, or information on groups of citizens that make up a civilian organization (such as a church congregation or parish). This restricts Army units under federal military command from collecting or retaining information that identifies individuals with businesses, voluntary organizations, or civilian agencies, except as authorized by DOD directives and regulations. The following individuals and groups are protected by intelligence oversight rules:

- U.S. citizens.
- Lawful permanent resident aliens.
- Unincorporated associations substantially composed of U.S. citizens or permanent resident aliens.
- Corporations incorporated in the United States, except for those directed and controlled by a foreign government.

7-41. Seven documents contain the core legal authorities for intelligence oversight:

- Constitution of the United States.
- Executive Order 12333 (1981).
- National Security Act of 1947.
- Foreign Intelligence Surveillance Act of 1978 (Public law 95-511).
- DODD 5240.01.
- DOD Publication 5240.1-R.
- Army Regulation (AR) 381-10.

The restrictions put in place by intelligence oversight directly affect specific Army elements and organizations conducting authorized intelligence activities.

7-42. Although units limit incident awareness and assessment operations in order to safeguard the rights of U.S. citizens, they may receive and retain intelligence concerning foreign intelligence and counter-intelligence. Commanders and intelligence personnel require further authorization, however, to continue to retain information if a foreign group or noncitizen is within the United States. The best practice for commanders is to limit intelligence capabilities to supporting situational awareness, assessment, and force protection unless they have a specified task to support civilian law enforcement agencies or national intelligence requirements.

7-43. Collection, retention, and further dissemination of law-enforcement-derived information and intelligence are permissible only according to DODD 5200.27, paragraphs 3, 4, and 5. For example, local police may know that a violent gang is active in a neighborhood affected in a disaster. The police may provide the Army unit with information on known locations used by the gang, peculiar paraphernalia associated with that gang, and the types of weapons and vehicles used by the gang members. Army units may only retain this information if there is a clear foreign intelligence or counterintelligence relationship or nexus. Military police or force protection units may only retain this information if these gangs constitute a direct and articulable threat to DOD missions, personnel, or resources, according to DODD 5200.27, paragraphs 3, 4, and 5. Civilian police may ask Soldiers to report any gang activity they observe through their chain of command to the police, although this information may only be acquired incidentally since federal military personnel may not directly assist civilian police in developing criminal information. Such information may be reported by Army intelligence or military police and force protection units according to DODD 5525.5; DOD Publication 5240.1-R, Procedure 12; and DODD 5200.27, paragraphs 3, 4, and 5. The unit may retain law enforcement intelligence provided by the police only according to DODD 5525.5; DOD Publication 5240.1-R, Procedure 3; and DODD 5200.27; and log any information provided to the police under intelligence oversight or other sensitive information program standards, as long as no specifically identifying information is retained regarding the United States persons collected on. Before any further dissemination, the staff should confirm with the staff judge advocate that they could distribute the information to subordinate units.

7-44. Airborne sensors and unmanned aircraft systems pose particular challenges for intelligence oversight. These systems provide commanders and civil authorities with powerful tools to help them assess the situation on the ground, particularly in the initial stages of response. However, information gathered by these systems can conflict with the intelligence oversight restrictions. For example, an Army helicopter equipped with forward looking infrared may be tasked to assess the stability of flood control constructed earlier in the day. During the course of the surveillance mission, the aircrew may spot a group of looters near the flooding. They may legally report this to their chain of command, without identifying the looters, according to DOD Publication 5240.1-R, Procedure 12. No identifying United States personal information may be retained by the Army unit. According to DOD Publication 5240.1-R, Procedure 3, information of this nature may be incidentally retained for this purpose of relaying it to civilian law enforcement, after which time it must be destroyed, not later than 90 days after acquisition.

7-45. Airborne support for incident awareness and assessment traditionally required specific Secretary of Defense approval on a case-by-case basis. In order to clarify the types of airborne support authorized, the CJCS DSCA EXORD contains pre-approved incident awareness and assessment support modules. Even though pre-approved, use of the capabilities for any purpose other than that specified in the CJCS DSCA EXORD requires specific Secretary of Defense approval. The 14 August 2009 CJCS DSCA EXORD contains the following incident awareness and assessment support modules:

- Situational Awareness Module.
- Damage Assessment Module.
- Evacuation Monitoring Module.
- Search and Rescue Module.
- Dynamic Ground Coordination Team.
- Hydrographic Survey Module.
- Chemical, Biological, Radiological, Nuclear, and High-Yield Explosives Assessment Module.

Chapter 7

SENSITIVE INFORMATION

7-46. Any information acquired on individual citizens and specific civilian organizations by military intelligence personnel and capabilities or by DOD law enforcement, antiterrorism, or force protection personnel is extremely sensitive. Its collection must be authorized, and all information collected must be provided directly to the supported law enforcement agency unless separate exceptions permit retention by DOD. Otherwise, the military unit may not retain this information. If commanders determine or suspect that these prohibitions have been violated, they report the violation in accordance with DOD Publication 5240.1-R, Procedure 15, for G-2 and intelligence violations; and according to DODD 5200.27 for improper collection activities by provost marshal, antiterrorism, or force protection personnel. DODD 5525.5, and Enclosure 2; DOD Publication 5240.1-R, and DODD 5200.27 govern the release of sensitive information. Any waivers or exceptions to these restrictions may only be granted by Secretary of Defense or the Secretary of the Army.

7-47. Sensitive information includes criminal intelligence generated by civilian law enforcement agencies and passed to military units involved in civil support. Similarly, it includes information and reports from Soldiers who witness what they believe to be criminal activity. Army forces may assist civilian and military law enforcement agencies through the dissemination of incidentally acquired information reasonably believed to reveal violations of federal, state or local law. Support must be consistent with DOD Publication 5240.1-R and DODD 5200.27, which provides the following guidance:

> *Operations Related to Civil Disturbance. The Attorney General is the chief civilian officer in charge of coordinating all Federal Government activities relating to civil disturbances. Upon specific prior authorization of the Secretary of Defense or his designee, information may be acquired that is essential to meet operational requirements flowing from the mission as to DOD to assist civil authorities in dealing with civil disturbances. Such authorization will only be granted when there is a distinct threat of a civil disturbance exceeding the law enforcement capabilities of State and local authorities.*
>
> DODD 5200.27

7-48. Military forces handle information developed by civilian law enforcement agencies regarding persons not affiliated with DOD during civil support operations according to DODD 5200.27 and AR 380-13. Most of this information is law-enforcement derived. DOD policy limits collecting, reporting, processing, or storing law-enforcement-derived information on individuals or organizations not affiliated with DOD. Chapter 6 provides additional information for handling intelligence and information related to citizens. This is a major difference between stability and civil support operations. These directives and regulations ensure compliance with various laws intended to protect the rights of citizens and restrict military intelligence collection to external threats. Although not discussed here, similar restrictions limit the activities of National Guard forces operating in either state active duty or Title 32 duty status. Each state and territory has specific instructions governing the collection and processing of information on U.S. citizens, legal aliens, and illegal aliens. In general, these are not as restrictive as DODDs and Service regulations applicable to federal military forces. The adjutant general of the state works with the state attorney general to clarify instructions pertaining to National Guard civil support.

7-49. There are legal restrictions on using information about individuals and organizations physically located within the United States and its possessions unless they are part of DOD (military, civilian, or contractor). The core regulations pertaining to these restrictions are DODD 5200.27 and AR 380-13. The restrictions on the use of law enforcement information govern the activities of all members of DOD (uniformed members and civilians). Like intelligence oversight program objectives, these restrictions are designed to ensure that the rights of, and information on, individuals or organizations not affiliated with DOD are protected unless such information is essential to the accomplishment of specified DOD missions. Any information collected on people not affiliated with DOD must pertain only to the protection of DOD functions and property, personnel security, or operations related to civil disturbance. Seven specific prohibitions regarding information acquisition are that—

- Information acquired on individuals or organizations not affiliated with DOD may be restricted to that which is essential to the accomplishment of assigned DOD missions.
- No information shall be acquired about a person or organization solely because he or she lawfully advocates measures in opposition to government policy.
- Physical or electronic surveillance of federal, state, or local officials or of candidates for such offices is prohibited.
- Electronic surveillance of any individual or organization is prohibited, except as otherwise authorized by law (such as, by warrant).
- Covert or otherwise deceptive surveillance or penetration of civilian organizations is strictly prohibited, unless specifically authorized by the Secretary of Defense (or designee).
- Absolutely no computerized data banks shall be maintained relating to individuals or organizations not affiliated with DOD, unless specifically authorized by the Secretary of Defense (or designee).
- No DOD personnel shall be assigned to attend public or private meetings, demonstrations, or other similar activities for the purpose of acquiring information, without specific prior approval by the Secretary of Defense (or designee).

However, an exception to the seventh item listed above may be made by the local commander concerned, or higher authority, when, in his or her judgment, the threat is direct and immediate and time precludes obtaining prior approval. In each such case a report is made immediately to the Secretary of Defense (or designee). (While permissible according to DODD 5200.27, paragraph 5.6, this is not recommended as it places the commander at great legal risk.)

SHARING INFORMATION

7-50. Because of these restrictions, commanders should ensure intelligence and sensitive information is not only lawfully collected or acquired, but is also is lawfully retained and disseminated. DOD operates under the common Congressional mandate to ensure all agencies, including DOD, share homeland security and homeland defense information and intelligence with the proper authorities to identify threats rapidly and effectively. However, the process requires careful compliance with existing laws and regulations. The key is to understand these requirements, their inherent complexities, and the requirement to protect civil rights. Because information acquired during civil support missions often refers to persons not affiliated with DOD, commanders should require their subordinates to segregate and label electronic and paper files generated during a civil support mission. This facilitates efficient disposal of all information on persons and organizations not affiliated with DOD following return to home station.

7-51. At the conclusion of any civil support mission, commanders should direct their subordinates to inspect printed and electronically stored information acquired during the operation. There is a 90-day window for disposal of sensitive information related to U.S. citizens not affiliated with DOD (measured from the time of acquisition). DODD 5200.27 states—

> *Information within the purview of this Directive, regardless of when acquired, shall be destroyed within 90 days unless its retention is required by law or unless its retention is specifically authorized under criteria established by the Secretary of Defense, or his designee.*

DODD 5200.27

All staff sections and subordinate units should inspect their paper and electronic archives. The purpose of this inspection is to ensure that the unit has not inadvertently retained personal information on any citizen or civilian organization. In general, units should only retain operational records and documents related to expenditures. They should delete or destroy any information containing civilian names, phone numbers, addresses, or any other personal identifying information, even if acquired incidental to the mission (such as from an aircraft manifest). Information on U.S. persons not affiliated with DOD contained in intelligence files, databases, and repositories is retained in accordance with disposition criteria in AR 25–400–2.

Information about U.S. persons deleted from user electronic files, but remaining on servers or archived files, may remain until systems administrators purge or retire them in accordance with systems maintenance policies, AR 25–400–2, or Archivist of the United States disposition instructions.

7-52. In combat, many units reconfigure command post configurations and processes to create a "fusion center" for different types of intelligence, particularly in a counterinsurgency mission. Any information received from a variety of sources is funneled to the fusion center where it is analyzed and used in data bases. While a powerful tool in combat situations, units engaged in civil support operations should not use a fusion center to combine operational information with any sensitive information, including criminal intelligence or law enforcement information. "Fusing" information using combat intelligence techniques and procedures with information received from civilian police authorities on United States persons or persons not affiliated with DOD will invariably lead to violations of intelligence oversight and sensitive information restrictions. In a civil support operation, commanders and their staffs segregate any sensitive information into appropriate law enforcement channels and keep it there.

ISOLATION AND QUARANTINE AUTHORITIES

7-53. *Isolation* refers to the separation and the restriction of movement of people who have an infectious illness from healthy people to stop the spread of that illness. *Quarantine* refers to the separation and restriction of movement of people who are not yet ill but have been exposed to an infectious agent and are therefore potentially infectious. A geographical quarantine, known as a "cordon sanitaire," is a sanitary barrier erected around an area. Both isolation and quarantine may be conducted on a voluntary basis or compelled on a mandatory basis through legal authority.

7-54. The federal government has the authority to prevent the spread of disease into the United States (foreign) or between states and territories (interstate). The Department of Health and Human Services is the lead federal agency for isolation and quarantine. The Secretary of Health and Human Services has delegated to the Director of the Centers for Disease Control and Prevention the authority to determine whether measures taken by health authorities of any state are insufficient to prevent the spread of any communicable diseases from that state to another state. The Director of the Centers for Disease Control and Prevention may take measures to prevent the spread of the disease interstate as he or she deems reasonably necessary.

7-55. The Secretary of Health and Human Services is authorized to accept from state and local authorities any assistance in the enforcement of federal quarantine regulations that those authorities are able and willing to provide. The Secretary of Health and Human Services shall cooperate with and aid States in the enforcement of their quarantine and other health regulations. At the request of state authorities, the Secretary of Health and Human Services may extend temporary assistance not to exceed six months to a state in meeting health emergencies of a nature warranting federal assistance. The Secretary of Health and Human Services may require reimbursement for any assistance provided as he may determine to be reasonable under the circumstances.

7-56. Apprehension, detention, examination, isolation and quarantine by federal civil authorities are authorized for a period of time and in such a manner as may be reasonably necessary, but only for those "communicable" diseases that are set forth in executive orders issued from time to time by the President. The current order's (E.O. 13295 as amended by E.O. 13375) list includes cholera, diphtheria, infectious tuberculosis, influenza caused by novel or re-emergent influenza viruses, plague, severe acute respiratory syndrome, smallpox, yellow fever, and viral hemorrhagic fevers.

7-57. Only one federal statute permits federal military forces to enforce quarantine laws, under very narrow circumstances. Section 97 of Title 42, USC, allows military commanders of any coastal fort or station to assist in the execution of state quarantines with respect to vessels arriving in or bound for the United States. Otherwise, there have been several legislative proposals to expand this enforcement authority to other situations, but Congress has always refused to consider them. Consequently, absent a Presidential decision under inherent authority or an exception to the Posse Comitatus Act (see chapter 7), federal military forces cannot be used to enforce quarantine or isolation.

7-58. Under Title 7, USC, the Secretary of Agriculture, to protect the agriculture, environment, economy, and health and welfare of the population by preventing, detecting, controlling, and eradicating diseases and pests of animals, is authorized to cooperate with foreign countries, states, and other jurisdictions, or other persons, to prevent, regulate, and eliminate burdens on interstate commerce and foreign commerce. When federal military support is requested, it is provided under the Economy Act.

PERSONAL LIABILITY

7-59. Federal military personnel are immune from personal liability if they cause death, injury, or property damage as a result of their negligent acts (not intentional misconduct) while carrying out duties under the Stafford Act or within the scope of employment under the Federal Tort Claims Act (Sections 1346(b) and 2671 through 2680 of Title 28, USC), respectively. As long as they are performing defense support of civil authorities under a valid mission authority, they are protected. If a negligent act causing the death, injury, or property damage was committed outside the scope of their duty or employment, a Soldier or civilian employee may face personal liability, criminal prosecution, or both.

7-60. In conclusion, civil support is governed by different laws and regulations than military operations conducted in foreign counties against a hostile force Legal issues will often arise and necessitate timely legal advice throughout the civil support operation. The character of the Constitution and laws enacted by successive Congresses create a complicated legal environment. Commanders should note that this chapter only provides a summary; this discussion is not a comprehensive review of every requirement and restriction. Commanders should always consult a staff judge advocate for legal advice.

This page intentionally left blank.

Chapter 8

Sustainment—Logistics and Personnel Services

This chapter begins by defining the sustainment warfighting function, including its three major subfunctions. This chapter discusses the first two subfunctions of the sustainment warfighting function—logistics and personnel services—in relation to civil support operations. This discussion builds on the doctrine in chapters 1, 2, and 3. Chapter 9 continues the discussion of the sustainment warfighting function with the third subfunction—health service support.

THE SUSTAINMENT WARFIGHTING FUNCTION

8-1. Army doctrine defines the *sustainment warfighting function* as the related tasks and systems that provide support and services to ensure freedom of action, extend operational reach, and prolong endurance (FM 3-0). The sustainment warfighting function includes logistics, personnel services, and health service support. Sustainment often determines the degree of success units conducting civil support can achieve. Effective sustainment, especially logistics, allows units to move into the operational area rapidly and commence operations quickly. *Logistics* is planning and executing the movement and support of forces. It includes those aspects of military operations that deal with: a. design and development, acquisition, storage, movement, distribution, maintenance, evacuation, and disposition of materiel; b. movement, evacuation, and hospitalization of personnel; c. acquisition or construction, maintenance, operation, and disposition of facilities; and d. acquisition or furnishing of services (Joint Publication (JP) 4-0). Personnel services are related to Soldiers' welfare, readiness, and quality of life.

LOGISTICS COORDINATION FOR CIVIL SUPPORT OPERATIONS

8-2. The principal logistics function of the military during disaster response is to move, maintain and secure logistical capabilities necessary for the response effort. The characteristics of the operational area must be taken into consideration by all levels of command in order to properly assist with the response effort and support military personnel. The military must be dependable in their ability to respond and provide assistance in the most austere and damaged environments. The unit will deploy with basic sustainment (food, water, and fuel), and coordinate with the higher headquarters for resupply. As the situation improves, contracted support plays a greater role within the affected area. The capability of the civilian population to provide for logistics decreases or eliminates the military requirement. In other missions, the supported state or federal agency may provide the full range of support, with easy access to amenities and rapid response to requirements. This might be the case during planned support to law enforcement agencies. The Army possesses significant logistical capability and is able to respond with its organic assets to assist civil support operations. Additionally, the Army is able to leverage other component and Service installations in order to support operations. Logistics capabilities determine to a significant extent the flexibility that the commander has to complete mission assignments quickly and accept other missions. The ground and rotary wing distribution capability of Army forces is often critical to alleviate suffering within the operational area.

8-3. Army units are expected to be self-sustaining during any civil support operations and individual units should deploy with their sustainment requirements for the initial phase of operations, usually 72 hours, unless prior coordination has been made and is in place. Units should arrive at the location of an incident with enough sustainment to conduct operations for at least 72 hours. This eases the sustainment requirements on the gaining headquarters during any rapid response situation. After the 72 hours, Army units must utilize the unit supply system, government purchase card or military contracting officers in order

Chapter 8

to provide sustained internal support that incorporates all classes of supply. Except in rare circumstances, the need for Class V (ammunition) is not required. Any deployment order will specify whether or not ammunition is required for the specific mission. Except in extreme circumstances, ammunition supply is not a factor; units deploy with small arms and ammunition as specified by their gaining headquarters and normally return with every round they took with them. In most cases, National Guard forces under state control receive sustainment from National Guard installations and supply centers, while federal military forces draw from Department of Defense (DOD) resources and installations. However, this may not always be the case.

8-4. A defense coordinating officer serves as a key link between the primary agency and joint (interagency) field office, state agencies, and the combatant commands providing forces and support (see chapter 2 for more information about the joint field office). Activities within a joint field office or regional coordination center involve more than requests for federal military support. A defense coordinating officer also coordinates for support to federal military forces supporting incident response. For example, if federal military forces require additional radios to communicate with civilian responders, the defense coordinating officer may coordinate a loan through the Federal Emergency Management Agency (FEMA) or other agency resources. The defense coordinating officer coordinates through the logistics section at the joint field office, which includes ground support, communications, supply, facilities, and medical support units for additional support available through FEMA and other agencies. (See also paragraph 8-10.)

8-5. Federal military and state National Guard forces receive logistical and personnel support through their controlling commands. Federal military forces receive support through DOD channels, primarily through their parent Service channels, while National Guard units in Title 32 or state active duty receive support through their state National Guard supply agencies. Both federal military and state National Guard obtain consumables through contracting to the maximum extent feasible. In practice, commanders adjust logistics support to the situation. Recent operations have featured federal military installations providing facilities and common user logistics to National Guard forces conducting civil support operations. In other instances, DOD may receive support such as basing and facilities from the National Guard through a memorandum of agreement coordinated between the adjutant general, National Guard Bureau, and DOD.

8-6. Federal statutes and DOD policy restrict DOD components from procuring or maintaining any supplies, materiel, or equipment exclusively for providing civil support, unless otherwise directed by the Secretary of Defense. Federal military forces may lease or hand receipt real property such as vehicles and generators, from other agencies or contracted vendors, but may not purchase these items without specific authority from DOD. The defense coordinating officer can coordinate through the federal coordinating officer to acquire certain items for use by federal military forces and then hand receipt the items to the deployed forces. All leased or borrowed property must be returned to the owning agency, transferred to other federal agencies as directed by the joint field office, or returned to the vendor as part of the unit's transition and redeployment.

8-7. For any disaster response, FEMA is responsible for the overall coordination of logistical support at the federal, interagency level during a disaster response operation. At this level, commercial, private, government, volunteer, and faith-based organizations work with FEMA using coordination guidance contained within the National Incident Management System (NIMS) and the National Response Framework (NRF). Note that some military organizations involved in logistical support may operate outside the federal military joint task force chain of command. For example, the United States Army Corps of Engineers, as an agency, draws directly upon its own and federal resources in coordination with FEMA. The Corps of Engineers will also support National Guard and Regular Army units when tasked, and may submit requests for assistance through the joint field office to the federal military or National Guard joint task force.

8-8. In a disaster response, FEMA coordinates and provides most of the sustainment needed by responding organizations and victims. Military forces may provide some support to disaster victims as part of a mission assignment. Officials from FEMA coordinate and sustain the majority of these people using the resources of the federal government and agencies such as the Red Cross. FEMA logistic centers (see figure 8-1, page 8-3) support responding agencies. These sites provide the resources for FEMA to manage any emergency. The sites are located near Atlanta, Georgia; Berryville, Virginia; Cumberland, Maryland;

Ft. Worth, Texas; Frederick, Maryland; Kansas City, Missouri; and San Jose, California. The three offshore storage sites are located in Guam, Hawaii, and Puerto Rico. With access to 50 additional cache storage facilities used by FEMA's National Disaster Medical System to store medical supplies and equipment across the country and 252 pre-positioned disaster supplies containers located in logistical centers and fourteen states, FEMA can expedite the shipment of emergency commodities to any disaster in the United States.

8-9. Most of the centers provide resources such as blankets, emergency meals, bottled water, generators, cots, blankets, tarps, and roof sheeting, all of which can be distributed through state and county distribution points in time of need. Two of the centers provide specialized resources: the Berryville, Virginia center maintains computer equipment and electronics for joint field office operations, and the Frederick, Maryland, center provides emergency medical supplies and equipment. FEMA also includes logistical planning as part of its national exercise program involving commercial, private, government, volunteer, and faith-based organizations.

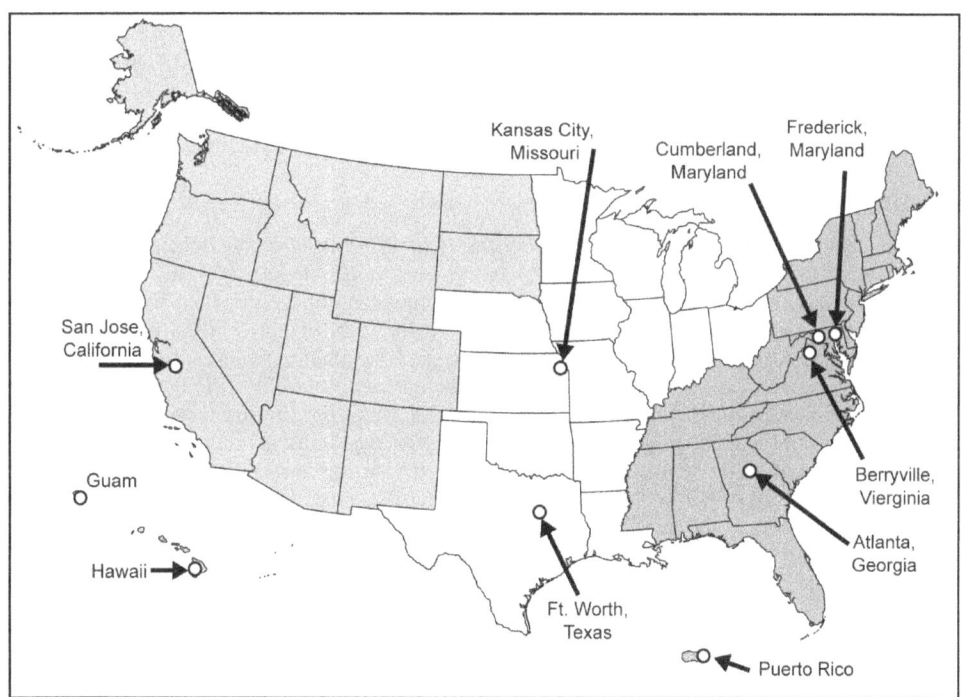

Figure 8-1. Federal Emergency Management Agency logistics centers

8-10. Federal disaster support under emergency support function annex (ESF) #5 (Emergency Management) includes a regional response coordination center and a joint field office. FEMA personnel coordinate the establishment of site facilities, supplies, and equipment to support federal government activities but may coordinate with the military for any identified shortfalls. The ongoing integration of the defense coordinating officer and defense coordinating element with FEMA helps facilitate logistical coordination during emergencies. When an incident occurs, the defense coordinating officer and the defense coordinating element coordinate with the resource staff in the joint field office. Each agency working in the joint field office is responsible for documenting the costs of its own activities and response efforts. Military forces coordinate with civil authorities and other partners based on the NIMS and the NRF to achieve unity of effort (see chapter 2). The response to floods in North Dakota in 2009, described on page 8-4, provides an excellent example of unity of effort in domestic disaster response.

> **Flooding in North Dakota**
>
> Severe flooding of the Red River in 2009 led to a response that featured innovative cooperation between all military forces in the disaster area. Grand Forks Air Force Base, a Regular Air Force installation located outside the flood plain near Grand Forks, North Dakota, became the nexus for federal and state response forces. The North Dakota National Guard provided most of the military forces, with assistance from federal military forces. Federal military force helicopters and unmanned aerial system providers used Grand Forks Air Force Base for basing and sustainment. The North Dakota National Guard used the Air Force emergency preparedness liaison officer to coordinate for use of the Air Force base for National Guard aircraft. The Federal Emergency Management Agency used the Air Force base to warehouse emergency supplies such as cots, food, and water. The National Guard used its working relationships with the base commander to accommodate all National Guard response forces, ground and air. During the response operation, when the status of National Guard aircraft crews transitioned from Title 32 status to state active duty status, the issue of financial reimbursement surfaced. The North Dakota adjutant general has since negotiated a memorandum of understanding with the Air Force so the North Dakota National Guard has a standing agreement for use of the Grand Forks Air Force Base for any future floods.

DEPLOYMENT OF FORCES

8-11. Deployment and redeployment of military forces to an incident requires planning and preparation that is similar to that used in deploying and redeploying from operations outside the United States. However, there are some notable differences. The most important difference is one of infrastructure—the United States has one of the most developed transportation infrastructures in the world. A robust and advanced communications network ties the transportation infrastructure together. In fact, in many ways, the commercial communications architecture exceeds the military's capability. For the deployment planner, this means that there are many options. There are also challenges. The most important of these is civilian control of the transportation system. All military movements using military transportation need coordination through military channels to civilian agencies such as the Federal Aviation Administration and state transportation authorities. In addition, movement of equipment and supplies needs to comply with any applicable federal and state transportation restrictions on oversized and hazardous materials. Movement to and from a disaster must comply with the same restrictions that apply to movement to and from a major training event; however, the priority accorded to the movement is much higher.

8-12. Deployment into the area of operations will be administrative in nature. Movement plans will be coordinated by the gaining headquarters through United States Transportation Command (USTRANSCOM) and the installation transportation officers for federal military forces. The state or territorial joint force headquarters will coordinate movement requirements for road movement with state transportation and highway patrol officials. The National Guard Bureau will also assist the supported and supporting adjutants general with air movement of additional National Guard units when required.

Deployment of National Guard Forces

8-13. Following an alert order, National Guard forces assemble at their designated marshalling point, which is normally their unit armory. Unit leaders conduct equipment issue and pre-movement inspections. As they do this, the joint force headquarters–state coordinates for movement clearance and support through the state transportation officials for road movements of military convoys, since movement for most equipment will be by road. Advance parties and liaison elements normally self-deploy in one or two vehicle elements and draw fuel using state credit cards or state agency facilities coordinated by the joint force headquarters–state. When required, the joint force headquarters–state directs movement of convoy support detachments (maintenance, fuel, and possible medical) to support areas coordinated with state transportation officials.

8-14. Reception, staging and onward movement of units normally occurs at a designated location that the joint force headquarters–state and joint task force–state commanders have selected as the base area for the support. This may be a National Guard air base, state maintenance facility, or contracted property. As they reach their assembly areas, unit commanders report their status and coordinate for logistical support and forward operating bases as required. They then self-deploy into their areas of operations and conduct civil support operations.

8-15. Air assets normally self-deploy to the area of operations using pre-established procedures managed by that state's Air National Guard. All air movement remains under the airspace control authority of the Federal Aviation Administration. Normally, fixed and rotary wing aircraft will deploy to the nearest Air National Guard facility; if that lies beyond supportable range, the joint force headquarters–state will contract for space and facilities at a commercial airport. The third option bases Air and Army Guard helicopters at a field location contracted through the state or local emergency mangers.

8-16. Emergency management assistance units from other states may move by either ground or air assets. When moved by Air National Guard assets, the supported state coordinates with the supporting state and the National Guard Bureau for necessary air movement. The National Guard Bureau coordinates with USTRANSCOM and the Joint Staff to ensure that Air Guard support to DOD operations continues. When moving by ground, the providing joint force headquarters–state coordinates with state transportation officials from the point of departure through any adjoining states until the supporting unit moves into the supported state, at which time the unit passes to the movement control of the gaining state.

Deployment of Federal Military Forces

8-17. Deployment of federal military assets to the area of operations in the continental United States is under the direction of the supported combatant commands, either United States Northern Command (USNORTHCOM) or United States Pacific Command (USPACOM). The combatant command determines deployment priorities and movement timelines in conjunction with its Service components or joint task force. USTRANSCOM executes the deployment plan and sources required transportation assets to move the required force. The joint movement control center coordinates with the state emergency operations center for necessary road clearances.

8-18. USTRANSCOM schedules movement by military aircraft and contracted commercial aircraft according to priorities established by the supported combatant commander. The supporting commander, normally United States Joint Forces Command, provides support to the aerial port of embarkation. Upon arrival at the aerial port of debarkation, the gaining commander conducts reception, staging, onward movement, and integration (RSOI) activities necessary to get the unit into the joint operations area. Competing worldwide strategic lift requirements, particularly during war, may prevent rapid air movement for the main body. Therefore, planners give priority movement to critical command and control elements necessary to support RSOI and initial phases of operations.

8-19. Road movement is often the most effective means to move personnel and equipment. Military convoys are coordinated between the deploying unit's installation and the defense movement coordinators in states where the convoys originate. A representative from the supporting base support installation's installation transportation office, in conjunction with a movement control team, coordinates military movements with a state's transportation, emergency management, and law enforcement officials. USTRANSCOM and USNORTHCOM coordinate liaison officers for more complex movements. National Guard forces coordinate their movements with the joint force headquarters–state and state officials. The latter serve as the nexus to coordinate with USTRANSCOM and state law enforcement for movements. Unit staffs coordinate with their parent commands and United States Army North (USARNORTH) for movement support.

8-20. Managing RSOI in the early stages of a disaster response requires flexible leaders and patience. Prior planning provides a framework for responding to contingencies but cannot capture all situations. Commanders need to be flexible and innovative to meet the demands of civil support operations. An essential component of contingency operations is effective command and control. As soon as possible following alert, the deploying unit headquarters should deploy an early entry command post to the designated RSOI location and liaison officers to the gaining headquarters. Liaison personnel should have cell phones, laptops, and unit information. The early entry command post should have tactical communications as well as commercial communications. The deploying command post reports to the RSOI commander at the aerial port of debarkation and coordinates for the reception of units.

8-21. During deployment and redeployment planning, units should consider the use of commercial assets in an effort to minimize overall transportation costs. The servicing installation transportation office in the area of operations procures the commercial transportation, prepares and issues shipping documentation, and monitors carrier performance.

NATIONAL GUARD LOGISTICS

8-22. National Guard forces continue to be supported through their state's military infrastructure. Initially, support comes from unit armories, but the joint force headquarters–state shifts bulk resupply of military items to resources maintained at the state level, normally at that state's military training facilities. The adjutant general and joint task force commander work through the state emergency manager and state coordinating officer to establish contracts for bulk consumables, temporary facilities, and commercially available services such as laundry and sanitation support (portable latrines). The joint task force staff coordinates with unit commanders, local officials and state contracting representatives to obtain facilities capable of providing field services or submits a request for forces for Army field service units. For example, the Army Corps of Engineers may respond to a National Guard request for specialized engineering equipment.

8-23. Out-of-state National Guard forces receive logistical support from the supported state. Because different state units may have different equipment, the supporting state headquarters remains prepared to respond to requests for assistance from the supported state.

FEDERAL MILITARY LOGISTICS

8-24. The primary Army Service component command (ASCC) for civil support is USARNORTH, providing logistical support within the continental states, Alaska, Puerto Rico and Virgin Islands. Although United States Army Pacific Command (USARPAC) has operational control of the federal military units located in Alaska, significant geographical barriers that have led to the implementation of Joint Task Force–Alaska. Joint Task Force–Alaska supports civil support operations within Alaska and is a subordinate command of United States Northern Command (USNORTHCOM).

8-25. USARNORTH makes extensive use of DOD and federal government capabilities to sustain deployed Army forces. As the ASCC, USARNORTH supports all deployed federal Army forces and provides common user logistics to other federal military forces as directed by the combatant commander. USARNORTH works with the deployed joint task force and the defense coordinating officer to coordinate for FEMA support, usually through a series of federally negotiated contracts. The keys to success are flexibility and coordination between logisticians from each Service element. Logisticians must keep in mind not only mission accomplishment, but also good stewardship of taxpayer dollars when determining the most effective and efficient method of support. USARNORTH coordinates with the Army staff, Army commands, and direct reporting units for Service-specific logistical support. Figure 8-2 shows and example of the sustainment structure USARNORTH may use to support a large incident.

8-26. The primary means for providing support at the ASCC level is a dedicated theater sustainment command. The theater sustainment command serves as the senior logistics command in the joint operations area. This support may include:
- Establishment of lines of communication
- Joint RSOI and integration of deploying forces as required
- Transportation and movement control of military and displaced civilian personnel, equipment, and supplies
- Distribution sources for water, food, ice, and other classes of supply
- Establishment of temporary shelter.
- Managing staging and throughput.

Sustainment—Logistics and Personnel Services

- Managing fuel support and distribution.
- Managing medical and veterinary support.
- Managing rotary and ground ambulance support.
- Mortuary affairs, explosive ordnance disposal.
- Vertical and horizontal engineering support.
- Military police support.

8-27. One of the most important functions of the ASCC is coordination with the Army commands and direct reporting units that lie outside the combatant commander's control. The ASCC provides the direct linkage to Department of the Army capabilities. For example, the ASCC coordinates with United States Army Installation Management Command for support provided by Army installations. Other support is coordinated through United States Army Materiel Command for distribution directly from strategic stocks to deployed Army forces.

8-28. Not all civil support operations involve large forces. The ASCC monitors the sustainment of small detachments providing civil support. The defense coordinating officer exercise tactical control of a small detachment deployed to an incident site, and will normally coordinate for any logistics, human resources support, and medical support that is not available from the parent installation or through the primary agency. While the situation may vary, the ASCC manages sustainment for company-sized formations and larger (approximately 250 personnel or more).

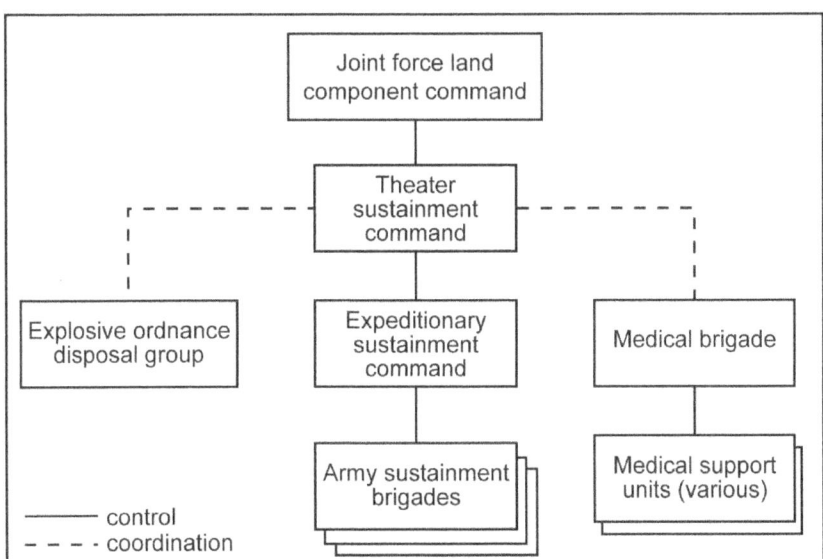

Figure 8-2. USARNORTH sustainment structure

Strategic and National Providers

8-29. Several organizations assist in sustainment activities. When requested, they can provide a liaison officer or team to provide support to the deployed joint task force. Some of the providers are Defense Logistics Agency, United States Army Materiel Command, USTRANSCOM, and Army and Air Force Exchange Service. Additionally, USARNORTH has a habitual relationship with 20th Support Group for explosive ordnance disposal and dog teams, 412th Contracting Support Brigade for contingency contracting teams, and 3rd Human Resources Command for personnel services. The Defense Contracting Agency and General Services Administration also provide support.

Phased Sustainment for Catastrophic Incident Response

8-30. USARNORTH plans for sustainment in Phase 0 and provides sustainment in the next five phases. Phase I involves coordinating and preparing for efficient flow of USARNORTH forces and materiel. Phase II includes establishment of logistic operations. Phase III involves the deployment of USARNORTH forces and materiel. Phase IV involves on-the-ground sustainment operations. Phase V involves transition of sustainment operations to appropriate local, state, and federal organizations.

8-31. During Phase I, the theater sustainment command and its expeditionary sustainment commands plan and prepare for RSOI of deploying federal military forces. During the initial phases of any response, the defense coordinating officer estimates the required capabilities, and USARNORTH assesses the sustainment needed. A USNORTHCOM assessment team may help assess federal government and DOD sustainment requirements. Phase I actions are—

- Gather information.
- Assess logistical support requirements.
- Assess required logistical capabilities.
- Identify unit capabilities required to support ground forces.

8-32. Phase II includes preparation for deploying sustainment for command and control elements that can open the theater for federal military assets. The joint force land component commander, in coordination with the federal coordinating officer, prioritizes essential units and equipment required to support of life saving operations. Phase II actions are—

- Plan and prepare for operation of distribution networks, base support installations, and support of displaced civilian centers. (State National Guard units prepare based on guidance from their state chain of command, while Regular Army units respond to mission assignments.)
- Plan and prepare to support sustainment of decontamination operations in support of a chemical, biological, radiological, nuclear, or high-yield explosives incident.
- Augment logistical command and control capability based upon mission analysis.
- Establish joint RSOI command and control, facilities, and procedures.
- Monitor force readiness of units.
- Conduct health service review.
- Review and adjust existing support contracts.
- Coordinate with the state to identify key distribution nodes in the affected region and alternate logistic routes.
- Identify status of key distribution nodes in the affected region; identify alternate logistic routes.
- Develop options for providing sustainment support to active component forces
- Coordinate sustainment actions with state National Guard forces, FEMA, General Services Administration, and other organizations to help optimize sustainment operations.

8-33. Phase III involves continuous support to deployed forces. During this phase, USARNORTH, serving in its roles as the joint force land component command and the ASCC, ensures that logistical support is as efficient as possible. When authorized by the Secretary of Defense and the adjutant general of the state, joint task force commanders of Service components develop common user logistics agreements and accounting procedures. In this phase, USARNORTH may also support ESFs as determined by the mission assignment process. Phase III actions are—

- Manage sustainment, establish and maintain a distribution network, manage the base installation sustainment as directed in mission assignments.
- Support decontamination operations.
- Conduct joint RSOI.
- Support force protection requirements of federal military (Title10) forces as required and authorized.

Sustainment—Logistics and Personnel Services

- Support force readiness.
- Plan and execute force rotation due to exposure to chemical, biological, radiological, nuclear, or high-yield explosives elements.

8-34. Phase IV encompasses preparation and planning for transition to civilian support throughout the joint operations area. This requires assessment at the joint field office of logistical support requirements for the deployed forces and continuing support needed for the civilian agencies once military assets redeploy. Phase IV actions are—

- Initiate logistical planning for redeployment and reset requirements.
- Manage sustainment operations, distribution networks, and support installations in preparation to return to civilian control.
- Remove debris.
- Decontaminate personnel and equipment.
- Distribute fuel.
- Coordinate, as required, actions for procurement, production, and distribution of water.
- Support dislocated civilian operations.
- Prepare for force redeployment.

8-35. Phase V involves a staged execution of sustainment to appropriate local, state, federal, or civilian organizations. USARNORTH does this in close coordination with the unified coordination group and specific ESF managers. When the mission nears completion, sustainment units continue to support other units awaiting redeployment. Military support is not curtailed before civil authorities assume the functions. Transportation is arranged through the appropriate movement control organization in accordance with established priorities.

Base Support Installation Selection

8-36. A crucial early decision is selection of the base support installation. Base support installation selection is a seven step process that follows guidance in DOD Publication 3025.1-M and the Chairman of the Joint Chiefs of Staff standing execute order for DSCA (referred to as the CJCS DSCA EXORD). Support provided by the designated base support installation may include, but is not limited to, general supply and maintenance, transportation, contracting, communications, personnel and equipment reception and staging, facilities, civil engineering, health, and other life support services such as billeting, food service, and force protection. The preferred location for the base support installation is at a DOD installation with these capabilities:

- Proximity to the incident site (less than 100 miles).
- Proximity to a major airfield that is suitable for use as an aerial port of debarkation.
- Life support services.
- Open and covered areas for staging of supplies and equipment.
- Adequate transportation infrastructure to and from incident site.
- Communications infrastructure sufficient to meet the surge of forces arriving in the area.

8-37. If a designated base support installation is a major installation within a reasonable travel time from the incident area, then that installation will augment joint task force common user support to all responding forces to the greatest extent possible. This will enable the responding joint task force to focus on the civil support mission. The installation staff should be able to assume responsibility for the majority of the joint reception and staging mission. As the ASCC, USARNORTH coordinates for Army-specific support through the base support installation.

Chapter 8

8-38. Figure 8-3, page 8-10, illustrates the base support installation selection process for DSCA missions. Base support installation selection is a seven-step sequence that ensures selection of the best possible location. The seven steps are—
- Data collection and coordination.
- Data reporting.
- Evaluation.
- Incident response.
- Base support installation nomination.
- Base support installation designation.
- Base support installation build-up and sustainment.

Data Collection and Coordination

8-39. The regional defense coordinating officer is the primary contact with installations near the affected area. Along with the defense coordinating element, state emergency preparedness liaison officer, and possibly a base support installation reconnaissance team from USARNORTH, the defense coordinating officer collects data on installation capabilities.

Data Reporting

8-40. USARNORTH provides installation commanders with its handbook for base support installations, along with the USNORTHCOM base support installation selection criteria. The data collected is reported to USARNORTH, consolidated, and sent to USNORTHCOM. General capabilities and shortfalls of potential base support installations are identified.

Evaluation

8-41. Potential base support installations are evaluated on their ability to provide the needed support. (Paragraph 8-36 lists general requirements.) Each situation is different; therefore, evaluation criteria are specific to the operation.

Incident Response

8-42. After the commander of USNORTHCOM designates the joint operations area, dialogue between USARNORTH staff, defense coordinating officer, United States Army Installation Management Command, and prospective base support installation locations will start to determine the exact nature of the capabilities that will be required or requested.

Base Support Installation Nomination

8-43. USARNORTH considers input from United States Army Installation Management Command, regional defense coordinating officer, and installation staff prior to submitting base support installation nomination to USNORTHCOM.

Base Support Installation Designation

8-44. For homeland defense missions, the Secretary of Defense designates primary and alternate base support installations. In DSCA operations, the USNORTHCOM commander can designate base support installations after conferring with and reaching an agreement with the owning Service component. If an agreement cannot be reached, the Secretary of Defense makes the final decision.

Base Support Installation Build-Up And Sustainment

8-45. When base support installation selection is approved, United States Army Installation Management Command informs USARNORTH of the specific installation capabilities and shortfalls. This allows the USARNORTH staff to submit a request for forces to augment the base support installation as needed.

Sustainment—Logistics and Personnel Services

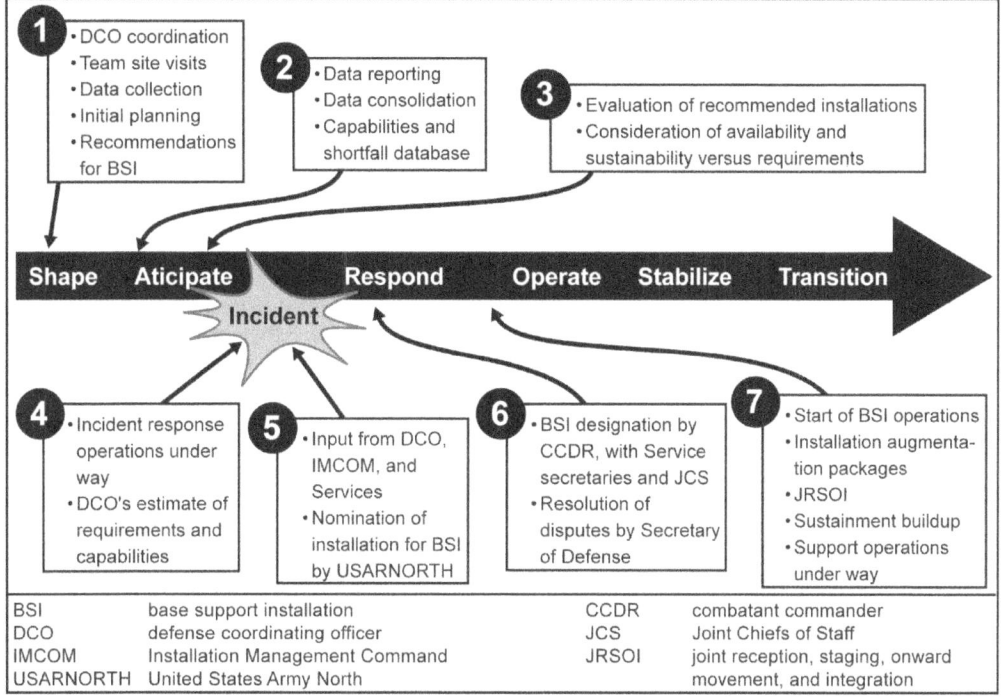

Figure 8-3. Illustration of base support installation selection

8-46. Depending on the location of a catastrophic incident, no major DOD installation may be close enough to support the operation. In these instances, the joint task force completes an estimate of the requirements and requests contract support or submits requests for forces to mitigate logistic capability shortfalls. In some cases, the Secretary of Defense may authorize USNORTHCOM to coordinate use of a state National Guard installation either as the base support installation or as a forward operating base. Commander, USNORTHCOM can designate base support installation(s) after conferring with and reaching an agreement with the owning Service component.

LOGISTICS CONSIDERATIONS FOR CIVIL SUPPORT OPERATIONS

8-47. There are several unique aspects to logistical support during domestic operations. By understanding these differences and applying initiative, logisticians can provide effective and efficient support to not only Soldiers, but also supported civilian organizations. Major advantages of domestic operations include—
- Rapid and reliable commercial transportation.
- A robust communications grid.
- Professional contracted support for most logistical requirements.
- Minimal language barriers.
- Honest public officials.
- A supportive civilian population.
- Straightforward access to national military support organizations (such as Defense Logistics Agency) and installations, including home stations.
- Readily available potable water and safe food (from outside a disaster area).

8-48. A major difference between foreign and domestic operations is the legal requirements concerning movement, handling, and storage of hazardous materials, including fuel, ammunition, and many other seemingly mundane support items. Commanders must consider environmental requirements; state and national environmental laws and regulations apply to all DSCA operations. Local installation transportation officers and movement control team personnel can also provide specific guidance on what may be required for military drivers to haul hazardous cargo. The Environmental Protection Agency and other agencies can provide guidance when requested. Additionally, commanders should also consider any specific environmental concerns for their particular operating area and noise abatement requirements for any space they occupy.

8-49. Fuel is readily available throughout the United States, barring temporary disruption of a power grid. However, it is not military grade JP-8. Tactical vehicles will require military refueling support, or a command waiver to use commercially available diesel fuel with attendant maintenance requirement upon redeployment. Military aircraft can normally obtain fuel from commercial or military airfields. Defense Logistics Agency representative can coordinate with the Defense Energy Supply Center. The Defense Energy Supply Center coordinates for direct bulk fuel delivery for ground or aviation operations to base support installations or airfields. Units should plan to deploy with sufficient tankers to support their tactical vehicles and coordinate with the joint task force for continued support. Any refueling operations must comply with environmental restrictions, and noncommissioned officers must emphasis safe handling and cleanup procedures.

8-50. Rental equipment and vehicles are quickly depleted near a disaster area. If the mission depends upon additional commercial equipment, units should be prepared to obtain it through providers well outside the disaster area.

8-51. Units should prepare to deploy items and personnel capable of executing a field arms room. The decision to deploy with weapons rests with the Secretary of Defense for federal military forces and with the adjutant general for National Guard forces. Unfortunately, many civil support operations involve aspects of law enforcement and infrastructure protection that may require arming some Soldiers. Depending on proximity to home station or armory, forces plan to establish a field arms room for at least some of the deploying units.

8-52. Sustainment officers should work closely with the joint task force to obtain adequate bath and laundry support for the force. One of the lessons of Hurricane Katrina is that bath and laundry is not just a morale booster—it is a critical force protection measure. For planning purposes, sustainment officers should contract or deploy sufficient resources to allow Soldiers to have a clean uniform and shower daily. Medical, food service, and mortuary affairs personnel receive priority for showers and laundry. Commanders should ensure that their Soldiers involved in disaster response have ready access to replacement uniforms or separate work clothing. Hurricane Katrina and other disasters demonstrated that expensive uniforms needed replacement after exposure to filthy water, contaminates, and jagged debris.

CONTRACTING

8-53. Operational contract support can be an effective and efficient method of rapidly augmenting organic military support capabilities in civil support actions if properly planned and executed. Contracted support can be especially viable as a source of base support installation augmentation support. Contracted support in civil support operations may include all classes of supply, labor, mortuary affairs, laundry, showers, food service, sanitation, billeting, transportation, maintenance and repair, access to communications networks, temporary real property leasing, and construction. In addition, while lessons learned from recent major DSCA operations clearly indicate contracting of supplies and services was an important source of support for these operations, there are some key limiting factors that must be kept in mind when planning for these types of operations. These limiting factors include:
- Limited pre-planning opportunities.
- Very short time requirement.
- Very limited availability of commercial supplies and services within or near the joint operational area.

- Numerous federal, state and local agencies competing for locally available commercial capabilities.
- Low priority to the military for any locally available commercial support.

8-54. In most DSCA missions, the Army will be the lead Service responsible to plan and execute contract support to the joint force. In these operations, the ASCC uses its aligned contracting support brigade to perform this task. This United States Army Materiel Command unit has unique capabilities to plan for and integrate contract support. A related contracting support brigade mission is to ensure any needed expansion of existing contracts or development of new contracts does not adversely impact other federal, state, or local responder contracting efforts. At the tactical level, the contracting support brigade's contracting battalions and teams, taking advantage of organic base support installation contracting support capabilities, award contracts, provide contract oversight, and assist in the overall integration of contract support effort. Additionally, the Army may also utilize the United States Army Material Command's logistic civil augmentation program and the United States Army Corps of Engineers contract support capabilities as necessary.

8-55. Commanders should understand DOD is not normally the lead contracting authority in DSCA missions. In most of these operations, FEMA leads the contract coordination effort between state agencies, local agencies, National Guard forces operating under Title 32 authority, and federal military forces. This centralized coordination effort is essential since numerous contracting agencies will be competing for the same locally available resources. Additionally, in DSCA operations, priority of commercial support will normally be to local emergency services (such as hospitals and fire and police services), displaced civilians, and support of deployed military forces, respectively. Because of this lower priority of support and the often short-term nature of DSCA missions, Army forces operating inside a disaster area must be prepared to deploy with their full modified table of organization and equipment sustainment capabilities and to live in field conditions. Deployed Army forces also must be prepared to provide sufficient trained contracting officer representatives with the required subject matter expertise to assist in contract oversight.

8-56. The key to successful contracting actions is operational contract support planning, requirements development, and adequate contracting capabilities to support the force. Failure to accomplish these critical tasks may lead to costly delays of materiel and services during civil support operations. Supported units must also be prepared to assist in contract oversight through the nomination of qualified contracting officer representatives and receiving officials as required by the responsible contracting officer.

NEGOTIATED SUPPORT

8-57. In some cases, civil agencies and organizations may have enough logistical resources to support not only themselves but also supporting Army forces. Such support is negotiated on a case-by-case basis with the appropriate civil authorities. Memorandums of agreement are established before an operation to reduce time of negotiation.

SUPPORT FROM OTHER ORGANIZATIONS

8-58. General Services Administration provides common general supplies and services to organizations of the federal government. General Services Administration may support DOD through its procurement and leasing service capability for supplies, office supplies and furniture, real property, service contracts, transportation, machine and hand tools, photo supplies, various types of batteries, and numerous other items. Commanders use the normal procurement process. However, military forces should not expect to be supported from other agencies providing assistance during DSCA operations.

8-59. The Defense Logistics Agency provides common user logistics and services used by the military when conducting civil support operations. Normally the classes of supply may consist of class I (subsistence, bottled water, etc.), class II (clothing, textiles, tents, etc), class III (packaged and bulk fuel), class IV (construction and barrier material), class VIII medical, dental and veterinary supplies, equipment and blood products, and class IX (spare parts). Services may include storage, distribution, disposal, document automation, and printing production. Normally, a Defense Logistics Agency response team co-locates with various logistical headquarters to coordinate supply and fuel support. Defense Logistics

Agency distribution depots are located strategically throughout the continental United States along major distribution networks to quickly launch needed supplies to its customers.

RESOURCE MANAGEMENT

8-60. Federal military forces provide civil support on a reimbursable basis unless directed otherwise by the President. Cost reimbursement for civil support is usually in accordance with the Economy Act, which mandates cost reimbursement by the federal agency requesting support (see chapter 7). However, when the President declares a disaster or emergency, the Robert T. Stafford Disaster Relief and Emergency Assistance Act sets the guidelines for reimbursements to federal agencies and states from federal funds set aside to support these missions.

8-61. When possible, resource management analysis precedes key operational decisions and actions. Army financial managers must seek early guidance regarding reimbursement from published orders, published guidance from Headquarters, Department of the Army, the USARNORTH reimbursement cell, or the USNORTHCOM financial management augmentation team. These sources provide guidance on the reimbursable process, specific accounting codes that have been established and allocation of reimbursable authority from funding received from other federal agencies.

REIMBURSABLE ACTIVITIES

8-62. In most cases, state, local, and federal agencies reimburse federal military forces for the costs of civil support missions. The reimbursement process requires the DOD components to capture and report total and incremental costs in accordance with applicable DOD financial management regulations. Supported agencies also maintain records of support received from military forces. To distinguish these costs from those related to training or normal operating expenses, resource managers must maintain accountability throughout an operation for equipment and material costs associated with operational support. Organizational record-keeping needed to support cost-capturing must begin at the start of the operation and extend to the lowest functional level.

8-63. Commanders must work closely with their financial management staff to ensure all reimbursable activities are documented and accounted for properly. Under current policy, DOD components shall not procure or maintain any supplies, materiel, or equipment exclusively for providing civil support, unless otherwise directed by the Secretary of Defense. Costs generally considered eligible for reimbursement are—

- Pay for personnel specifically hired for disaster response support.
- Regular pay and allowances for Economy Act Orders only—military and civilian.
- Overtime.
- Travel and per diem.
- Cost of consumables (such as fuel, rations) requisitioned to support disaster operations.
- Transportation of personnel, supplies, and equipment.
- Cost to pack and crate supplies and equipment lost, destroyed, or damaged as a result of civil support operations (except aircraft, motor vehicles, and water craft).
- Cost of aircraft flight hours.
- Cost of port (air, ocean, inland-waterway) loading, off-loading, and handling.
- Cost to repair or recondition non-consumable items returned (allocated according to percentage of repair costs attributable to the support provided).
- Replacement costs of supplies and equipment furnished and not returned.
- Cost of parts used to repair end-items used in disaster relief (excluding depot or field maintenance on a time compliance basis).

8-64. Additional guidance in this area for federal military forces can be found in DOD Publication 7000.14-R. A second source of additional federal military information is JP 1-06.

Nonreimbursable Activities

8-65. Expenses not considered reimbursable in the context of civil support operations are—
- Generally, regular pay and allowances of military and civilian personnel (when not under Economy Act orders), except United States Army Corps of Engineers.
- Charges for use of military vehicles and watercraft.
- Aircraft, vehicles, or watercraft damaged, lost, destroyed, or abandoned.
- Administrative overhead.
- Annual and sick leave, retirement, and other benefits.
- Cost of telephone, telegram, or other transmissions used to requisition items in a disaster area to replenish depot stocks.

Planning Guidance for Accounting Procedures

8-66. Accounting codes, for use in accumulating costs, are requested at the onset of a disaster relief effort. The key is to maintain accounting records and monitor expenses. All organizations supporting operations—such as United States Army Materiel Command, theater sustainment command elements, sustainment brigades, or medical brigades—that receive, store, issue, and account for DOD material ensure complete accountability of all supplies. Commanders and staff integrate financial management into all phases of the operation. Early involvement is essential for advice and review procedures. Responsive financial management calls for detailed planning procedures to account for the expenditure of all resources supporting sustainment for a civil support operation with the expectation of being audited. By requesting early on-site involvement and advice from external functional experts, such as the Army Audit Agency and General Accounting Office, resource managers can head off major accounting problems that may occur later in the operation. Specific financial guidance and point-of-contact information is included in operation orders, execute orders, and deployment orders published by USNORTHCOM, USARNORTH and Service command channels.

Critical Services during Civil Support Operations

8-67. The supported state and federal coordinating officers identify certain critical sustainment functions to reduce loss of life, limb and property, and to meet basic logistic requirements. These critical services include mortuary affairs, establishment of temporary facilities and relief supplies. Commanders providing these capabilities should:
- Tailor the package for the mission.
- Contract for support and services early.
- Use local resources when possible.

Mortuary Affairs

8-68. Disasters may create high casualty rates that initially overwhelm civilian facilities. When requested, Army mortuary affairs units can provide assistance. Army mortuary affairs units normally provide collection point, transport to designated storage area, and identification services in support of civil authority. Ensure there is link-up between mortuary affairs and local morgues, medical facilities, funeral parlors and ensure cultural considerations are considered during operations. Chapter 2 of JP 4-06 outlines additional information for mortuary affairs for DSCA. Chapter 9 provides additional discussion on the handling of human and animal remains.

8-69. The local, territorial, tribal, or state medical examiner or coroner normally maintains jurisdiction over fatalities, and military forces support that official when authorized. Within the United States, the civil jurisdiction has authority to order and perform an investigation, including an autopsy or an appropriate examination of human remains. This local authority can waive jurisdiction to the military or request an Armed Forces medical examiner. This is a sensitive topic and requires analysis and legal advice on case-by-case basis.

8-70. Because mortuary affairs capabilities within DOD are extremely limited, mortuary affairs units support civil authorities only when response or recovery requirements are beyond the capabilities of civil authorities. When directed by the President or Secretary of Defense, DOD can provide advisory support, search, recovery, receiving, decontamination, identification, processing, storage, and transportation assistance of the remains. DOD mortuary affairs personnel integrate into federal, state, and local operations to assist and augment the medical examiner or coroner according to state laws. It is DOD guidance that only mortuary affairs personnel handle human remains, with the reverence, care, and dignity befitting them and the circumstances.

8-71. In most states, the state medical examiner or coroner is legally responsible for operations associated with the identification, processing, and disposition of human remains. Each state and territory has different laws for processing human remains. DOD personnel may assist National Guard and civilian law enforcement authorities in locating human remains and transporting them after processing. The search, recovery, and movement of human remains may become a law enforcement issue when there is a requirement to enter private property or when the location is clearly a crime scene. In the former, a law enforcement official must enter the private premises first to conduct a search to determine if any deceased persons are inside. In the latter, permission from law enforcement authorities must be received before moving human remains.

8-72. The National Response Framework under ESF #8 gives Department of Health and Human Services the lead in providing mortuary services. Mortuary services under ESF #8 are—
- Identifying victims (by means such as fingerprint, dental, DNA, pathological, and anthropological).
- Providing temporary morgue facilities.
- Processing, preparation, and disposition of remains.
- Returning personal effects.
- If necessary, making remains and personal effects available to law enforcement.

8-73. There are three types of searches for victims and for human remains. Soldiers may conduct an immediate or hasty search in the aftermath of a disaster, such as a flood or hurricane, to find and rescue living personnel who are on rooftops, front porches, or trees, for example, waiting for rescue. A primary search follows, by going house-to-house, knocking on doors, looking into windows, and listening for sounds to determine if someone inside needs assistance. Federal military forces may accompany National Guard or civilian law enforcement authorities and stand by to assist while they do the initial entry into the house or private business. A deliberate or secondary search follows later by going house-to-house and entering the premises to determine if any deceased persons are inside. Federal military forces again may accompany and stand ready to assist National Guard or civilian law enforcement authorities.

Temporary Facilities

8-74. The United States Army Corps of Engineers, Army, and other Service engineers may prepare temporary facilities or improve existing facilities to house military and supporting civilian personnel, and for additional support basing. Mission assignments determine the support provided to civilian agencies, while USARNORTH coordinates with the base support installation and subordinate Army commanders for additional facilities to support military forces. USARNORTH and the joint force headquarters–state may also coordinate for shared logistical facilities and housing; a memorandum of agreement may follow that assigns shared costs and responsibilities. The USARNORTH and subordinate engineer staff coordinate with Service engineer agencies (such as Naval Facilities Engineering Command) to analyze cost, availability, and schedules for construction of temporary facilities. Normally, housing for displaced citizens comes through the joint field office under ESF #6, coordinated by FEMA and assisted by other federal agencies, United States Army Corps of Engineers, and the American Red Cross. In situations involving a mass evacuation or refugee crisis, DOD may receive mission assignments to provide shelter to civilians.

8-75. Service capabilities developed and procured for rapid global deployment may prove useful in domestic emergencies. Such capabilities may include Air Force Red Horse and Prime Beef; Army rapid deployment logistics and medical modules such as Force Provider; or pre-packaged Marine logistics sets stored in the United States or on sea lift currently in U.S. waters.

OTHER LOGISTICS REQUIREMENTS FOR CIVIL SUPPORT OPERATIONS

8-76. Army units may require an extensive storage complex based on mission requirements and flow of supplies. During an incident response, federal and state agencies and civilian partners distribute large quantities food, water, ice, and clothing to affected citizens. Frequently, stockpiles of military supplies supplement resources from civilian emergency stockpiles. When tasked, Soldiers assist in distribution. Leaders need to understand that the law requires an accurate accounting for both the supplies and the Soldiers' effort.

Real Property

8-77. When requested and approved by their respective headquarters, National Guard and federal military bases may support civilian agencies. Vacant warehouses, parking lots, open fields, potential staging areas, universities, airports and airfields, hospitals, and other facilities may be used for support and service activities, and temporary resettlement of dislocated persons. The Secretary of Defense, in coordination with the owning service secretary, commits active military installations to support civilian agencies. The adjutant general of the state exercises decision authority for use of National Guard bases and armories.

8-78. Permanent or temporary transfer of any accountable equipment from an Army unit to a sister Service, other service component, or civilian agency requires Department of the Army approval. Loans require proper authorization and documentation. The borrower signs a statement assuming liability for equipment during the period of the loan, and for care, custody, security and safeguarding, proper use and maintenance, and responsibility for all incremental costs accrued to the Army. Before issue, the Army clearly defines condition standards for return and how and where to find the agency or organization that borrowed the item. In an emergency situation, Soldiers may provide items of equipment to their military counterparts or a civilian organization. They should document the transfer either in writing, or in an operations log at their TOC. One expedient means of documentation is to record it digitally on cell phone cameras. Transfer of weapons, combat or tactical vehicles, water vessels, or aircraft requires the approval of the Secretary of the Army.

Maintenance

8-79. Army commanders and staff cooperate with the lead civil authority. Commanders consider support for their own equipment and support for civilian equipment such as buses, trucks, ambulances, and power generation equipment. Federal military forces require a mission assignment in order to provide maintenance assistance to civilian equipment. National Guard assets provide support through immediate response or upon approval by their joint task force. Commanders consider providing maintenance support to nearby civilian responders (such as nongovernmental organizations); this can be one of the most effective means of building unity of effort while improving support. As soon as possible, however, contractors should replace military maintenance support to civilian agencies.

Transportation

8-80. USARNORTH planners assist USNORTHCOM and USTRANSCOM to plan, schedule, and control federal military movements into, within, and out of an area of operations. They support joint movement control and coordinate support with civilian agencies in the joint operating area. When tasked by a mission assignment, Army movement control personnel may augment and assist civilian authorities manage traffic into and out of a declared disaster area. The preferred means of manning traffic control points is through National Guard forces, in order to avoid any conflict with the Posse Comitatus Act. Regular Army personnel may support in a staff capacity or in a liaison capacity with law enforcement and National Guard elements. The joint task force–state and federal military joint task force may establish a joint movement center to ensure efficient movement within declared disaster areas. Federal military and state National Guard commanders coordinate manning requirements. Transportation units may serve as part of a joint force headquarters or as part of a pure Army force transportation headquarters (see figure 8-5).

8-81. Transportation units may serve as part of a joint headquarters or a pure Army transportation headquarters. Units serve as part of forces (except for small table of organization and equipment staff elements), not as part of the headquarters. They may provide services in unity of effort with civilian transportation assets. Wheeled military units can distribute large quantities of essential cargoes over terrain normally impassable to most civilian trucking. Inland cargo transfer companies prepare cargo for transshipment at distribution centers. Seaport operations companies operate water ports, load and offload ships, or assist civilian port operators. Watercraft companies move units, supplies, and equipment along intra-coastal and inland waterways.

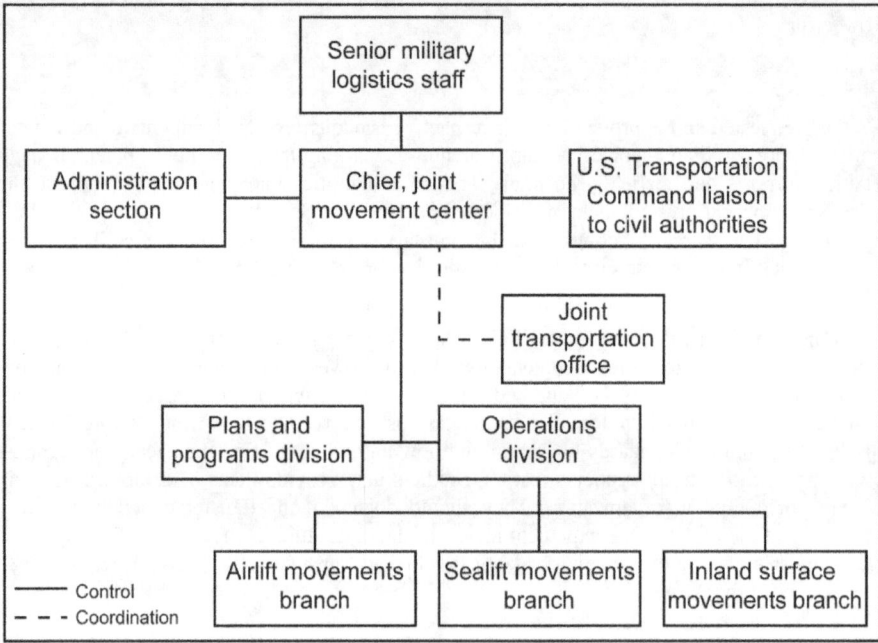

Figure 8-5. Example of joint movement center organization

Geospatial Support

8-82. In civil support operations, map coverage is critical to responding military and civil agencies. When possible, all controlling headquarters operate from the same geographic reference(s). In many cases, locally produced large-scale (1:10,000 or 1:5,000) maps are optimal. Many of the local residents and first responders are familiar with such local products. Local planning agencies, realtor associations, travel agencies, or utility company records may be able to provide such detailed map coverage. Army geospatial engineer units, federal mapping agencies or local topographic or printing companies may be able to reproduce or modify these products as required. If map coverage does not exist over the area of operations, agencies can request image-based products, which can be produced in a relatively short period.

8-83. The United States Army Geospatial Center at Fort Belvoir provides direct geospatial support and products to deployed forces conducting civil support operations. This includes products such as maps, hydrological studies, and "flyover capabilities." These products can support the unit's incident awareness and assessment before, during, and after deployment.

PERSONNEL SERVICES IN CIVIL SUPPORT OPERATIONS

8-84. During a civil support operation, personnel support to military forces should not be overlooked. Personnel support activities encompass the elements of postal operations management; morale, welfare and recreation (MWR); and band operations. For DSCA operations, personnel support operations not only support the military, but can also assist civil authorities in restoring capabilities that may be degraded.

8-85. The ability of the Army to support the United States Postal Service is important. Army support may be requested to augment postal operations until normal postal services are restored in the affected area.

8-86. The MWR network, in coordination with servicing base support installations, provides DOD personnel with an opportunity to relax and unwind while deployed normally through opportunities for sports and recreation. While human resources organizations are not the executors of MWR centers, acknowledging this aspect of personnel support during DSCA operations is essential to provide military and civilians alike with an outlet that improves morale.

8-87. Administrative control over personnel remains with the parent Service and providing headquarters unless otherwise specified by the supported combatant commander. National Guardsmen remain under the administrative control of their respective state. The Army Reserve Command continues to exercise administrative control over mobilized Army Reserve Soldiers. Active Component Soldiers receive administrative support through their home station. The supporting commander may attach a human resources team with the deploying unit to assist with administrative actions and coordinate with home station for additional support as required. Adequate personnel support to the deployed force must be a planning consideration for commanders and human resources providers.

HUMAN RESOURCES CONSIDERATIONS FOR CIVIL SUPPORT OPERATIONS

8-88. Human resources support requirements for DSCA operations depend on the operational environment. Some human resources support can be coordinated at home station, at the base support installation, when deployed with the organization, or from multiple deployed locations. Human resources planners must consider the numbers and type of organizations involved, task-organization of the force, level of support needed, and the operational environment (including the technological capabilities available).

Personnel Accountability

8-89. Civil support operations may require additional planning and preparation by the personnel staff officer. The biggest single challenge is maintaining accurate strength accountability. This is a challenge for both National Guard and federal military forces. Commanders take several steps to maintain personnel accountability. These include—

- Establish and maintain a central control point through which all Soldiers report and depart from the operational area. This is not easy to control, since there are numerous ways to arrive and depart.
- Ensure accountability procedures and reporting requirements are accurate and integrated with not only with the higher headquarters, but also the rear detachment.
- Manage units provided by other states under Emergency Management Assistance Compact Agreements carefully, since these units normally have a 30-day employment window. (This applies to National Guard joint task force commanders.)
- If possible, maintain unit integrity at as high a level as feasible, and specify a support relationships between dissimilar units. This allows the parent unit commanders to mange missions and accountability more effectively.
- Remain aware of Soldiers in within the command that may be affected personally by a disaster response mission. These Soldiers may have family in the affected area.
- Consider bringing in one or more human resources platoons or teams to support civil authorities in accomplishing their mission, using civilian agency systems. These elements may include postal platoons to assist the United States Postal Service or casualty liaison teams to assist in casualty operations.

Mail Services and Connectivity

8-90. The entire chain of command should ensure that basic services continue, with particular attention to mail and internet connectivity. The latter becomes increasingly important each year as more Soldiers depend upon online services for banking and communications. The commander should contract for connectivity (such as wireless networks) sufficient for Soldiers to use their own devices, or leased terminals to remain connected when off duty.

Time Off

8-91. During extended operations, commanders should develop rotational plans to allow Soldiers and civilians to spend a short time back at home station to deal with personal and professional issues. In most civil support operations, there will be numerous courier vehicles and flights, and a well-managed personnel control system can ensure that Soldiers get to where they need to go and back again efficiently.

Policy for Alcohol Use

8-92. One of the key policies that the supported commander must establish concerns the use of alcohol. Commanders and leaders need to understand and enforce the personal conduct rules on consumption of alcohol.

Awards

8-93. Personnel officers should review the awards and decorations that the command may award for service, achievement, and heroism during civil support operations. Careful personnel accountability will help ensure that Soldiers receive service ribbons authorized for civil support missions. Personnel officers provide information to subordinate commanders on the criteria for awards and decorations and assist in their expeditious submission and approval.

Casualty Reporting

8-94. Even during DSCA operations, there may be a requirement for casualty reporting and operations. For military and civilian members who are killed or injured while performing a DSCA mission, the nearest military installation coordinates with the home station casualty area center for family notification and transportation. DOD civilians are treated similar to military members while deployed in support of DSCA operations

8-95. Casualty reporting procedures during a DSCA operation are just as important as if in a combat environment. It must also be understood that domestic media access can potentially be greater than in overseas operations, and any delays in reporting can undermine the family notification process.

FINANCIAL MANAGEMENT CONSIDERATIONS FOR CIVIL SUPPORT OPERATIONS

8-96. When developing command resource requirements, the appropriate staff section must determine if there are any existing agreements, regulations, or policy guidance that the financial manager must support. Based on this staff review, the financial managers ensure adherence to proper billing and reimbursement procedures. Resource requirements include, but are not limited to, contracting, transportation, support to other agencies and force sustainment. The financial manager determines the method to fund these requirements and what appropriations, authorities, and fiscal laws apply during the mission.

Sustainment—Logistics and Personnel Services

8-97. Accounting systems track costs (by event, program, unit, military department, and Army management structure code for each transaction) based on the accounting classification associated with transactions. Financial managers use the accounting classification for two main purposes. First, it helps track expenditures at a detailed level. Second, it helps prepare and present fiscal information to the command and staff, including the status of funds, mission or event cost, status of unfunded requirements, and obligations rates.

8-98. Reimbursable costs may occur because of providing support to other organizations, units, and Services, or agencies. Financial managers normally seek reimbursable authority by contacting the USARNORTH reimbursement cell or the USNORTHCOM financial management augmentation team. The reimbursement cell and financial management augmentation team manage reimbursable budget authority for DSCA events and document expenses associated with these events.

8-99. Deployed units depend on support provided to the logistical system and to contingency contracting efforts. A large percentage of financial management wartime efforts support the procurement process and oversight is critical in preventing improper or illegal payments. Financial managers coordinate with contracting officers and the staff judge advocate regarding local business practices. Procurement support includes two areas: contracting support and commercial vendor services support.

8-100. Civil support operations may require additional financial management support. Financial management consists of two core functions, resource management and finance operations. Resource management support is found in the support brigade budget section. Finance operations support is arranged based on analysis of the mission variables (METT-TC). Additional resource management and finance operations support should be included in planning requirements for the support brigade. Financial managers will coordinate with contracting officers and the staff judge advocate regarding local business practices. Financial management detachment operations may include support to procurement, pay, disbursing, and accounting.

8-101. Financial management detachment operations may include procurement and disbursing support. Deployed units depend on support provided to the logistical system and to contingency contracting efforts. A large percentage of financial management wartime efforts support the procurement process and oversight is critical in preventing improper or illegal payments. Financial managers coordinate with contracting officers and the staff judge advocate regarding local business practices. Procurement support includes two areas: contracting support and commercial vendor services support.

8-102. Not every civil support mission requires a large operation. Often the support provided may consist of a small element such as a dive team (such as the Navy element that responded to the Minneapolis bridge collapse) or a pair of helicopters. Temporary duty status remains an effective means of deploying and sustaining Soldiers performing limited missions. Depending on the situation, the supported agency may contract the necessary support, the defense coordinating officer may provide for their support, or the Soldiers may make arrangements following normal travel procedures.

RELIGIOUS SUPPORT CONSIDERATIONS FOR CIVIL SUPPORT OPERATIONS

8-103. The unit ministry team deploys during civil support operations for the primary purpose of providing religious support to authorized DOD personnel. In this context, authorized DOD personnel is defined as military members, their families and other authorized DOD civilians (both assigned and contracted) as determined by the joint forces command. Laws implementing the Establishment Clause of the Constitution of the United States generally prohibit chaplains from providing religious services to the civilian population. However, following certain rare and catastrophic large-scale disasters, local and state capabilities of all types, including spiritual care, may be overwhelmed. In these situations unit ministry teams may serve as liaison to nongovernmental organizations (including faith-based organizations) when directed by the joint forces command. In addition, the primary supported agency, in coordination with local and state authorities, may determine that additional caregivers are needed and may request federal military chaplains to provide care, counseling, or informational services to persons not affiliated with DOD. Commitment requires meeting four criteria:

- Such support is incidental, there is generally no significant cost, and support does not significantly detract from the primary role of the unit ministry team as defined above.
- Such support is during a Presidential emergency or disaster declaration.
- There is an acute need for immediate ministry recognized by appropriate civilian authorities and directed by a federal military commander.
- There is a government-imposed burden of some sort, such as quarantine on a federal facility, or there is no reasonable civilian alternative to meet the needs of persons not affiliated with DOD who are affected by the emergency.

Chapter 9

Sustainment—Health Service Support

This chapter provides information on health service support during civil support operations. It discusses coordination of military and civilian medical capabilities, health service support considerations, and medical logistics. This discussion builds on the doctrine presented in chapters 2, 3, and 8.

MEDICAL CAPABIILITY COORDINATION FOR CIVIL SUPPORT OPERATIONS

9-1. Army health service support includes all medical services performed, provided, or arranged by the Army Medical Department to meet health service support and force health protection requirements for the Army and, as directed, for civilian agencies during civil support operations. Commanders review considerations for transition to civilian medical organizations throughout operations. Department of Defense (DOD) provides medical support for declared emergencies and major disasters under the guidance of the National Response Framework's emergency support function annex (ESF) #8, led by Department of Health and Human Services (see chapter 2). The coordinated effort includes Department of Health and Human Services, Federal Emergency Management Agency, DOD, Department of Veterans Affairs, state and local governments, and the private sector. Generally, the primary coordination of local, state, and federal medical assets occurs in a joint field office (discussed in chapter 2). Interagency coordination helps determine the Army health service support capabilities required in response to an incident. A defense coordinating officer, working in a joint field office, coordinates civil authorities' requests for federal military medical capabilities, including Army. Primary authorities within a joint field office can include state and federal ESF #8 representatives, state National Guard surgeon(s), a joint regional medical plans and operations officer, and the supported combatant command surgeons.

9-2. ESF #8 of the National Response Framework discusses multiagency public health and medical support to state, tribal, and local governments. The National Response Framework continues to evolve; the most up-to-date information is available online at http://www.fema.gov. The functional support areas covered by ESF #8 are—

- Assessment of public health and medical needs.
- Health surveillance.
- Medical care personnel.
- Health, medical, and veterinary equipment and supplies.
- Patient evacuation.
- Patient care.
- Safety and security of drugs, biologics, and medical devices.
- Blood and blood products.
- Food safety and security.
- Agriculture safety and security.
- All-hazard public health and medical consultation, technical assistance, and support.
- Behavioral health care.
- Public health and medical information.
- Vector control.
- Potable water and wastewater and solid waste disposal.

Chapter 9

- Mass fatality management, victim identification, and decontaminating remains.
- Veterinary medical support.

9-3. Medical response efforts begin at the local level and increase based on requests from local and state authorities. A broad response may include federal military assets. Per ESF #8, DOD performs the following support functions:

- Alerts DOD National Disaster Medical System federal coordinating centers (Army, Navy, and Air Force) and provides specific reporting and regulating instructions to support incident relief efforts.
- Alerts DOD National Disaster Medical System federal coordinating centers to activate National Disaster Medical System patient reception plans in a phased, regional approach, and when appropriate, in a national approach.
- At the request of the Department of Health and Human Services, provides support for the evacuation of patients and medical needs populations to locations where hospital care or outpatient services are available.
- Using available DOD transportation resources, in coordination with the National Disaster Medical System Medical Interagency Coordination Group, evacuates and manages victims and patients from the regional evacuation point in the vicinity of the incident site to National Disaster Medical System patient reception areas.
- Provides available logistical support to public health and medical response operations.
- Provides available medical personnel for casualty clearing and staging and other missions as needed, including aeromedical evacuation and medical treatment. Mobilizes and deploys available Reserve and National Guard medical units, when authorized and necessary to provide support.
- Coordinates patient reception, tracking, and management to nearby National Disaster Medical System hospitals, Veterans Administration hospitals, and DOD military treatment facilities that are available and can provide appropriate care.
- Provides available military medical personnel to assist ESF #8 in the protection of public health (such as food, water, wastewater, solid waste disposal, vectors, hygiene, and other environmental conditions).
- Provides available military veterinary personnel to assist ESF #8 personnel in the evacuation, triage, medical treatment and temporary sheltering of pets, companion animals and livestock.
- Provides available DOD medical supplies for distribution to mass care centers and medical care locations being operated for incident victims with reimbursement to DOD.
- Provides available emergency medical support to assist state, tribal, or local officials within the disaster area and the surrounding vicinity. Such services may include triage, medical treatment, behavioral health support, and the use of surviving DOD medical facilities within or near the incident area.
- Provides assistance, as available, in managing human remains, including victim identification and mortuary affairs and temporary internment of the dead.
- Provides evaluation and risk management support through use of defense coordinating officers, emergency preparedness liaison officers, and joint regional medical planners.
- Provides available blood products in coordination with the Department of Health and Human Services.
- Provides medical surveillance and laboratory diagnostic and confirmatory testing in coordination with the Department of Health and Human Services.

(This list omits the United States Army Corps of Engineers.)

9-4. Most states have a statutory provision that addresses the recognition of medical licenses issued by another state or the waiver of the states' licensure requirements for military health care providers who enter the state to provide medical treatment to civilians during an emergency or disaster. Military health care providers will be covered by the Federal Tort Claims Act and the Medical Malpractice Immunity Act (see chapter 7 for a discussion of legal considerations). The Emergency Management Assistance Compact agreements include license requirements for medical professionals from other states.

9-5. Initial federal-level incident response actions begin with assessment of public health and medical needs and health surveillance requirements. Department of Health and Human Services deploys teams and assets based on requests and the situation.

NATIONAL DISASTER MEDICAL SYSTEM

9-6. The Department of Health and Human Services' Office of Preparedness and Response activates the National Disaster Medical System when requested by local and state authorities. This system integrates federal medical support into a unified medical response to augment state and local capabilities. The system activates in preparation for or in response to a declared major disaster or emergency, for a specific period. Requests for federal military support are processed as requests for assistance. Normally, requests for assistance are developed into approved mission assignments.

9-7. The National Disaster Medical System has three major components:
- Deployable medical response to a disaster area in the form of individuals and teams, supplies, and equipment.
- Patient movement from a disaster site to unaffected areas of the nation.
- Definitive medical care at participating hospitals in unaffected areas.

In contrast to the Army health system, the National Response Framework and the National Disaster Medical System classify mortuary services under public health and medical care (see paragraphs 8-67 to 8-72).

Deployable Medical Response

9-8. The deployable medical response capability for domestic incidents includes civilian response teams and equipment organized for rapid deployment. Team members are non-federal volunteers who may be federalized as part-time employees when activated. They are principally a community resource available to support local, regional, or state requirements. DOD medical teams may support these teams in emergency situations.

Patient Movement

9-9. To move patients out of a disaster area, local authorities initially set up casualty collection points. Initially transportation support may include commercial aviation companies, private organizations, and individual citizens. If local medical services are inadequate, local authorities request state assistance. A state may operate regional evacuation points. When local authorities request state assistance, support may include the National Guard ground and aviation assets. If state and local authorities are unable to establish casualty collection points or regional evacuation points, they may request federal authorities to rapidly deploy teams, such as U.S. Public Health Service Commissioned Corps teams, to assist. If resources still are inadequate, local and state authorities can request additional federal medical evacuation assistance.

9-10. When necessary, the Department of Health and Human Services requests federal military support through ESF #8 for evacuating seriously ill or injured patients. Federal military support may include providing transportation assets, operating and staffing National Disaster Medical System federal coordinating centers, and processing and tracking patient movements from regional evacuation points to reception facilities. DOD takes the lead for federally managed evacuation efforts.

9-11. The United States Transportation Command (USTRANSCOM) Global Patient Movement Requirements Center may deploy a joint patient movement team. A joint patient movement team regulates and tracks all patients, including civilians, transported on DOD assets to reception facilities. The team regulates and tracks patients using the USTRANSCOM regulating and command and control evacuation system.

9-12. USTRANSCOM coordinates DOD transportation assets. Most seriously ill patients are evacuated by air. USTRANSCOM establishes aeromedical evacuation centers. Depending on the nature and scope of the disaster, transportation may be by air, surface, or sea:
- Air Mobility Command.
- Military Surface Deployment and Distribution Command.
- Military Sealift Command.

9-13. Civilian medical teams meet patients at the reception facilities. These teams determine which patients will go to which National Disaster Medical System hospitals. Procedures are based on local agreements and advance coordination among National Disaster Medical System federal coordinating centers and hospitals. Transportation directly to the hospitals is by local ground and air transport.

Definitive Medical Care

9-14. The National Disaster Medical System provides a nationwide network of nonfederal acute care hospitals. These hospitals provide definitive care for disaster victims when the need exceeds the capabilities of the affected local, state, or federal medical systems.

9-15. Sixty-two federal coordinating centers coordinate with a network of approximately 1,800 nonfederal National Disaster Medical System member hospitals and eighty-two patient reception areas to provide an 80,000-bed capability for definitive acute medical care.

9-16. Within this system, the federal coordinating center roles include—
- Soliciting participation in the National Disaster Medical System by nonfederal area hospitals.
- Assisting in coordination of area disaster plans with hospital representatives.
- Arranging annual National Disaster Medical System exercises, and developing procedures for participants to report on bed availability.
- Triaging.
- Transporting and tracking of incoming patients to area hospitals.

UNITED STATES ARMY MEDICAL COMMAND SPECIALIZED INCIDENT RESPONSE CAPABILITIES

9-17. United States Army Medical Command (USAMEDCOM) has the capability to task-organize its table of distribution and allowances assets and deploy them in support of Army Medical Department missions. These capabilities are not intended to supplant table of organization and equipment units but can be used to support domestic disasters, chemical, biological, radiological, nuclear, or high-yield explosives incidents, and other designated support. The table of distribution and allowances assets of the USAMEDCOM and its subordinate commands is used to provide the capabilities needed. USAMEDCOM capabilities include—
- Health facilities planning.
- Investigational new drug capability.
- Radiological advisory medical capability.
- Theater lead agent for medical materiel (TLAMM) support.
- Medical command, control, communications, and telemedicine capability.
- Behavioral health and religious support capability.
- Public health support.
- Burn capability.

9-18. Health facilities planning provides a rapid deployable capability to address, assess, and assist in the comprehensive evaluation of health facility support systems and medical facility issues.

9-19. Investigational new drug capability provides guidance in the administration of investigational new drugs and vaccines as biological threat countermeasures in mass casualty incidents (such as anthrax, botulinum, and smallpox).

9-20. Radiological advisory medical capability provides direct comprehensive radiological health and medical guidance and specialized services to the combatant commander, on-scene commander and local medical officials responding to a radiological nuclear event.

9-21. TLAMM support provides rapidly deployable medical logisticians to base support installations in support of the United States Northern Command (USNORTHCOM) joint task force–medical, DOD installations, and various civil support requirements. The TLAMM capability coordinates linkage of medical supply chain support from the base support installation to class VIII supply sources.

9-22. Medical command, control, communications, and telemedicine capability provides an intuitive, compact, and deployable medical command, control, communication and telemedicine information technology package as augmentation for incident response.

9-23. Behavioral health and religious support capability provides behavioral health care and religious support to local, state, federal, and other government authorities in response to man-made and environmental disasters. These capabilities augment behavioral health and religious support to local medical authorities. They support trauma ministry, mass casualty ministry, and spiritual assessment.

9-24. Public health support is a multifunctional capability that combines preventive medicine, veterinary services, and smallpox epidemiological response. This capability is still being refined but will be able to provide initial disease and occupational and environmental health threat assessments, conduct or assist in the field investigations of disease or injury outbreaks or clusters, and assess environmental destruction or risk related to animal health and food safety.

9-25. Burn capability provides expert worldwide aeromedical evacuation for any critical illness or injury, with particular expertise in the stabilization and management of trauma and burn patients.

HEALTH SERVICE SUPPORT CONSIDERATIONS FOR CIVIL SUPPORT OPERATIONS

9-26. This section briefly discusses special considerations for health service support during civil support operations. This discussion is not exhaustive. The overarching consideration is that disaster response operations are multiagency operations in support of civil authorities. Army health system units support and cooperate with various nonmilitary organizations, consistent with ESF #8 and under appropriate local, state, and federal laws. Army health system units support and cooperate with various nonmilitary organizations, consistent with ESF #8 and under appropriate local, state, and federal laws. Continuous coordination helps avoid duplication of effort. In each situation, the nature and scope of the response depends on the requirements of the incident. Refer to Field Manual (FM) 8-42 for additional information.

9-27. Public health authorities conduct surveillance and rapid needs assessment immediately after an incident. Army health system personnel review all relevant intelligence products from the Armed Forces Medical Intelligence Center, Centers for Disease Control and Prevention, U.S. Army Center for Health Promotion and Preventive Medicine, and other public health entities before deployment and employment. Army health system personnel should deploy as part of the military advance party detachments. Medical units acquire information as rapidly as possible for developing medical courses of action.

9-28. Commanders ensure that medical personnel conduct pre and post-deployment assessments for all Soldiers according to DOD and Service policies. On-scene, following the emergency treatment or evacuation of civilian patients, Army health system units emphasize preventive medicine and force health protection.

COMMAND RELATIONSHIPS

9-29. Based on the size of the disaster and capability of local and state assets, federal medical personnel may be under the command of a defense coordinating officer, a task force commander, or a joint task force commander. The normal command relationship will be operational control. Army medical forces that deploy under immediate response authority remain under the command parent unit or installation until the defense coordinating officer or joint task force assumes operational control of forces. Under a joint task force, medical forces may be aligned functionally, geographically or by Service (such as a joint force land component command or a joint force air component command) depending on the joint task force commander's concept of support and intent. Likely tasks remain the same as those listed in this chapter. Task force–medical, for example, is a component of the federal military chemical, biological, radiological, nuclear, and high-yield explosives consequence management response forces. Task force–medical and its subordinate units are organized to accomplish assigned medical tasks for disasters.

Medical Surveillance

9-30. Medical surveillance and sharing of health-related intelligence help guide decisions for incident response operations. Medical personnel gather data and monitor health threat indicators throughout operations. Integrated medical surveillance tasks include—
- Describing and monitoring medical, public health, and psycho-social effects.
- Identifying changes in agents and host factors.
- Detecting changes in health practices.
- Detecting illness or injuries, including sudden changes in disease occurrence.
- Detecting, investigating, and analyzing collected data to identify necessary interventions.
- Monitoring long-term disease trends.
- Providing evidence for establishment of response protocols.
- Providing information about probable adverse health effects for decisionmaking.
- Investigating rumors.
- Determining needs and match resources in affected communities.

9-31. Medical personnel identify potential health hazards and develop and implement countermeasures. They provide education and training to personnel on potential health threat exposures. They perform environmental and personal monitoring and sampling to document exposure. They monitor the health of the force, gauge the pre-deployment health status of units, and identify preexisting (baseline) health characteristics of assigned Service members. They ensure sampling data, reports, and assessments are evaluated, reported, and archived. They ensure that occupational and environmental hazard exposure incident data and reports are submitted to the Defense Occupational and Environmental Health Readiness System (DOEHRS) portal. Refer to DODI 6490.03 for more information.

9-32. Additionally, veterinary personnel develop a vigorous veterinary surveillance program that includes food, water and ice inspections, suspected animal-to-human disease outbreak investigations, animals treated, and any other veterinary-related events. They archive veterinarian-related sampling data for analysis.

MEDICAL RISK ASSESSMENT

9-33. A Medical health risk assessment is developed as part of the preventive medicine estimate. Army units coordinate risk assessments with civil authorities. The intent is to identify any health threat and its potential impact on the mission. The assessment includes analysis of weather, altitude, terrain, endemic diseases, local food and water sources, zoonotic diseases (disease transmitted from animals to humans), parasites, hazardous plants and animals, and potential exposure to hazardous and toxic materials. Refer to FM 4-02.17 for Army doctrine on preventative medical services. See also Army Regulation (AR) 11-35.

9-34. The completed medical risk assessment is used to—
- Determine immunization and chemoprophylaxis requirements.
- Determine personal protective equipment requirements.
- Conduct health threat briefings on the health hazards.
- Provide individual training to all deploying personnel on health and specific protective measures.
- Educate medical support personnel on recognition, prevention, and treatment of potential diseases, injuries, exposures.

The primary disaster related health threats include—
- Contaminated food.
- Contaminated water.
- Environmental conditions (heat and cold).
- Environmental contamination (air, water, soil).
- Inadequate living or sleeping conditions (crowding and ventilation, for example).
- Disease vectors.
- Accidents.
- Stress.

Assisting Civil Authorities with Inspections of Water, Food, And Waste

9-35. Army health system units assist civil authorities with water, food and waste disposal inspections as requested. This includes monitoring approved sources of food, water, and ice products as well as production, distribution and storage systems. Waste disposal site inspections include solid, medical and hazardous waste streams and will comply with state and federal standards. Public health hazards caused by inadequate or contaminated services may pose a greater threat than the initial incident. Medical units, when requested, support civil authorities with sanitation inspections of potable water sites, systems, and containers. Inspections or surveys are conducted using civilian forms in accordance with local, state and federal guidelines.

9-36. Under most conditions, threats posed by contaminated water and food are interrelated. Medical personnel may support civil authorities with food service sanitation inspections, food service sanitation training, and illness outbreak investigations. Inspections are performed according to local, state, and federal standards.

9-37. Medical personnel may help civil authorities to conduct sanitation inspections of waste handling operations to determine health threats. Medical personnel may also assist with training on countermeasures and use of personal protective equipment, sanitation inspections, or environmental surveillance of affected areas.

Behavioral Health

9-38. Disasters produce strong and unpleasant emotional and physical responses in victims and rescuers. Common symptoms are—
- Confusion.
- Fear.
- Anxiety.
- Hopelessness.
- Helplessness.
- Sleeplessness.
- Anger.
- Grief.
- Guilt.

- Shock
- Aggressiveness.
- Mistrustfulness.
- Loss of confidence.
- Physical pain.
- Over-dedication to mission.

9-39. Behavioral health personnel play a vital role in any DOD force performing civil support operations. Behavioral health personnel apply psychological first aid when required and advise leaders on preventive measures. Examples of preventive measures for behavioral health during disaster response operations are—

- Providing basic needs for food, shelter, and health care.
- Listening to peoples' stories.
- Keeping families together.
- Providing frequent, clear, updated information to victims.
- Helping maintain connection with friends and family.
- Providing responders with regular communication with family members back home.
- Maintaining awareness of the stress levels of others.
- Providing responders with a rest area for sleep, hygiene, and food that is separate from the public and media.
- Insisting on proper sleep, nutrition, and exercise among responders.
- Not forcing people to share stories.
- Not giving simple, generalized reassurances (such as "everything will be ok").
- Not telling people how they may feel, or "why" things happened to them.
- Not making promises one cannot keep.
- Not criticizing current relief efforts in front of those needing help.

9-40. Handling of human remains is particularly stressful. Examples of behavioral health preventive measures used during handling of human remains are—

- Providing basic needs for food, shelter, and health care.
- Listening to peoples' stories.
- Keeping families together.
- Providing frequent, clear, updated information to victims.
- Helping maintain connection with friends and family.
- Providing responders with regular communication with family members back home.
- Maintaining awareness of the stress levels of others.
- Providing responders with a rest area for sleep, hygiene, and food that is separate from the public and media.
- Insisting on proper sleep, nutrition, and exercise among responders.
- Not forcing people to share stories.
- Avoiding simple, generalized reassurances (such as "everything will be ok").
- Not telling people how they may feel, or "why" things happened to them.
- Not making promises one cannot keep.
- Not criticizing current relief efforts in front of those needing help.

9-41. Additional stress management personnel may be required to meet health requirements. Combat and operational stress control and behavioral health teams educate Soldiers about recognition and treatment of stress prior to operations. During deployment, they conduct investigations of suspected stress outbreaks. They use results of the investigations to identify corrective measures. Stress management personnel inform commanders of the impact stress may have on operations and of any irregularities in stress statistics or trends. They conduct briefings to newcomers arriving in the area of operations about stress threats and countermeasures. They brief personnel exiting the area of operations on possible stress-related conditions that may manifest and procedures for follow-up.

VETERINARY SUPPORT

9-42. Pets and livestock require veterinary care during incident response operations. Veterinary issues should be anticipated and planned for. Preventive measures help reduce the spread of disease and minimize injuries. Veterinary concerns affecting public health include—

- Spoilage of human food and water supply (through contamination by animals).
- Animal bites.
- Outbreaks of diseases transmitted between animals and humans.
- Impact on public behavioral health due to the emotions owners feel for their animals. (This is more evident in seniors and children.)
- Overall health of pets, companion animals, and livestock.

Military Working Dogs

9-43. Veterinarians care for working animals during operations (military and interagency). They ensure follow-up care upon redeployment. Based on risk assessments and potential exposures to medical threats additional immunization and chemoprophylaxis may be required for working animals prior to or during deployment. Veterinarians also ensure follow-up care and health surveillance upon redeployment. Additional immunization and chemoprophylaxis may be required for military working dogs prior to deployment.

Animal Remains

9-44. To avoid potential spread of disease, animal remains should be disposed of properly and as expeditiously as possible. Army units may be tasked to assist civil authorities with carcass disposal operations. Carcass disposal methods and locations are determined by local and state authorities. Considerations related to animal carcass disposal are similar to those listed in paragraph. 9-42. Waivers may be required.

MEDICAL LOGISTICS FOR CIVIL SUPPORT OPERATIONS

9-45. During civil support operations, USAMEDCOM continues medical logistics support to Army installations through its medical treatment facilities and clinics and serves as the TLAMM for USNORTHCOM. As the TLAMM, USAMEDCOM coordinates directly with USNORTHCOM, Defense Logistics Agency (as the DOD executive agent for medical materiel), and the single integrated medical logistics manager to ensure the appropriate level of medical logistics support. Medical logistics support is normally a Service responsibility. However, in joint operations, the USNORTHCOM commander designates one of the Service components to serve as the single integrated medical logistics manager responsible for providing centralized medical logistics support to USNORTHCOM joint task forces and other government agencies.

Chapter 9

9-46. USAMEDCOM uses existing Army medical logistics automated systems, infrastructure (including installation medical supply activities at Army medical treatment facilities in the continental United States), Defense Logistics Agency contracts, and support relationships with regional DOD logistics organizations and supply support activities to execute the TLAMM mission. As the TLAMM, USAMEDCOM's medical logistics capability is ready to deploy for civil support operations. Support includes providing class VIII supply chain and medical logistics support to deployed medical joint task forces. When directed, USAMEDCOM medical logistics enablers can assist a joint task force in coordinating for the receipt and distribution of resources from the Centers for Disease Control and Prevention's Strategic National Stockpile. The Strategic National Stockpile is a national repository of antibiotics, chemical antidotes, antitoxins, life-support medications, IV administration, airway maintenance supplies, and medical and surgical items. The Strategic National Stockpile is designed to re-supply state and local public health agencies in a biological or chemical incident.

9-47. Federal military class VIII requisitions flow from the supported units, through the TLAMM master ordering facilities, to the prime vendor contracted to provide the requested item. The designated prime vendor delivers the requested item to the supporting medical logistics company. Joint task force–medical units are expected to deploy with their full unit basic load of class VIII supplies. Service components are responsible to resupply its forces for the first ten days of the operation or until the TLAMM and joint task force–medical logistics unit are operational. Once the medical logistics units are operational, supported units will establish accounts with the deployed medical logistics company for class VIII resupply support. Requisitions are forwarded using existing automated systems. The primary DOD requisitioning system is the Defense Medical Logistics Standard Support System's Customer Assistance Module. The TLAMM conducts post-operational financial reconciliation with other Service components and USNORTHCOM for reimbursement.

BLOOD AVAILABILITY

9-48. Department of Health and Human Services monitors blood availability nationally. It maintains contact with the American Red Cross, American Association of Blood Banks Inter-organizational Task Force on Domestic Disasters and Acts of Terrorism, and the Armed Services Blood Program Office. The Department of Health and Human Services determines—
- The need for blood, blood products, and supplies used in their manufacture, testing, and storage.
- The ability of existing supply chain resources to meet needs.
- Emergency measures needed to augment or replenish existing supplies.

9-49. Department of Health and Human Services sends a request for assistance through military channels when blood product requirements exceed capacity. The USNORTHCOM Joint Blood Program Office, in coordination with the Armed Services Blood Program Office, manages blood products within DOD.

9-50. The Armed Services Blood Program has blood distribution and storage assets in the continental United States. The Armed Services Whole Blood Processing Laboratories are the major blood product distribution hubs. Deployable blood distribution assets include Blood Support Detachment and Blood Transshipment Systems. In addition, medical treatment facilities on DOD installations can be used for limited expanded blood product storage.

9-51. When Department of Health and Human Services requests blood distribution assets, the USNORTHCOM joint blood program office coordinates with United States Army North (USARNORTH), joint task force-medical and Joint Forces Command to accommodate blood distribution and storage.

SPECIAL NEEDS POPULATIONS

9-52. The National Response Framework defines a special needs population as a group with special functional needs before, during, and after an incident. Special functional needs include maintaining independence, communication, transportation, supervision, and medical care. For example, individuals in need of additional assistance may have disabilities, live in institutionalized settings, be very young or very old, or have limited English proficiency. Army medical and nonmedical personnel may support response efforts for special needs populations.

MANAGEMENT OF MASS CASUALTY EVENTS

9-53. The military may be tasked to support civilian medical capabilities as needed in the handling of mass casualties. DOD coordinates closely with Department of Health and Human Services and other public health providers in the joint operations area. Army medical planning staffs cooperate closely with responding organizations under the guidelines of the National Incident Management System and the National Response Framework. The military augments civilian medical capabilities as needed in the handling of mass casualties resulting from chemical, biological, radiological, nuclear, and high-yield explosives attacks) or other toxic material contamination. For pertinent Army doctrine, refer to FMs 4-02.283, 4-02.285, 4-02.7, and 8-284. Also see the *Field Management of Chemical Casualties Handbook*, Third Edition, for additional information.

9-54. In a mass casualty situation, triage establishes who receives treatment first by placing casualties into four categories. Terminology and priorities for these categories differ in military and civilian environments, but the basic concepts are similar. See FM 3-28.1, table VII-2 and table VII-3 for more information about triage in civil support operations. The Army's senior medical commander coordinates treatment priorities with the lead civil medical authority.

This page intentionally left blank.

Appendix A
Planning Checklists

This appendix contains a variety of checklists designed to help unit commanders and staffs with their military decisionmaking process during a civil support operation. The appendix provides general checklists for situational assessment (overall, joint task force, organizational, and local agency) and individual staff section checklists. These checklists are not prescriptive.

INITIAL SITUATIONAL AWARENESS AND ASSESSMENT

A-1. Table A-1, pages A-1 to A-2, lists items to consider for initial situational awareness and assessment. This list is not all inclusive; items need not be considered in the sequence shown.

Table A-1. Initial planning checklist for situational awareness and assessment

Number	Brief description of items to consider for initial situational awareness and assessment
1.	Damage assessment estimates from incident commanders and situational assessment teams
2.	Homes, especially those with light construction, such as mobile homes
3.	Status of roads, rail lines, airports, airfields, communications nodes and seaports.
4.	Other factors associated with the local community and the nature of the disaster (Refer to appendix B for more information on safety considerations.)
5.	Status of first responders and their assets (such as vehicles, communications, and fuel)
6.	Debris removal and clearing lines of communication
7.	Environmental hazards, natural or manmade
8.	Fires, toxic chemical spills (toxic and nontoxic), ruptured pipelines, downed power lines
9.	Weather or geographic hazards
10.	New and emerging threats (such as civil disorder, or another natural disaster)
11.	Further evacuations needed or taking place
12.	Sustainment
13.	Medical capacity
14.	Communication status
15.	Aviation facilities
16.	Search and rescue efforts underway
17.	Water purification, ice, and means of delivery
18.	Availability of basic personal hygiene and cleaning materials
19.	Sanitation capabilities
20.	Security
21.	Available shelter
22.	Availability of food and means of distribution
23.	Electrical power and electrical grid
24.	Availability of gasoline and diesel fuel
25.	Availability of JP-8
26.	Command and control
27.	Incident command structure in place

Table A-1. Initial planning checklist for situational awareness and assessment, continued

Number	Brief description of items to consider for initial situational awareness and assessment
28.	Liaison and planning staff for headquarters
29.	Counselors for citizens affected by the disaster
30.	Communications
31.	Chains of command and positions of authority
32.	Types of communication and information management systems in use by first responders and other responding organizations
33.	Communication assets required for Soldiers to communicate with the joint task force HQ and other responding groups
34.	Identifying alternatives when communication systems are not operating or not compatible
35.	Identification of responding organizations not yet integrated with the overall effort; facilitating cooperation with these groups (including volunteer groups)
36.	Maps, global positioning system (GPS), and other topographic resources to navigate to specific locations when roads and landmarks are destroyed. Map products used by local organizations and first responders. Identifying a map system useable by most organizations
37.	Electronic and hard copy products used to portray the common operational picture across boundaries or jurisdictions and all organizations
38.	Location for the Army headquarters and where to place supporting staff and liaisons
39.	Existing staff and liaisons needing augmentation
40.	Public affairs assets required to acquire and relay accurate, useable information to the public
41.	Synchronization of public affairs operations with the lead civil authority and local news media
42.	Resource requirements
43.	Document actions to assure prompt acquisition of resources and timely reimbursements (Refer to chapter 6 for information required for reimbursement.)
44.	Resources available now and later in the operation
45.	Contracting management and support
46.	How to synchronize civil and military resource prioritization
47.	Communication assets required to obtain resources during the operation
48.	Transportation assets available to move resources and transport personnel
49.	Accounting systems to activate for military reimbursement
50.	Procedures to track expenditures within funding systems
51.	Legal
52.	Initial plans and orders review by staff judge advocate
53.	Review standing rules of the use of force
54.	Permissible actions according to military status of Soldiers (federal Title 10 Active Duty, National Guard Title 32, and state active duty)
55.	Pertinent local, state, and federal laws
56.	Coordination and planning with other responding groups
57.	Obtain a copy of the most up-to-date disaster plan from the lead civil authority with the applicable emergency
58.	Obtain a copy of the applicable joint force land component command contingency plan
59.	Extract how the plan covers the tasks and responsibilities of all organizations based on METT-TC
60.	Determine where Army support is required
61.	Review the makeup and focus of the other organizations
62.	Designate staff responsibility to collect lessons learned

JOINT TASK FORCE CHECKLIST

A-2. Table A-2 provides a list of initial tasks for a joint task force. This list is not all inclusive; items need not be considered in the sequence shown.

Table A-2. Initial planning checklist for a joint task force

Number	Brief description of initial tasks for consideration for a joint task force
1.	Coordinate with military (Air National Guard, Army National Guard, Coast Guard, Air Force, Navy, Marine Corps), local, state, federal agencies and organizations and nongovernmental organizations and volunteers. The bottom line is command control systems coordinate with virtually any agency, organization or individual that can help support the mission to reduce loss of life, limb and property. Determine the most feasible solutions for effective communication.
2.	Ensure that initial communications capabilities are self-sufficient and interoperable with both first responders and local authorities. This usually means commercial internet and telephone capability.
3.	Bring all communications equipment, to include computers, cables, routers, switches, and power supply. Procure and plan for the use of additional communication devices: telephone (satellite, cellular or land line), radio (military maritime, and civilian, in all bandwidths), Non-Secure Internet Protocol Router Network, SECRET Internet Protocol Router Network, video equipment, video teleconferencing, and satellite-based commercial Internet systems. The goal is to communicate effectively and reduce restrictions to effective communication.
4.	Ensure all equipment has operators, essential repair parts, operating and repair manuals, tools, initial fuel and power generation required.
5.	Send qualified signal leaders to ensure operators and equipment are used effectively.
6.	Prepare to provide a limited amount of critical communications equipment (cell phones, radios, base sets, etc.) to first responders.
7.	Plan and coordinate for additional, extended logistical and maintenance support for equipment and personnel as well as unexpected requirements including generator support; maintenance of equipment; fuel requirements of vehicles, systems, and generators; and support for others' equipment (such as charging cell phones from your power source, charging satellite phones, identify internal and external electronic repair capabilities).
8.	Ensure that communications structures are expandable and flexible to meet future needs. Remember that military units and civilian agencies may require extended communications support.
9.	Conduct a synchronization meeting between all primary entities that have impact as soon as possible.

ORGANIZATIONAL AND UNIT CHECKLIST

A-3. Table A-3 lists initial tasks for Army units. This list is not all inclusive; items need not be considered in the sequence shown.

Table A-3. Initial planning checklist for Army units

Number	Brief description of initial tasks for consideration for Army units
1.	Bring all communications equipment, to include computers, cables, routers, switches, and power. Ensure all equipment has operators, essential repair parts, operating and repair manuals, tools, initial fuel and power generation required.
2.	Send qualified signal leaders to integrate signal systems and to ensure operators and equipment are used effectively.
3.	Plan and coordinate for additional, extended logistical and maintenance support for equipment and personnel.
4.	Ensure that communications structures are expandable and flexible to meet future needs.
5.	Establish reach-back capability.

Appendix A

LOCAL AGENCIES

A-4. A complete or precise list of potential responding groups is not practical. Initial disaster response efforts tend to be chaotic, and responders in various regions or types of disasters are different. At the beginning, no one knows exactly who is responding. Therefore, these lists provide a starting point for Army staffs to seek and obtain precise information during a given mission so they can establish communication. Most local government contact information is available in local phone books under "government." Some information is available by internet searches or even word of mouth.

CIVILIAN LEADERSHIP

A-5. Local civil authorities normally can be found at these locations:
- Local town hall (local government employees and elected officials).
- County seat (county government employees and elected officials).
- Emergency operations centers.

PRIMARY EMERGENCY RESOURCES

A-6. Primary emergency resources may come from—
- Law enforcement (local sheriff or chief of police).
- Fire department.
- Ambulance district.
- Department of public works or engineering, including geospatial information and services offices.
- Search and rescue teams.
- Hazardous materials response teams.
- Local transportation assets (private or public).
- Bomb disposal (locations of bombs, bomb disposal assets).
- Local medical centers and hospitals.
- County, city, or town transportation departments.
- Department of public works or engineering.
- Finance officers (such as a city or county treasurer).
- Public safety center.

OTHER RESOURCES

A-7. Additional resources may come from—
- Local library (source for maps, specific local information).
- Recreation and tourism center (source for maps and specific, local information).
- Chief medical examiner.
- Local and regional religious and service club organizations
- Morgue.
- Forensic specialists.
- Department of education (temporary infrastructure, storm and fallout shelters).
- Labor center (hiring of local workers).
- LP gas and petroleum boards (location of damaged gas and oil lines, oil spills).
- Historical preservation society.
- Local Chamber of Commerce

VOLUNTEER RESPONDERS

A-8. Examples of volunteer responders may include—
- Volunteer security.
- Volunteer fire fighters.
- Volunteer and commercial security and law enforcement.
- Volunteer and commercial skilled labor with equipment.
- Volunteer and commercial transportation with knowledge of locations.
- Volunteer and commercial medical services and search and rescue crews.
- Volunteer and commercial organizations providing food, water, and shelter.
- Corporate and independent agriculture.
- Private education facilities and staff.
- Local veterinarians, animal shelters, and wildlife volunteers.
- Commercial gas and petroleum companies.
- American Red Cross.
- Salvation Army.
- Volunteer responders.
- Young Lawyers Association.
- Catholic Charities.

STAFF CHECKLISTS

A-9. Tables A-4 through A-8 provide checklists to assist with initial planning for S-1, S-2, S-3, S-4, and S-6 staffs. Staffs use the military decisionmaking process and ensure the use simple, concise statements in language all parties (including civilians) understand. The Army uses the National Incident Management System and National Response Framework for planning and coordination with other organizations as much as possible.

A-10. Table A-4 lists initial planning items for the S-1. This list is not all inclusive; items need not be considered in the sequence given.

Table A-4. Initial planning checklist for the S-1

Number	Brief description of items for initial consideration by the S-1
1.	Soldier readiness processing
2.	Personnel accountability, including government and contractor personnel and volunteers
3.	Coordination for postal service with the local postal office
4.	Requests for military pay support
5.	Coordination for chaplain activities
6.	Automation equipment including power generation, back-up battery packs with surge protection, photo copiers, printing capability with backup printer, field filing systems, supplies, tool kit, mobile shelving, tables, chairs, waterproof shelter, heating, cooling.

A-11. Table A-5 lists initial planning items for S-2. This list is not all inclusive; items need not be considered in the sequence given.

Table A-5. Initial planning checklist for the S-2

Number	Brief description of items for initial consideration by the S-2
1.	Intelligence preparation of the battlefield (modified intelligence preparation of the battlefield). NOTE: This is an analysis of the environment and civil considerations under incident awareness and assessment.
2.	Maps (paper and electronic) both civilian and military, electronic topographic capability. Knowledge to incorporate systems to build map products useable to help locate personnel and critical facilities or infrastructure in areas where road signs, roads, and landmarks are destroyed. Do military and Army civilian areas of responsibility correlate?
3.	Population demographics of residential areas. Residents of economically distressed areas are more likely to remain in the area and require support.
4.	Ethnic distribution of population in disaster areas; identify types of linguists required.
5.	Areas without electricity.
6.	Areas without water, status of water purification systems, and availability of commercial purification equipment and products, improvised water purification systems.
7.	Location and capabilities of medical facilities.
8.	Status of sanitation systems.
9.	Relief and drainage systems. Effects on mobility for unit vehicles in rescue and relief efforts. Estimated time to drain flooded areas; include bridging requirements if applicable.
10.	Obstacles. Identify areas where debris impedes mobility.
11.	Surface materials. Type and distribution of soils and subsoils in area and soil trafficability.
12.	Manmade features. Identify roads, railroads, bridges, tunnels, mines, towns, industrial areas, and piers. Identify unsafe structures requiring demolition.
13.	Availability of unmanned aircraft systems.
14.	Topographic systems with global positioning system and software.
15.	Operations and physical security.
16.	Arms room.
17.	Automation equipment including power generation, back-up battery packs with surge protection, photo copiers, printing capability with backup printer, field filing systems, supplies, tool kit, mobile shelving, tables, chairs, waterproof shelter, heating, cooling.
18.	Local criminal activity and gangs for Force Protection purposes. Note this may contain Sensitive information—check with the staff judge advocate.
19.	Coordination with local law enforcement to proscribe registered sex offenders from family sections of emergency shelters. Note this will contain Sensitive Information – check with the staff judge advocate.
20.	Special needs populations such as retirement homes and group homes. Note this may contain sensitive information—check with the staff judge advocate.

A-12. Table A-6, on page A-7, lists initial planning items for the S-3. This list is not all inclusive; items need not be considered in the sequence given.

Table A-6. Initial planning checklist for the S-3

Number	Brief description of items for initial consideration by the S-3
1.	Simple, concise definition of command and support relationships (Army and coordinating organizations).
2.	Priority: location of victims requiring rescue, evacuation, and medical treatment; status of local emergency medical capabilities; hazards or potential threats; and facilities (such as schools or warehouses) for temporary housing.
3.	Status of lines of communication, major roads, railroads, waterways, ports, and airports, and airfields in the area. State the nature and extent of damage and projected repairs.
4.	Characteristics of physical damage in specific areas: housing, commercial, industrial, public utilities, and so on. Start damage assessment in high-density and low-income areas: mobile homes, high-rise apartment buildings, and business offices.
5.	Numbers and locations of dislocated persons. Economically distressed areas tend to have more victims. These areas may be near industrial areas containing hazardous materials. Identify hazards such as fires, chemical spills, or ruptured pipelines.
6.	Local sources of media reproduction, especially high-speed, large-format printing.
7.	Availability of civilian engineer equipment and personnel.
8.	Advance party. Include signal officer, engineer, provost marshal, JAG, contracting officer, information operations officer, and internal logistical planner.
9.	Daily schedule.
10.	Briefings and reports.
11.	Points of contact for subject matter experts.
12.	Packing lists.
13.	Transportation (tactical) and convoy operations.
14.	Mission-related training and mission rehearsal exercises.
15.	Weapons qualification.
16.	After action reviews.
17.	Composite risk management. See FM 5-19 and Appendix B.
18.	Liaison officers.
19.	Airspace command and control. See appendix F.
20.	Checks with S-6 on dedicated satellite and cell phones and satellite, cable, or Internet capability.
21.	Automation equipment including power generation, back-up battery packs with surge protection, photocopiers, printing capability, field filing systems, supplies, tool kit, mobile shelving, tables, chairs, waterproof shelter, heating, cooling.
22.	End state and exit strategy. Set end state conditions as soon as possible and recognizing when the unit's work is complete. Coordinate these conditions with other organizations. (The Army responds to disasters when conditions temporarily overwhelm state and local governments.) Include the following checks: • Be attentive to measures of performance and the conditions the Army achieves to declare mission success and the end state. • Make clear to state and local governments that the Army presence is limited and temporary. • Agree with state and local governments on the acceptable end state, usually recognized as when state and local governments can re-establish normal operations. • Use commercial vendors and contractors. • Unit training before civil support mission
NOTE: Army forces avoid allowing state or local governments to become dependent on Army assistance (which could impede long-term recovery). Army forces return tasks to civilian organizations as soon as feasible. If local businesses and contractors can perform tasks assigned to Army forces, the continued employment of the Army may become unnecessary or illegal. It may deprive local citizens of employment opportunities. The primary role of the Army is to train, prepare for, and execute combat operations. Even a short absence from this focus on combat operations may degrade a unit's preparedness.	

Appendix A

A-13. Table A-7 provides planning items for the S-4. This list is not all inclusive; items need not be considered in the sequence given.

Table A-7. Initial planning checklist for the S-4

Number	Brief description of items for consideration by the S-4
1.	Sources of all classes of supply needed for critical restoration activities.
2.	Life support: mobile weatherproof shelters with all required equipment, billeting, mess, rations, water, bath and laundry.
3.	Funding. Units capture costs for reimbursement. Reimbursable authority may be provided.
4.	Transportation (administration). See chapter 2 of *Coordinating Military Deployments on Roads and Highways: A Guide for State and Local Agencies*, May 2005, published by the U.S. Department of Transportation, Federal Highway Department, Petroleum, Oils, and Lubricants.
5.	Fuel access and fuel requirements.
6.	Minimum of a 90-day supply of repair parts based upon weather and increased use of certain types of equipment in unique environments.
7.	Locations or sources to purchase parts, fuel, oils, lubricants.
8.	Maintenance and recovery.
9.	Reception, staging, onward movement, and integration.
10.	Ammunition storage.
11.	Automation accessories required for austere environment.
12.	Maintain an accurate record of the mission. Items to include:
13.	Record of missions performed.
14.	Rosters of personnel involved.
15.	Travel and per diem (military and civil service).
16.	Civilian employee overtime
17.	Temporary personnel wages, travel, and per diem.
18.	Lodging cost.
19.	Transportation cost (car and bus rentals, chartered aircraft, and fuel).
20.	Contracting cost.
21.	Equipment provided or operated (estimated hourly cost for operation).
22.	Material provided from regular stock. (all classes of supply).
23.	Laundry expenses.
24.	Official or morale phone calls.
25.	Retain receipts and other supporting documents. Supporting documents include:
26.	Unit orders.
27.	Temporary duty (TDY) orders.
28.	TDY payment vouchers. (Refer to unit procedures for Defense Travel System Management)
29.	Vehicle dispatch logs.
30.	Fuel card receipts.
31.	Hand receipts.
32.	Request and receipt of supplies.
33.	Government credit card receipts.
34.	Copy of contracts.
35.	Memorandums and other documentation of exceptions to policy and regulations.
36.	Mortuary services

A-14. Table A-8 shows initial planning items for S-6 (or G-6). This list is not all inclusive; items need not be considered in the sequence given.

Table A-8. Initial planning checklist for the S-6

Number	Brief description of items for consideration by the S-6
1.	Incorporate local and state responders into exercises prior to an incident to identify likely communications challenges.
2.	Establish liaison with military (Air National Guard, Army National Guard, Coast Guard, Air Force, Navy, Marine Corps), local, state, federal agencies and organizations and nongovernmental organizations and volunteers. The bottom line is command control systems coordinate with virtually any agency, organization or individual that can help support the mission to reduce loss of life, limb and property. Determine the most feasible solutions for effective communication.
3.	Initial communications capabilities are self-sufficient and interoperable with both first responders and local authorities.
4.	If operating as a joint task force headquarters, the Joint Communication Control Center (JCCC) should incorporate and co-locate technical representatives from subordinate units (task force S-6s, assigned signal battalion etc) with JCCC to facilitate planning and collaboration.
5.	Plan for all means of communications and purchasing of additional communication devices: telephone (satellite, cellular or land line), radio (military maritime, and civilian, in all bandwidths), Non-Secure Internet Protocol Router Network, SECRET Internet Protocol Router Network, video equipment, video teleconferencing, and satellite-based commercial Internet systems. The goal is to communicate effectively and reduce restrictions to effective communication.
6.	Do not send equipment without operators, essential repair parts, operating and repair manuals, tools, initial fuel and power generation required.
7.	Send qualified signal leaders to ensure operators and equipment are used effectively.
8.	Prepare to provide communications equipment (cell phones, radios, base sets, etc.) to first responders based on mission assignments.
9.	Plan and coordinate for additional, extended logistical and maintenance support for equipment and personnel as well as unexpected requirements including generator support; maintenance of equipment; fuel requirements of vehicles, systems, and generators; and support for others' equipment (such as charging cell phones from your power source, charging satellite phones, identify internal and external electronic repair capabilities).
10.	Know the power requirements for your equipment. Always bring your own power generation equipment, parts and fuel for essential communication equipment.
11.	Communications (voice, data, video) with various emergency operations centers including military (Air National Guard, Army National Guard, Coast Guard, Air Force, Navy, Marines), local, state, or federal.
12.	Communications structures are expandable and flexible to meet future needs. What can be established initially and expanded to handle a greater demand? Small deployable packages ahead of larger deployable command posts for immediate feedback of requirements.
13.	Establish reach-back capability.
14.	Conduct a synchronization meeting between all primary entities that have impact as soon as possible.
15.	Realize that geography and weather affects signal performance. A communications system that worked well at one location might not work in another.

This page intentionally left blank.

Appendix B
Safety

This appendix highlights safety concerns during civil support operations. It focuses on composite risk management and accident reporting. National Guard and federal military forces adhere to similar safety requirements.

SAFETY AND INTERAGENCY INCIDENT RESPONSE

B-1. Several official Web sites contain excellent safety information to assist incident responders at all levels identify hazards and protect the civilian population. Examples are—
- Occupational Safety and Health Administration (OSHA) (http://www.osha.gov/).
- Centers for Disease Control and Prevention (http://www.cdc.gov/).
- Federal Emergency Management Agency (http://www.fema.gov/).
- Ready Army (http://www.acsim.army.mil/readyarmy/).

These Web sites contain information for specific types of disasters to ensure responders at all levels have the safety tools to provide support and to aid the rapid return to normalcy after incidents.

B-2. During interagency incident response operations, an incident action plan identifies the incident action safety officer. Appropriate DOD personnel must contact the incident action safety officer and participate in any safety boards or meetings.

COMPOSITE RISK MANAGEMENT IN CIVIL SUPPORT OPERATIONS

B-3. Disaster response involves numerous hazards. Composite risk management is the Army's primary process for identifying hazards and managing risks. Composite risk management is integrated into all phases of mission or operational planning, preparation, execution, and assessment. Composite risk management is a process used to mitigate risks associated with all hazards that have the potential to injure or kill personnel, damage or destroy equipment, or otherwise impair mission effectiveness.

B-4. Hazard identification, mitigation, and management of risk are key factors in safely conducting civil support operations. The Army uses composite risk management program as the primary decisionmaking tool for the commander and staff, while the other Services use operational risk management. Both programs are used to identify hazards associated with operations and to mitigate risks. Commanders implement both throughout the operations process.

B-5. Field Manual (FM) 5-19 provides in-depth guidance in composite risk management, with examples for required staff estimates (see also FM 5-0). The Army Combat Readiness/Safety Center created the Ground Risk Assessment Tool (for both classified and unclassified networks) as a tool for commanders and staff to integrate the composite risk management process. Fewer accidents occur when Soldiers are aware of hazards and hazard prevention measures. The intent of this information is to increase awareness and reduce risk.

B-6. In a civil support operation, safety and accident prevention are critical to mission accomplishment. Training and operating to standard are key elements in ensuring safe and effective mission accomplishment. Responses to any of the incidents addressed in this publication do not imply a need for participants to cast aside safety and standards in order to accomplish the assigned tasks. Commanders, leaders at all levels, Soldiers, and Army civilians are responsible for safety and safe completion of all tasks while conducting civil support operations.

Appendix B

B-7. The Department of Defense Instruction (DODI) 6055 series is the basis for Department of Defense (DOD) safety and occupational health programs. The Army safety program is addressed in Army Regulation (AR) 385-10, Department of the Army Pamphlet (DA PAM) 385-10, and supporting publications. The Air Force uses the Air Force Instruction (or AFI) 91 series; the Navy uses the Chief of Naval Operations Instruction (or OPNAVINST) 5100 series; and the Marine Corps uses the Marine Corps Orders (or MCO) 5100 series in applying the DODIs.

B-8. Hazards associated with civil support operations vary greatly based on the incident. For each situation, the Army uses appropriate equipment and procedures to prevent injury and equipment loss. This translates to effective and efficient mission accomplishment. Safety equipment can include hard hats, combat helmets, gloves, personal protective equipment, biohazard protection, respirators, water hazard protection, personal flotation devices, goggles, face shields, and knee and elbow pads. Subordinate units should coordinate with their joint task force safety officer regarding the type of personal protective equipment, and ensure that the S-4 or G-4 submit the requisitions.

B-9. In general, disaster response operations require Soldiers to—
- Be aware of the surroundings and know how to enter damaged structures as required.
- Be alert for exposed electrical, gas, other utility lines, fallen or flying debris and raw sewage.
- Wear appropriate protective gear.
- Avoid moving or tampering with propane tanks unless necessary.
- Watch for nails, glass, and other sharp objects.
- Follow appropriate procedures when they discover human remains.
- Do not attempt to recover human remains (unless serving as a trained member of a recovery crew.)
- Avoid domestic and wild animals when possible. Leave handling of such animals to trained personnel.

Note: Soldiers should not attempt to enter collapsed structures except under the supervision of trained rescue personnel. Untrained personnel risk endangering themselves as well as any survivors.

HAZARDS

B-10. To identify hazards, the Army obtains information about the characteristics of the specific geographical region and the overall effects of the disaster. For example, flooding of buildings has significant secondary effects in hot, humid environments. Toxic mold and fungus thrive in these conditions. Standing, water-damaged structures can become uninhabitable for humans but may shelter dangerous stray or wild animals, insects, and reptiles.

B-11. Specific types of disasters require specific types of safety equipment. For example, safety equipment for disasters triggered by high winds and water includes life preservers and other marine-specific safety gear, waterproof boots, and special handling equipment for stray pets. Engineering safety equipment for assessment of damaged infrastructure includes equipment for safe repair of damaged electrical facilities, towers, buildings, and bridges. Disasters triggered by chemical, nuclear, and biological terrorist events or accidents require both Army and civilian protective clothing and masks. The Army uses civilian masks and clothing because the Army protective mask does not filter certain chemicals and the mission oriented protective posture suit may not protect against some chemical hazards. Purchase or issue of civilian OSHA-approved filtration masks and clothing is required for specific contamination agents.

B-12. The pace of work in a disaster response and other incidents is demanding. Leaders monitor their Soldiers to avoid physical exhaustion. Rotating personnel between more demanding tasks and less demanding tasks mitigates the accumulation of fatigue. Leaders need to establish and enforce viable sleep plans.

Personal Hygiene

B-13. Personal hygiene requires every leader's personal attention. Many natural and manmade contaminants pose risks during civil support operations. Precautions include providing potable water, sanitary laundry and bath facilities, and latrines. Soldiers should wash their hands often, and make sure that waste is disposed of properly.

Food Safety

B-14. Trained personnel should inspect food and water sources frequently for safety. Contamination may come from sources such as extreme heat, chemicals, biohazards, pest infestations, smoke, and flooding.

Preventable Injuries

B-15. Many injuries to the eyes, ears, head, hands, back, and feet are preventable with appropriate safety gear. When appropriate, Soldiers wear protective lenses, goggles, or face shields. Leaders enforce the use of hearing protection when personnel are operating heavy equipment, generators, or chain saws. Helmets or hard hats must be worn in construction areas in accordance with civilian requirements. Combat helmets (such as Kevlar helmets) do not provide the same protection as civilian hardhats. Soldiers must remove rings or other jewelry that conduct electricity or may become hooked or snagged or interact adversely with chemicals or heat. Soldiers must wear gloves as required. Soldiers must use proper lifting techniques and lifting equipment to avoid back injuries. Soldiers must wear the correct footwear for the job and follow preventative measures for trench foot and fungal infections.

Respiratory Hazards

B-16. Respiratory hazards are common in any disaster area. These include smoke, ash, molds, various airborne contaminants, toxic chemicals, and radiation. Soldiers can be exposed to asbestos, carbon monoxide, nuisance dust, or other caustic vapors. Qualified individuals should conduct tests to identify hazards. When needed, Soldiers must use the appropriate Army or civilian gas, mist, fume, or dust protective masks to remove airborne toxins. Commanders and leaders must understand that current mission-oriented protective posture or JSLIST gear does not provide adequate protection against most toxic industrial chemicals and toxic industrial materials.

Blood-borne Pathogens and Diseases Such as Tetanus

B-17. Everyone involved in disaster response operations must be aware of the risk from blood-borne pathogens. At a minimum, Soldiers must have up-to-date hepatitis and tetanus immunizations. Soldiers must observe basic preventive medicine precautions. Soldiers must use the following equipment, whenever required:

- Latex or rubber gloves.
- Over-garments for clothing protection.
- Face masks for respiratory protection.
- Goggles for eye protection from splashes or spills.
- Bleach and chlorine for cleanup and decontamination of biohazards.
- Biohazard bags.

Stress

B-18. Everyone involved in rescue and recovery operations experiences increased stress and anxiety. Medical combat and operational stress teams, Army Chaplains, leaders, and Soldiers are trained to manage stress. For information on control of combat stressors and for details about specific leader and individual actions to control stress, see FM 4-02.51, and FM 6-22.5. Primary stress management support channels for civilians include local churches and the American Red Cross. The Red Cross can send stress management teams to help citizens affected by the disaster.

Appendix B

ANIMALS

B-19. Disaster conditions increase the risk of bites and scratches from domestic or wild animals, including venomous snakes and rats. Soldiers can become infested with lice and fleas. The danger from diseases such as rabies increases. Household pets can become more aggressive or dangerous than usual. Soldiers take precautions to avoid animal and snakebites. They do not taunt, play with, or handle animals unless trained and authorized.

BITING OR STINGING INSECTS AND SPIDERS

B-20. Soldiers need to be aware of and protect themselves from mosquitoes, ticks, chiggers, ants, venomous spiders, fleas, lice, wasps, and bees. Refer to Army Center for Health Promotion and Preventive Medicine at http://phc.amedd.army.mil/home/ for information on health and personal safety.

HAZARDOUS PLANTS

B-21. Numerous hazardous plants require special handling and safety procedures. Some species of brush, such as oleander, are poisonous. Oleander is used as an ornamental plant around parks and residential areas. Burning it releases toxic chemicals. Poison ivy and poison oak are harmful when touched or burned. Refer to the Army Center for Health Promotion and Preventive Medicine website at http://phc.amedd.army.mil/home/.

ELECTRICAL HAZARDS

B-22. All electrical transformers pose severe risks. Electrical lines can present a lethal shock hazard. To avoid injuries, Soldiers—
- Do not attempt to move transformers during cleanup.
- Mark transformers and report locations to the chain of command.
- Do not touch, work or operate equipment near downed power lines. Electricity might be restored to downed power lines without notice.

B-23. As commercial power is re-supplied, all emergency generators should be taken offline. Only qualified utility or engineer personnel conduct the changeover. If a downed power line is difficult to see but is in a traffic area, Soldiers clearly mark the area so no one touches the downed wire.

B-24. Soldiers use caution when antennas are near power lines. They should avoid erecting antennas near power lines. They identify antennas that may fall on power lines or on people and take appropriate action to prevent accidents or injury.

POWER GENERATOR SAFETY

B-25. Generator usage during Civil Support operations can create special concerns. Soldiers entering homes and buildings need to be aware of the carbon monoxide threat posed by generators used indoors with inadequate ventilation. Military personnel using generators should ensure—
- Generators are only operated by trained personnel.
- Safe refueling.
- Proper grounding and bonding of generators.
- Carbon Monoxide hazards.
- Generator fire hazards and fire protection.
- Generator electrical load limits and capacity.
- Electrocution hazards, prevention and first aid.

Handling Contaminated Items

B-26. Soldiers take precautions when handling and collecting contaminated items. A collection site for contaminated items is established. In addition, sites are designated for showering and clothing changes before Soldiers move to non-contaminated areas. For more information, see the following websites:
- United States Army Maneuver Support Center of Excellence: http://www.wood.army.mil/wood_cms/.
- Occupational Safety and Health Administration: www.osha.gov.
- Chemical, Biological, Radiological, and Nuclear Defense Information Analysis Center: https://www.cbrniac.apgea.army.mil/Pages/default.aspx.
- Center for Disease Control and Prevention: http://www.cdc.gov.

Fire

B-27. Fires trigger extreme heat, toxic gases, fumes, and toxic dust hazards. Most Army units do not have all the equipment required to fight large fires. Special breathing and burn prevention equipment is required. For further information, refer to the United States Army Maneuver Support Center of Excellence Web site (above) and Fire Rescue 1 at http://www.firerescue1.com.

Use of Chain Saws

B-28. Chain saws are inherently dangerous. Chain saw safety guidance is available through every chain saw manufacturer and the Occupational Safety and Health Administration website, www.osha.gov. They require maintenance and prudent use to reduce risk of injury and death. Leaders ensure chainsaw operators—
- Receive training before operation. This includes procedures for chain saw use and maintenance, and how to ensure cut trees fall safely.
- Use personal protective equipment including eye protection, hearing protection, leg guards, and gloves (adjusted according to weather conditions).
- Check for nails, wire, and other metal objects before cutting.

Use of Vehicles and Transportation

B-29. Soldiers must drive defensively and remain alert to potential hazards. Leaders and operators of vehicles—
- Pair experienced drivers with inexperienced drivers for supervision and hands-on training.
- Use experienced drivers in difficult terrain.
- Remind drivers to slow down in limited visibility, on rough terrain, and during inclement weather.
- Secure vehicle antennas to prevent contact with power lines and other objects.
- Take into account the maximum fording depth for each vehicle type, and ensure proper fording equipment and accessories are installed before entering water areas.
- Use ground guides during periods of limited visibility.
- Ensure operators are licensed on their vehicle. Operators designated to transport hazardous materials and ammunition must be licensed to load, transport and off-load these materials.

B-30. All operators of vehicles perform—
- Preventive maintenance checks and services, especially under adverse or unusual conditions.
- Special requirements covered in the "Operating under Unusual Conditions" section of their respective operator's manual.

B-31. Leaders conduct convoy briefings before movement. Additionally, leaders ensure all vehicle operators know how to—
- Conduct a physical reconnaissance of the route to avoid hazards. Mark unavoidable hazards on a strip map and include them in the convoy briefing.
- Reconnoiter the route for bridges or underpasses that might be too low for large vehicles.
- Assess roads, bridges, and overpasses that may not be posted with weight or height restrictions.
- Reconnoiter routes for hazards below the water line before operations begin.
- Check water height before driving on submerged surfaces. (A good rule of thumb is not to drive into running water deeper than the vehicle axle.)

ACCIDENT REPORTING

B-32. AR 385-10 and DA PAM 385-40 address accident reporting requirements. All accidents will be reported within 24 hours to the task force safety office. Accidents meeting the following criteria may require more in-depth investigations and/or Army Combat Readiness/Safety Center investigator support—
- Injury to any military personnel that results in a lost workday.
- Estimated damage of $2,000 or more to any military property or equipment.
- Nonfatal injury or illness to any civilian resulting from military operations that requires either hospitalization of 24 hours or more or the loss of work.
- Estimated damage to civilian property of $2,000 or more resulting from military operations.

B-33. At a minimum the following information is provided for each accident reported:
- Point of contact for the accident information and their duty.
- Point of contact telephone number.
- Unit involved in the accident.
- Location of the accident.
- Date and time of the accident.
- Name and rank of personnel involved.
- Extent of injuries.
- Type of property or equipment damage.
- Estimated cost of damage.
- Estimated environmental cost.
- Description of circumstances and events.

Appendix C
National Guard Weapons of Mass Destruction–Civil Support Teams

Weapons of mass destruction—civil support teams of the state National Guard can respond to a chemical, biological, radiological, nuclear, or high-yield explosives incident. They provide immediate response capabilities to assist local and state agencies. They can also respond to other types of disasters. A weapons of mass destruction—civil support team often provides support for smaller-scale incidents where specific technical capabilities are required.

ORGANIZATION OF THE WEAPONS OF MASS DESTRUCTION–CIVIL SUPPORT TEAM

C-1. A weapons of mass destruction—civil support team (WMD–CST) includes twenty-two full-time Title 32 team members from Army and Air National Guard, Active Guard, and Reserve personnel. It comprises six sections: command, operations, communications, medical and analytical, administration, and logistical, and survey. WMD–CST members receive specialized training and state-of-the-art equipment (both commercial and military) so they can rapidly and accurately identify and model the extent of chemical, biological, or radiological contamination in a given area. They can provide a technical reach-back capability to other experts. The specialization within the team contains a greater number of senior personnel than normally found in a similar-sized military unit.

MISSION OF THE WEAPONS OF MASS DESTRUCTION–CIVIL SUPPORT TEAM

C-2. The mission of the WMD–CST is to support civil authorities at domestic chemical, biological, radiological, nuclear, or high-yield explosives incident (CBRNE incident) sites by identifying chemical, biological, radiological, nuclear, and high-yield explosives (CBRNE) agents and substances, assessing current and projected consequences, advising on response measures, and assisting with appropriate requests for additional support. This includes incidents involving the intentional or unintentional release of CBRNE materials, including toxic industrial chemicals and materials, and other disasters that result or could result in the catastrophic loss of life or property in the United States.

EMPLOYMENT OF THE WEAPONS OF MASS DESTRUCTION–CIVIL SUPPORT TEAM

C-3. In the event of an emergency resulting from actual or suspected use of a weapon of mass destruction, the National Guard Bureau facilitates WMD–CST employment through the response management plan. The response management plan prescribes national response categories assigned by the National Guard Bureau for each WMD–CST, consisting of three mission categories: Priority (gold), Ready (silver), or Standby (bronze). The assigned response category directs how rapidly a WMD–CST must be prepared to deploy to an incident scene after official notification. Non-mission-capable teams receive a "black" status, which alerts the National Guard Bureau to cover that state with other teams. Note that the legislation creating the WMD–CST program permits WMD–CSTs to deploy across state boundaries in Title 32 status without a formal written agreement, but based simply on a verbal agreement between the affected governors. Up to 22 WMD–CST's, for example, deployed to states affected by Hurricane Katrina over a 45-day period in 2005.

Appendix C

C-4. Priority response (gold) requires the deployment of an advanced party of the WMD–CST no later than 90 minutes after the official time of notification (N-hour) and deployment of the remaining WMD–CST no later than N + 3 hours to support a response anywhere within the Nation. Ready response (silver) requires units to focus on preparing for possible priority response missions outside their home state. WMD–CSTs in this response category, once directed, must deploy to the event no later than N + 24 hours. Standby response (bronze) requires units to focus on areas such as training requirements and leave. WMD–CSTs in this category, once directed, must prepare for and deploy no later than N + 72 hours.

CAPABILITIES OF THE WEAPONS OF MASS DESTRUCTION–CIVIL SUPPORT TEAM

C-5. The Analytical Laboratory System is a self-contained, C-130 transportable, mobile, analytical platform. The Analytical Laboratory System provides advanced technologies with enhanced sensitivity and selectivity for identification and characterization of CBRNE agents. Within the compartments of the Analytical Laboratory System, operators have the ability to prepare, extract, analyze, and store environmental samples and to document the contaminated environmental conditions. They may also prepare samples for possible law enforcement evidence in the event of a criminal or terrorist incident, and send them to other national laboratory networks. The members of the Analytical Laboratory System team provide the incident commander with the best available on-site analysis of hazards. This allows the state and federal agencies to determine appropriate follow-on response to a CBRNE incident. When linked to the Unified Command Suite, the Analytical Laboratory System provides on-site data and analysis to national laboratories and subject matter experts.

C-6. The Unified Command Suite is a self-contained, stand-alone C-130 air-mobile, fielded communications system that operates in urban and undeveloped areas using portable and fixed equipment. The Unified Command Suite provides real-time voice, data, and video communications reach back (unclassified and classified) among WMD–CST members, local and state emergency response agencies, lead federal agents, and supporting military activities. This enhanced communications system allows technicians with the WMD–CST to share on-scene data and analysis with any responding or supporting agency.

C-7. The advanced echelon of the team deploys using a specially equipped sport utility vehicle with capabilities similar to the Unified Command Suite, but with limited encryption. It is interoperable with the Unified Command Suite and first responders. En route, advanced echelon capabilities allow mobile voice and data international maritime satellite, satellite telephone communications, a media center with onboard navigational information, and intra-team communications.

C-8. Because it was designed to comply with incident command system specifications, the WMD–CST's integrated command, operations, medical, and communications sections can form the support nucleus of a much larger incident command staff. During large terrorist incidents and natural disasters these teams have provided incident commanders critical communications, hazard predication modeling, medical assessments and support staff. Joint and interagency CBRNE incident response task forces of over 200 people have been structured around the WMD–CST's sections.

LIMITATIONS OF THE WEAPONS OF MASS DESTRUCTION–CIVIL SUPPORT TEAM

C-9. Although WMD–CST can provide a wide array of support, the teams have limited endurance without follow-on support. The WMD–CST can conduct 24-hour continuous operations for limited periods. (Extended CST deployments have lasted 60 days during sustained response operations.) However, commanders should consider providing the team additional personnel for continuous operations extending beyond 18 hours. The WMD–CST is one-deep in most specialty functions. Factors such as ongoing training (including required schools), mission preparation requirements, leave, illness, and personal emergencies reduce the number of personnel available for contingency missions. Required response times require careful management by the adjutant general to ensure mission readiness. To meet increased force requirements or sustained mission duration multiple WMD–CSTs are frequently employed to an incident.

C-10. WMD–CST equipment receives rapid resupply in the form of push packages from the consequence management support center. Equipped with CBRNE detection and protection equipment found in many government and civilian agencies the WMD–CST can also purchase needed equipment during a response. These packages typically move by commercial carrier to the response location.

C-11. The civil support team usually deploys using organic vehicles. Teams routinely practice airlift movement to reinforce responses in more remote states and territories. Normally, the Air National Guard moves the teams using C-130 transports. Interstate movement times can vary widely due to distance, available airlift, and weather. Although WMD–CST equipment is rail mobile, that mode is the least timely.

C-12. WMD–CST is capable mainly of self-decontamination. Limited capabilities and supplies exist for decontamination of other first responders.

C-13. The organic medical capability of WMD–CST, including formulary, is very limited. The team only has enough medical capability to support team personnel.

C-14. The WMD–CST is a National Guard response asset. Strategic planning normally excludes them from Army contingency force packages deployed outside the United States and its territories. However, United States Northern Command or United States Pacific Command may request one or more WMD–CST as part of a civil support mission.

This page intentionally left blank.

Appendix D
CBRNE Enhanced Response Force Package

The National Guard chemical, biological, radiological, nuclear, and high-yield explosives enhanced response force package provide specialized consequence management capabilities required by local, state, or federal authorities. It is the "medium" Army response package, considerable larger than the weapons of mass destruction–civil support teams but much smaller than the chemical, biological, radiological, nuclear, and high-yield explosives consequence management response force. Seventeen chemical, biological, radiological, nuclear, and high-yield explosives enhanced response force packages, distributed among the National Guards of Massachusetts, New York, Pennsylvania, West Virginia, Florida, Illinois, Texas, Missouri, Colorado, California, Hawaii, Ohio, Minnesota, Georgia, Virginia, Nebraska, and Washington, ensure that every Federal Emergency Management Agency region has at least one available.

CAPABILITY OF THE CBRNE ENHANCED RESPONSE FORCE PACKAGE

D-1. The National Guard chemical, biological, radiological, nuclear, and high-yield explosives (CBRNE) enhanced response force packages support mass casualty decontamination at or near chemical, biological, radiological, nuclear, or high-yield explosives incident (CBRNE incident) sites, casualty search and extraction, emergency medical treatment, triage, and patient stabilization. A request for a CBRNE enhanced response force package can originate from a variety of state sources. Requests are channeled through the joint force headquarters–state and coordinated with the state emergency management agency or equivalent. A CBRNE enhanced response force package can deploy within 6 hours of alert and perform their mission upon arrival at the incident site. With augmentation and support, the CBRNE enhanced response force package can continue operations for 72 hours or longer, at which time much larger federal military forces will have arrived to continue the mission.

ORGANIZATION OF THE CBRNE ENHANCED RESPONSE FORCE PACKAGE

D-2. National Guard Soldiers and Airmen form a CBRNE enhanced response force package. Unlike the Weapons of Mass Destruction–Civil Support Team (WMD–CST) personnel, however, they are not full-time active guard and reserve, but must be called up by their governor. They organize and train for no-notice CBRNE consequence management. A CBRNE enhanced response force package deploys to an incident site and provides command and control, casualty decontamination operations, casualty search and extraction, and emergency medical triage and patient stabilization. When reinforced with a security element, a CBRNE enhanced response force package also conducts cordon and entry control point missions. A CBRNE enhanced response force package can be task-organized with almost any National Guard or Regular Army headquarters. Operational parameters include—
- A CBRNE enhanced response force package will normally operate under state command and control as an element of the National Guard (Title 32).
- A CBRNE enhanced response force package supports the state's incident command system when requested through the state emergency management system.

Appendix D

- A CBRNE enhanced response force package may be federalized (placed in Title 10 status), and pass to the attachment or operational control of a federal military joint task force or other higher headquarters. The modular combat support brigade is optimum force headquarters for a CBRNE enhanced response force package.
- A single CBRNE enhanced response force package can operate a maximum capacity for up to 12 hours, with subsequent rest periods. If the incident commander requires 24-hour operational support, the force headquarters requests one or more additional CBRNE enhanced response force package.

D-3. A CBRNE enhanced response force package comprises four response elements: medical treatment, decontamination, search and extraction, and a command and control team. Typical attachments may include a Fire Fighting Element, a Fatality Search and Recovery Team, Air and Ground Casualty Transportation assets, and Air National Guard Expeditionary Medical Support Teams. The joint force headquarters–state (JFHQ–state) is responsible for coordinating administrative and logistic requirements that will be required for training certification, orders, travel, equipment maintenance, and storage. Figure D-1 shows an example of a CBRNE enhanced response force package organization.

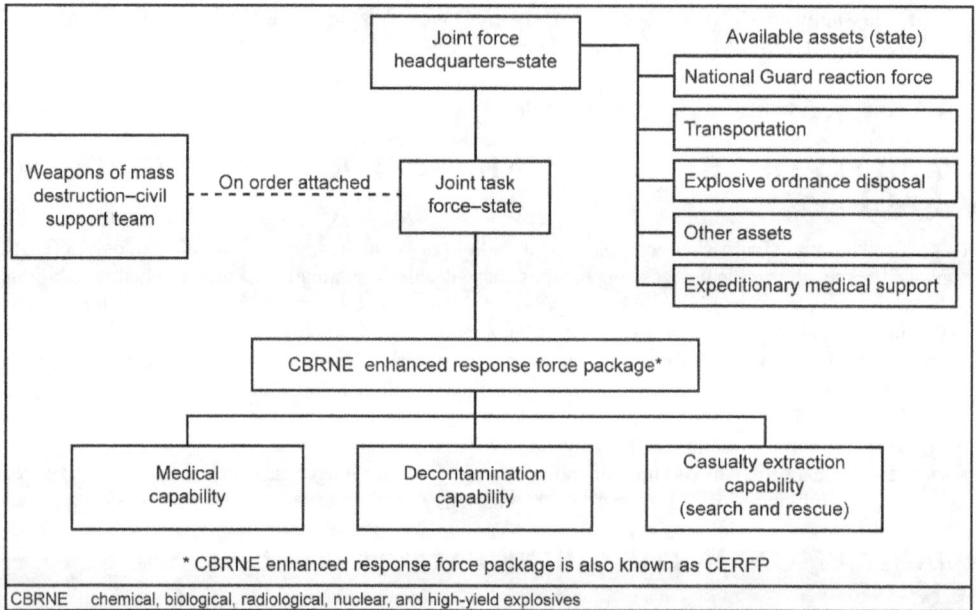

Figure D-1. Example of CBRNE enhanced response force package organization

D-4. The command and control element must be prepared to execute recall of a CBRNE enhanced response force package and coordinate adequate transportation for CBRNE enhanced response force package personnel and equipment to the incident site. At the incident site, the command and control element coordinates with the incident or task force commander.

D-5. The medical element provides short duration, pre-hospital emergency medical treatment during a CBRNE response mission and at rescue sites. Specifically, the team works with decontamination or casualty extraction teams to provide emergency medical treatment and triage in a contaminated environment and stabilization and treatment in the cold zone prior to evacuation.

D-6. The decontamination element conducts ambulatory and non-ambulatory patient decontamination under supervision of medical personnel. The decontamination element will don appropriate personal protective equipment (defined as a minimum of Level C) when conducting decontamination.

D-7. Unlike most search and rescue teams, search and extraction element has capability to identify and recover casualties from a contaminated environment. As a type II collapse search and rescue team, a CBRNE enhanced response force package can conduct medium intensity operations for 12 to 24 hours.

D-8. The parent National Guard joint force headquarters may attach a security element as shown. This normally comes out of that state's National Guard Response Force. The security element receives training in contaminated environment operating procedures. Note that if a WMD–CST is on scene, a CBRNE enhanced response force package may assume operational control of it. Although not shown, the Defense Threat Reduction Agency can support a CBRNE enhanced response force package with technical information on contaminants and other hazards through reach-back to subject matter experts. States should be prepared to task-organize explosive ordnance disposal and CBRNE enhanced response force package capabilities to respond to situations involving explosives. Detachments of the 52nd Ordnance Group (EOD), located around the country, provide explosive ordnance disposal capability in response to requests for federal assistance. Many civilian law enforcement agencies also possess explosive ordnance disposal capability.

MISSION OF THE CBRNE ENHANCED RESPONSE FORCE PACKAGE

D-9. The search and extraction element locates and removes the casualties from a contaminated area (the "hot zone") to an initial decontamination area known as a "warm zone." Medical personnel with the search element perform initial triage and prioritize casualties before decontamination. The decontamination element moves the patient to decontamination, records the casualty, and decontaminates the patient. Once decontaminated, the medical team provides medical treatment and stabilization in a contaminant-free area (the "cold zone") prior to evacuation to an area hospital. If required, the security detachment controls all entry and exit from a CBRNE enhanced response force package area. Figure D-2 depicts a typical flow of patients.

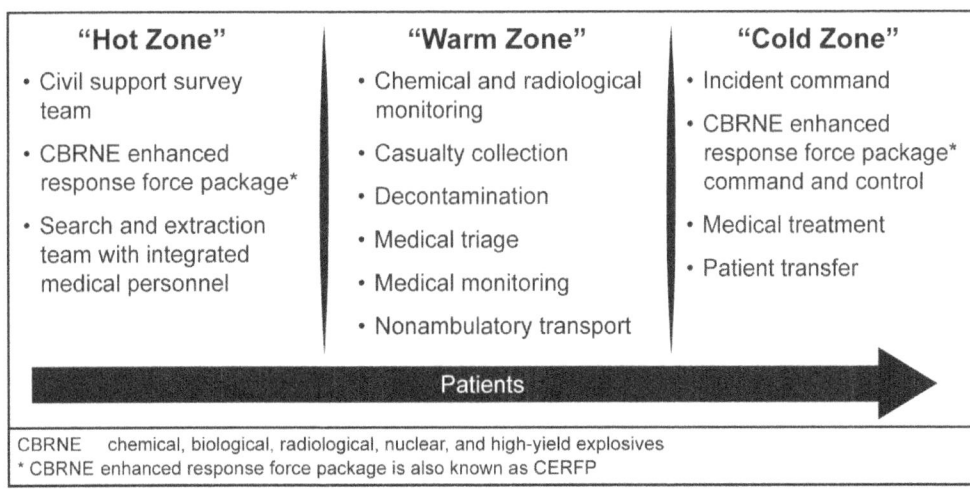

Figure D-2. Example of patient flow

DEPLOYMENT OF THE CBRNE ENHANCED RESPONSE FORCE PACKAGE

D-10. When alerted, CBRNE enhanced response force package members report to designated armories or staging areas and will deploy by the fastest means available to the incident site. A CBRNE enhanced response force package command and control element will establish liaison with the incident command staff and the National Guard task force commander. A CBRNE enhanced response force package will deploy with equipment to the incident site or staging area using organic transportation, or designated

Appendix D

National Guard ground or air assets. An additional command element from the supporting state may deploy to coordinate a CBRNE enhanced response force package's employment and sustainment with the supported JFHQ–state.

SUSTAINMENT OF THE CBRNE ENHANCED RESPONSE FORCE PACKAGE

D-11. The CBRNE enhanced response force package leadership works with the JTF–state, the JFHQ–state, the nearest consequence management support center and the National Guard Support Center in Lexington, Kentucky to sustain extended operations. The consequence management support center should be prepared to provide immediate service and sustainment support for nonstandard, commercial off-the-shelf equipment, as requested. Additionally, United States property and fiscal officer, surgeon, chaplain, public affairs, operations, and state logistic staffs must be prepared to support CBRNE enhanced response force package operations. Chaplain and surgeon activities should comply with state and federal guidelines for employment. If federalized, the CBRNE enhanced response force package will receive support from the gaining unit commander.

Appendix E
CBRNE Consequence Management Response Force

This appendix discusses chemical, biological, radiological, nuclear, and high-yield explosives consequence management response force organization, operations, and considerations.

ORGANIZATION OF THE CBRNE CONSEQUENCE MANAGEMENT RESPONSE FORCE

E-1. The chemical, biological, radiological, nuclear, and high-yield explosives (CBRNE) consequence management response force provides the Department of Defense response to a chemical, biological, radiological, nuclear, or high-yield explosives incident. It is a multicomponent and multi-Service force package; however, all forces are federal military forces (under Title 10, United States Code).

E-2. The CBRNE consequence management response force is the largest of the military forces trained for CBRNE consequence management. Should a significant chemical, biological, radiological, nuclear, or high-yield explosives incident (CBRNE incident) occur within the United States, United States Northern Command (USNORTHCOM) would alert and prepare to deploy the CBRNE consequence management response force to augment federal consequence management efforts. For planning purposes the force includes about 5,000 personnel task-organized into three subordinate task forces. Units may vary depending upon forces provided by United States Joint Forces Command (USJFCOM) to USNORTHCOM, but the capabilities remain constant. Joint Task Force–Civil Support, a standing USNORTHCOM joint task force, normally commands the initial CBRNE consequence management response force committed. Additional CBRNE consequence management response forces will be employed under the command of other joint task forces (JTF-51 or JTF-52 in the continental United States) as the forces become available to the supported combatant command. Figure E-1, page E-2, illustrates the state (National Guard) CBRNE response elements and the CBRNE consequence management response force.

Appendix E

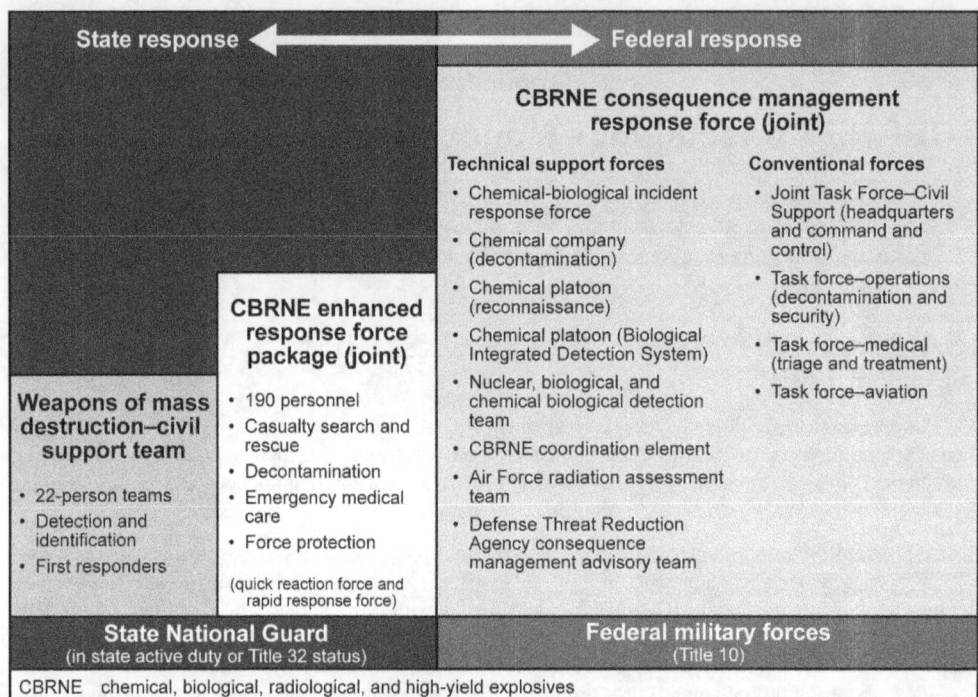

Figure E-1. State and federal CBRNE incident response forces

E-3. The CBRNE consequence management response force is a multi-Service force drawn from the active and reserve components of the Air Force, Army, Navy, and Marines. Forces designated for the CBRNE consequence management response force remain under the administrative control of the parent Service. The commander of USNORTHCOM exercises coordinating authority for training of these forces through commander of USJFCOM. The commander of USNORTHCOM reviews training readiness, and mobilization plans for reserve component forces in the CBRNE consequence management response force.

JOINT TASK FORCE–CIVIL SUPPORT

E-4. Joint Task Force–Civil Support is a USNORTHCOM standing joint task force headquarters, commanded by a two-star officer. Joint Task Force–Civil Support is assigned to United States Army North (USARNORTH). The task force consists of active, Guard and Reserve military members drawn from all Service branches, as well as civilian personnel, commanded by a federalized (Title 10) National Guard general officer. Joint Task Force–Civil Support plans and integrates federal military support to the designated primary agency for domestic CBRNE consequence management. Joint Task Force–Civil Support trains to respond to a CBRNE incident beyond the capability of civilian agencies. When directed by USNORTHCOM, Joint Task Force–Civil Support alerts and deploys to the incident site and commands forces federal military forces provided by the combatant commander. Joint Task Force–Civil Support provides support to civil authorities to save lives, prevent injury and provide temporary critical life support. Some typical Joint Task Force–Civil Support tasks include incident site support, casualty medical assistance and treatment, displaced populace support, mortuary affairs support, logistical support, and air operations. Additional CBRNE consequence management response forces will be commanded by a joint task force with similar capabilities to Joint Task Force–Civil Support. The role of the Joint Task Force–Civil Support within the CBRNE consequence management response force construct is illustrated in Figure E-2.

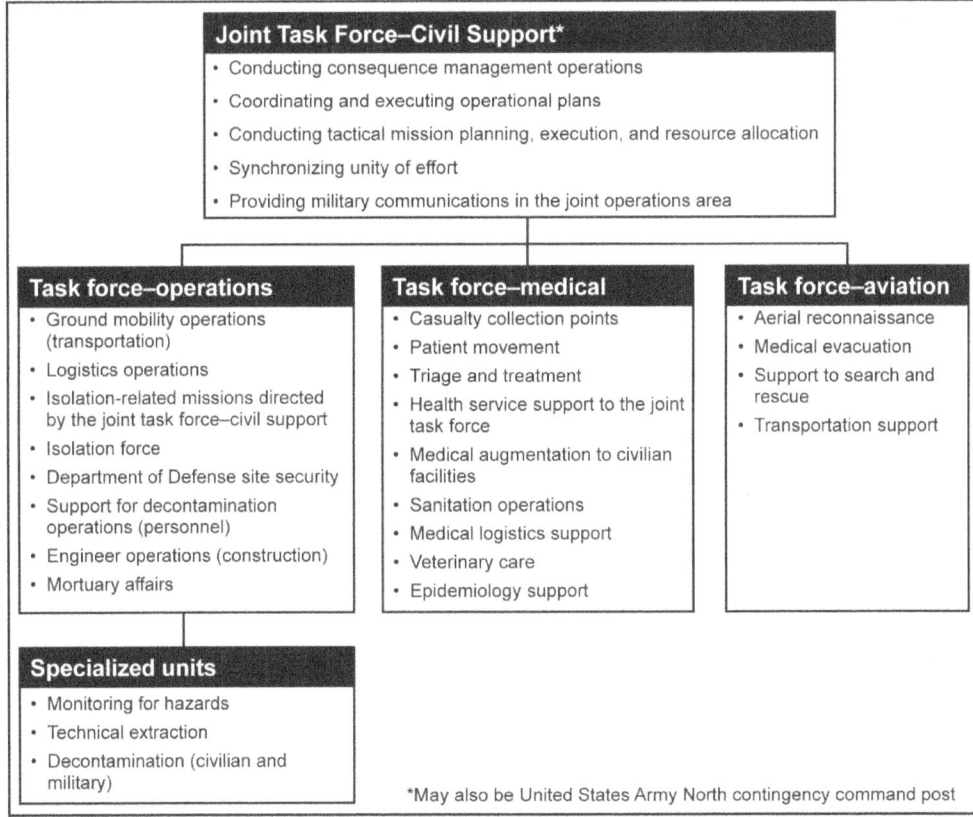

Figure E-2. Organization of the CBRNE consequence management response force

Appendix E

CBRNE CONSEQUENCE MANAGEMENT RESPONSE FORCE SUBORDINATE TASK FORCES

E-5. The CBRNE consequence management response force is a tailored force based on the specialized requirements for CBRNE incident response. It becomes the base organization to which additional federal military forces may be attached or under operational control, based upon the requirements at the incident site. The CBRNE consequence management response force normally consists of three subordinate, multi-Service task forces: task force–operations, task force–medical, and task force–aviation. Each task force has a colonel or equivalent (O-6) in command and is organized around a brigade or equivalent headquarters. The composition of each task force varies according to the availability and organization of forces selected for the CBRNE consequence management response force. Subsequent paragraphs describe the CBRNE consequence management response force using example forces. It is important to note that the logistic support to this force is limited and dependent on the theater logistic support established by USARNORTH.

Task Force–Operations

E-6. The largest task force in the CBRNE consequence management response force is task force–operations. The basic organization comes from an infantry brigade combat team or a combat support brigade (maneuver enhancement) although USJFCOM may designate other brigades. A Marine expeditionary brigade may also become task force–operations, but this manual uses the Army for illustration. The brigade commander task-organizes the brigade and any attachments into subordinate task forces intended for area support, and functional task forces intended for specialized activities such as decontamination or mortuary affairs support. The brigade commander organizes subordinate task force elements around the battalion headquarters available within the brigade.

E-7. In addition to the organic elements of the brigade, task force–operations normally receives specialized CBRNE response units and additional engineer assets. In the case of an Army brigade combat team, the Marines may provide a chemical–biological incident response force—a multifunctional task force. The Air Force and Navy may provide engineer assets in addition to any Army units organic or attached to the Army brigade.

Task Force–Aviation

E-8. Task force–aviation provides rotary wing lift capabilities to the joint task force. Task force–aviation normally includes an Army aviation brigade, minus its assigned attack aviation units. Task force–aviation also deploys with an aviation maintenance battalion tailored to support the mix of aircraft deployed. The task force also includes an air traffic control element to assist the joint force air component commander with Army airfield operations. The aviation brigade provides direct support to joint task force elements and general support as directed to the federal agencies directing various emergency support functions. When deployed, task force–aviation may receive tactical control of Marine or Navy aircraft.

Task Force–Medical

E-9. Task force–medical is a multi-Service task force that provides medical support to Joint Task Force–Civil Support. Typically, task force–medical includes two battalion-equivalent capabilities: a patient treatment and evacuation unit and a medical support unit which provides logistical support and also includes ground evacuation assets. Specialized detachments unique to the CBRNE consequence management response force round out the medical capability. These may include contaminated patient care capabilities, laboratory support, mental health specialists, veterinary care, and disease control sections.

E-10. Task force–medical has three priorities of care. The first is to provide medical care to deployed forces within the Joint Task Force–Civil Support. The second is to provide reinforcing medical capabilities to civilian responders for collection, screening, emergency treatment, and evacuation of patients. The third priority is to provide health service support to federal and state personnel when their medical requirements outstrip their agencies' capacity.

CBRNE CONSEQUENCE MANAGEMENT OPERATIONS

E-11. CBRNE consequence management response force response is rapid, flexible, and provides a designated chain of command for federal military CBRNE consequence management operations. The CBRNE consequence management response force provides capabilities necessary to execute the initial set of anticipated mission assignments. As required, the joint task force commander requests additional forces using the request for forces process. In general, the CBRNE consequence management response force conducts operations according to the six USNORTHCOM phases shown in figure E-3. These phases are not rigid; forces perform actions as needed.

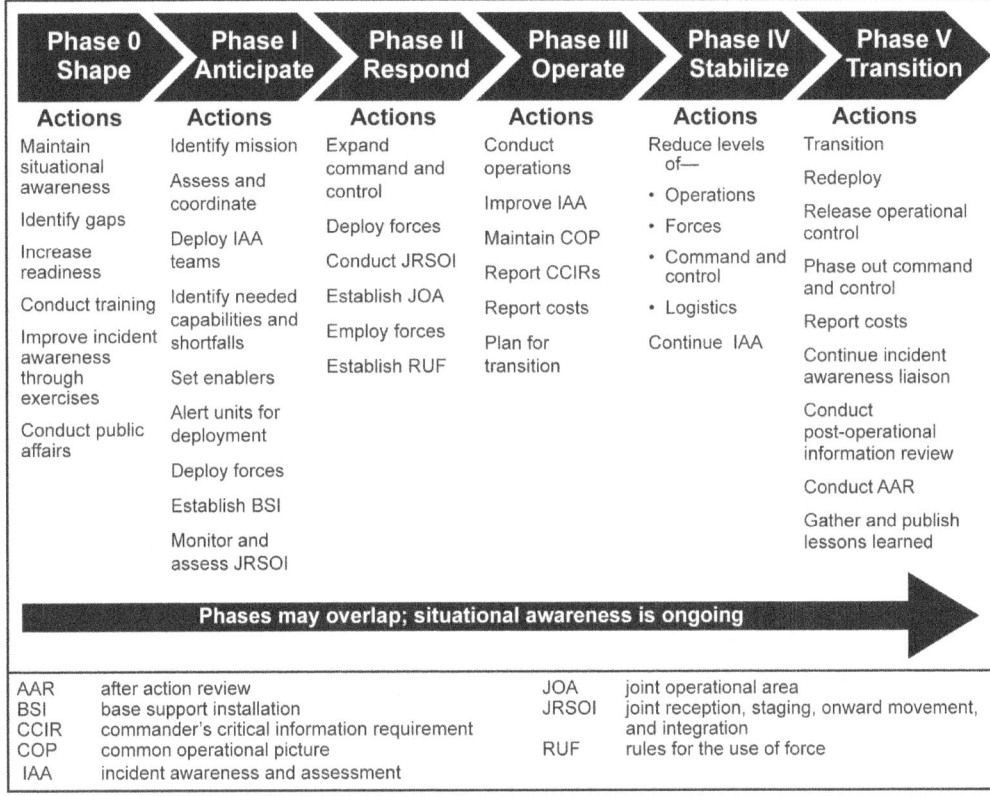

Figure E-3. USNORTHCOM disaster response phases and actions

PHASE 0—SHAPE

E-12. Phase 0 involves continuous situational awareness and preparedness. Actions in this phase include interagency coordination, planning, identification of gaps, exercises, and public affairs outreach. This phase sets conditions for increased CBRNE consequence management interoperability and cooperation with interagency partners and designated CBRNE consequence management response force units. This requires participation in planning, conferences, and exercises while simultaneously supporting USNORTHCOM's Theater Security Cooperation Plan with bordering nations. These activities continue through all phases.

E-13. Response force is the focus during this phase with priority on CBRNE consequence management operations and building command relationships. Commanders focus on training and rehearsals for CBRNE incidents, based on the training priorities provided through USARNORTH. Selected commanders and staff

Appendix E

participate in training provided by USARNORTH (defense support of civil authorities (DSCA) courses I and II). Individuals and detachments receive training from experts on operations in a contaminated environment. The subordinate unit staffs carefully review interoperability challenges, concentrating on command and control systems and liaison requirements with their headquarters and the supported combatant command. They identify shortfalls and submit requests for additional capabilities through their parent headquarters. The staffs also modify existing plans to fit their particular organization and capabilities, and review the plans with the joint task force commander. This includes updating and submitting time phased force deployment data through their parent headquarters and USARNORTH to United States Transportation Command (USTRANSCOM). Each task force commander pays particular attention to interoperability between elements from the other Services, and includes liaison requirements in all planning and exercises. Finally, the shaping phase includes a mission rehearsal exercise. The phase ends with the identification of a potential CBRNE incident through indicators and warning, Secretary of Defense direction, or an actual CBRNE incident.

PHASE I—ANTICIPATE

E-14. The objective of this phase is to minimize the response time of federal military forces and provide the combatant commander with assessments that allow rapid and effective tailoring of the CBRNE consequence management response force, and identify additional requirements for forces. During Phase 1 the defense coordinating officer and USNORTHCOM Situational Awareness Teams) assess the situation and provide reports to USNORTHCOM. The assessments determine the scope and magnitude of the incident, identify potential theater response forces, determine which forces need to be expedited to the incident, and identify potential command and control requirements. This phase ends when CBRNE consequence management response force and follow-on forces receive prepare-to-deploy orders and are staged and ready to deploy, or when the combatant commander determines that the scope and magnitude of the incident does not warrant deployment. In the former case, USNORTHCOM deploys consequence management forces. In the latter case, the combatant commander directs the return to Phase 0 operations.

E-15. At the tactical level, once units receive a deployment order, operational control passes from the supporting commander to the gaining commander. Each subordinate task force deploys liaisons to a location designated by the joint task force commander. These liaisons provide communications connectivity for dissimilar systems and pass situational assessments back to their task forces as the situation develops. Simultaneously, each task force deploys an advance party to the base support installation identified by USARNORTH for reception and logistics support. The task force commanders coordinates with the joint task force commander on rules for use of force, arming status, law enforcement missions, intelligence support and restrictions, public affairs guidance, deployment priorities, and mission assignments (if known). Because of the nature of the most likely CBRNE incidents, forces will deploy into and remain in the joint operational area for the duration of the CBRNE incident response. For a catastrophic incident, the commander plans for force rotation of units within the CBRNE consequence management response force.

PHASE II—RESPOND

E-16. During Phase II, the joint task force deploys forces to key theater nodes and to the joint operational area. The joint task force establishes command and control of all assigned, attached, and operational control federal military forces; develops a common operational picture; and conducts joint reception, staging, onward movement, and integration (JRSOI). Commanders of subordinate units appoint a capable officer and small staff to continue to manage unit arrival and JRSOI. As units arrive and reassemble, they occupy their assigned operating bases and prepare for mission assignments. Leaders take every available opportunity to reinforce Soldier skills they will need when operating in the area of operations. They stress protective measures, rules for the use of force, and situation awareness and reporting. Task force commanders receive and integrate additional forces identified during Phase II. They provide updates to Joint Task Force–Civil Support and keep the supporting installations informed. Phase II success equals forces deployed with enough command and control and consequence management capability to safely and effectively conduct operations. This phase ends when 1) response forces are prepared to conduct operations in the joint operations area, 2) when theater support and incident response forces are postured to conduct consequence management operations, and 3) the joint force land component command and joint task force establish command and control of federal military forces and begin execution of mission assignments.

PHASE III—OPERATE

E-17. Phase III begins when CBRNE consequence management operations commence. Operations focus on mitigating CBRNE incident effects, saving lives, preventing further injury, and providing temporary critical life support. The aim of operations is to enable community recovery through efficient employment of available capabilities. All commanders pay particular attention to safety and force health protection of their personnel.

E-18. At the tactical level, the joint task force commander will begin assigning missions to units as soon as the units complete assembly and integration. Each task force can expect to receive multiple missions in the form of fragmentary orders together with a priority of effort. Commanders circulate constantly between their subordinates in order to experience and assess for themselves the situation on the ground. They also conduct information engagement actions with residents and responders working near CBRNE consequence management response force units. Further, federal military commanders at every level from company to brigade should personally coordinate with state National Guard commanders and other DOD asset leaders operating in proximity to CBRNE consequence management response force. The operation plan, fragmentary orders, and e-mails cannot substitute for face-to-face coordination between commanders to increase situational understanding and achieve unity of effort. If possible, federal military commanders should meet with their Guard counterparts at least once a day.

E-19. Certain units of the CBRNE consequence management response force may work closely with highly specialized personnel from other agencies, such as the Defense Threats Reduction Agency and the Department of Energy as part of their mission assignment. The commander should designate a subordinate commander to provide any required support to these agencies and personally visit them to assess the progress of operations.

E-20. For many missions, Army tactics, techniques, and procedures and mission-essential task list conditions and standards are adequate to meet the requirements of civil authorities developed in mission assignments. However in some circumstances, additional requirements will be established. Army forces should expect some civilian agency coordination and periodic oversight to confirm that projects are progressing on time and to acceptable civil standards.

E-21. Phase III ends when deployed federal military forces are present in sufficient strength that no additional forces are required to perform mission assignments. Further, Phase III ends with CBRNE incident effects are reduced and conditions are set for transition to stabilizing operations in preparation for transition to civil authorities or designated command.

PHASE IV—STABILIZE

E-22. Phase IV begins when the requirements for CBRNE consequence management response force capabilities decline and the majority of assigned missions have been completed, or are under execution, and no other significant CBRNE incident response mission assignments are anticipated. The purpose of this phase is to allow the joint task force to scale down operations. Determining whether federal military forces have met transition criteria will require close coordination and day-to-day interaction with the primary agency. Forces begin preparation of any special equipment and loaned items for turn in. Planning begins for movement to staging areas for redeployment to home-station. Selective redeployment of forces that are no longer required for operations may occur. Phase IV ends successfully when civil authorities can sustain consequence management operations with reduced federal military support.

PHASE V—TRANSITION

E-23. Phase V begins with the transition of operational responsibilities to designated civil authority or follow-on military forces. Civil authorities are postured for full recovery operations and have the ability to accommodate surge requirements. Well before this phase begins, joint task force planners develop transition criteria with specific measures of effectiveness for each mission assignment. As required, they modify reporting formats to indicate readiness for transition. Resource managers should assign particular attention to accountability for non-expendable items that are to be turned over to a civilian agency as part of transition. Site clean-up and turnover of hazardous material protective items and equipment is coordinated with federal, state, local authorities for disposition. Lessons learned and after action reports are completed. Commanders review redeployment schedules and mode of transport details with their subordinates and ensure that leaders understand the schedule and requirements for a safe and efficient redeployment. Forces safely redeploy to home-station to reset and reconstitute.

E-24. The phase ends when the CBRNE consequence management response force has moved out of the joint operations area and is released from USNORTHCOM command. Success in Phase V is achieved when federal military forces have transitioned all operations back to civil authorities and redeployed to home station.

CONSIDERATIONS FOR THE CBRNE CONSEQUENCE MANAGEMENT RESPONSE FORCE

E-25. A terrorist attack on U.S. soil would present daunting challenges for civilian authorities. Unintentional CBRNE releases, whether the result of accidents or natural events, could create catastrophes. CBRNE incidents may cause overwhelming loss of life, extensive environmental and infrastructure devastation, and general service disruptions for long periods. Incidents may occur at one or many locations, simultaneously or sequentially, overwhelming local resources.

E-26. Initial task-organization for the task force should stress unit integrity above capability management. The CBRNE consequence management response force brings together many different elements in a dangerous environment with limited experience working with each other. Exercising command and control through a familiar chain of command, using mission orders, will improve mission effectiveness, even though it will appear to be less efficient. Whenever possible, commanders should specify a tactical control or support relationship between units from different components and Services. This also simplifies logistical support. As the operations progresses, subordinate elements will become accustomed to the mission and the environment, and commanders may change the task organization more frequently. Other considerations include:

- Request and integrate experts in CBRNE training and operations. Use them to assess training and mission preparation.
- Strike a balance between mission accomplishment and risk. In order to evaluate the risks, commanders need to understand the hazards. This often requires individual study and expert advice. Some of the hazards will be difficult to understand, but commanders should press for explanations until they are satisfied that they understand both what the experts know, and what they don't know. Require subordinates to become familiar with the risks associated with the mission and the steps their subordinates need to take to mitigate potential hazards.
- Stay flexible and be prepared to adapt to unforeseen circumstances. Keep in mind that previous CBRNE incidents differ in many ways from the current mission, and that what the units find on the ground may differ from what they expected.
- Be prepared to deal with panic-stricken citizens, many of whom will be very difficult to control.

Appendix F
Airspace Command and Control

This appendix provides guidance on civilian airspace control requirements and military airspace command and control during civil support. Numerous organizations use aircraft during disaster response operations. Army leaders and staff must coordinate airspace command and control procedures to operate effectively along with other organizations to reduce the chance of accident or injury.

COORDINATING AIRSPACE IN CIVIL SUPPORT OPERATIONS

F-1. Army aviation support for civil support operations includes air movement of logistics; transportation of personnel and equipment; command and control support to federal, state, and local authorities; air evacuation; and reconnaissance and surveillance support to civilian law enforcement operations. Federal military and National Guard aviation units support civil authorities for counterdrug programs, civil disturbances, and border surveillance operations. Several emergency support function annexes (ESFs) of the National Response Framework may apply to aviation support, depending on the mission. ESF #1 discusses transportation, including airspace command and control. ESF #9 discusses interagency search and rescue operations. ESF #7 discusses logistics management. ESF #5 discusses emergency management. Aviation support during disaster assistance concentrates on air movement, medical evacuation, and command and control. Disasters may temporarily close ground lines of communication due to debris or higher priority traffic. Large metropolitan areas may experience traffic gridlock. Aviation units may include medium lift assets in the initial response to enhance distribution of critical personnel, supplies, and equipment over these obstacles. Early aerial incident awareness of the disaster area by federal, state, and local authorities helps to assess relief priorities.

F-2. The guiding rule for airspace control in civil support operations is that the Federal Aviation Administration is always the airspace coordinating authority. (Federal Aviation Administration is part of the Department of Transportation.) The national airspace remains under the control of the Federal Aviation Administration. The airspace control plan developed by the Federal Aviation Administration for emergencies provides specific planning guidance and procedures that all organizations, civilian and military, follow for airspace control during civil support operations.

F-3. Each state should have an airspace control plan signed by the adjutant general, maintained by 1st Air Force. As required, the joint force air component commander coordinates with the Federal Aviation Administration and issues supplementary instructions to air commanders to accommodate changes required for emergency operations by military aircraft.

F-4. The airspace control plan assumes that civilian air traffic control facilities and communications will control all air traffic to provide visual and instrument flight rules separation. If requested, federal military command and control assets will augment Federal Aviation Administration capabilities when an incident disrupts civilian air command and control facilities. For large civil support operations, the military plan outlines airspace procedures for assessment, search, rescue, recovery, and reconstitution operations for all military organizations. The airspace control plan describes processes and procedures for the safe employment of air assets, both military and civilian, operating within the rescue and recovery area. The airspace control plan is used for other military operations within the scope directed by the joint force air component command.

F-5. The airspace control plan is directive for all assets, military or civilian, operating in or through the disaster area. Strict adherence to the airspace control plan and Federal Aviation Administration air traffic procedures ensures safe, efficient, and expeditious use of airspace while still allowing all participants the

Appendix F

ability to complete their respective missions. The air component command for United States Northern Command (USNORTHCOM) is Air Force North (1st Air Force, headquartered at Tyndall Air Force Base, Florida). The air tasking order is used to build and promulgate the plan and pass information for air support during a specified period. Airspace control measures can be adjusted daily according to mission requirements by making changes in the special instructions within the air tasking order. To assist with coordination, all military and civilian agencies and organizations provide liaisons to the joint force air component command, and all air activities are coordinated with Federal Aviation Administration representatives. While this is true for federal military missions, Air Force North offers the Contingency Response Air Support Schedule to all agencies supporting disaster response operations. Participation is voluntary; civil and other federal agencies are not required to participate with the Contingency Response Air Support Schedule but are highly encouraged.

F-6. The Regional Air Movement Coordination Center located at Tyndall Air Force Base, assists Department of Defense (DOD) to provide assets and coordinate with the primary federal agency controlling predictability of arrival of transient (originating outside the joint operations area) federal military air assets. Federal military aircraft providing support based within the joint operations area are not included in the Regional Air Movement Coordination Center.

F-7. Information flow during a major civil support operation can be challenging due to the rapidly changing nature of the situation and the resources available. It is imperative that information flow freely between DOD and other participating agencies to ensure all units are operating on the most current information. The joint field office air operations branch is the new and correct structure at the federal level. The air operations branch is designed to facilitate coordination of aviation assets during disaster operations.

F-8. When an Army aircraft supports a defense support of civil authorities (DSCA) mission, airspace control is transferred to the joint force air component command. All military aircraft in the joint operations area are line-tasked in the air tasking order. For those assets not directly tasked by the joint force air component command, applicable mission information appears in the air control plan and special instructions section of the air tasking order for command, control, and coordination purposes. All participating military aircraft adhere to the air control plan and applicable air tasking order special instructions.

JOINT AIRSPACE CONTROL

F-9. The daily air domain and civil support operations are conducted by Air Force North. The 1st Air Force standing air operations center is carefully tailored and particularly suited for all homeland security operations taking place within the USNORTHCOM area of responsibility. Additional tactical command and control systems (ground based or airborne) may be required to deploy to the area based on the availability of the local communications and command and control nodes.

> Note: 1st Air Force controls military airspace within the USNORTHCOM area of responsibility except in Alaska, where the 11th Air Force Air and Space Operations Center supports Joint Task Force–Alaska.

F-10. 1st Air Force is responsible for coordinating DOD search and rescue support within the continental United States (See appendix G). In support of civil support operations, Air Force North is prepared to deploy numerous air component coordination element elements as well as additional liaison elements to support other major commands.

F-11. Air National Guard air control squadrons provide operationally ready command and reporting center mission control elements for support of theater air operations. These elements include radar surveillance and tracking, radar service to tactical aircraft, supervision of subordinate deployed air control units, and data-link of a combined air picture to higher headquarters.

F-12. Many Navy ships are well suited for air command and control support during civil support operations. They possess robust communications capabilities. For example, Navy tactical air command and control centers are located on amphibious naval assault ships. They are able to assist the joint force air component command in air space planning, integration, and deconfliction of multiagency air assets.

F-13. A Marine air support squadron provides a direct air support center cell for coordination and control of aircraft operating in direct support of Marine air-ground task force. The entire direct air support center, or a portion of it, may deploy for civil support operations.

F-14. Air Force airborne warning and airspace control aircraft may deploy to provide a detailed air picture to the airspace control authority. These airborne control centers can become the link between the Federal Aviation Administration controllers on the ground, working out of a military facility, and aircraft in and around the incident site.

RESTRICTIONS ON UNMANNED AIRCRAFT SYSTEMS

F-15. Unmanned aircraft systems have become an indispensable combat multiplier for U.S. forces in combat. However, in civil support operations the Federal Aviation Administration may severely restrict their use due to safety and control issues associated with an unmanned aircraft. See appendix H for more information about these restrictions.

PLANNING CHECKLIST FOR AIRSPACE COORDINATION

F-16. This list provides some primary considerations for airspace coordination in domestic operations. This list is not all inclusive.

- Locate and establish contact with the air component coordination element and air command center.
- Identify the base support installation and determine its capabilities.
- Locate the combined air operations center.
- Identify the centralized command for all military air assets and other federal air assets.
- Locate and establish contact with air operations branch in the joint field office (each joint field office will be organized differently).
- Get a copy of the airspace control plan, and get Web site addresses for updated information.
- Locate the Federal Aviation Administration representatives.
- Find out what assets are controlled by the joint force air component command (such as Air Force, Army, and Navy) or other Services and organizations (such as Coast Guard and Marine Corps).
- Develop contacts with supported and controlling agencies within the operational area.

This page intentionally left blank.

Appendix G
Search and Rescue

This appendix provides an overview of search and rescue performed by Army forces during civil support. It describes the general process used by federal military forces for search and rescue, and provides a comparison between civilian search and rescue and military efforts. The appendix then describes the specialized area of urban search and rescue.

STANDARDS FOR INTERAGENCY SEARCH AND RESCUE OPERATIONS

G-1. Search and rescue involves assisting persons and property in potential or actual distress. Types of search and rescue missions include mountain rescue, wilderness rescue, urban search and rescue, combat search and rescue, air-sea rescue, and mass rescue operations. Conducting search and rescue is hazardous. Search and rescue should only be undertaken by competent individuals under the supervision of skilled instructors and in accordance with Federal Emergency Management Agency (FEMA) standards for search and rescue personnel and equipment. The U.S. government has developed the *National Search and Rescue Plan of the United States* to identify the roles and responsibilities of various agencies conducting or supporting search and rescue.

G-2. As a participant in the *National Search and Rescue Plan of the United States*, Department of Defense (DOD) provides federal military support to civil search and rescue within the continental United States. The *National Search and Rescue Plan of the United States* supports standards prescribed in the *International Aeronautical and Maritime Search and Rescue (IAMSAR) Manual*, various international agreements, and DOD policy—all of which provide the authoritative basis for military participation in civil search and rescue efforts. DOD provides this support only when it does not interfere with ongoing military operations. Emergency Support Function #1 of the National Response Framework discusses transportation, including airspace command and control. Emergency Support Function # 9 discusses interagency search and rescue operations.

COORDINATING SEARCH AND RESCUE SUPPORT

G-3. The Air Force Rescue Coordination Center at Tyndall Air Force Base, Florida, coordinates military support to search and rescue efforts within the United States. The 11th Air Force (Alaska Air National Guard) oversees search and rescue in Alaska. The Coast Guard also oversees search and rescue in the United States maritime environment, including Hawaii. The National Park Service has primary responsibility for search and rescue in national parks. State and local authorities designate a search and rescue coordinator for their respective jurisdictions to work with the agency having primary search and rescue responsibility. Each state coordinates search and rescue differently. The Air Force Rescue Coordination Center ties into to the Federal Aviation Administration's alerting system and the U.S. Mission Control Center. In addition to the search and rescue satellite aided tracking information, the Air Force Rescue Coordination Center computer system contains resource files that list federal and state organizations which can conduct or assist in search and rescue efforts throughout North America

G-4. While every search and rescue assignment is unique, search and rescue missions follows the pattern discussed in the succeeding paragraphs. Response usually begins at the local level with first responders. If the emergency (or disaster) is great enough, the local emergency manager requests assistance from the state.

Appendix G

G-5. Following the disaster, the local emergency manager requests assistance from the state, the state in turn can request DOD assistance through the through the defense coordinating officer. A hasty search and rescue reconnaissance mission may be supported by federal military and state National Guard rotary wing, unmanned aircraft systems, or Civil Air Patrol assets. Coordination between DOD agencies allows prioritization of timely support to urgent needs. The DOD Global Area Reference System combines with local search and rescue grid systems to give a visual representation of areas where search and rescue has been completed.

DISASTER RESPONSE AND CIVIL SEARCH AND RESCUE

G-6. Aspects of domestic disaster response and civil search and rescue tend to be confused. This is because they overlap in certain aspects, such as responsible agencies and resources used, and both involve emergency response. Table G-1, pages G-2 to G-3, points out some of the basic differences between domestic disaster response and search and rescue in a way that may be helpful to Army personnel involved in both operations. However, it does not address how states or localities deal with these missions and their differences.

Table G-1. Disaster response and civil search and rescue comparison chart

Criteria	Disaster Response	Civil Search and Rescue
Nature of operations	Typically responds to events involving large-scale loss of lives or property, with lifesaving efforts (mostly urban SAR). First responders are rapidly overwhelmed and need substantial help from outside the affected area.	Locates and rescues persons in distress in land (wilderness, caves, and such), maritime (mostly oceanic environment), and aeronautical (involving persons in distress in aircraft on land or water) scenarios, including possible mass rescue operations. U.S. forces typically save 4,000–5,000 lives annually.
Main concept	Federal backup to the 28 states with self-sufficient, deployable, urban SAR task forces. Supplemented by mitigation and recovery efforts. Does not cover beyond 3 miles from shore (for example, a sinking passenger ship).	Divides globe into a patchwork of SAR regions, each with one RCC that arranges for SAR services within its region. Part of a global system of two specialized bodies of United Nations.
Caseload	Typically 5–12 cases annually.	Typically 40,000–50,000 cases annually.
Alerts or requests for assistance	May start with initial contact by a government official to FEMA or to a local, federal, or military entity for assistance. Either initially or eventually involves a governor request to FEMA for a "major disaster" declaration by the President.	Usually initiated automatically by communications equipment with distress alerting as a primary or secondary function (providing data to the responsible RCC) or by person in distress.
Common basis for federal involvement	Declared a disaster or emergency by the President based on request and justification from a governor. Default response responsibility is with local and state authorities.	Received distress alert by any means. Default response responsibility is federal military except where other arrangements are made, for example, via agreements with states to handle inland SAR.
Coordination of federal response	By a designated lead federal agency before a disaster declaration to ensure unity of effort. Often has involvement of local military command or other federal agency (for example, National Park Service) before a disaster declaration and by FEMA after such declaration.	By the responsible RCC, using own or arranged local, national, or international resources or by delegation based on plans or agreements.
Primary legal authorities	The Stafford Act[1], Presidential Directives, the NRF, and authorizing legislation relevant to various federal agencies (there are many) to provide or support federal response.	NRF and agency-specific legislation authorizing conduct or support of SAR.
Supplemental authorities	NRF.	National Search and Rescue Plan (NSP), available at www.uscg.mil/.

G-2 FM 3-28 20 August 2010

Table G-1. Comparison of disaster response and civil search and rescue, continued

Criteria	Disaster Response	Civil Search and Rescue
Implementing guidance for NRF and NSP[2]	Mainly the NIMS.	Mainly the IAMSAR Manual and the National Search and Rescue Supplement to the IAMSAR Manual.
Terminology	Mainly per NRF and NIMS.	Mainly per IAMSAR Manual.
Primary policy and oversight authorities	Department of Homeland Security and FEMA.	International Civil Aviation Organization, International Maritime Organization, and the National Search and Rescue Committee.
Typical operational coordination	NIMS.	Mainly international SAR procedures at the federal level, with NIMS and incident command system used mainly within (or when coordinating with) state and local levels. RCC Langley also uses incident command.
Compatibility of disaster response with SAR	Disaster response is carried out per the NRF and civil SAR (including mass rescue operations), if any. SAR coordination is separate from but "plugs into" the NIMS command structure.	SAR procedures achieve compatibility with NIMS by assigning a SAR representative to the incident commander in the operations section of the incident command post.
Command structure	Incident commander of incident command post or unified command.	SAR mission coordinator (usually in an RCC) and on-scene coordinator.
Factors affecting involvement of states	Primary responsibility for disaster response belongs to state. State sovereignty, laws, plans, and agreements. State capabilities. Responsibilities assigned to state agencies. Interstate organizations for governors, emergency managers, and so on. Mutual-aid arrangements among states.	RCC Langley agreements with each state. Various other agreements, where appropriate. RCC plans. NSP provides for states to assume aeronautical and maritime SAR responsibilities that default to the federal government.
Primary civilian agencies	Per Presidential Directives, all federal agencies follow the NRF, with Department of Homeland Security and FEMA as the lead.	The Coast Guard operates 10 RCCs and arranges SAR services for waters around the United States. National Park Service handles SAR in national parks. Primary supporting agencies are the National Oceanic and Atmospheric Administration, Federal Communications Commission, and National Aeronautics and Space Administration.
Department of Defense role	Defense support of civil authorities usually, but not limited to, actions under the Stafford Act.	Per NSP (not defense support of civil authorities), primary responsibility for RCC functions in continental United States (RCC Langley) and Alaska (RCC Elmendorf); secondary support of civil SAR in rest of the world; local military commands have authority for immediate response.
Search and rescue units	Mainly federal urban SAR task forces deployed under the NRF to support local efforts in the United States.	For sea, aircraft and boats with SAR-trained crews and specialized SAR equipment, ships at sea, and all other available resources. For land SAR, mostly state and local resources.
Funding	Mainly various types of funding available under the Stafford Act.	Agency-appropriated SAR; each entity funds own services. No charge to survivors.
FEMA Federal Emergency Management Agency IAMSAR International Aeronautical and Maritime Search and Rescue NIMS National Incident Management System NRF National Response Framework RCC regional coordination center SAR search and rescue		
Note[1]. The Stafford Act is the "Robert T. Stafford Disaster Relief and Emergency Assistance Act." Note[2]. NSP or National Search and Rescue Plan is "The National Search and Rescue Plan of the United States." Note[3]. Includes half of the North Atlantic and three-fourths of the North Pacific.		

Appendix G

URBAN SEARCH AND RESCUE

G-7. *Urban search and rescue* refers to searching for, extricating, and providing immediate medical treatment for victims of structural collapse or other hazards. Urban search and rescue falls under ESF #6 of the National Response Framework. Urban search and rescue is dangerous and highly specialized. Military units normally support specialized urban search and rescue teams and work under the direction of highly trained experts.

G-8. A catastrophic disaster, such as an earthquake, tornado, or a high-yield explosion, would result in a high degree of devastation in urban areas. Substantial numbers of persons could be in life-threatening situations requiring prompt rescue and medical care. Because the mortality rate dramatically increases beyond 72 hours, search and rescue must begin immediately. Rescue personnel will encounter extensive damage to buildings, roadways, public works, communications, and utilities. In an earthquake, aftershocks, secondary events, and other effects such as fires, tsunami, landslides, flooding, and hazardous materials releases will compound problems and may threaten both survivors and rescue personnel.

G-9. FEMA civilian urban search and rescue task forces, and other federal agencies, as well as DOD, will provide support to state and local urban search and rescue operations under three execution phases, in addition to planning and preparation for potential incidents. The execution phases include notification, initial response actions, and continuing actions. Because of the urgency to rescue trapped victims, the first two phases must be accomplished within 72 hours of the event. After arriving at a disaster site, structural specialists (licensed professional engineers) provide direct input to FEMA rescue task force members about the structural integrity of buildings and the risk of secondary collapses when applicable. Search teams venture around and into collapsed structures, shoring up structures and locating trapped personnel. Teams use electronic listening devices, search cameras, and specially trained search dogs to locate victims. When a victim is located, the search group begins the task of breaking and cutting through the damaged structures to reach victims. They stabilize and support the entry and work areas. Army engineers may participate in these activities.

G-10. Medical teams, composed of trauma physicians, emergency room nurses, and paramedics provide medical care for the victims as well as the rescuers, if necessary. A fully stocked mobile emergency room is part of the task force equipment cache. Army medics may be required to enter the unstable interior of the collapsed structure to render immediate aid. Throughout the effort, hazardous material specialists evaluate the disaster site and decontaminate rescue and medical members who may be exposed to hazardous chemicals or decaying bodies. Army chemical, biological, radiological, nuclear, and high-yield-explosives assets may be required.

G-11. Heavy rigging specialists direct the use of heavy machinery, such as cranes and bulldozers. These specialists understand the special dangers of working in a collapsed structure and help to ensure the safety of the victims and rescuers inside. Army engineers may be required. Technical information and communication specialists ensure all team members can communicate with each other and the task force leaders, facilitating search efforts and coordinating evacuation in the event of a secondary collapse. Army signal corps assets may be required.

G-12. Logistics specialists handle the more than 16,000 pieces of equipment to support urban search and extrication of the victims. The equipment cache includes such essentials as concrete cutting saws, search cameras, medical supplies, and tents, cots, food, and water to keep the task force self-sufficient for 72 or 96 hours. Army sustainment assets may be required.

G-13. During planning and preparation, DOD components and supporting federal agencies will plan support for urban search and rescue, and as required, engage in training and other related activities in order to expeditiously execute urban search and rescue. An example of this is the Army's 911th Engineer Company (Technical Rescue). It is the only unit in the Army that specializes in collapsed structure, vertical, confined space, and mine rescue. The unit is located at Fort Belvoir, Virginia. The unit regularly trains with local, state, and federal first responders in the National Capitol Region as part of Joint Force Headquarters–National Capital Region.

G-14. If a disaster response operation requires urban search and rescue, FEMA alerts the joint director of military support, the civilian urban search and rescue task forces, and the Department of Health and Human

Services (U.S. Public Health Service). Each civilian task force alerts its members regarding activation. The joint director of military support designates a supported combatant commander and issues a warning order to all supporting commanders.

G-15. FEMA headquarters, the joint director of military support, and the supported combatant commander take initial actions by assessing the situation. Based on this analysis, the joint director of military support determines the allocation of civilian task forces for the response. FEMA activates the civilian task forces and directs them to deploy to the scene. The joint director of military support evaluates alternatives and may direct the geographic combatant commander or United States Transportation Command (USTRANSCOM) to move some civilian task forces by military aircraft. Other civilian task forces may move to the disaster area by their own ground transportation.

G-16. The joint director of military support directs the supported combatant commander to execute urban search and rescue. The combatant commander deploys one or more tailored joint task forces to control the federal military effort and conduct basic and light urban search and rescue. Each joint task force will consist of a number of medium and heavy rescue teams, basic and light rescue units, and Service support. The basic and light rescue unit is a military unit (it may be augmented with civilian urban search and rescue specialists coordinated by FEMA and United States Army Corps of Engineers personnel tasked to conduct basic and light urban search and rescue).

G-17. The joint task force receives its mission assignments from the defense coordinating officer. The state coordinating officer, or territorial counterpart, provides the defense coordinating officer with requirements for the urban search and rescue. The defense coordinating officer coordinates these requirements with the joint task force, which assigns urban search and rescue units to one or more specific jurisdictions. In each jurisdiction, a local incident commander (or commanders) directs the specific operations of the subordinate units of the joint task force. The state coordinating officer may provide the defense coordinating officer with additional requirements or change the priority for support. The defense coordinating officer coordinates with the joint task force to provide civilian or military urban search and rescue units to other locations. If requested and made available, foreign urban search and rescue teams are integrated into the operation. Units are reassigned to other jurisdictions as required. Upon completion of the urban search and rescue mission, the joint task force, if not needed for follow-on missions, redeploys.

This page intentionally left blank.

Appendix H
Unmanned Aircraft Systems in Civil Support

This appendix addresses the use of unmanned aircraft systems in civil support operations. It identifies the basic types of systems and provides considerations for their employment. This document uses Joint Unmanned Aircraft Systems Center of Excellence categories to distinguish types of unmanned aircraft systems.

TYPES OF UNMANNED AIRCRAFT SYSTEMS

H-1. In full spectrum operations in different areas of the globe, the use of unmanned aircraft has grown exponentially. However, within the United States and its territories, the use of unmanned aircraft is severely restricted. Any use of unmanned aircraft systems must be approved at very high levels by both the Department of Defense and the Federal Aviation Administration prior to employment in civil support operations. This appendix provides some considerations for the employment of unmanned aircraft systems in support of civil authorities.

H-2. Unmanned aircraft systems (sometimes called unmanned aerial systems) employment considerations vary among the different types of systems. Army unmanned aircraft systems that may be suitable for domestic operations include groups 1, 3, and 4. Group 1 unmanned aircraft systems (such as Raven), by virtue of size and portability, have limited range and ability to support large areas of operation. Normally man-pack portable, hand-launched, and controlled with its own individual controller, the Group 1 unmanned aircraft systems have a normal range of less than 20 miles. Group 1 unmanned aircraft systems may be teamed with unmanned ground vehicles, utilizing the same controller for both the unmanned ground vehicle and the unmanned aircraft systems, and may be tracked using blue force tracker. Group 1 unmanned aircraft systems have fairly limited endurance (typically two hours or less). Simplicity of launch and recovery operations allows the unit to employ group 1 assets quickly, within constraints of airspace coordination. Group 3 unmanned aircraft systems (such as Shadow) require a fairly robust command and control and support element, but may have employment advantages over larger unmanned aircraft systems. Group 3 unmanned aircraft systems are normally launched from a catapult, have increased payloads and weapons capabilities, and are controlled by a ground and shipboard control system. Based on weight, power, and size restrictions, this group can be tracked by either blue force tracking or a transponder and becomes a combat multiplier utilizing manned-unmanned teaming. Although still limited by line of sight to the ground control stations, groups 3 and 4 unmanned aircraft systems can provide support in a larger geographic area than group 1 unmanned aircraft systems. Group 4 (Hunter MQ-5B and Sky Warrior) possesses increased size and capabilities over group 1 unmanned aircraft systems but have increased airspace management requirements.

MISSIONS FOR UNMANNED AIRCRAFT SYSTEMS

H-3. Five missions are normally associated with unmanned aircraft systems during civil support: provide incident awareness assessment, support search and rescue, support civilian law enforcement agencies, support communications, and support detection of chemical, biological, radiological, nuclear, or high-yield explosive materials. (Emergency Support Function #1 of the National Response Framework discusses transportation, including airspace command and control. Emergency Support Function # 9 discusses interagency search and rescue operations.)

Appendix H

SUPPORT INCIDENT AWARENESS AND ASSESSMENT

H-4. Incident awareness assessment capabilities include electro-optical, infra-red and synthetic aperture radar imagery, as well as full motion video. Incident awareness and assessment requirements are based on the nature of the support requested, and these requirements will derive from the primary federal agency. For example, after an earthquake, the primary federal agency may wish to ascertain the damage to a major highway running through the affected area for ground-based relief efforts. Broad area and point damage assessments are also components of incident awareness and assessment, and all activities must be fully compliant with the Posse Comitatus Act, intelligence oversight policy, and other U.S. laws and policies regarding the use of U.S. Armed Forces in a domestic setting. (See chapters 3 and 7.)

SUPPORT SEARCH AND RESCUE

H-5. In some situations, military forces supporting a search and rescue mission may plan for the use of unmanned aircraft systems platforms in concert with manned platforms and ground teams. Unmanned aircraft systems can perform the "search" portion of this mission, locating and identifying victims in need of rescue, while manned aircraft and ground systems can complete the mission by performing the actual rescue. The use of unmanned aircraft systems for surveillance and detection allows the manned aircraft to concentrate on rescue of survivors. Emergency Support Function # 9 discusses interagency search and rescue operations. (See appendix G for more information about search and rescue).

SUPPORT CIVILIAN LAW ENFORCEMENT AGENCIES

H-6. Any non-traditional use of intelligence assets must be approved by Secretary of Defense. This includes the use of unmanned aircraft systems with intelligence, surveillance, and reconnaissance capabilities, especially if domestic imaging is involved. Army forces may provide unmanned aircraft systems support to civilian law enforcement agencies (such as the Federal Bureau of Investigation or Drug Enforcement Agency) during counterterrorism, foreign intelligence, counterintelligence, or counternarcotics support. However, all of these missions require approval by the Secretary of Defense. Law and policy dictate permissible use of information and data gathered by unmanned aircraft systems operating in support of civilian law enforcement agencies. Each use is subject to different authorities, procedures and law and policy limitations. All requests for military unmanned aircraft systems to support to civilian law enforcement agencies must be processed in accordance with Department of Defense Directive (DODD) 5525.5; DOD Publication 5240.1-R, Procedure 12; and Chairman of the Joint Chiefs of Staff Instruction (CJCSI) 3710.01B, as appropriate. (See chapters 3 and 7 for more information about intelligence. See chapter 5 for more information about law enforcement.)

SUPPORT COMMUNICATIONS

H-7. Unmanned aircraft systems can fill gaps and extend communication ranges within the area of operations. For example, after a natural disaster cellular phone communications may be disrupted due to power outages or antenna damage. Unmanned aircraft systems could be employed to fill these gaps in coverage, serving as airborne antennas. Communications relay services could also be provided by unmanned aircraft systems, extending the range of emergency first responder land mobile radio systems.

SUPPORT CBRNE INCIDENTS

H-8. Unmanned aircraft systems offer a significant advantage in detection of chemical, biological, radiological, nuclear, or high-yield explosive materials over manned aircraft due to the danger involved and the risk of contamination to the aircraft. Unmanned aircraft systems could gather data used to identify and track toxicity plumes, radiation fields, or collect damage assessment imagery without risk to human life. Additionally, decontamination of the unmanned aircraft system is much easier than with a manned aircraft.

EMPLOYMENT CONSIDERATIONS FOR UNMANNED AIRCRAFT SYSTEMS

H-9. The preferred means of unmanned aircraft systems employment during civil support is in direct support of a civilian agency. In direct support, the military unit generating the unmanned aircraft systems Missions receives the tasks and priorities from the supported agency. The unmanned aircraft system collects the data and the data is downloaded to the military detachment, which in turn passes the information directly to the supported agency. If required the military unit may provide on-site analysis of the data, but does not retain the data once provided to the supported agency.

H-10. Use of unmanned aircraft systems during civil support should be a last resort when manned assets are not available or not practical. The driving force behind a decision to employ an unmanned aircraft system must be the capability required for the operation in question. These systems give the commander many capabilities, but in many cases unmanned aircraft systems may not be the most efficient, timely, or practical method of achieving the commander's desired effect. There may be cases where a manned platform can provide the desired capability in a much more timely and efficient manner. The decision to employ unmanned aircraft systems must be judicious. Unmanned aircraft systems are well-suited for those missions characterized as dull, dirty or dangerous. Dull missions are those where persistence or long on-station dwell times are required. Persistence gives unmanned aircraft systems an advantage over manned systems. Dirty missions are those missions that risk contamination to the vehicle or crew. An obvious application of a dirty mission is the detection of chemical, biological, radiological, nuclear, or high-yield explosive materials. Finally, dangerous missions are those missions where there is substantial risk to the airframe and operator of the system. This risk may come from an adversary or the environment itself. The "dull, dirty or dangerous" standard is a good rule of thumb for planners and commanders to use when considering unmanned aircraft system employment. The temptation to use unmanned aircraft systems simply because they are available should be avoided. The unmanned aircraft system needs to be the best available asset that enables the commander to provide the necessary capability.

H-11. The joint force air component command remains the approving authority for Army unmanned aircraft system missions; there is no "free space" below coordinating altitudes for small tactical systems. The Secretary of Defense approves unmanned aircraft system missions, not the joint force air component command. Deconfliction of airspace below the coordinating altitude is the responsibility of the Federal Aviation Administration and local authorities, unless the entire national airspace is put under military control. Army National Guard unmanned aircraft systems, with the approval of the Secretary of Defense, can be used in support of local authorities.

H-12. Certain unmanned aircraft systems such as Global Hawk can operate far above normal commercial traffic while providing situation assessment to ground commanders. Intermediate systems such as the Predator have supported recent disaster operations, dramatically increasing situational awareness at the field office level. If available and authorized, these systems can provide real time surveillance to command posts for extended periods. The approval process is not automatic. Requests for unmanned aircraft system surveillance support goes through the joint force air component command and joint task force to the joint field office for joint staff approval. The joint force air component command coordinates with the Federal Aviation Administration and includes the mission on the air taking order when approved. The Federal Aviation Administration issues notices to Airmen as required.

COMMAND AND CONTROL OF UNMANNED AIRCRAFT SYSTEMS

H-13. Command and control relationships for unmanned aircraft systems operations should be defined in advance of execution of the mission. In general, the controlling joint task force will typically exercise operational control of the available unmanned aircraft systems.

H-14. Unmanned aircraft system operators supporting domestic missions should anticipate coordinating their actions through the joint task force to supporting the joint force air component commander and be prepared for inclusion of their operations in the air tasking order. Regardless of the nature of operations, unmanned aircraft systems command and control structures must be thoroughly planned (well in advance,

Appendix H

when possible), responsive to both operator and user inputs, and flexible enough to handle changes to the operation. This is particularly important for re-tasking of unmanned aircraft systems assets.

H-15. The joint force air component command will provide guidance regarding the certification of authorization approval process due to their long-term relationship established with the Federal Aviation Administration. Regardless of the status of a certification of authorization application, active coordination with the Federal Aviation Administration when planning to operate military unmanned aircraft systems in the domestic airspace of the United States cannot be overemphasized. Timely coordination with the Federal Aviation Administration will give the operator a greater chance of gaining approval to operate unmanned aircraft systems where and when required. In those instances where no pre-existing certification of authorization is in place, a process is in place between joint force air component command and the Federal Aviation Administration to expedite certification of authorization approval for in extremis cases.

UNMANNED AIRCRAFT SYSTEMS AND DISASTER SUPPORT

H-16. Before an incident with some warning (such as a hurricane) units with unmanned aircraft systems assets should evaluate the requirement and environment to determine whether unmanned aircraft systems operations will be available to support possible requests for assistance. Unmanned aircraft systems normally do not have the speed or the range to allow for operations directly from their home station. They must deploy to a base support installation near the incident area. Deployment considerations include site surveys for possible operating locations. Planners should ensure unmanned aircraft system operations are conducted at smaller or remote sites, away from other disaster relief aircraft. Initial coordination for temporary flight restriction or Certification of Authorization should be staffed through United States Northern Command (USNORTHCOM) or United States Pacific Command (USPACOM) and then through the joint force air component command to the Federal Aviation Administration. An Army Regional Representative to the Federal Aviation Administration is located at each of the Federal Aviation Administration service centers to provide day-to-day unmanned aircraft systems coordination.

H-17. During an immediate response situation or the initial stages of a larger response, designated units move their unmanned aircraft systems to their operating locations. Additionally, units should be prepared to meet and coordinate with local airspace users to facilitate safe operations within the unmanned aircraft systems operating area. Under ideal conditions, the Federal Aviation Administration will issue a temporary flight restriction for disaster relief operations that authorize unmanned aircraft systems operations. With or without a temporary flight restriction, unmanned aircraft systems operations will require a certification of authorization from the Federal Aviation Administration to conduct operations. Units should ensure an additional site survey is conducted if their previously selected operating location sustained damage. Additions, modifications, or changes to the final certification of authorization must be coordinated with the joint force air component command for inclusion in the airspace control plan and the air tasking order.

H-18. In the aftermath of a disaster, the primary mission for unmanned aircraft systems will become assessment of the extent of the disaster. Additional unmanned aircraft systems missions include conducting initial damage assessment of critical locations and infrastructure, and identification of those areas hardest hit. Unmanned aircraft systems operations may be used to assist with locating and identifying personnel requiring rescue. Unmanned aircraft systems operations may provide critical information to law enforcement agencies by providing persistent observation of critical facilities and affected areas.

LIMITATIONS ON THE USE OF UNMANNED AIRCRAFT SYSTEMS

H-19. There are numerous limitations involving unmanned aircraft systems operations in United States. The three most important are legal restrictions, Federal Aviation Administration restrictions, and weather restrictions.

Legal Restrictions

H-20. Restrictions on the use of unmanned aircraft systems in domestic operations are numerous. Use of DOD intelligence capabilities for civil support missions, such incident awareness and assessment, damage assessment, and search and rescue, requires prior Secretary of Defense approval, together with approval of both the mission and use of the specific DOD intelligence community capabilities. Certain missions may require not only approval of the Secretary of Defense, but also coordination, certification, and possibly, prior approval by the Attorney General of the United States. Additionally, there are several DOD directives and CJCSIs covering military support to civil authorities. For example, DODDs 3025.12 and 5525.5 and CJCSI 3710.01B may apply to domestic unmanned aircraft systems operations. The Chairman of the Joint Chiefs of Staff standing execute order for DSCA (referred to as the CJCS DSCA EXORD) provides guidance on operational parameters and limitations on use of DOD intelligence capabilities for DSCA missions. Further, per DODD 5525.5, military systems are not to be used for surveillance and pursuit of individuals.

H-21. All requests for unmanned aircraft systems must be approved by Secretary of Defense. Operators of unmanned aircraft systems supporting civilian law enforcement agencies must be cognizant of, and fully comply with, DODD 5525.5 (see paragraph H-6) and any operational parameters and limitations specified in the CJCS DSCA EXORD regarding collection, retention, and dissemination of unmanned aircraft systems sensor data and imagery. Operators cannot conduct surveillance on specifically identified U.S. persons, unless expressly approved by the Secretary of Defense, consistent with U.S. laws and regulations. Additionally, civilian law enforcement agencies will handle any data collected by such surveillance operations. Finally, per current Office of the Secretary of Defense guidance, National Guard forces conducting domestic unmanned aircraft systems operations are normally in Title 10 (United States Code) status, unless the Secretary of Defense determines Title 32 status is more appropriate.

Federal Aviation Administration Restrictions

H-22. By far the biggest challenge to operating unmanned aircraft systems in the United States, its territories and possessions is access to the National Airspace System. Since unmanned aircraft systems are by their very nature different from manned systems, unmanned aircraft systems do not meet the same standards for operations in the National Airspace System that are required for manned systems (the ability to "see and avoid" other aircraft, for example). In order to fly unmanned aircraft systems in other than military restricted airspace or warning areas, unmanned aircraft systems operators must apply for a certificate of waiver or authorization (certification of authorization) from the Federal Aviation Administration granting specific permission to fly the unmanned aircraft systems in the National Airspace System. This certification of authorization process can take up to 60 days, although work is underway to shorten this process. Emergency certification of authorizations timeline can be reduced to hours if conditions dictate. Additionally, unmanned aircraft systems operators should be prepared to meet other Federal Aviation Administration requirements such as qualification training for operators and knowledge of the airspace regulations for the type of airspace the unmanned aircraft systems will operate in.

H-23. The Federal Aviation Administration will activate a temporary flight restriction in the vicinity of disaster and hazard areas, or approve an emergency certification of authorization for the unmanned aircraft systems to operate. Unmanned aircraft systems operations within an approved temporary flight restriction should be added to the verbiage contained in the temporary flight restriction. For operations outside the temporary flight restriction, an additional certification of authorization will be required.

Weather Restrictions

H-24. Severe weather presents operational challenges to most unmanned aircraft systems. Planners have to carefully consider the weather in the intended area of operations to determine if manned systems are more suitable for the desired mission. In-flight conditions such as icing, heavy precipitation or instrument meteorological conditions at the launch and recovery site will likely preclude unmanned aircraft systems operations. Throughout the civil support mission, unmanned aircraft systems employment depends on the current and forecasted weather conditions of the affected area.

This page intentionally left blank.

Appendix I
Joint Field Office Sections

This appendix illustrates examples of the four sections of a joint field office fully manned for operations, with all emergency support functions activated. This appendix provides a breakout diagram of each section, based on the incident command system. "Joint," in this context, refers to an interagency organization based on national policy documents.

EMERGENCY SUPPORT FUNCTIONS

I-1. The National Response Framework contains the emergency support function annexes that specify lead and supporting agencies for interagency incident response operations. The National Incident Management System describes the incident command system used for organizing the participating organizations. Chapter 2 of this field manual discusses the emergency support functions, joint field office, and incident management system.

I-2. As the primary agency (normally the Federal Emergency Management Agency, or FEMA) activates each emergency support function (ESF), the lead agency for each ESF deploys personnel for the joint field office. In addition, each ESF lead agency also assigns personnel as required to other functions and incident command system staff elements. (See table 2-1 for a listing of the 15 ESFs and their coordinating agencies.) Per the National Response Framework, participating agencies may have primary and support responsibilities. Department of Defense is a supporting agency for all ESFs except ESF #3, which is led by the United States Army Corps of Engineers.

Appendix I

I-3. This excerpt from the *National Response Framework: Overview* summarizes how ESFs work during an interagency response:

> *The Federal Government and many State governments organize much of their resources and capabilities—as well as those of certain private-sector and nongovernmental organizations—under 15 Emergency Support Functions (ESFs). ESFs align categories of resources and provide strategic objectives for their use.*
>
> *During a response, ESFs are a critical mechanism to coordinate functional capabilities and resources provided by Federal departments and agencies, along with certain private-sector and nongovernmental organizations. ESFs may be selectively activated for both Stafford Act and non-Stafford Act incidents where Federal departments or agencies request DHS [Department of Homeland Security] assistance or under other circumstances. Not all incidents result in the activation of ESFs.*
>
> *ESFs may be activated to support headquarters, regional, and/or field activities. The Incident Command System provides for the flexibility to assign ESF and other stakeholder resources according to their capabilities, tasking, and requirements to augment and support the other sections of the Joint Field Office (JFO)/Regional Response Coordination Center (RRCC) or National Response Coordination Center (NRCC) in order to respond to incidents in a more collaborative and cross-cutting manner.*
>
> *While ESFs are typically assigned to a specific section at the NRCC or in the JFO/RRCC for management purposes, resources may be assigned anywhere within the Unified Coordination structure. Regardless of the section in which an ESF may reside, that entity works in conjunction with other JFO sections to ensure that appropriate planning and execution of missions occur. For example, if a State requests assistance with a mass evacuation, the JFO would request personnel from ESF #1 (Transportation), ESF #6 (Mass Care, Emergency Assistance, Housing, and Human Services), and ESF #8 (Public Health and Medical Services). These would then be integrated into a single branch or group within the Operations Section to ensure effective coordination of evacuation services.*
>
> National Response Framework: Overview, January 2008

THE MAIN SECTIONS OF A JOINT FIELD OFFICE

I-4. Figure I-1 illustrates an example of the four main sections of a fully manned joint field office, based on the flexible principles of the incident command system. In this illustration, all 15 ESFs have been activated. The four sections are operations, planning, logistics, and finance and administration. Normally, a unified coordination group oversees the joint field office (refer to chapter 2). (Each joint field office will have these four sections, but each section will be organized to accommodate the situation.)

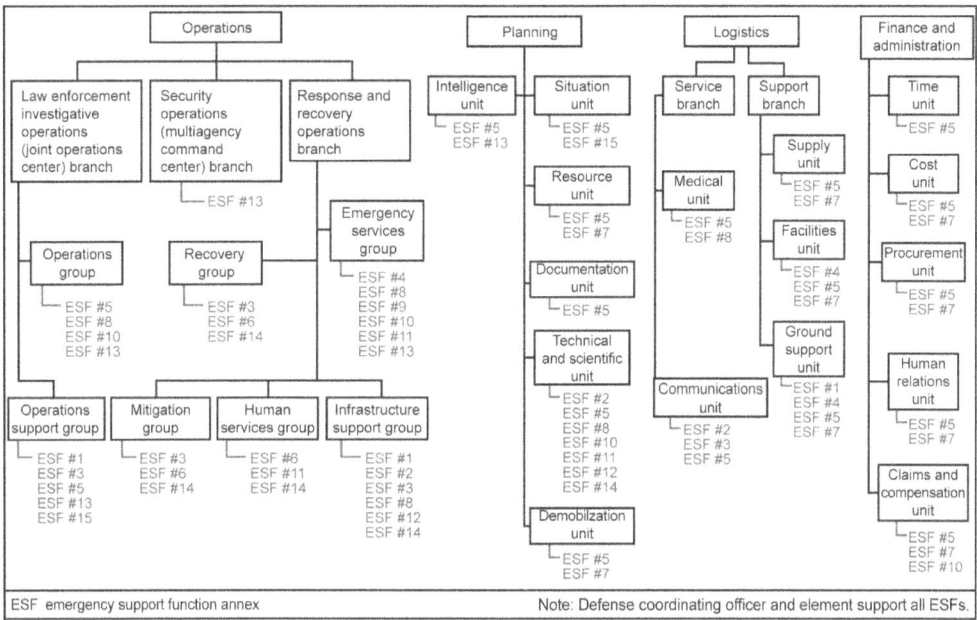

Figure I-1. Example of a fully manned joint field office

Appendix I

THE OPERATIONS SECTION OF A JOINT FIELD OFFICE

I-5. Figure I-2 illustrates an example of the operations section of a joint field office. The operations section has the most incident resources. It develops and implements strategy and tactics to carry out the incident objectives. Each joint field office is organized according to the flexible principles of the incident command system, so each operations section will be somewhat different depending on the situation. It expands from the bottom up. The operations section—

- Organizes, assigns, and supervises the tactical field resources.
- Supervises air operations and those resources in a staging area.
- Directs and coordinates all incident tactical operations.
- Normally the first organizations to be assigned to the incident.
- May include staging areas and special organizations.

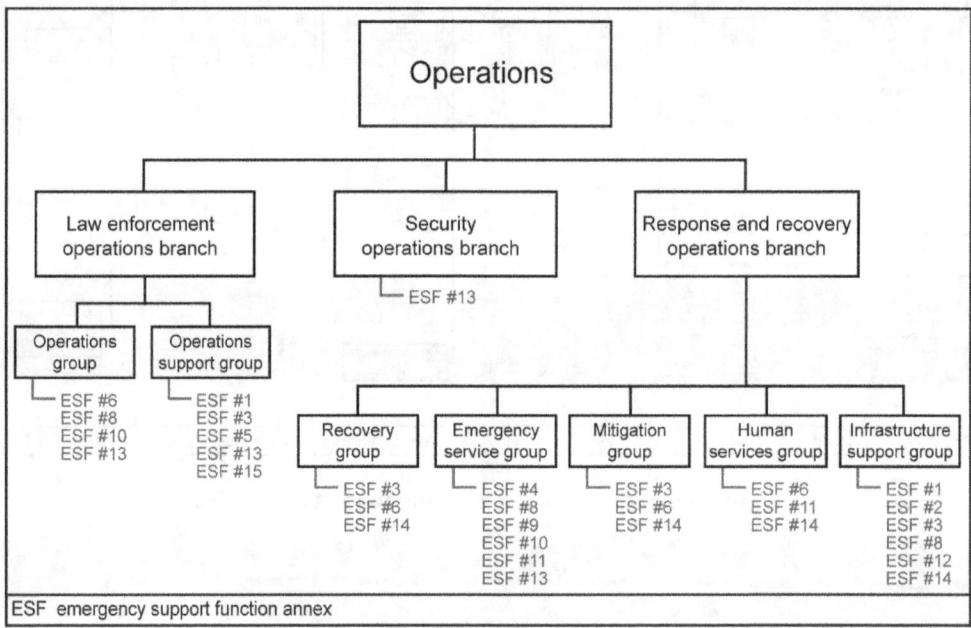

Figure I-2. Example of the operations section of a joint field office

THE PLANNING SECTION OF A JOINT FIELD OFFICE

I-6. The planning section gathers, analyzes, and disseminates information and intelligence. The planning section—

- Manages the planning process.
- Compiles the incident action plan.
- Manages Technical Specialists.
- Maintains resource status.
- Maintains and displays situation status.
- Prepares the Incident action plan.
- Develops alternative strategies.
- Provides documentation services.
- Prepares the Demobilization plan.
- Provides a primary location for technical specialists assigned to an incident.

Figure I-3 illustrates an example of the planning section of a joint field office. Each planning section is organized to accommodate the situation, according to the flexible principles of the incident command system.

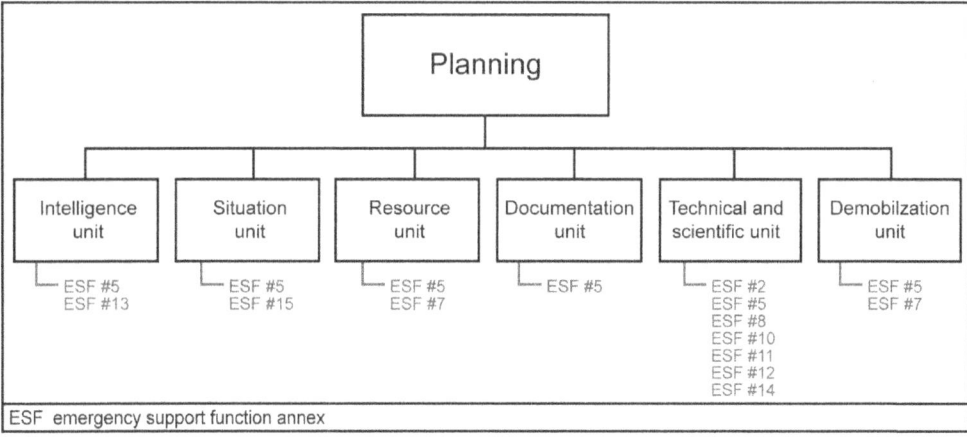

Figure I-3. Example of the planning section of a joint field office

Appendix I

THE LOGISTICS SECTION OF A JOINT FIELD OFFICE

I-7. The logistics section provides resources and services required to support incident activities. The logistics section develops portions of incident action plan and forwards them to planning section. The logistics section—

- Contracts for and purchases goods and services needed at the incident.
- Coordinates communications support.
- Provides medical support to incident personnel.
- Provides food for incident personnel.
- Provides supplies.
- Provides facilities.
- Oversees ground support.

Figure I-4 illustrates an example of the logistics section of a joint field office. Each logistics section is organized to accommodate the situation, according to the flexible principles of the incident command system.

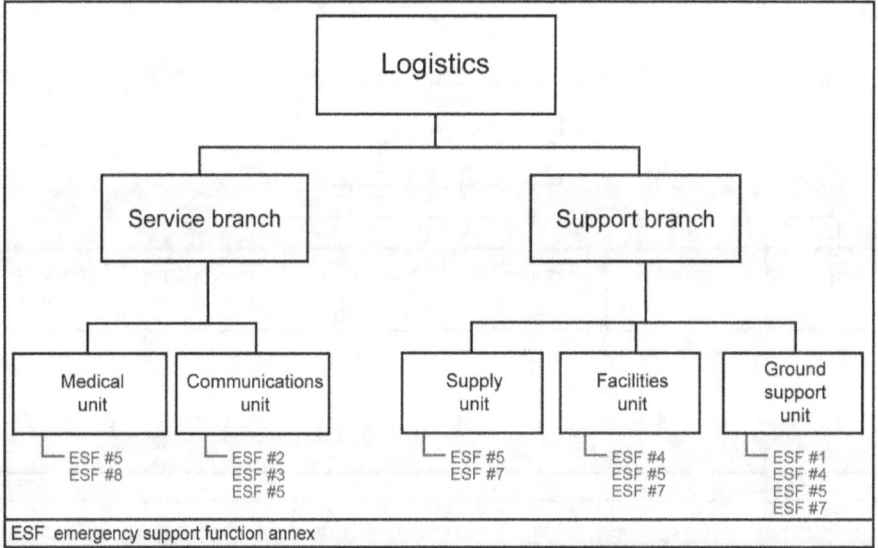

Figure I-4. Example of the logistics section of a joint field office

THE FINANCE AND ADMINISTRATION SECTION OF A JOINT FIELD OFFICE

I-8. The finance and administration section handles financial transactions, accounting, and human resources support. This includes—

- Contract negotiation and monitoring.
- Timekeeping.
- Cost analysis.
- Compensation for injury or damage to property.

Figure I-5 illustrates an example of the finance and administration section of a joint field office. Each finance and administration section is organized to accommodate the situation, according to the flexible principles of the incident command system.

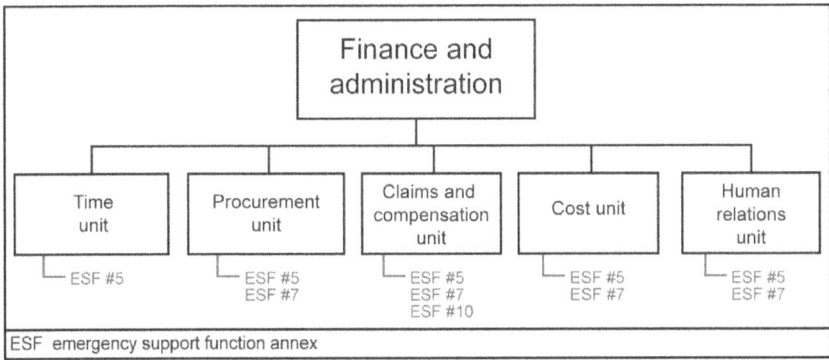

Figure I-5. Example of the finance and administration section of a joint field office

This page intentionally left blank.

Appendix J
Comparison of Stability and Civil Support Tasks

Table J-1, pages J-1 to J-22, lists tactical tasks from *The Army Universal Task List* (AUTL), Field Manual (FM) 7-15, by warfighting function and their relationship to full spectrum operations. Tasks that apply in stability operations and civil support are shown with a white background. Tasks that only apply to stability operations are shown light grey shading. Tasks that only apply to civil support operations appear in dark grey with white lettering. Tasks for the fires warfighting function are omitted because none applies directly to civil support or stability operations.

Table J-1. Stability and civil support task comparison chart

AUTL #	Title	Stability	Civil Support	Remarks
1.1	Perform Tactical Actions Associated with Force Projection and Deployment	X	X	
1.1.1	Conduct Mobilization of Tactical Units	X	X	
1.1.1.1	Conduct Alert and Recall	X	X	
1.1.1.2	Conduct Home Station Mobilization	X	X	
1.1.1.3	Conduct Mobilization Station Activities	X	X	
1.1.2	Conduct Tactical Deployment/Redeployment	X	X	
1.1.2.1	Conduct Pre-deployment Activities	X	X	
1.1.2.2	Conduct RSOI	X	X	
1.1.2.3	Conduct Redeployment Activities	X	X	
1.1.3	Conduct Demobilization of Tactical Units	X	X	
1.1.4	Conduct Rear Detachment Activities	X	X	
1.2.2.7	Conduct Actions on Contact	X		
1.2.3	Employ Combat Patrols	X		
1.2.4	Conduct Counter-ambush Actions	X		
1.2.5	Exploit Terrain to Expedite Tactical Movements	X		
1.2.6	Cross a Danger Area	X		
1.2.7	Linkup with Other Tactical Forces	X	X	
1.2.9	Conduct a Relief in Place	X	X	
1.2.10	Navigate From One Point to Another	X	X	
1.2.12	Conduct Sniper Active Countermeasures	X	X	
1.2.13	Conduct Sniper Passive Countermeasures	X	X	
1.3	Conduct Tactical Troop Movements	X		
1.3.1	Prepare Forces for Movement	X	X	
1.3.1.1	Conduct Advance Party Activities	X	X	
1.3.1.2	Conduct Quartering Party Activities	X	X	

Table J-1. Stability and civil support task comparison chart, continued

AUTL #	Title	Stability	Civil Support	Remarks
1.3.1.4	Conduct Pickup Zone Operations	X	X	
1.3.2	Conduct Tactical Road March	X		
1.3.3	Conduct Tactical Convoy	X		
1.4	Conduct Direct Fires	X		
1.4.1	Conduct Lethal Direct Fire Against a Surface Target	X		
1.4.2	Conduct Nonlethal Direct Fire Against a Surface Target	X	X	Nonlethal weapons only
1.5	Occupy an Area	X	X	
1.5.1	Occupy an Assembly Area	X	X	
1.5.5	Conduct Landing Zone Operations	X	X	
1.6	Conduct Mobility Operations.	X	X	
1.6.1	Overcome Barriers, Obstacles, and Mines	X		
1.6.1.1	Conduct Breaching Operations	X		
1.6.1.2	Conduct Clearing Operations	X	X	
1.6.1.2.1	Conduct Area Clearance	X	X	
1.6.1.2.2	Conduct Route Clearance	X	X	
1.6.1.3	Conduct Gap Crossing Operations	X	X	
1.6.1.3.2	Conduct Line of Communications Gap Crossing Support	X	X	
1.6.2	Enhance Movement and Maneuver	X	X	
1.6.2.1	Construct/Maintain Combat Roads and Trails	X	X	
1.6.2.2	Construct and Maintain Forward Airfields and Landing Zones	X	X	
1.6.3	Negotiate a Tactical Area of Operations	X	X	
1.6.4	Provide Diver Support	X	X	
1.6.5	Conduct Non-Tactical Movement	X	X	
1.7.1	Site Obstacles	X	X	
1.7.2	Construct, Emplace, or Detonate Obstacles	X	X	
2.1	Support to Force Generation	X		
2.1.1	Provide Intelligence Readiness	X		
2.1.1.1	Perform Indications and Warnings	X		
2.1.1.2	Ensure Intelligence Readiness Operations	X	X	According to intelligence oversight laws for civil support
2.1.2	Establish Intelligence Architecture	X	X	According to intelligence oversight laws for civil support
2.1.2.1	Conduct Intelligence Reach	X	X	According to intelligence oversight laws for civil support
2.1.2.2	Develop/Maintain Automated Intelligence Networks	X	X	According to intelligence oversight laws for civil support

Comparison of Stability and Civil Support Tasks

Table J-1. Stability and civil support task comparison chart, continued

AUTL #	Title	Stability	Civil Support	Remarks
2.1.2.3	Establish and Maintain Access	X	X	According to intelligence oversight laws for civil support
2.1.2.4	Create/Maintain Intelligence Databases	X	X	According to intelligence oversight laws for civil support
2.1.3	Provide Intelligence Over watch	X	X	According to intelligence oversight laws for civil support
2.1.4	Generate Knowledge	X	X	According to intelligence oversight laws for civil support
2.1.4.1	Develop the foundation to Define Threat Characteristics	X		
2.1.4.2	Obtain Detailed Terrain Information and Intelligence	X	X	According to intelligence oversight laws for civil support
2.1.4.3	Obtain Detailed Weather and Weather Effects Information and Intelligence	X	X	According to intelligence oversight laws for civil support
2.1.4.4	Obtain Detailed Civil Considerations Information and Intelligence	X	X	According to intelligence oversight laws for civil support
2.1.4.5	Complete Studies	X	X	According to intelligence oversight laws for civil support
2.1.4.5.1	Conduct Area, Regional, or Country Study of a Foreign Country	X		
2.1.4.5.2	Conduct Specified Study	X	X	According to intelligence oversight laws for civil support
2.1.5	Tailor the Intelligence Force	X	X	According to intelligence oversight laws for civil support
2.2	Support to Situational Understanding	X	X	According to intelligence oversight laws for civil support
2.2.1	Perform Intelligence Preparation of the Battlefield	X	X	According to intelligence oversight laws for civil support
2.2.1.1	Define the Operational Environment	X	X	According to intelligence oversight laws for civil support
2.2.1.2	Describe Environmental Effects on Operations	X	X	According to intelligence oversight laws for civil support
2.2.1.3	Evaluate the Threat	X	X	According to intelligence oversight laws for civil support
2.2.1.4	Determine Threat Courses of Action	X	X	According to intelligence oversight laws for civil support

Appendix J

Table J-1. Stability and civil support task comparison chart, continued

AUTL #	Title	Stability	Civil Support	Remarks
2.2.1.5	Conduct Geospatial Engineering Operations and Functions	X	X	According to intelligence oversight laws for civil support
2.2.2	Perform Situation Development	X	X	According to intelligence oversight laws for civil support
2.2.3	Provide Intelligence Support to Protection	X	X	According to intelligence oversight laws for civil support
2.2.4	Provide Tactical Intelligence Over watch	X		
2.2.5	Conduct Police Intelligence Operations	X		
2.2.5.1	Collect Police Information	X		
2.2.5.2	Complete Police Information Assessment	X		
2.2.5.3	Develop Police Intelligence Products	X		
2.2.6	Provide Intelligence Support to Civil-Affairs Operations	X	X	According to intelligence oversight laws for civil support
2.3	Perform Intelligence, Surveillance, and Reconnaissance	X	X	According to intelligence oversight laws for civil support
2.3.1	Perform ISR Synchronization	X	X	According to intelligence oversight laws for civil support
2.3.1.1	Develop Requirements	X	X	According to intelligence oversight laws for civil support
2.3.1.2	Develop the ISR Synchronization Plan	X	X	According to intelligence oversight laws for civil support
2.3.2	Perform Intelligence, Surveillance, and Reconnaissance Integration	X	X	According to intelligence oversight laws for civil support
2.3.2.1	Develop the Intelligence, Surveillance, and Reconnaissance Plan	X	X	According to intelligence oversight laws for civil support
2.3.2.2	Execute/evaluate and update the ISR Plan	X	X	According to intelligence oversight laws for civil support
2.3.3	Conduct Reconnaissance	X	X	According to intelligence oversight laws for civil support
2.3.3.1	Conduct a Route Reconnaissance	X	X	According to intelligence oversight laws for civil support
2.3.3.2	Conduct A Zone Reconnaissance	X	X	According to intelligence oversight laws for civil support
2.3.3.3	Conduct An Area Reconnaissance	X	X	According to intelligence oversight laws for civil support
2.3.3.5	Conduct A Reconnaissance Patrol	X	X	According to intelligence oversight laws for civil support

Table J-1. Stability and civil support task comparison chart, continued

AUTL #	Title	Stability	Civil Support	Remarks
2.3.4	Conduct Surveillance	X	X	According to intelligence oversight laws for civil support
2.3.5	Conduct Related Missions and Operations	X	X	According to intelligence oversight laws for civil support
2.3.5.1	Establish a Mission Intelligence Briefing and Debriefing Program	X	X	According to intelligence oversight laws for civil support
2.3.5.1.1	Establish a Mission Intelligence Briefing Plan	X	X	According to intelligence oversight laws for civil support
2.3.5.1.2	Establish a Debriefing Plan	X	X	According to intelligence oversight laws for civil support
2.3.5.2	Conduct Intelligence Coordination	X	X	According to intelligence oversight laws for civil support
2.3.5.2.1	Establish and Maintain Technical Authority and Channels	X	X	According to intelligence oversight laws for civil support
2.3.5.2.2	Conduct Deconfliction and Coordination	X	X	According to intelligence oversight laws for civil support
2.3.5.3	Support Sensitive Site Exploitation	X		
2.3.5.4	Intelligence Support to Personnel Recovery	X		
2.3.5.4.1	Conduct PR Focused Intelligence Preparation of the Battlefield	X		
2.3.5.4.2	Conduct Support to PR Planning, Preparation, and Execution	X		
2.4	Provide Intelligence Support to Targeting and Information Superiority	X		
2.4.1	Provide Intelligence Support to Targeting	X		
2.4.1.1	Provide Intelligence Support to Target Development	X		
2.4.1.2	Provide Intelligence Support to Target Detection	X		
2.4.2	Provide Intelligence Support to Information Tasks	X	X	According to intelligence oversight laws for civil support
2.4.2.1	Provide Intelligence Support to Activities Related to Information Engagement	X		
2.4.2.1.1	Provide Intelligence Support to Public Affairs	X		
2.4.2.1.2	Provide Intelligence Support to Psychological Operations	X		
2.4.2.2	Provide Intelligence Support to Command and Control Warfare	X		
2.4.2.3	Provide Intelligence Support to Electronic Attack	X		

Table J-1. Stability and civil support task comparison chart, continued

AUTL #	Title	Stability	Civil Support	Remarks
2.4.2.4	Provide Intelligence Support to Information Protection	X	X	According to intelligence oversight laws for civil support
4.1	Provide Logistics Support	X	X	
4.1.1	Provide Maintenance Support	X	X	
4.1.1.1	Perform Preventative Maintenance Checks and Services	X	X	
4.1.1.2	Recover/Evacuate Disabled Equipment	X	X	
4.1.1.3	Diagnose Equipment Faults	X	X	
4.1.1.4	Substitute Parts	X	X	
4.1.1.5	Exchange Parts	X	X	
4.1.1.6	Repair Equipment	X	X	
4.1.1.7	Return Repaired Equipment to the User	X	X	
4.1.1.8	Provide Maintenance Management	X	X	
4.1.2	Provide Transportation Support	X	X	
4.1.2.1	Provide Movement Control	X	X	
4.1.2.1.1	Provide Highway and Main Supply Route Regulation	X	X	
4.1.2.1.2	Regulate Movement	X	X	
4.1.2.1.3	Conduct Support to Movement Operations	X	X	
4.1.2.2	Conduct Terminal Operations	X	X	
4.1.2.2.1	Conduct Arrival and Departure Airfield Control Group Activities	X	X	
4.1.2.2.2	Conduct Trailer, Container, and Flatrack Transfer Operations	X	X	
4.1.2.2.3	Conduct Rail Transfer Operations	X	X	
4.1.2.2.4	Conduct Marine Terminal Operations	X	X	
4.1.2.3	Conduct Mode Operations	X	X	
4.1.2.3.1	Move by Surface	X	X	
4.1.2.3.2	Move by Air	X	X	
4.1.2.3.3	Move by Water	X	X	
4.1.3	Provide Supplies	X	X	
4.1.3.1	Provide Subsistence (Class I)	X	X	
4.1.3.2	Provide Clothing, Individual Equipment, Tools, and Administrative Supplies (Class II)	X	X	
4.1.3.3	Provide Petroleum, Oil, and Lubricants	X	X	
4.1.3.3.1	Provide Bulk Fuel	X	X	
4.1.3.3.2	Provide Packaged Petroleum, Oils, and Lubricants Products	X	X	
4.1.3.3.3	Provide Petroleum Quality Assurance and Quality Surveillance	X	X	
4.1.3.3.5	Provide RETAIL Fuel	X	X	
4.1.3.4	Provide Barrier and Construction Material	X	X	
4.1.3.5	Provide Ammunition	X	X	

Comparison of Stability and Civil Support Tasks

Table J-1. Stability and civil support task comparison chart, continued

AUTL #	Title	Stability	Civil Support	Remarks
4.1.3.5.1	Provide Munitions	X		
4.1.3.5.2	Provide Separate Loading Munitions	X		
4.1.3.5.3	Provide Pyrotechnic and Specialty Items	X	X	
4.1.3.6	Provide Personal Demand Items	X	X	
4.1.3.7	Provide Major End Items	X	X	
4.1.3.8	Provide Medical Material and Repair Parts	X	X	
4.1.3.9	Provide Repair Parts	X	X	
4.1.3.10	Provide Supplies for Civilian Use	X	X	
4.1.3.11	Provide Water Support	X	X	
4.1.3.11.1	Purify Water	X	X	
4.1.3.11.2	Provide Packaged Water	X	X	
4.1.3.12	Provide Miscellaneous Supplies	X	X	
4.1.3.13	Conduct Forward Arming and Refueling Point Activities	X	X	
4.1.3.15	Provide Supply Management	X	X	
4.1.3.15.1	Request Supplies	X	X	
4.1.3.15.2	Receive Supplies	X	X	
4.1.3.15.3	Procure Supplies	X	X	
4.1.3.15.4	Issue Supplies	X	X	
4.1.3.16	Salvage and Retrograde Equipment and Materiel	X	X	
4.1.3.17	Prepare Configured Loads	X	X	
4.1.4	Provide field Services	X	X	
4.1.4.1	Conduct Mortuary Affairs	X	X	
4.1.4.2	Conduct Aerial Delivery Support	X	X	
4.1.4.3	Provide Base Camp Sustainment	X	X	
4.1.4.3.1	Provide Clothing and Textile Repair Support	X	X	
4.1.4.3.2	Provide Hygiene Support	X	X	
4.1.4.3.3	Provide Nutrition Support	X	X	
4.1.4.3.4	Provide General Purpose Shelters and Systems	X	X	
4.1.5	Provide Contracting Support	X	X	
4.1.5.1	Request Contracting Support	X	X	
4.1.5.2	Provide Logistics Civilian Augmentation Program (LOGCAP) Support	X		
4.1.6	Provide Distribution	X	X	
4.1.6.1	Conduct Distribution Management	X	X	
4.1.6.2	Provide In transit Visibility /Asset Visibility	X	X	
4.1.6.3	Conduct Unit Logistics Package Operations	X	X	
4.1.6.4	Establish Hub/Node	X	X	
4.1.6.4.1	Conduct APOD Operations	X	X	
4.1.6.4.2	Conduct SPOD Operations	X	X	

Appendix J

Table J-1. Stability and civil support task comparison chart, continued

AUTL #	Title	Stability	Civil Support	Remarks
4.1.6.4.3	Conduct Hub Operations	X	X	
4.1.7	Provide General Engineer Support	X	X	
4.1.7.1	Restore Damaged Areas	X	X	
4.1.7.2	Construct and Maintain Sustainment Lines of Communications	X	X	
4.1.7.2.1	Construct and Maintain Roads and Highways	X	X	
4.1.7.2.2	Construct and Maintain Over-the-Shore Facilities	X	X	
4.1.7.2.3	Construct and Maintain Ports	X		
4.1.7.2.4	Construct and Maintain Railroad Facilities	X		
4.1.7.2.5	Construct and Expand Airfield Facilities	X		
4.1.7.2.6	Construct and Maintain Pipelines and Tank Farms	X		
4.1.7.2.7	Construct and Maintain Standard and Nonstandard Fixed Bridges	X		
4.1.7.3	Provide Engineer Construction Support	X	X	
4.1.7.4	Supply Mobile Electric Power	X	X	
4.1.7.5	Provide Facilities Engineering Support	X	X	
4.1.7.5.1	Provide Waste Management	X	X	
4.1.7.5.2	Acquire, Manage, and Dispose of Real Estate	X	X	
4.1.7.5.3	Provide Fire-Fighting Support	X	X	
4.1.7.5.4	Construct, Manage, Maintain Bases and Installations	X	X	
4.2	Provide Personnel Services Support	X	X	
4.2.1	Provide Human Resource Support	X	X	
4.2.1.1	Man the Force	X	X	
4.2.1.1.1	Perform Personnel Readiness Management	X	X	
4.2.1.1.2	Conduct Personnel Accounting and Strength Reporting	X	X	
4.2.1.1.2.1	Conduct Personnel Accounting	X	X	
4.2.1.1.2.2	Conduct Strength Reporting	X	X	
4.2.1.1.3	Provide Personnel Information Management	X	X	
4.2.1.1.4	Conduct Reception, Replacement, Return-to-Duty Operations, Rest and Recuperation and Redeployment Operations	X	X	
4.2.1.2	Provide Human Resource Services	X	X	
4.2.1.2.1	Conduct Casualty Operations	X	X	
4.2.1.2.2	Perform Essential Personnel Services	X	X	
4.2.1.2.2.1	Provide Identification Documents	X	X	
4.2.1.2.2.2	Operate Award and Decorations Programs	X	X	
4.2.1.2.2.3	Provide Promotions and Reduction Support	X	X	
4.2.1.2.2.4	Control Personnel Evaluations	X	X	

Table J-1. Stability and civil support task comparison chart, continued

AUTL #	Title	Stability	Civil Support	Remarks
4.2.1.2.2.5	Operate Leave and Pass Program	X	X	
4.2.1.2.2.6	Complete Line of Duty Investigations	X	X	
4.2.1.2.2.7	Conduct Military Pay Transactions	X	X	
4.2.1.3	Provide Personnel Support	X	X	
4.2.1.3.1	Conduct Human Resource Programs	X	X	
4.2.1.3.2	Conduct Postal Operations	X	X	
4.2.1.3.3	Provide Morale, Welfare, and Recreation and Community Support Activities	X	X	
4.2.1.3.4	Conduct Retention Operations	X	X	
4.2.1.4	Conduct Human Resource Planning and Operations	X	X	
4.2.1.4.1	Perform Human Resource Planning and Mission Preparation	X	X	
4.2.1.4.2	Operate Human Resource Command and Control Nodes	X	X	
4.2.2	Provide Financial Management Support	X	X	
4.2.2.1	Provide Support to the Procurement Process	X	X	
4.2.2.2	Provide Limited Pay Support	X	X	
4.2.2.3	Provide Disbursing Support	X	X	
4.2.2.4	Provide Accounting Support	X	X	
4.2.2.5	Provide Banking and Currency Support	X		
4.2.2.6	Develop Resource Requirements	X	X	
4.2.2.7	Provide Support to Identify, Acquire, Distribute and Control Funds	X	X	
4.2.2.8	Provide Support to Track, Analyze and Report Budget Execution	X	X	
4.2.2.9	Conduct Financial Management Planning and Operations	X	X	
4.2.3	Provide Legal Support	X	X	
4.2.3.1	Provide Military Judge Support	X		Installation task
4.2.3.2	Provide Trial Defense Support	X		Installation task
4.2.3.3	Provide International Law Support	X		Installation task
4.2.3.4	Provide Administrative and Civil Law Support	X	X	
4.2.3.5	Provide Contract and Fiscal Law Support	X	X	
4.2.3.6	Provide Claims Support	X	X	
4.2.3.7	Provide Legal Assistance	X	X	
4.2.4	Provide Religious Support Operations	X	X	
4.2.4.1	Deliver Religious Services	X	X	
4.2.4.2	Provide Spiritual Care and Counseling	X	X	
4.2.4.3	Provide Religious Support to the Command	X	X	
4.2.4.4	Provide Rites, Sacraments, and Ordinances	X	X	
4.2.4.5	Coordinate Military Religious Support	X	X	

Table J-1. Stability and civil support task comparison chart, continued

AUTL #	Title	Stability	Civil Support	Remarks
4.2.4.6	Provide Religious Crisis Response	X	X	
4.2.4.7	Provide Religious Management and Administrative Support	X	X	
4.2.4.8	Provide Religious Education	X	X	
4.2.5	Provide Band Support	X	X	
4.3	Provide Health Service Support	X	X	
4.3.1	Provide Combat Casualty Care	X		
4.3.1.1	Provide Medical Treatment (Organic and Area Medical Support)	X	X	
4.3.1.2	Provide Hospitalization	X	X	
4.3.1.3	Provide Dental Services	X	X	
4.3.1.4	Provide Clinical Laboratory Services	X	X	
4.3.1.5	Provide Behavioral Health/Neuropsychiatric Treatment	X	X	
4.3.2	Provide Medical Evacuation (Air/Ground)	X	X	
4.3.3	Provide Medical Regulating Support	X	X	
4.3.4	Provide Medical Logistics	X	X	
4.3.4.1	Provide Medical Equipment Maintenance and Repair	X	X	
4.3.4.2	Provide Optical Fabrication	X	X	
4.3.4.3	Supply Blood and Blood Products	X	X	
4.4	Conduct Internment/Resettlement Operations	X		
4.4.1	Perform Detainee Operations	X		
4.4.2	Perform Enemy Prisoner of War Operations	X		
4.4.3	Conduct Resettlement Operations	X		
5.1	Execute the Operations Process	X	X	
5.1.1	Plan Operations	X	X	
5.1.1.1	Conduct the Military Decision Making Process	X	X	
5.1.1.1.1	Receive the Mission	X	X	
5.1.1.1.2	Perform Mission Analysis	X	X	
5.1.1.1.3	Develop Courses of Action	X	X	
5.1.1.1.4	Analyze Courses of Action	X	X	
5.1.1.1.5	Compare Courses of Action	X	X	
5.1.1.1.6	Approve Course of Action	X	X	
5.1.1.1.7	Produce plans and orders	X	X	
5.1.1.2	Integrate Requirements and Capabilities	X	X	
5.1.1.3	Develop Commander's Critical Information Requirements Recommendations (CCIR)	X	X	
5.1.1.4	Establish Target Priorities	X		
5.1.1.5	Integrate Space Capabilities	X	X	
5.1.2	Prepare for Tactical Operations	X	X	

Table J-1. Stability and civil support task comparison chart, continued

AUTL #	Title	Stability	Civil Support	Remarks
5.1.2.1	Establish Coordination and Liaison	X	X	
5.1.2.2	Perform Rehearsals	X	X	
5.1.2.3	Task-Organize for Operations	X	X	
5.1.2.4	Revise the Plan	X	X	
5.1.2.5	Conduct Pre-operations Checks and Inspections	X	X	
5.1.2.6	Integrate New Units and Soldiers into the Force	X	X	
5.1.3	Execute Tactical Operations	X	X	
5.1.3.1	Perform Ongoing Functions	X	X	
5.1.3.1.1	Focus Assets on Decisive Operation	X	X	
5.1.3.1.2	Adjust CCIR and EEFI	X	X	
5.1.3.1.3	Adjust Graphic Control Measures	X	X	
5.1.3.1.4	Manage Sustainment Force Positioning	X	X	
5.1.3.1.5	Manage Use and Assignment of Terrain	X	X	
5.1.3.1.6	Maintain Synchronization	X	X	
5.1.3.1.7	Control Tactical Airspace	X		Federal Aviation Administration maintains Airspace Control; Military may do airspace coordination
5.1.3.1.8	Control a Tactical Insertion of Forces	X		
5.1.3.2	Perform Planned Actions, Sequels, and Branches	X	X	
5.1.3.3	Adjust Resources, Concept of Operations, or Mission	X	X	
5.1.3.4	Synchronize Actions to Produce Maximum Effective Application of Military Power	X	X	
5.1.3.4.1	Coordinate Actions Within a Staff Section	X	X	
5.1.3.4.2	Synchronize Actions Among Staff Sections (Coordinating, Special, and Personal)	X	X	
5.1.3.4.3	Review Orders of Subordinate Organizations	X	X	
5.1.3.4.4	Synchronize Force Operations	X	X	
5.1.3.5	Conduct Transitions	X	X	
5.1.4	Assess Tactical Situation and Operations	X	X	
5.1.4.1	Monitor Situation or Progress of Operations	X	X	
5.1.4.2	Evaluate Situation or Operation	X	X	
5.1.4.2.1	Develop Running Estimates	X	X	
5.1.4.2.2	Evaluate Progress	X	X	
5.2	Conduct Command Post Operations	X	X	
5.2.1	Conduct Command Post Operations	X	X	
5.2.1.1	Organize People, Information Management Procedures, and Equipment and Facilities	X	X	

Appendix J

Table J-1. Stability and civil support task comparison chart, continued

AUTL #	Title	Stability	Civil Support	Remarks
5.2.1.2	Organize Command Post to Support Command and Control Functions	X	X	
5.2.1.3	Establish or Revise Standing Operating Procedures	X	X	
5.2.2	Displace the Command Post	X	X	
5.2.2.1	Prepare the Command Post for Displacement	X	X	
5.2.2.2	Select, Reconnoiter, and Evaluate the New Command Post Location	X	X	
5.2.2.3	Occupy the New Command Post Location	X	X	
5.2.2.4	Transfer Command and Control Functions During Displacement	X	X	
5.2.3	Execute Sleep Plans	X	X	
5.2.4	Manage Stress	X	X	
5.2.5	Maintain Continuity of Command and Control	X	X	
5.3	Integrate Information Superiority Contributors	X	X	
5.3.1	Integrate Information Engagement Capabilities	X	X	
5.3.1.1	Conduct Leader and Soldier Engagement	X	X	
5.3.1.2	Conduct Psychological Operations	X		
5.3.1.3	Provide Visual Information Support	X	X	
5.3.1.4	Conduct Operations in Support of Diplomatic Efforts	X		
5.3.2	Conduct Military Deception	X		
5.3.3	Facilitate Situational Understanding Through Knowledge Management	X	X	
5.3.4	Manage Tactical Information and Data	X	X	
5.3.5	Establish a Tactical Information Network and System	X	X	Add condition / task: establish interoperable systems with civilian responders
5.3.5.1	Conduct Network Operations	X	X	
5.3.5.2	Collect Relevant Information	X	X	
5.3.5.2.1	Collect Friendly Force Information Requirements	X	X	
5.3.5.2.2	Integrate Intelligence Products	X	X	According to intelligence oversight laws for civil support
5.3.5.2.3	Assess quality of Collected Information	X	X	According to intelligence oversight laws for civil support
5.3.5.2.4	Process Relevant Information to Create a COP	X	X	According to intelligence oversight laws for civil support
5.3.5.2.5	Display a COP Tailored to User Needs	X	X	

Table J-1. Stability and civil support task comparison chart, continued

AUTL #	Title	Stability	Civil Support	Remarks
5.3.5.2.6	Store Relevant Information	X	X	According to intelligence oversight laws for civil support
5.3.5.2.7	Disseminate COP and Execution Information	X	X	
5.3.5.2.8	Communicate with Non-English Speaking Forces and Agencies	X		
5.3.6	Conduct Electromagnetic Spectrum Management Operations	X		
5.3.6.1	Perform Spectrum Management	X	X	
5.3.6.2	Perform Frequency Assignment	X	X	
5.3.6.3	Perform Host Nation Electromagnetic Spectrum Coordination	X		
5.3.6.4	Monitor Spectrum Management Policy Adherence	X	X	
5.4	Conduct Civil-Military Operations	X	X	
5.4.1	Provide Interface/Liaison between U.S. Military Forces and Local Authorities/Nongovernmental Organizations	X	X	
5.4.2	Locate and identify Population Centers	X	X	
5.4.3	Identify Local Resources/Facilities/Support	X	X	
5.4.4	Advise Commanders of Obligations to Civilian Population	X	X	
5.4.5	Conduct Negotiations With and Between Other Governmental and Nongovernmental Organizations	X	X	
5.4.6	Conduct Civil Affairs Operations	X	X	
5.4.6.1	Provide Public Legal Support	X		
5.4.6.1.1	Provide Support to Indigenous judicial Systems	X		
5.4.6.1.2	Provide Property Control Support	X		
5.4.6.2	Provide Economic and Commerce Support	X		
5.4.6.2.1	Provide Food and Agricultural Support	X		
5.4.6.2.2	Provide Civilian Supply Support	X	X	
5.4.6.3	Provide Infrastructure Support	X	X	
5.4.6.3.1	Provide Public Communications Support	X	X	
5.4.6.3.2	Provide Public Transportation Support	X	X	
5.4.6.3.3	Provide Public Works and Facilities Support	X	X	USACE
5.4.6.4	Provide Government Support	X	X	
5.4.6.4.1	Provide Public Safety Support	X	X	
5.4.6.4.2	Provide Public Administration Support	X		
5.4.6.5	Provide Health and Welfare Support	X	X	
5.4.6.5.1	Provide Public Health Support	X	X	
5.4.6.5.2	Provide Cultural Relations Support	X		
5.4.6.5.3	Resettle Dislocated Civilians	X	X	

Appendix J

Table J-1. Stability and civil support task comparison chart, continued

AUTL #	Title	Stability	Civil Support	Remarks
5.4.6.5.4	Provide Arts, Monuments, and Archives Support	X		
5.4.6.6	Provide Public Education and Information Support	X		
5.4.6.6.1	Provide Public Education Support	X		
5.4.6.6.2	Provide Civil Information Support	X	X	
5.5	Execute Command Programs	X	X	
5.5.1	Support the Commander's Leadership Responsibilities for Morale, Welfare, and Discipline	X	X	
5.5.1.1	Determine Morale and Moral Climate of Organization	X	X	
5.5.1.2	Establish and Maintain Discipline	X	X	
5.5.1.2.1	Provide Law and Order	X	X	
5.5.1.2.2	Perform Law Enforcement	X	X	
5.5.1.2.3	Conduct Criminal Investigations	X	X	
5.5.1.2.4	Intern U.S. Military Prisoners	X		Installation task in United States
5.5.1.2.5	Provide Customs Support	X	X	
5.5.1.2.6	Provide Straggler Movement Control	X		
5.5.1.3	Provide Military Justice Support	X	X	
5.5.1.4	Provide Operational Law	X	X	
5.5.1.5	Train Subordinates and Units	X	X	
5.5.1.5.1	Develop Mission Essential Task List	X	X	
5.5.1.5.2	Plan Training	X	X	
5.5.1.5.3	Prepare for Training	X	X	
5.5.1.5.4	Execute Training	X	X	
5.5.1.5.5	Assess Training	X	X	
5.5.2	Preserve Historical Documentation and Artifacts	X	X	
5.5.2.1	Collect Historical Documentation and Artifacts	X	X	
5.5.2.2	Protect Historical Documents and Artifacts	X	X	
5.5.2.3	Prepare Historical Reports of Military Operations	X	X	
5.5.2.4	Ship Historical Documents and Artifacts	X	X	
5.5.3	Conduct Official Ceremonial, Musical, Public, and Special Events	X	X	
5.5.4	Develop a Command Environmental Program	X	X	
5.6	Integrate Space Operations	X	X	
5.6.1	Provide Space Force Enhancement	X	X	
5.6.1.1	Provide Space Based Position, Navigation, and Timing Support	X	X	

Table J-1. Stability and civil support task comparison chart, continued

AUTL #	Title	Stability	Civil Support	Remarks
5.6.1.2	Provide Reconnaissance and Surveillance Support	X	X	According to intelligence oversight laws for civil support
5.6.1.3	Provide Satellite Communications Support	X	X	
5.6.1.4	Provide Weather and Environmental Monitoring Support	X	X	
5.6.3	Provide Army Space Control	X	X	
5.6.4	Provide Space Situational Awareness	X	X	
5.6.5	Coordinate Army Space Capabilities	X	X	
5.7	Conduct Public Affairs Operations	X	X	
5.7.1	Plan Public Affairs Operations	X	X	
5.7.2	Execute Information Strategies	X	X	
5.7.3	Facilitate Media Operations	X	X	
5.7.4	Maintain Community Relations	X	X	
5.7.5	Conduct Internal Information Program	X	X	
5.7.6	Implement Higher Headquarters Public Affairs Themes	X	X	
6.2	Conduct Personnel Recovery Operations	X	X	
6.2.1	Ensure Personnel Recovery Readiness during Pre-Mobilization	X		
6.2.1.1	Coordinate Code of Conduct, SERE (Survival, Escape, Resistance, and Escape) and Theater-related Personnel Recovery Education and Training	X		
6.2.1.2	Plan Personnel Recovery Coordination Cell/Personnel Recovery Officer Capability	X		
6.2.2	Perform Personnel Recovery Related Force Projection Tasks	X		
6.2.2.1	Conduct Personnel Recovery Related Mobilization Activities	X		
6.2.2.2	Deploy Personnel Recovery Capability and Build Combat Power Through Reception, Staging, Onward Movement and Integration	X		
6.2.2.3	Sustain Personnel Recovery Capabilities	X		
6.2.2.4	Redeploy Personnel Recovery Capabilities	X		
6.2.3	Plan Personnel Recovery Operations	X		
6.2.3.1	Conduct Unassisted Personnel Recovery	X		
6.2.3.2	Conduct Immediate Personnel Recovery	X		
6.2.3.3	Conduct Deliberate Personnel Recovery	X		
6.2.3.4	Conduct External Supported Personnel Recovery	X		
6.2.3.5	Conduct Army Special Operations Forces Personnel Recovery	X		
6.2.4	Provide Personnel Recovery Support to Civil search and rescue on Non-Interference Basis	X	X	
6.2.5	Conduct Homeland Security Personnel Recovery Operations		X	

Table J-1. Stability and civil support task comparison chart, continued

AUTL #	Title	Stability	Civil Support	Remarks
6.3	Conduct Information Protection	X	X	
6.3.1	Provide Information Assurance	X	X	
6.3.1.1	Ensure Information Security	X	X	
6.3.1.2	Employ Communication Security	X	X	
6.3.1.3	Maintain Emission Security	X		
6.3.2	Perform Computer Network Defense	X	X	
6.3.3	Perform Electronic Protection Actions	X	X	
6.3.4	Conduct Electronic Protection	X	X	
6.4	Perform Fratricide Avoidance	X		
Art 6.4.1	Detect and Establish Positive Identification of Friend, Foe, and Noncombatants	X	X	
6.4.2	Maintain Constant Situational Awareness	X	X	
6.5	Conduct Operational Area Security	X	X	
6.5.1	Conduct Area and Base Security Operations	X	X	
6.5.2	Conduct Critical Installations and Facilities Security	X	X	
6.5.3	Establish Local Security	X	X	
6.5.3.1	Establish Guard Posts	X	X	
6.5.3.2	Establish Checkpoints	X	X	
6.5.3.3	Establish Perimeter Security	X	X	
6.5.3.4	Establish Observation Posts	X	X	
6.5.3.5	Control Access to Equipment, Installations, Materiel, and Documents	X	X	
6.5.3.6	Employ Intrusion Detection Devices	X	X	
6.5.3.7	Conduct Command Post Security	X	X	
6.5.4	Provide Protective Services for Selected Individuals	X		
6.5.5	Conduct Response Force Operations	X		
6.5.5.1	Conduct Battle Handover From Base/Base Cluster Security Forces to Response Forces	X		
6.5.5.2	Conduct Battle Handover From Response Forces to Tactical Combat Forces	X		
6.5.6	Secure Supply Routes and Convoys	X		
6.5.6.1	Conduct Convoy Security Operations	X		
6.5.6.2	Conduct Route Security Operations	X		
6.6	Apply Antiterrorism Activities	X	X	
6.6.1	Identify Potential Terrorist Threats and Other Threat Activities	X	X	
6.6.2	Reduce Vulnerabilities to Terrorist Acts/Attack	X	X	
6.6.3	React to a Terrorist Incident	X	X	
6.7	Conduct Survivability Operations	X		
6.7.1	Protect Against Enemy Hazards within the area of operations	X		

Table J-1. Stability and civil support task comparison chart, continued

AUTL #	Title	Stability	Civil Support	Remarks
6.7.1.1	Protect Individuals and Systems	X		
6.7.1.2	Prepare Fighting Positions	X		
6.7.1.2.1	Construct Vehicle Fighting Positions	X		
6.7.1.2.2	Construct Crew-Served Weapon Fighting Positions	X		
6.7.1.2.3	Construct Individual Fighting Positions	X		
6.7.1.3	Prepare Protective Positions	X		
6.7.1.3.1	Construct Protective Earth Walls and Revetments	X	X	
6.7.1.4	Employ Protective Equipment	X	X	
6.7.1.4.1	Install Bridge Protective Devices	X		
6.7.1.4.2	Install or Remove Protective Obstacles	X	X	
6.7.1.5	React to Enemy Direct Fire	X	X	
6.7.1.6	React to Enemy Indirect Fire	X		
6.7.1.7	Conduct Improvised Explosive Device Defeat Operations	X		
6.7.1.7.1	Plan for Possible IED Threats	X		
6.7.1.7.2	Prepare for IED Defeat (Predict, Detect, Prevent, Neutralize, and Mitigate)	X		
6.7.1.7.3	Prepare for a Suspected IED Attack Against Static Position	X		
6.7.1.7.4	React to IED	X		
6.7.2	Disperse Tactical Forces	X		
6.7.3	Conduct Security Operations	X	X	
6.7.4	Conduct Actions to Control Pollution and Hazardous Materials	X	X	
6.8	Provide Force Health Protection	X	X	
6.8.1	Provide Preventive Medicine Support	X	X	
6.8.1.1	Perform Medical Surveillance	X	X	
6.8.1.2	Perform Occupational and Environmental Health Hazard Surveillance	X	X	
6.8.2	Provide Veterinary Services	X	X	
6.8.3	Provide Combat and Operational Stress Control Prevention	X	X	
6.8.4	Provide Preventive Dentistry Support	X	X	
6.8.5	Provide Area Medical Laboratory Services	X	X	
6.9	Conduct Chemical, Biological, Radiological, Nuclear and High-Yield Explosives Operations	X	X	
6.9.1	Support Threat Reduction Cooperation	X		
6.9.4	Provide Chemical, Biological, Radiological, and Nuclear Passive Defense	X	X	
6.9.4.1	Provide Chemical, Biological, Radiological, Nuclear Protection to Friendly Forces	X	X	
6.9.4.1.1	Employ Contamination Avoidance	X	X	

Table J-1. Stability and civil support task comparison chart, continued

AUTL #	Title	Stability	Civil Support	Remarks
6.9.4.1.2	Identify Chemical, Biological, Radiological, Nuclear Hazards	X	X	
6.9.4.1.3	Warn Personnel/Units of Contaminated Areas	X	X	
6.9.4.1.4	Report Chemical, Biological, Radiological, Nuclear Hazards Throughout the area of operations	X	X	
6.9.4.2	Decontaminate Personnel and Systems	X	X	
6.9.4.2.1	Perform Immediate Decontamination	X	X	
6.9.4.2.2	Perform Operational Decontamination	X	X	
6.9.4.2.3	Perform Thorough Decontamination	X	X	
6.9.4.2.4	Perform Area Decontamination	X	X	
6.9.4.2.5	Perform Patient Decontamination	X	X	
6.9.5	Conduct Chemical, Biological, Radiological, Nuclear, and High-Yield Explosive Consequence Management	X	X	
6.9.5.1	Provide logistical and engineering support of operations for weapons of mass destruction protection	X	X	
6.9.5.2	Handle, process, store, and transport CBRN contaminants	X	X	
6.9.5.3	Handle, process, store, and transport Chemical, Biological, Radiological, Nuclear-contaminated human remains	X	X	
6.9.5.4	Protect against exposure and effects of high-yield explosives	X	X	
6.9.5.5	Conduct Tactical Chemical, Biological, Radiological, Nuclear, and High-Yield Explosives Consequence Management Crisis Action Planning	X	X	
6.9.5.6	Assess the Chemical, Biological, Radiological, Nuclear, and High-Yield Explosives operations environment	X	X	
6.9.5.7	Conduct tactical Chemical, Biological, Radiological, Nuclear, and High-Yield Explosives Consequence Management command and control	X	X	
6.9.5.8	Perform Chemical, Biological, Radiological, Nuclear, and High-Yield Explosives incident/hazard risk communication	X	X	
6.9.5.9	Establish and maintain access/egress controls and hazard zone perimeter	X	X	
6.9.5.10	Conduct CBRNE victim and casualty search, rescue, and extraction	X	X	
6.9.5.11	Provide temporary housing, processing operations, and evacuation of affected population	X	X	
6.9.5.12	Conduct decontamination operations	X	X	
6.9.5.13	Isolate, quarantine, and manage potentially contaminated/infectious human and animal population	X	X	

Table J-1. Stability and civil support task comparison chart, continued

AUTL #	Title	Stability	Civil Support	Remarks
6.9.7.5	Plan for mitigation of potential tactical weapons of mass destruction elimination collateral effects.	X		
6.9.7.7	Exercise command and control in the preparation for and conduct of weapons of mass destruction elimination operations.	X		
6.9.7.12	Conduct security support for weapons of mass destruction elimination			
6.9.7.13	Search facilities and spaces for weapons of mass destruction materials.	X	X	
6.9.7.17	Contain weapons of mass destruction-related material for final disposition to include defeat, neutralization, storage, or transport.	X	X	
6.9.7.18	Conduct neutralization of suspect weapons of mass destruction-related agent or material.	X	X	
6.9.7.19	Store weapons of mass destruction-related material for final disposition.	X	X	
6.9.7.20	Transport weapons of mass destruction-related material for final disposition.	X	X	
6.9.7.21	Gather forensic evidence in support of elimination mission.	X		
6.9.7.22	Maintain control of materials related to weapons of mass destruction elimination mission.	X		
6.9.7.23	Establish tactical containment and temporary safe storage of suspect materials.	X	X	
6.10	Employ Safety Techniques	X	X	
6.10.1	Conduct Composite Risk Management	X	X	
6.10.2	Develop and Implement Command Safety Program	X	X	
6.10.3	Minimize Safety Risks	X	X	
6.11	Implement Operations Security	X	X	Select units, NSSE
6.11.1	Conduct Operations Security	X	X	Select units, NSSE
6.11.1.1	Identify EEFI	X	X	Select units, NSSE
6.11.1.2	Apply Appropriate OPSEC Measures	X	X	Select units, NSSE
6.11.2	Implement Physical Security Procedures	X	X	
6.11.2.1	Employ Camouflage, Concealment, and Decoy Techniques	X		
6.11.2.2	Employ Noise, Light, Thermal, and Physical Evidence Controls	X		
6.11.3.1	Conduct Counterintelligence Operations	X		
6.11.3.3	Perform Counterintelligence	X		
6.12	Provide Explosive Ordnance Disposal Protection Support	X	X	
6.12.1	Conduct Unexploded Ordnance and Explosive Remnants of War Operations	X	X	
6.12.4	Conduct Explosive Ordnance Chemical Operations	X	X	

Appendix J

Table J-1. Stability and civil support task comparison chart, continued

AUTL #	Title	Stability	Civil Support	Remarks
6.12.5	Conduct Weapons of Mass Destruction Operations	X	X	
6.12.6	Conduct IED/UXO Protection	X	X	UXO support provided by explosive ordnance disposal
6.12.6.1	Provide Chemical, Biological, Radiological, Nuclear and High-Yield Explosive Site Surveys	X	X	
6.12.6.2	Provide Explosive Ordnance Disposal Support to Weapons Storage Site Inspections	X	X	
6.11.6.3	Provide Explosive Ordnance Disposal Support to Amnesty and Weapons Buy Back Programs	X		
6.12.6.5	Conduct Technical Intelligence on unexploded explosive ordnance; Improved Explosive Devices; and Chemical, Biological, Radiological and Nuclear Hazards	X	X	Explosive ordnance disposal support, with Federal military support
6.12.6.6	Conduct Crater, Fragmentation and Post blast Analysis	X		
6.12.7	Respond to Accidents or Incidents involving Military Chemical, Biological, Radiological, and Nuclear Munitions	X	X	
6.12.8	Provide Explosive Ordnance Disposal Sustainment Support	X	X	
6.12.8.3	Provide Explosive Ordnance Disposal Support to the Defense Environment Restoration Program		X	
6.12.8.4	Provide Explosive Ordnance Disposal Support to Homeland Security Operations		X	
6.12.8.5	Provide Explosive Ordnance Disposal Support to Civil Authorities	X	X	
6.12.8.6	Provide Specific Training to Personnel on Explosive Ordnance	X	X	
6.12.8.7	Provide Explosive Ordnance Disposal Support to the Secret Service		X	
7.3.1	Establish Civil Security	X	X	Selected measures only
7.3.1.1	Restore and Maintain Order	X	X	Civil disturbance operations
7.3.1.2	Conduct Disarmament, Demobilization, and Reintegration of ex-Combatants	X		
7.3.1.2.1	Forcibly Separate Belligerents	X		
7.3.1.2.2	Disarm Belligerents	X		
7.3.1.2.3	Demobilize Belligerents	X		
7.3.1.2.4	Establish Protected Areas	X		
7.3.1.3	Establish Border Patrol, Border Security, and Freedom of Movement	X	X	Select measures only
7.3.1.4	Protect Reconstruction and Stabilization Personnel and Facilities	X	X	Select measures only
7.3.2	Establish Civil Control	X	X	Select measures only

Table J-1. Stability and civil support task comparison chart, continued

AUTL #	Title	Stability	Civil Support	Remarks
7.3.2.1	Restore Public Safety and Order	X	X	Select measures only
7.3.2.2	Establish Interim Criminal Justice System	X		
7.3.2.3	Perform Host Nation Police Training and Support	X		
7.3.2.4	Support Judicial Reform	X		
7.3.2.5	Support Dispute Resolution Process	X		
7.3.2.6	Support Human Rights Initiatives	X		
7.3.2.7	Support War Crimes Courts and Tribunals	X		
7.3.3	Restore Essential Services	X	X	
7.3.3.1	Provide Essential Civil Services	X	X	
7.3.3.2	Control Movement of Dislocated Civilians	X	X	
7.3.3.3	Resettle Dislocated Civilians	X		
7.3.3.4	Conduct Populace and Resource Control	X	X	
7.3.3.5	Support Famine Prevention and Emergency Food Relief Programs	X		
7.3.3.6	Support Shelter and Non Food Relief Programs	X	X	
7.3.3.7	Conduct Medical Stability Operations	X		
7.3.3.8	Provide Public Health Support	X	X	
7.3.4	Support Governance	X		
7.3.4.1	Support Transitional Administration	X		
7.3.4.2	Support Development of Local Governance	X		
7.3.4.3	Support Elections	X		
7.3.5	Support Economic and Infrastructure Development	X		
7.3.5.1	Support Economic Development and Stabilization	X		
7.3.5.2	Support Private Sector Development	X		
7.3.5.3	Protect Natural Resources and Environment	X	X	
7.3.5.4	Support Infrastructure Reconstruction Programs	X	X	
7.4.1	Provide Support in Response to Disaster or Terrorist Attack	X	X	
7.4.1.1	Provide Disaster Relief	X	X	
7.4.1.2	Provide Humanitarian Relief	X	X	
7.4.2	Provide Support to Civil Law Enforcement	X	X	
7.4.2.1	Support Department of Justice Counterterrorism	X	X	
7.4.2.2	Conduct Civil Disturbance Operations	X	X	
7.4.2.3	Provide General Support to Civil Law Enforcement	X	X	
7.4.3	Provide Other Support as Required		X	
7.6.1.5	Military Support to Counterdrug Operations	X	X	
7.6.1.5.1	Detection and Monitoring of Drug Shipments	X	X	

Appendix J

Table J-1. Stability and civil support task comparison chart, continued

AUTL #	Title	Stability	Civil Support	Remarks
7.6.1.5.2	Provide C4 & ISR to Counterdrug Efforts	X	X	
7.6.1.5.3	Provide Planning Support to Counterdrug Efforts	X		
7.6.1.5.4	Provide Logistic Support to Counterdrug Efforts	X	X	
7.6.1.5.5	Provide Training Support to Counterdrug Efforts	X	X	
7.6.1.5.6	Provide Manpower for Counterdrug Efforts	X	X	
7.6.1.5.7	R&D Acquisition Support to Counterdrug Efforts	X		

Appendix K
Media Considerations

This appendix provides an overview of the interaction between the media and the military during a disaster or other serious incident. It emphasizes interagency coordination, coordination with the media, and general considerations for commanders and Soldiers when dealing with the domestic media.

INTERAGENCY COORDINATION

K-1. Modern news reporting provides valuable information to citizens before, during, and after a civil disaster or other civil support event. The news media are a key, independent asset that can assist or impede civil support. Army leadership and public affairs planners, in coordination with the lead federal authority, coordinate closely with the news media and help them obtain information to inform the public accurately and rapidly. Military public affairs activities support the lead federal and state agencies and conform to their guidance. Civil support by the military is secondary to the overall task of the supported government leader. Therefore public affairs officers establish and maintain close contact with the information director supporting the federal and state coordinating officers. News media organizations collect and report information from virtually any location. Unlike journalists reporting on combat operations, local and national media representatives report freely on civil support activities. Interagency coordination of public affairs information by the lead civil authority ensures accurate information is communicated to the news media. Civil and Army leadership, public affairs officers, and Soldiers must understand the primary mission and end state and how this information is conveyed to the media. Every organization and individual working for the government, including the Army, should coordinate messages to ensure that they are accurate and confined to their sphere of responsibility when dealing with the media.

K-2. Within civil support operations, Army leadership and public affairs officers operate in an interagency environment with emphasis on unity of effort. The lead civil authority establishes guidance for release of public affairs information. This follows the guidelines within emergency support function #15 for public affairs. Generally a local and federal joint information center is established by to provide accurate and timely information. The joint information centers are usually collocated with the state or local emergency operations center. Army public affairs officers work in concert with the joint information centers.

K-3. To the public, a Soldier in a camouflage uniform is in the Army; most citizens do not understand the differences between the National Guard and Regular Army in domestic situations. Therefore, Regular Army and state National Guard public affairs officers coordinate closely with one another. They discuss common ground and differences before speaking to the news media. While working together, regular Army and National Guard public affairs officers ensure compliance with the doctrine and procedures contained within the National Incident Management System (NIMS) and the National Response Framework (NRF).

COORDINATION WITH THE NEWS MEDIA

K-4. Most news media organizations are willing to work with the Army to convey vital information to the public. Soldiers should understand how the media function and be prepared to help news media organizations obtain accurate information on civil support operations to inform the public. Experience garnered in combat dealing with the media provides useful lessons, but may need review as part of an ongoing civil support operation. A first rule of thumb is to assume that the domestic media will "get the story" sooner rather than later, so they might as well have the whole story initially. The second rule of thumb is to "stick to your lane" and discuss only those things for which the unit is responsible and has

Appendix K

experienced. Avoid speculation or opinion, and always refer the media to the supported civilian agency responsible for public information.

K-5. Members of the media will be present in large numbers during the initial stages of any disaster or civil disturbance. Depending on the situation, Army leaders assist members of the media to the extent they can, without impeding higher priority work. For example, the Army may provide shower facilities, a cup of coffee, a place to park, or other essential needs for media personnel. Other needs include latrines, meals, power generation, lighting, sleeping facilities, office areas with phone and internet access, access to plans and operations centers (when security is not jeopardized), and involvement in certain planning events. Before providing the media with any support not readily available to citizens and relief workers, commanders obtain clearance from their controlling headquarters. If media control procedures require accreditation in order to work in the area, local commanders should assist members of the media with getting that accreditation from the issuing authority, normally the local disaster coordination center.

Providing Appropriate Information

K-6. Different media outlets, such as television, radio, internet, newspapers and magazines, have varying information requirements. Media information and packaging requirements are discussed below, to enable Soldiers to help the media get accurate information to the public on time.

K-7. Television and commercial radio are the two media systems used the most by the general public for dissemination of domestic disaster information. People often react to warning sirens with disbelief until confirmation through radio or television is obtained. Television and radio usually cover the same types of information. Packaging methods are different. For example, the television medium prefers visuals, and a telephone conversation is not an adequate substitute. Television is predisposed to a headline approach that emphasizes succinct, easily remembered twenty-to-thirty-second statements. Radio reaches audiences almost anywhere and tends to broadcast information almost as soon as received. Radio reporters generally limit reports to a short duration and are selective in detail for civil disasters or other significant events. These media are essential for successful dissemination of high priority information to the public.

K-8. Generally, print news does not have the same time constraint experienced by radio and television. Therefore it allows for more background and in-depth material. Print media reports include analysis and commentary, and stories may build day-after-day as the disaster response progresses. Print news editors want depth and graphics. With the use of the internet to distribute information and stories, many newspapers are now much like television and radio in capability. The internet enables rapid dissemination of real time domestic disaster information worldwide. The World Wide Web is also used to collect information about an incident for later reference. In general, information packaging for the internet is a combination of the material used by television, radio, newspapers, and magazines. During disaster support missions, Soldiers remain aware that information they send with cell phone, email, or internet links may not remain private. It may be intercepted or shared beyond the intended recipient.

K-9. Local news organizations are interested in all phases of the actual disaster since they may have long-range, home-town concerns. They attempt to provide specific information to area residents to help them face the disaster: warning information, evacuation advice, where help is available, and how long utilities are expected to be out of service. National news media organizations are more concerned with the overall picture, such as the scope of the impact, the number of dead and injured, and the activities of federal response organizations. National news media concern with long-term recovery from the disaster is unlikely. Almost all reporters present at a disaster, regardless of their news medium, share information with one another. Therefore, the Army must coordinate with the primary agency to give accurate and consistent information.

Referring Questions to the Joint Information Center

K-10. Soldiers should anticipate a mixture ranging from very credible reporting by experienced professional teams through "niche" outlets focused on the outlandish. Ideally, every Soldier understands the media guidance provided by the joint information center. However, as the operation continues around the clock, Soldiers on the street may not receive timely guidance. Therefore leaders at each level should remind their subordinates to limit their discussion to their personal experiences. "What did you see? Were you scared? How did you feel after you rescued the animals?" Leaders should also anticipate that media members will ask questions that Soldiers should always defer to the controlling civil authorities. Common examples include—

- **Casualty Information.** How many were killed or injured? Of those injured, how serious is their condition? How many escaped? How was escape hindered? Were any of the victims prominent persons? Where were they taken? What was the disposition of the dead?
- **Property Damage.** What is the estimated value of property loss? What kinds of structures are involved? Did the damage include any particularly important property (such as, historical buildings, art treasures, homes of prominent figures)? Is other property threatened? What measures are being undertaken to protect property? Is the damage covered by insurance? Has this area been damaged by disasters before?
- **Response and Relief Activities.** Who discovered the emergency? Who summoned the alarm? How quickly were response units on the scene? What agencies responded? How many are engaged in the response? What acts of heroism occurred? How was the emergency kept from spreading? How are the displaced and homeless being cared for?
- **Other Characteristics of the Crisis.** Did you hear about any blasts or explosions? Do you think this was terrorism? Collapse of structures? Crimes or violence? Attempts at escape or self rescue? What was the extent of the disaster? The duration? Number of spectators? Crowd problems? Were there other unusual happenings? What accompanying accidents have occurred? What were the resulting effects (such as anxiety, stress) on the families and survivors?
- **Causes of the Disaster.** Were there any previous indications of danger? Could the disaster have been prevented? How? (Questions about blame are more likely to surface in technological disasters such as nuclear or other hazardous materials accidents). Is there a coroner's inquest? Lawsuits? Insurance company actions? Criminal investigation?

K-11. In addition to inappropriate questions, Soldiers should be prepared to deal with inappropriate behavior. Most members of the media are experienced professionals and very good at their jobs. Occasionally the media oversteps its limits and Soldiers should be prepared to deal professionally with the situation before it becomes a major news story in itself. Considerations include—

- Police or National Guard forces should intercede to control members of the media whenever their presence interferes with mission accomplishment. If time permits, Army forces coordinate with the incident commander for assistance. If external assistance is not available, the unit leaders should confer with the media and ask them to modify their activity to allow the Soldiers to complete their mission. Unless life or limb is at risk, Soldiers avoid using any level of force.
- Army forces never attempt to seize cameras or other media equipment. If it is necessary, this is a task for civilian law enforcement.
- Soldiers remember that the rights of citizens outweigh the rights of the press. Should the activities of the press upset citizens, Soldiers remain prepared to offer assistance to all parties. Civilians view members of the military as neutral parties, and the respect that media and citizens give them can allow them to diffuse emotional situations.
- In a major disaster, members of the press become just as exhausted as Soldiers. Commanders should remind Soldiers that the media are also professionals with an important job, and that Soldiers will respect fellow professionals. Soldiers are courteous and offer hospitality if possible. They keep in mind that the American media has an underlying respect for Soldiers and Marines.

BASIC CONSIDERATIONS FOR IMPROVING NEWS COVERAGE

K-12. The news media are more effective when their personnel understand the nature of the disaster and what information may be communicated to the public. Army public affairs officers work with the media to help them understand what information the public requires during civil disasters. For example, newscasters may be encouraged not to withhold news information, warnings, and instructions to the public for fear of causing panic. Evidence indicates the public is capable of handling facts.

- The news media may know that a disaster warning is less likely to be taken seriously if it is followed by resumption of normal programming.
- Newscasters may know the importance of announcing the areas not affected by the disaster. The effect of this information may be a reduction of the number of calls by persons who believe they have loved ones in the impact zone.
- Reporters should know that acquisition of precise information and accurate figures on deaths, injuries, and damage in the initial aftermath of a disaster is not possible.
- Previously inaccurate information that was conveyed to the public is corrected as soon as possible.

BASIC MEDIA GUIDELINES FOR SOLDIERS

K-13. Some basic guidelines for media contact include—
- Commanders or senior staff should be ready for interviews. Interviews serve as opportunities to ensure the public receives accurate, timely, and useful information concerning the Army's response to the situation.
- Soldiers use simple, concise language free of military jargon and acronyms.
- Soldiers doing their duty always make a good impression. When questioned, they try to ignore the cameras and talk directly to the reporter. They remove sunglasses and headgear if appropriate. They use appropriate posture and gestures.
- Soldiers should pause and think before answering a question. They answer questions accurately, but not necessarily instantly. They answer one question at a time.
- If a question seems unclear, a Soldier asks the reporter to rephrase it.
- Soldiers assume everything is on the record.
- Soldiers should be friendly but businesslike. The interviewer chooses the questions; the Soldier chooses the answers.
- Soldiers speak about what they know. If a Soldier doesn't know the answer, the Soldier's reply is, "I don't know." When possible, Soldiers direct a reporter to the most appropriate individual with the required knowledge.
- Soldiers keep in mind that it is never appropriate to lie to the media.
- A Soldier does not divulge or confirm classified information even when a reporter may have knowledge of such information.

MEDIA CARDS

K-14. Media cards include the basic information Soldiers are required to know for dealing with news media organizations. The public affairs officer is responsible for their development. Items to include in a media card are—
- The appropriate person to contact and how to contact him or her if a reporter arrives in the unit's area.
- Responsibilities of a media escort.
- What information can and cannot be discussed.
- When to allow a media interview.
- How to treat reporters.
- How to conduct an interview.
- The best techniques to use in telling the correct information.

Glossary

SECTION I – ACRONYMS AND ABBREVIATIONS

AR	Army regulation
ART	Army tactical task
ASCC	Army Service component command
ASD(HD&ASA)	Assistant Secretary of Defense (Homeland Defense and America's Security Affairs)
AUTL	Army Universal Task List
CBRNE	chemical, biological, radiological, nuclear, and high-yield explosives
CBRNE incident	chemical, biological, radiological, nuclear, or high-yield explosives incident
CJCS	Chairman of the Joint Chiefs of Staff
CJCS DSCA EXORD	Chairman of the Joint Chiefs of Staff standing execute order for defense support of civil authorities
CJCSI	Chairman of the Joint Chiefs of Staff instruction
DCO	defense coordinating officer
DHS	Department of Homeland Security
DOD	Department of Defense
DODD	Department of Defense directive
DODI	Department of Defense instruction
DSCA	defense support of civil authorities
EMAC	Emergency Management Assistance Compact
ESF	emergency support function (or emergency support function annex)
EXORD	execute order
FBI	Federal Bureau of Investigation
FEMA	Federal Emergency Management Agency
FM	field manual
HSPD	homeland security Presidential directive
JFHQ–state	joint force headquarters–state
JP	joint publication
JTF–state	joint task force–state
NIMS	National Incident Management System
NRF	National Response Framework
S-1	personnel staff officer
S-2	intelligence staff officer
S-3	operations staff officer
S-4	logistics staff officer
S-6	signal staff officer
SRUF	standing rules for the use of force
TLAMM	theater lead agent for medical materiel

Glossary

USACE	United States Army Corps of Engineers
USAMEDCOM	United States Army Medical Command
USARNORTH	United States Army North
USC	United States Code
USJFCOM	United States Joint Forces Command
USNORTHCOM	United States Northern Command
USPACOM	United States Pacific Command
USTRANSCOM	United States Transportation Command
WMD–CST	weapons of mass destruction–civil support team
9/11	referring to the attack on the United States that occurred on 11 September 2001

SECTION II – TERMS

This manual uses numerous civilian terms, to facilitate interagency coordination. The Federal Emergency Management Agency is the proponent for civilian terms related to incident management and response. In general, definitions given of civilian terms within this manual have been summarized or paraphrased from the National Incident Management System and the National Response Framework. The National Incident Management System and the National Response Framework continue to evolve. Readers can find full and up-to-date definitions for civilian terms discussed in this manual at http://www.fema.gov/emergency/nrf/

References

REQUIRED PUBLICATIONS

These documents must be available to intended users of this publication.

FM 1-02. *Operational Terms and Graphics*. 21 September 2004.

JP 1-02. *Department of Defense Dictionary of Military and Associated Terms*. 12 April 2001. (As amended through April 2010).

National Incident Management System. http://www.fema.gov/emergency/nims/.

National Response Framework. January 2008. http://www.fema.gov/emergency/nrf/.

RELATED PUBLICATIONS

These documents contain relevant supplemental information.

JOINT AND DEPARTMENT OF DEFENSE PUBLICATIONS

Find joint and Department of Defense publications at http://www.dtic.mil/doctrine/doctrine/doctrine.htm.

CJCSI 3710.01B. *DOD Counterdrug Support*. 26 January 2007.

DODD 1200.17. *Managing the Reserve Components as an Operational Force*. 29 October 2008.

DODD 3025.1. *Military Support to Civil Authorities (MSCA)*. 15 January 1993.

DODD 3025.12. *Military Assistance for Civil Disturbances (MACDIS)*. 4 February 1994.

DODD 3025.15. *Military Assistance to Civil Authorities*. 18 February 1997.

DODD 5111.13. *Assistant Secretary of Defense for Homeland Defense and Americas' Security Affairs (ASD (HD&ASA))*. 16 January 2009.

DODD 5200.27. *Acquisition of Information Concerning Persons and Organizations not Affiliated with the Department of Defense*. 7 January 1980.

DODD 5240.01. *DOD Intelligence Activities*. 27 August 2007.

DODD 5525.5. *DOD Cooperation with Civilian Law Enforcement Officials*. 15 January 1986.

DODI 6490.03. *Deployment Health*. 11 August 2006.

DOD 3025.1-M. *Manual for Civil Emergencies*. 2 June 1994.

DOD 5240.1-R. *Procedures Governing the Activities of DOD Intelligence Components That Affect United States Persons*. 1 December 1982.

DOD 7000.14-R. *Department of Defense Financial Management Regulations*, volumes 1-15. Date varies per volume.

JP 1-06. *Financial Management Support in Joint Operations*. 4 March 2008.

JP 3-0. *Joint Operations*. 17 September 2006.

JP 3-27. *Homeland Defense*. 12 July 2007.

JP 3-28. *Civil Support*. 14 September 2007.

JP 3-41. *Chemical, Biological, Radiological, Nuclear, and High-Yield Explosives Consequence Management*. 2 October 2006.

JP 4-0. *Joint Logistics*. 18 July 2008.

JP 4-06. *Mortuary Affairs in Joint Operations*. 5 June 2006.

JP 5-0. *Joint Operation Planning*. 26 December 2006.

DEPARTMENT OF THE ARMY PUBLICATIONS

Find Department of the Army publications at https://akocomm.us.army.mil/usapa/index.html.

AR 11-35. *Deployment Occupational and Environmental Health Risk Management*. 16 May 2007.

AR 25-400-2. *The Army Records Information Management System (ARIMS)*. 12 August 2010

AR 380-13. *Acquisition and Storage of Information Concerning Non-Affiliated Persons and Organizations*. 30 September 1974.

AR 381-10. *U.S. Army Intelligence Activities*. 3 May 2007.

AR 385-10. *The Army Safety Program*. 23 June 2010.

DA PAM 385-10. *Army Safety Program*. 23 May 2008.

DA PAM 385-40. Army *Accident Investigations and Reporting*. 6 March 2009.

FM 3-0. *Operations*. 27 February 2008

FM 3-11. *Multiservice Tactics, Techniques, and Procedures for Nuclear, Biological, and Chemical Defense Operations*. 10 March 2003.

FM 3-19.15. *Civil Disturbance Operations*. 18 April 2005

FM 3-22.40. *Multi-Service Tactics, Techniques, and Procedures for the Tactical Employment of Nonlethal Weapons*. 24 October 2007.

FM 3-28.1. *Multi-Service Tactics, Techniques, and Procedures for Civil Support (CS) Operations*. 3 December 2007.

FM 4-02.7. *Multiservice Tactics, Techniques, and Procedures for Health Service Support in a Chemical, Biological, Radiological, and Nuclear Environment*. 15 July 2009.

FM 4-02.17. *Preventive Medicine Services*. 28 August 2000.

FM 4-02.51. *Combat and Operational Stress Control*. 6 July 2006.

FM 4-02.283. *Treatment of Nuclear and Radiological Casualties*. 20 December 2001.

FM 4-02.285. *Multiservice Tactics, Techniques and Procedures for Treatment of Chemical Agent Casualties and Conventional Military Chemical Injuries*. 18 September 2007.

FM 5-0. *The Operations Process*. 26 March 2010.

FM 5-19. *Composite Risk Management*. 21 August 2006.

FM 6-22.5 *Combat and Operational Stress Control Manual for Leaders and Soldiers*. 18 March 2009.

FM 7-15. *The Army Universal Task List*. 27 February 2009.

FM 8-42. *Combat Health Support in Stability Operations and Support Operations*. 27 October 1997.

FM 8-284. *Treatment of Biological Warfare Agent Casualties*. 17 July 2000.

TC 3-19.5. *Nonlethal Weapons Training*. 5 November 2009.

References

UNITED STATES LAW

Specific laws are grouped according to where they are found in United States law.

Code of Federal Regulations

Find the Code of Federal Regulations (CFR) at http://www.gpoaccess.gov/cfr/index.html.

Hazardous waste operations and emergency response standard. Title 29, Part 1910. Occupational Safety and Health Standard Number 1910.120. View at http://www.access.gpo.gov/nara/cfr/waisidx_09/29cfr1910_09.html.

National Oil and Hazardous Substances Pollution Contingency Plan. Title 40, Part 300. View at http://www.access.gpo.gov/nara/cfr/waisidx_09/40cfr300_09.html.

United States Code

Find the United States Code (USC) at http://uscode.house.gov/lawrevisioncounsel.shtml.

Foundational Documents

Articles of Confederation. 1777.

Constitution of the United States of America. 1787.

Titles and Laws in the United States Code

Title 6, Domestic Security.

> Homeland Security Act of 2002. Public Law 107-296. Codified predominantly at Sections 101 to 557.
>
> Post-Katrina Emergency Management Reform Act of 2006. Public Law 109-295. Title VI of the Department of Homeland Security Appropriations Act of 2006.

Title 7, Agriculture.

Title 10, Armed Forces.

> Emergency Situations Involving Chemical or Biological Weapons of Mass Destruction. Section 382.
>
> Insurrection Act. Sections 331 to 335.
>
> Uniform Code of Military Justice. Sections 801 to 941.

Title 28, Judiciary and Judicial Procedure.

> Federal Tort Claims Act. Sections 1346(b) 2761 through 2680.
>
> Medical Malpractice Immunity Act. Public Law 94-464.

Title 14, Coast Guard.

Title 18, Crimes and Criminal Procedure.

> Prohibited Transactions Involving Nuclear Materials. Section 831.
>
> Posse Comitatus Act, Section 1385.

Title 31, Money and Finance.

> Economy Act. Sections 1535 and 9701.

Title 32, National Guard.

Title 42, The Public Health and Welfare.

> Comprehensive Environmental Response, Compensation, and Liability Act of 1980. Sections 9601-9675
>
> Public Health Service Act. Section 201 et seq.
>
> Robert T. Stafford Disaster Relief and Emergency Assistance Act. Sections 300hh-11 and 5121 et seq, and chapter 15A.

References

Title 50, War and National Defense.

Defense Against Weapons of Mass Destruction Act of 1996. Sections 2301 et seq.

National Security Act of 1947. Section 401 et seq.

National Emergencies Act. Sections 1601 to 1651.

Foreign Intelligence and Surveillance Act, 1978. Section 1801.

National Defense Authorization Act for Fiscal Year 1991, Public Law 101-510, Nov. 5, 1990, 104 Stat. 1485.

EXECUTIVE ORDERS AND PRESIDENTIAL DIRECTIVES

Executive Order 12333. *United States Intelligence Activities*. 4 December 1981. Available at http://www.archives.gov/federal-register/executive-orders/1981-reagan.html.

Executive Order 13295. *Revised List of Quarantinable Communicable Diseases*. 4 April 2003, amended by Executive Order 13375. Available at http://www.archives.gov/federal-register/executive-orders/2003.html.

Executive Order 13375. *Amendment to Executive Order 13295 Relating to Certain Influenza Viruses and Quarantinable Communicable Diseases*. 1 April 2005. http://www.archives.gov/federal-register/executive-orders/2005.html.

Homeland Security Presidential Directive 5. *Management of Domestic Incidents*. 28 February 2003. Available at http://www.dhs.gov/xabout/laws/gc_1214592333605.shtm.

Homeland Security Presidential Directive 8. *National Preparedness*. 17 December 2003. Available at http://www.dhs.gov/xabout/laws/gc_1215444247124.shtm.

NATIONAL GUARD PUBLICATIONS

See http://www.ngbpdc.ngb.army.mil/pubs/ARNG%20Series/arngseries.htm#500arng for National Guard regulations.

NGR 500-1/ANGI 10-8101. *National Guard Domestic Operations*. 13 June 2008.

NGR 500-2/ANGI 10-801. *National Guard Counterdrug Support*. 29 August 2008.

OTHER DOCUMENTS AND PUBLICATIONS

Web sites listed were current as of July 2010.

CJCS (SC) "Defense Support of Civil Authorities (DSCA)" other-organizational message. Standing execute order for DSCA operations, addressed to Joint Staff, Commander of United States Northern Command, Commander of United States Joint Forces Command, Commander of United States Pacific Command, Commander of North American Aerospace Defense Command, Commander of United States Southern Command, Commander of United States Transportation Command, Secretary of the Army, Secretary of the Navy, and Secretary of the Air Force. 141745Z August 2009.

Coordinating Military Deployments on Roads and Highways: A Guide for State and Local Agencies. U.S. Dept. of Transportation, Federal Highway Administration. May 2005. Available at http://ops.fhwa.dot.gov/publications/fhwahop05029/index.htm .

Field Management of Chemical Casualties Handbook, second edition. U. S. Army Medical Research Institute of Chemical Defense (USAMRICD), Chemical Casualty Care Division. July 2000.

International Aeronautical and Maritime Search and Rescue Manual (IAMSAR). 2010 edition. Available from the International Maritime Organization: http://www.imo.org/.

National Drug Control Strategy. 2010. Available at http://www.whitehousedrugpolicy.gov/policy/ndcs.html.

National Fire Protection Association Standard 472, *Standard for Competence of Responders to Hazardous Materials/Weapons of Mass Destruction Incidents*, 2008 edition. Available at http://www.nfpa.org/aboutthecodes/AboutTheCodes.asp?DocNum=472.

National Infrastructure Protection Plan. 2009. Available at
http://www.dhs.gov/files/programs/editorial_0827.shtm.

National Preparedness Guidelines. September 2007. Available at
http://www.dhs.gov/files/publications/gc_1189788256647.shtm.

National Search and Rescue Plan of the United States. 2007. National Search and Rescue Committee.
Available at http://www.uscg.mil/hq/cg5/cg534/nsarc/SAR_publications.asp.

Quadrennial Defense Review Report. Department of Defense. 1 February 2010. Available at
http://www.defense.gov/qdr.

Quadrennial Homeland Security Review Report. Department of Homeland Security. February 2010.
Available at http://www.dhs.gov/xabout/gc_1208534155450.shtm.

*United States National Search and Rescue Supplement to the International Aeronautical and Maritime
Search and Rescue Manual.* National Search and Rescue Committee. May 2000. Available at
http://www.uscg.mil/hq/cg5/cg534/nsarc/SAR_publications.asp.

REFERENCED FORMS

DA forms are available on the Army Publishing Directorate Web site: www.apd.army.mil. DD forms are available on the OSD website (www.dtic.mil/whs/directives/infomgt/forms/formsprogram.htm).

DA Form 2028. *Recommended Changes to Publications and Blank Forms.*

DD Form 2535. *Request for Military Aerial Support.*

DD Form 2536. *Request for Armed Forces Participation in Public Events (Non-Aviation).*

PRESCRIBED FORMS

None.

WEB SITES

Web sites listed were current as of July 2010.

Army Center for Health Promotion and Preventive Medicine. http://phc.amedd.army.mil/home/.

Centers for Disease Control and Prevention. http://www.cdc.gov/.

Chemical, Biological, Radiological, and Nuclear Defense Information Analysis Center/
https://www.cbrniac.apgea.army.mil/Pages/default.aspx.

Department of Defense contact information. http://www.defense.gov/faq/comment.html.

Department of Defense travel regulations. http://www.defensetravel.dod.mil/perdiem/trvlregs.html.

Department of Homeland Security. http://www.dhs.gov/index.shtm.

Emergency Management Assistance Compact. http://www.emacweb.org/.

Federal Emergency Management Agency. http://www.fema.gov.

Fire Rescue I. http://www.firerescue1.com.

Innovative Readiness Training. http://irt.defense.gov/index.html.

Occupational Safety and Health Administration. http://www.osha.gov/.

Ready Army. http://www.acsim.army.mil/readyarmy/.

United States Coast Guard. www.uscg.mil/.

United States Army Corps of Engineers. www.usace.army.mil.

United States Army Maneuver Support Center of Excellence. http://www.wood.army.mil/wood_cms/.

United States Northern Command. http://www.northcom.mil/.

RECOMMENDED READING

Web sites listed were current as of July 2010.

DODD 5210.56. *Use of Deadly Force and the Carrying of Firearms by DOD Personnel Engaged in Law Enforcement and Security Duties*. 1 November 2001. (Incorporating Change 1, 1 January 2002).

DODI 6055.06. *DOD Fire and Emergency Services (F&ES) Program*. 21 December 2006.

FM 3-07. *Stability Operations*. 6 October 2008.

A Governor's Guide to Homeland Security. National Governors Association Center for Best Practices. Washington, DC. 2007. Available at http://www.nga.org/portal/site/nga/menuitem.9123e83a1f6786440ddcbeeb501010a0/?vgnextoid=58b4aee432d41110VgnVCM1000001a01010aRCRD.

Military Use Handbook. National Interagency Fire Center. July 2006. Available at http://www.nifc.gov/nicc/logistics/references.htm.

Index

Entries are by paragraph number unless otherwise specified.

A

accident reporting, B-32–B-33

accounting procedures, planning guidance for, 8-66

adjutant general, National Guard civil support and, 2-83–2-84

agricultural diseases, outbreak and response to, 4-59- 4-60

Air National Guard, National Guard civil support and, 1-14, 1-23, 1-26, 3-16, 3-106, 4-23, 8-15–8-16

airspace coordination planning checklist, F-16

airspace in civil support, coordination of, F-1–F-8

area command, brief explanation of, 2-13

areas of operations, disaster response and, 3-91–3-95

Army National Guard, civil support and, 1-21–1-24

Army Reserve,
civil support and, 1-18–1-20;
mobilization of for civil support, 7-31–7-32

Army unit initial planning checklist, table A-3

Army Universal Task List, use in civil support training, 1-72–1-74, table J-1

B

base support installation, selection of, 8-36–8-46, figure 8-3

battle command, the operations process and, 3-63–3-68

border security, law enforcement support and, 5-22–5-24

C

CBRNE consequence management response force, considerations for, E-25–E-26; operations of, E-11–E-24, figure E-3; organization of, E-1–E-10; See also Joint Task Force–Civil Support.

CBRNE enhanced response force package,
capability of, D-1;
mission of, D-9–D-11;
organization of, D-2–D-8, figure D-1

CBRNE incidents, considerations for, 4-61–4-88

CCMRF. See CBRNE consequence management response force.

CERFP. See CBRNE enhanced response force package.

Chairman of the Joint Chiefs of Staff defense support of civil authorities standing execute order,
pre-scripted mission assignments and, 2-121;
United States Northern Command response and, 2-103;
United States Pacific Command response and, 2-113

chemical, biological, radiological, nuclear, and high-yield explosives enhanced response force package. See CBRNE enhanced response force package.

chemical, biological, radiological, nuclear, and high-yield explosives consequence management response force. See CBRNE consequence management response force.

chemical, biological, radiological, nuclear, or high-yield explosives incident, definition of, 4-1

chemical, biological, radiological, nuclear, or high-yield explosives incident response, considerations for, 4-61–4-88

chemical, biological, radiological, nuclear, or high-yield explosives incidents,
National Guard response to, 4-22–4-25, table 4-2;
federal military response to, 4-26–4-37, table 4-3

Chief of the National Guard Bureau, National Guard civil support and, 2-88–2-89

civil disturbance, law enforcement support and, 5-26–5-35

civil search and rescue, comparison of disaster response and, table G-1

civil support, definition of, 1-4

civil support operations, fundamentals of, 1-54–1-70

civilian officials, civil support and, 1-63–1-67

Coast Guard, federal government response and, 2-65–2-68

combatant commands, federal military response and, 2-101–2-115

command and control, disaster response and, 3-69–3-95

command and support relationships, disaster response and, 3-75–3-78

command of military forces, multistate disaster and, 3-72–3-74, figure 3-9

command post operations, disaster response and, 3-79–3-83

command, civilian usage of, 2-8

common tasks by warfighting function, 1-72–1-74

communications, disaster response and, 3-84–3-87

components of the Army, civil support and, 1-14–1-24

composite risk management, civil support and, B-3–B-31

Constitution of the United States, the Army and, 1-10–1-13

contracting, considerations for, 8-53–8-56

costs, accounting and reimbursement for. See reimbursable activities.

counterdrug support, law enforcement support and, 5-17–5-24

Index

D

defense coordinating officer, explanation of, 2-94–2-97, figure 2-8

defense support of civil authorities, definition of, 1-4–1-5

Department of Homeland Security, federal government response and, 2-60–2-68

Department of Justice, federal government response and, 2-69

Department of State, federal government response and, 2-70

deployment of forces, civil support and, 8-11–8-21

differences between stability and civil support operations, 1-37–1-40

disaster declaration. *See* presidential disaster declaration.

disaster response, responsibility for, 3-5–3-9

disaster response operations, considerations for, 3-61–3-121

disaster response operations, phases of, 3-50–3-56, figure 3-7

disasters, federal military response to, 3-30–3-49

disasters, initial local and state response to, 3-10–3-12

disasters, state National Guard response to, 3-13–3-29

documenting costs, civil support and the importance of, 1-68–1-69

domestic emergencies, national policy for, 2-1–2-37

domestic operations, key aspects of, 1-34–1-36, table 1-2

DSCA EXORD. *See* Chairman of the Joint Chiefs of Staff defense support of civil authorities standing execute order.

duty status,
  civil support and, 1-25–1-33, table 1-1;
  federal military forces and, 1-26–1-27;
  state national guard forces and, 1-28–1-32, table 1-1

E–F

emergency authority, law enforcement and, 5-8 – 5-11

Emergency Management Assistance Compact, explanation of, 3-24–3-29

emergency operations center, explanation of, 2-19, figure 2-2

emergency preparedness liaison officer, explanation of, 2-98–2-100

emergency support function, explanation of, 2-36, table 2-1

ESF. *See* emergency support function.

federal coordinating officer, explanation of, 2-78

Federal Emergency Management Agency,
  federal government response and, 2-63–2-64, figure 2-5;
  regions, 2-63–2-64, figure 2-5

federal government incident response, 2-59–2-81

federal military forces, national response and, 2-90–2-121

FEMA. *See* Federal Emergency Management Agency.

financial management, considerations, civil support operations and, 8-96–8-102

first responders, local- to state-level, 2-40–2-58

fundamentals of civil support operations, 1-54–1-70

H–I

homeland security and homeland defense, defined, 1-41–1-44

immediate response authority, disaster response and, 3-31-3-33

incident awareness and assessment, 3-116–3-119

incident command staff, explanation of, 2-14–2-16, figure 2-1

incident command system, explanation of, 2-7–2-13

incident management team, explanation of, 2-14

intelligence oversight, rules and restrictions for, 7-40–7-52

intelligence, civil support tasks and, 3-115–3-121

isolation and quarantine, enforcement of, 4-51–4-58, 7-53–7-58

J

joint airspace control, F-9-F-14

joint field office,
  explanation of, 2-79, figure 2-6, figure I-1;
  finance and administration section of, figure I-5;
  logistics section of, figure I-4;
  operations section of, figure I-2;
  planning section of, figure I-3

Joint Force Headquarters–National Capitol Region, explanation of, 2-109

joint force headquarters–state, disaster response and, 3-15–3-18, figure 3-3, figure 3-4

joint information center, explanation of, 2-21

Joint Interagency Task Force–West, explanation of, 2-114

joint task force, federal military response and, 2-118–2-120

joint task force, initial planning checklist, table A-2

Joint Task Force–Alaska, explanation of, 2-110

Joint Task Force–Civil Support, explanation of, 2-107

Joint Task Force–Civil Support, CBRNE consequence management response force and, 2-107, 4-29–4-33

Joint Task Force–Homeland Defense, explanation of, 2-115
Joint Task Force–North, explanation of, 2-108

K–L

key aspects of domestic operations, 1-34–1-36, table 1-2
law enforcement support, considerations for, 5-43–5-62
law, civil support and the importance of, 1-56–1-62
liaison officers, disaster response and, 3-88–3-90
logistic support from other organizations, 8-58–8-59
logistics considerations, civil support and, 8-47–8-83
logistics coordination, civil support and, 8-2–8-46

M

martial law, use of, 5-12–5-14
mass casualty incidents, medical logistics and, 9-53–9-54
medical capabilities for civil support, coordination of, 9-1–9-25
medical considerations, civil support and, 9-26–9-44
medical logistics, civil support and, 9-45–9-54
military end state, civil support and, 1-70
mission assignments, federal military forces and, 3-46–3-49
mortuary affairs, critical services and, 8-68–8-73
movement and maneuver, disaster response and, 3-102
multiagency coordination group, definition of, 2-18
multiagency coordination systems, explained, 2-17–2-19

N

National Disaster Medical System, civil support and, 9-6–9-16
National Guard civil support, definition of, 1-6
National Guard civil support, organization of forces and, 2-85–2-87, figure 2-7
National Guard civil support, state response and, 2-82–2-87, figure 2-7

National Incident Management System, planning process for, 2-22–2-31
National Incident Management System, summary of command and management component, 2-6–2-31, figure 2-1, figure 2-2, figure 2-3
National Planning Scenarios, 2-37, table 2-2, 4-4, table 4-1
national policy for domestic emergencies, 2-1–2-37
National Response Framework, explanation of, 2-32–2-37, figure 2-4
National Response Framework, principles of, 2-35
National Response Plan. See National Response Framework.
national special security events. See special events, support for.
Native American reservations, incident response and, 2-46–2-48
NIMS. See National Incident Management System.
nonlethal force, civil support and, 3-96–3-101
Nonlethal weapons, use of for law enforcement, 5-57–5-60
nonreimbursable activities, logistics and, 8-65
NRF. See National Response Framework.

P

pandemic disease outbreaks, support for, 4-38–4-60
parallel command, disaster response and, 3-70–3-71, figure 3-8
personal liability, civil support and, 7-59
personnel services, civil support and, 8-84–8-103
phases of disaster response. See disaster response, phases of.
Posse Comitatus Act, 1-26, 1-30, table 1-1, 3-31, 5-5–5-7, 5-32, 5-51, 6-11, 7-20, 7-23–7-28, 8-80, H-4
pre-scripted mission assignments, explanation of, 2-121, figure 2-10
presidential disaster declaration, Stafford Act, 3-34

primary civil support tasks, 1-45–1-53, figure 1-2
primary purposes of civil support, 1-55
protection considerations, CBRNE incident response and, 4-67–4-74
protection considerations, disaster response and, 3-96–3-101
public information, explanation of, 2-20

R–S

range of response, 1-7–1-8, figure 1-1
regional team leader, explanation of, 2-80–2-81
Regular Army, civil support and, 1-15–1-17
reimbursable activities, logistics and, 8-62–8-64
religious support, civil support and, 8-103
request for assistance, federal military forces and, 3-34–3-44, figure 3-5
resource management, logistics and, 8-60–8-61
rules for the use of force, 1-59, 3-96–3-99, 5-31, 5-49, 5-54–5-60, 6-11, 7-33–7-39
S-1 initial planning checklist, table A-4
S-2 initial planning checklist, table A-5
S-3 initial planning checklist, table A-6
S-4 initial planning checklist, table A-7
S-6 initial planning checklist, table A-8
search and rescue, coordination of, G-3–G-5; interagency standards for, G-1–G-2; urban, G-7–G-17
sensitive information, civil support and, 7-46–7-49
single incident command, brief explanation of, 2-10
situational awareness and assessment checklist, table A-1
special events, support for, 6-2–6-6
stability tasks, compared to civil support tasks, table J-1

Index

Stafford Act, presidential disaster declaration, 3-34

state active duty status, 1-29

state coordinating officer, explanation of, 2-53

state defense forces, 1-33

support to domestic civilian law enforcement agencies, authorities for, 5-1–5-14; types of missions and, 5-15–5-42

sustainment, disaster response and, 3-103–3-114

T–U

terrorism, protection against, 5-36–5-42

tiered response, 2-38–2-81

title 10 status, 1-26–1-27

title 32 status, 1-30–1-32

training for civil support operations, 1-71–1-75

training priority for civil support tasks, 1-75

transition from military to civilian support, disaster response phases and, 3-58–3-60

unified command, brief explanation of, 2-11

United States Army Corps of Engineers, federal military response and, 2-116–2-117

United States Army Medical Command, incident response capabilities and, 9-17–9-25

United States Army North, federal military response and, 2-105–2-108, figure 2-9

United States Northern Command, federal military response and, 2-102–2-111

United States Pacific Command, federal military response and, 2-112–2-115

unmanned aircraft systems, considerations for employment of, H-9–H-24; missions for, H-3–H-8; types of, H-1–H-2

urban search and rescue. *See* search and rescue, urban.

V–W

veterinary support, considerations for, 9-42–9-44

weapons of mass destruction–civil support team, mission of, C-2–C-14; organization of, C-1

wildland firefighting, support for, 6-15–6-19

www.ingramcontent.com/pod-product-compliance
Lightning Source LLC
Chambersburg PA
CBHW082113230426
43671CB00015B/2687